The Director

THE
Director

An Oral Biography of

J. EDGAR HOOVER

by Ovid Demaris

HARPER'S MAGAZINE PRESS
Published in Association with Harper & Row
New York

Portions of this work originally appeared in *Esquire* and *Argosy*.

Grateful acknowledgment is made for permission to reprint the following:

Excerpts from *American Agent* by Melvin H. Purvis. Copyright 1936 by Melvin H. Purvis. Reprinted by permission of Doubleday & Company. Excerpt from *Dillinger: A Short and Violent Life* by Robert Cromie and Joseph Pinkston. Copyright © 1962 by Robert Cromie. Reprinted by permission of the authors. Excerpt from *We Band of Brothers* by Ed Guthman. Copyright © 1971 by Edwin Guthman. Reprinted by permission of Harper & Row Publishers, Inc. Excerpts from *The F.B.I. Story* by Don Whitehead. Copyright © 1963 by Don Whitehead. Published by Random House, Inc.

CONTENTS

Preface   ix

PART I

PRIVATE LIFE   3

PART II

PUBLIC LIFE   51

PART III

SECRET LIFE   245

Afterword   321

APPENDIXES

1. Last Will and Testament of J. Edgar Hoover   327
2. Petition of Clyde A. Tolson   328
3. Inventory, Appraisal and Re-appraisal   333
4. Money and Debts Due to Deceased   390

Index   391

PREFACE

Not long before the death of J. Edgar Hoover, as demands for his resignation grew louder, there were many in Washington who agreed with Tom Wicker that the Director of the Federal Bureau of Investigation had "wielded more power, longer, than any man in American history." Wicker even suggested that Hoover's replacement would be "one of the single most important Presidential appointments of this century." That Nixon would pick L. Patrick Gray III says as much about the pitfalls of political prognostication as it does about the former President's selection mechanism.

As to Wicker's assessment of Hoover's power, it will be many years before anyone can produce anything approaching a "definitive" biography. Untold numbers of words have been written about Hoover, more perhaps than about anybody else in this century, but the public record is so replete with distortions, embellishments, half-truths and outright lies that it will take a genius with the patience of Job and the wisdom of Solomon to sift through it.

For a half century, he defended himself and his Bureau against a constant barrage of attacks from the extreme right and extreme left, from the Ku Klux Klan and the Mafia, from fascists and Communists, from racists and integrationists; in fact, through the various stages of the Bureau's history, the attacks have come from nearly every sector of our society. Because of his emotional attachment to the Bureau and his tendentious compulsion to respond to all attacks, however marginal, it is probably true, as critics have charged, that the most prolific weaver of this ghostly cocoon of myths was the Director himself. He spoke and wrote (mostly had ghostwritten) millions of words, a paroxysm of opinions on the nature of political and moral deviates, of bums, rats, diseased women, craven beasts, vermin, vultures, slobs, kooks, misfits, pinkos, rabble-rousers, commies, bleeding-heart judges, sob-sister parole boards, sentimental yammerheads, pseudo intellectuals, so-called liberals—in fact, all the enemies of law and order, as he saw it—but in the process told us next to nothing about the nature of the Director, except, of course, that he was America's foremost bulwark against evil, foreign or domestic.

For most people, the real J. Edgar Hoover was more metaphor than substance. Art Buchwald once suggested that Hoover was a "mythical person first thought up by the *Reader's Digest*." He was Mr. FBI, the indomitable G-man, for so many years that it is quite possible that history will fuse the person with the institution and punch out a statistical chart instead of a three-dimensional portrait of the first cop to have his flag-covered coffin placed on Abraham Lincoln's black catafalque in the Capitol rotunda, and to be eulogized on network television by the President and the Chief Justice of the United States.

Once, in 1963, I had a chance to meet him. An FBI agent called at my home to say that the Director would be pleased to see me the next time I was in Washington. A few weeks later, during a television interview, I called attention to the Bureau's desultory performance in organized crime and civil rights cases and forever became persona non grata. There was a time when I contemplated doing a full-length study of his life and times, but after a few months of unbelievable agony in the archives, I settled for something less ambitious and, from a working standpoint at least, far more interesting. In the spring of 1972, some two months before his death, I began a series of interviews with the thought that oral sketches would lend color and depth to the flat monochrome that would evolve from the written record.

First, however, I had to penetrate that wall of silence Hoover had so carefully erected around himself and his Bureau. Even after his death, the air was so charged with fear that anyone not acquainted with his methods would think it was galloping paranoia. This atmosphere was best expressed in a telephone conversation with Sam Noisette, the Negro who worked forty years as Hoover's valet while officially classified in later years as a special agent. It took several calls before Sam loosened up and told me what was on his mind.

"If you do come to Washington," he said, "I wouldn't want anybody to know that I know you and you know me. I wouldn't want a damn soul to know it but you and me. It's just that touchy. If any man talks to me I wouldn't want him to know that I had been knowing you or whether I had ever just said how-de-do to you. It's just that way. I can't explain in the short time here what the difference is, but there is that difference. I have reasons and naturally I can't discuss them over the telephone, not even a little bit, because the telephone with that sort of information around here is so damn hot you can't hardly sit on the seat next to it and look out the window." Unfortunately, Sam died before he could explain the difference.

There were others, of course, who talked more freely, and much of what they had to say will not be found in any archives. Yet it is tricky business to resort to the memories of others to flesh out the factual skeleton concealed in the cocoon, but with a subject as complex as Hoover it is perhaps the only way. As you will see in reading this book, no effort is made to reconcile reminiscences and opinions with the written record. This is an oral biography, and, as such, it focuses almost exclusively on the recollections of family, colleagues, acquaintances, both admirers and detractors, contemporaries whose firsthand accounts, it is hoped, add a third dimension to the life and times of J. Edgar Hoover.

OVID DEMARIS

PART
I

PRIVATE
LIFE

In Love with Company A

John Edgar Hoover was born in Washington, D.C., on New Year's Day in 1895, the youngest of three children of Dickerson N. Hoover and Annie M. Scheitlin. His father was of old American stock and of British and German origins, and his mother came from a long line of Swiss mercenary soldiers; her uncle, John Hitz, had been the Honorary Consul General of Switzerland. Both Hoover's father and grandfather worked for the Coast and Geodetic Survey, and his brother, Dickerson, Jr., who was fifteen years older, became Inspector General of the Steamboat Inspection Service.

All three children—Dickerson, Jr., Lillian and John Edgar—were born in a small stucco dwelling at 413 Seward Square, a muddy section of row houses occupied mostly by government clerks and their families. It was known locally as Pipetown. As a boy, Hoover was nicknamed Speed, a tribute either to his fleetness of foot or his rapid staccato manner of speech. He was too small to be an athlete, but there is the story that his flattened nose was the result of a hard-hit baseball. Because of his diminutive size when he entered Central High School in 1909, the football coach rejected him on sight, a memory that allegedly evoked twinges ever after. This led to his joining the school's cadet corps, and at the commencement-day dress parade four years later he stepped out as the captain of his company. He was so proud of his cadet uniform that he wore it on Sundays when he sang in the choir and taught a Sunday school class at the Church of the Covenant, a Presbyterian church to which the family belonged.

The story that he seriously considered becoming a minister was repeated so often that in later years Hoover himself came to accept it as fact, frequently alluding to it in interviews.

It was his mother, Jack Alexander wrote in a 1937 *New Yorker* profile, who was the disciplinarian, "rewarding obedience and punishing disobedience with military impartiality. Her domestic justice set up in John a pattern of scrupulous regard for law and zeal for punishing wrongdoing, a pattern which as Director he is now trying to impress upon the American mind." Alexander went on to observe that "the discipline in the Hoover home had little effect on John's brother, Dickerson, Jr.," whom he described as "amiable and easygoing."

In high school John Edgar was known for his morality and celibacy. He never went out with girls, and friends accused him of being in love with Company A, an institutional attachment that biographers came to regard as foreshadowing his marriage to the FBI. As a debater, he successfully argued "The Fallacies of Women Suffrage," and he was described in the school yearbook as "a gentleman of dauntless courage and stainless honor."

Following his graduation in 1913, he took a thirty-dollar-a-month job as an indexer at the Library of Congress and studied law at night at George Washington University, where he earned a Bachelor of Laws degree in 1916 and a Master's in 1917.

A Case of Dominating the Situation

The above summary contains just about all the fact and fiction on his early life available in the archives. As inconceivable as it may seem, no writer—at least, to my knowledge—has ever added a single glimmer of information to Alexander's meager findings. For forty years, Alexander has had the first and last word on Hoover's private life for that period. As a result, it is quite possible that he's been the most plagiarized writer in America. Since plagiarism requires some fancy deception, it is not surprising to find that horrendous distortions have resulted, particularly in the more critical Hoover books.

One thing is certain. Nothing exciting or revealing will ever surface from the written record, which has all the freshness of the Dead Sea Scrolls. This is not the stuff that inspires biographers. There will be no suspenseful weaving of an intricate web of fact and fiction, built around some great dramatic denouement that keeps the reader turning pages until the final word is digested. On the contrary, Hoover would emerge precisely as he's been portrayed throughout most of his lifetime: a cardboard tyrant on a papier-mâché pedestal.

But that is not the real J. Edgar Hoover, not the flesh and blood human being who started out in life as a child like the rest of us, growing up with likes and dislikes, fears and longings, tears and laughter, and leaving impressions for others to cherish or despise. That is the J. Edgar Hoover that I was after and the only place I could find him was in the memories of those who knew him.

What is remarkable about the interviews is that no other writers had availed themselves of the opportunity to speak with most of the people you will meet in these pages. For example, I was amazed to discover that no writer had sought out his two nieces, Mrs. Margaret Fennell and Mrs. Anna Kienast, who probably knew him better when he was a young man than anybody else. In their pleasant recollections the humanity of this seemingly formidable personality comes out in a way that any number of press releases or critical books cannot conceivably reveal. Their revelations are not mind-boggling, but they do show that the inscrutable hero on Abraham Lincoln's black catafalque did indeed at one point have human dimensions.

As the daughters of the elder brother, Dickerson, both Mrs. Fennell and Mrs. Kienast were born at 411 Seward Square, in 1908 and 1915 respectively, and both at various times lived in the same house with J. E., as they called him, and his mother, whom they called Nanny. "Our houses shared a common wall," Mrs. Fennell recalled. "They were nice houses, two stories, with three bedrooms upstairs; downstairs there was a dining room, kitchen, and front and back parlors that were separated by an invisible line—you simply did not go into the front parlor. There was a big back yard that was really nice. Nanny loved flowers and she was always gardening. There was a grape arbor, there were roses, bleeding hearts, lilies-of-the-valley."

His prizefighter profile, they said, was due to a boil on his nose when he was growing up. Although he was named John Edgar, Nanny always called him Edgar, and so did everyone else in the family. I asked about Nanny and of his relationship with his mother.

Mrs. Fennell: "She wasn't dull at all. She was a person who made herself felt. She was a very forceful kind of person, and I think that she always expected that J. E. was going to be successful. And probably encouraged him as much as she could. Now whether it's encouraging or pushing, I don't know, but pushing doesn't hurt sometimes."

MRS. KIENAST: "You had two very strong personalities here. There was never any real fighting. It was a case of dominating the situation. She ran a beautiful home for him, but he provided the wherewithal to run it beautifully. And he was very good to her. He'd give her gifts—jewelry, some very nice jewelry. I remember he also gave her a canary that she always called her jailbird because J. E. bought it from the Birdman of Alcatraz. On the other hand, Nanny always liked to leave the shades down all through the back and front parlors so it was always a very cool, dark atmosphere when J. E. came home in the evening. Then up went the shades. There was no argument about it. He simply would go around and raise the shades and go up to his room. It was a kind of battle of wits on the part of two very intelligent people."

MRS. FENNELL: "He was quite a tyrant about food, I remember. His breakfast—and this goes back to Nanny running the house for him, although they had a cook—was a full-scale operation. She was up and dressed and seated at the breakfast table when he came downstairs. They had breakfast together every morning. His favorite breakfast was a poached egg on toast, and if that egg was broken, he wouldn't eat it. It went back to the kitchen and another egg was prepared. This was pretty funny, because he'd eat one bite of it, then cut it up and put the dish on the floor for Spee Dee Bozo to finish up.

"Spee Dee was his first dog, but I think he was more Nanny's dog. She just thought he was wonderful. She always sort of put down Scottie, sort of made fun of him. Spee Dee was an Airedale, and Scottie was a Scotch terrier. G-boy, who came later, was a cairn. I remember he used to take Spee Dee for a walk every single evening. He took him with him in the morning when he walked over to Pennsylvania Avenue to get the morning paper. When he came in the front door, he'd roll it up and put it in Spee Dee's mouth and he would roar up the steps and take it to Nanny.*

"J. E. liked to walk at night. There were many evenings when we would take a streetcar up to Eighteenth and Columbia Road, which is not such hot territory now, but there was an ice cream place there, and we'd

---

* By February 1972, Hoover's dogs filled seven little graves in the Aspen Hill Pet Cemetery. One headstone bore the inscription "In Memory of Spee Dee Bozo. Born July 3, 1922. Died May 24, 1934. Our best friend." "A man buries his wife because he has to," the cemetery's director observed, "but he buries his dog because he wants to."

get off the streetcar and have ice cream. Our favorites were pistachio and chocolate, and then we'd walk all the way back home. It was quite a hike, but he enjoyed walking. That's something we did two or three times a week.

"Oh, I must tell you that when I was a baby—J. E. was thirteen when I was born—his services were commandeered—seldom volunteered—as a baby-sitter for me, because he frequently told rather embarrassing stories about things that happened on those occasions when he had to push me in my baby carriage for walks on Capitol Hill.

"Thinking back on the years I lived there, this was during Prohibition, and, as I remember, I was enjoying life as most people who are seventeen and eighteen, and I was going out a lot. Nanny liked young people around the house. He cautioned me one evening when I was going out to be careful where I went, and he said, 'If you're in a place that's raided, kindly don't give your right name.' In those days, J. E.'s closest friend was Frank Baughman. It was about that time that J. E. became quite a sharp dresser. I remember he and Frank used to wear white linen suits. And it was around that time too that his doctor had recommended that he smoke a cigarette after dinner to relax. The problem was that he didn't like to smoke alone. I was about sixteen and so he suggested that I smoke too. Well, I'm still smoking, and he stopped years ago.

"Those were busy years for him. And he worked very hard, always bringing home a briefcase full of work. I remember he had a problem with stuttering, and there were many evenings—his bedroom was next to mine—this was at the beginning of his career when he was just beginning to be asked to speak to groups—and I can remember hearing him practice whatever it was he was going to say. He had quite a problem there, which he overcame."

As I sat listening to these two gracious ladies in the Maryland home of Mrs. Kienast, I couldn't help but wonder at the incongruities they were inflicting on my subconscious. My God, the nemesis of draft dodgers, enemy aliens and anarchists was human after all. He liked dogs, ice cream and stuttered. Not only that, but these happy failings had been kept from us, his public, all these years. Later, of course, there would be more important revelations, but meanwhile, back in Mrs. Kienast's living room, the atmosphere was warm and congenial.

MRS. KIENAST: "When the neighborhood began to deteriorate, he became very anxious to move away. He wanted to find a house in Chevy

Chase, but he never was able to get Nanny to agree to any of the houses he looked at. They would go on Sunday afternoons and look at two or three houses, and when they came home there was always a flaw in whatever they looked at. I remember on one occasion, they had come back from looking at what was probably a very lovely home, and Nanny said, yes, it had lots of things about it she liked, but there was one step down from the hall into the living room and that ruled it out—it couldn't be considered. He must have found this very frustrating, considering the fact they had a parquet floor in the dining room that was kept waxed to within an inch of your life, and Nanny would get up from a chair in the back parlor and go headlong through that room to the kitchen without taking a breath. She was sure-footed as a deer."

"He Had a Fear of Becoming too Personally Involved with People"

Mrs. Fennell: "Of course, there is something you have to remember. J. E. had the responsibility of caring for his mother during the last years of her life, but there was also a period much earlier when my grandfather was ill and while J. E. was still in school, when things were not so easy financially for his father and mother, and this responsibility fell on our father. Grandfather died of pneumonia when he was still quite young. I know he had a nervous breakdown there at one time. He was up at Laurel at the sanitarium. Why, I really don't know. I've never heard any reason advanced for it."

Mrs. Kienast: "Nanny was around seventy-eight when she died [in 1938]. We always thought it was cancer, but it was in the days when nobody mentioned cancer. She was bedridden nearly three years. I often thought this was one reason he never married. He didn't have a chance. When he might have married, there was his mother and there was no room in the house for another woman and he simply did not have the money to run two establishments."

Mrs. Fennell: "I think he regarded women as a kind of hindrance. You know, they sort of got in your way when you were going places. I think this is the difference between him and Father. Father married, he had a family, he had other considerations. In many ways, they were quite alike, but I think that early in his career, J. E. decided that he was going to achieve something big and I don't think he let himself be distracted from that. To me this is a very important quality in one who is headed for the top. And I sometimes have thought that he really—I don't know how to put it—had a fear of becoming too personally involved with people. He was always very gracious and fed you a lot of kidding and everything, but I think a lot of it was surface. And it's this kidding business that carried on into his adult life. He was known for his practical jokes.

"I think you would have to say that he was not a family person. I don't remember Aunt Lillian too well. She married a man called Robinette and moved out to the country. She used to come visit, bringing the young children, Fred and Marjorie, but I have only a very faint recollection of that. I know she had a hard time. Her husband died and she was crippled for many years. I've heard that J. E. never visited her, but I don't have any personal knowledge of it. I do know that he got to her funeral late and left early. He and Clyde Tolson came together. In all fairness, I must say that J. E. was always accessible if we wanted to see him, but he didn't initiate contacts with his family. I've never known of any instance when he was not available if you wanted to see him—if not available that day, he would be available the next day."

Were you surprised that he left the bulk of his estate to Clyde Tolson?

MRS. KIENAST: "Yes, I was. I had no idea that he would remember anyone in the family, and none of us really wanted it that way, but it was my feeling that he would leave his estate to charity, and it was quite a surprise to all of us to see it go to Clyde Tolson, who must be pretty well-off himself. But again that was his business."

Did you attend his funeral?

MRS. FENNELL: "Yes, they kept the coffin open for the family. I thought he looked very well. This is one of the advantages of dying suddenly. Of course, he always took real good care of himself. He was always careful to get his checkups every year. He looked very good, I thought, but smaller than I remembered. I guess death does that to you."

Adulation Bordering on the Fanatical

Many acquaintances have called themselves his friend, but throughout his lifetime Hoover had only two close friends, Frank Baughman and Clyde Tolson, both Bureau subordinates. It is possible that Baughman, who was a law school classmate of Hoover's, was less a subordinate than Tolson, whose tenure as Associate Director, the Bureau's number two spot, was a direct result of Hoover's friendship—or was it vice versa? Baughman, who became the Bureau's ballistics expert when the laboratory was created in 1932, lost his inside track when he got married.

Many agents have tried to up their status through social contacts with the Boss, as most of his friends addressed him, but no one else really succeeded. Louis B. Nichols, who devoted his prodigious promotional talents to lionizing Hoover, even named one of his children J. Edgar.

Outside of the Bureau, however, there are many who count themselves as his friend, and I have tried to talk to as many of them as I could. Unfortunately, too many were entirely too selective in the memories they wished to impart. They delicately tiptoed around unpleasant questions, their eyes going suddenly wary, a warning that I soon learned to respect. Their adulation, in some instances, bordered on the fanatical. Movie director Mervyn LeRoy tried to recant his reflections when it suddenly occurred to him that the book might not be 100 percent favorable. "If there is one derogatory word in that book, I don't want to be in it," he frantically informed me on the telephone weeks after his interview. When I told him that it was going to be as objective as I could make it, he threatened to forbid all of his friends from talking to me. The image many wished to convey was that of a man with no weakness or vice, unsoiled by any sexual desire (he never fell in love, heterosexually or homosexually), who was totally disciplined (he never got drunk, never took the Lord's name in vain), with the result that the image projected became emotionally sterile, more of a freak than a saint. Yet even the most biased reflection can sometimes add insight where none at all existed before. It is with this reservation in mind that excerpts from some of the more loyalist interviews are included in this section dealing with his private life.

Part of the problem, I think, is that most of his friends enjoyed a rather tenuous relationship. For example, George E. Allen, a wealthy Washington lobbyist, told me that their friendship went back forty years. They went to the races together just about every week, they had dinner at Harvey's Restaurant a couple of times a week, they vacationed in Florida in the winter and in California in the summer, and yet he never had the courage to question Hoover on anything he said. "Let me explain something to you," Allen said. "The worst thing you can do with a man like Hoover is bore him to death. So I couldn't ask him all those questions, you see. This just had to come naturally as he was talking. So a lot of things I can't give you a definite reason for, because I don't know what his reasons were."

As it so happens, George Allen is not the shy retiring type. He is the author of a book entitled *Presidents Who Have Known Me*. Allen began his Washington career as FDR's court jester and graduated to being Ike's golf and bridge partner. In between, he played a lot of poker with Harry Truman. Allen and two Texas oilmen, W. Alton Jones and B. B. (Billy) Byars, contributed more than $500,000 to the upkeep of Eisenhower's Gettysburg farm at a time when he, as President, was doing all within his power to enhance the profits of the oil industry. President Truman, who appointed Allen to the Reconstruction Finance Corporation, later referred to him as a "fixer" willing to do anything to ingratiate himself with someone in power.

I interviewed Allen in his Washington law offices in June 1972, some ten months before his death, and if anyone ever looked the part of a crafty country lawyer, the roly-poly cracker-barrel wit in the baggy suit, the back-slapping hail-fellow-well-met, it was George Allen. When I continued to press him for answers, he got angry: "Listen, if Hoover hadn't died, I wouldn't even be talking to you. I've never talked to the press, because Hoover wouldn't have liked it. He didn't like for people to talk to the press. He had another terrific trait and I'm not sure it wasn't good—Tolson used to do this quite a bit himself. If you ever wrote an article that was critical of the FBI, he answered you. He came right back. He answered anybody in the world. I'm not sure I approve. I've always gone on the theory that people will forget it in two weeks. But he would get incensed, called them scavengers, garbage collectors, all that stuff, but he was never vulgar, never used foul language."

The instinct to protect and defend appears almost genetic in most of his friends. At the first sight of blood, they retreat, but sometimes it's too late. Dorothy Lamour's husband, Bill Howard, knew Hoover some thirty-odd years. Every year when Hoover and Tolson visited La Jolla, they would spend a few days in Beverly Hills with friends.

HOWARD: "We would give a barbecue at our house and there would be just Edgar and Clyde, and Dorothy and myself. Nobody else was invited. He so enjoyed privacy where he could relax. He would do the cooking and be the bartender. He would mix what he called the G-man drink, which was a nice strong one, but not too many of them. Then he would do the barbecuing and we'd sit in the back yard. One night Louella Parsons, who lived right around the corner, decided to stop by and pay us a visit. And she rang the doorbell, and you couldn't say, 'Don't come in,' to

Louella Parsons. So Louise [Lester], our maid, gave her every excuse in the world and she said, 'Well, there's something going on here if you're giving me all these excuses, Louise, so I'm coming in,' and in she walked. Well, she was also very fond of Edgar and Clyde, and so she never did publish anything about it but that was a little ticklish situation."

In what way?

HOWARD: "Well, you didn't know what a person of the press might publish about a man who was as prominent as the Director was. What if she saw him with a drink in his hand or a steak in his hand, or what if he happened to mention some name that she might be interested in, she might use it. So that was a ticklish point. You had to be very careful about that. I remember once Edgar had his picture taken with Dorothy at a very famous nightclub called Mocambo, but there were no drinks in front of him or anything else. They cleared the whole table."

Judged by today's standards, this is hard to comprehend. Meanwhile, nobody gave a second thought to Jesse Strider, Hoover's black FBI chauffeur in Los Angeles, who was waiting out in the limousine. Howard wasn't sure Hoover had a chauffeur, but his maid knew it: "I remember because he used to sit in the car, he wouldn't come inside, and we used to take him sandwiches, remember, Mr. Bill."

Hoover just overwhelmed most of his—I hate to use this word—*so-called* friends. For Lawrence Welk, "It was one of the highlights of my lifetime that I had a chance to know him and to be acquainted with him, and I have always felt very flattered that he and the type of person he is would listen to my show. I have a very warm feeling for the people who have worked for the FBI. As a general group of people, I have felt that they were possibly the most dedicated and loyal and honest people that I've ever known in a group of people bunched together like that. I was invited to see him and I was very flattered when I found out he was a fan of mine, and I used to call him when I would go through there."

Don Smith, who has been general manager of the Del Mar racetrack since the days when Bing Crosby operated it, considers himself a friend of Hoover's, but he is convinced that Hoover was "not the sort of man you can become intimate with."

SMITH: "I know a lot of people like that who have many, many friends, but no real close friends. I mean, they don't get attached to one person—except for Tolson, who did everything for him, and they were as close as anybody can be, I guess; but as far as other people were concerned, he was always very friendly, but you never could get that close to him. He was a very disciplined man. All the time I've seen him, I've never seen him out of place, or offensive, or difficult with anybody. Always a perfect gentleman with everybody."

A Question of Freeloading

Much has been written about Hoover's hobnobbing with Texas oilmen in La Jolla, California. Columnist Jack Anderson was the first to charge that Hoover and Tolson had freeloaded in La Jolla. In a column dated May 12, 1971, Anderson wrote, "They stayed in $100-a-day suites at the Hotel Del Charro near the Del Mar track. The FBI pair never paid their bills, which were picked up by Texas oil millionaire Clint Murchison, the hotel owner. The former hotel manager, Allan Witwer, told us that while Hoover was there he ran up a total tab of over $15,000 picked up by Murchison."

What Witwer neglected to tell Anderson was that he was running around the country with, in his own words, "suitcases full of documentation" which he was trying to peddle to the highest bidder. I know because I was on his list. By the time he got to me, I knew he had already struck out with *Life,* the Los Angeles *Times,* and *Ramparts,* for God's sake. "Well, sir, I'll tell you something," Witwer told me in a telephone conversation. "You're talking to the man who has the only documentation in existence about this man, and this is no extravagant boast. I was president of the Del Charro from 1953 to 1959, when it all happened, the important years. Let me tell you something. There is so much documentation that I would be on the phone with you for a day, you see. It is all extensively and thoroughly documented, backup correspondence, *Life* contract which I declined, so much it's exhausting, but I pursued it for years."

When I asked if Murchison had picked up the tab, Witwer said, "He picked up part, an insurance company picked up part, and an oil company picked up part. And I have the originals and the duplicates. I have it all down, you know, letters, travel expenses, summit meetings with Sid Richardson and Murchison, and Murchison's personal letters to me asking for Hoover's bills—the whole damn thing."

Witwer's failure to sell the Hoover documentation was not due to inexperience. He had pulled off a pretty good coup in the Bahamas, where he had worked in the first casino on Grand Bahama Island. Jim Bishop described what happened in his syndicated column: "So I got him [Witwer] a job as a publicity agent. He worked a couple of years, smiling his way from one typewriter to another. Then he showed me a jumble of the most incoherent writing I've ever seen. It was an exposé of his boss. I'm a slow thinker. He didn't want to publish the junk; he wanted the boss to buy it from him. The boss did: for $60,000. So I lost two friends in one shot." But Witwer, it turned out, had kept copies of his documentation. Somehow it was leaked to the *Wall Street Journal*, winning that newspaper the Pulitzer Prize.

In an outline entitled *Now It Can Be Told*, Witwer charged that the "services of Nixon's man, Herb Klein, were used to euchre me out of the Murchison empire painlessly . . . [sic] but finally." Witwer said he was asked to attend a "settlement meeting at the Los Angeles Town House [now the Sheraton West] to be attended by Ed Crowley . . . and George Anson, Clint Murchison's chief counsel."

I talked with Edward J. Crowley back in March 1972, some two months before Hoover's death. If this interview shows anything, it emphasizes once more how remote Hoover really was with certain of his friends.

CROWLEY: "My first meetings with Mr. Hoover were with Clint Murchison and Sid Richardson, the fabulous Texas oilmen. In the old days when they went to the Scripps Clinic, we all used to stay at the Casa Mañana Hotel. That was before 1954, when we built—Mr. Murchison—the Del Charro Hotel. We built four bungalows there in the back of the hotel. Mr. Richardson had one, the Murchisons had one, Mr. Hoover had one, and we moved from the Casa Mañana to our little hotel. The Texans would come out in the summer and we'd gather around the pool for breakfast and talk over old times and the races and then we'd go to Del Mar. Mr. Hoover and Clyde Tolson would go a couple times a week and sit up there in their own little booth. And this went on summer after summer after summer."

Who were the Texans?

CROWLEY: "Clint and Sid, of course, and Billy Byars, Wofford Cain, Buddy Fogelson and his wife, Greer Garson, Don Harrington, Robert Thompson, and a few others. They'd fly in and out in their own planes. And, of course, my friendship grew with both Mr. Hoover and Clyde Tolson. But I didn't ever bother him. I'd go to the track with our gang and we'd be on one side and he and Clyde would sit up a way. In other words, we had boxes and we spent a lot of time being directors in the directors' room. Mr. Murchison in his later years was crippled and had to sit up in the directors' room with us so we could wheel him in, but Clyde and Mr. Hoover would sit kind of up there on their own. Everybody would kind of stop by, you know, and say hello, but they let him alone, they didn't bother him. I never went up and said, 'You got a good one?' or any of that jazz. But don't get the wrong impression. He's very outgoing, he's very warm. I'd go fishing with Phil Harris and Bing Crosby and I'd send salmon to Wofford and Effie Cain and they'd have Mr. Hoover over for dinner at their home on the beach near Del Mar. He'd have dinner there and the next day he'd send a bunch of flowers—you see, that's the kind of fellow he is.

"Let me tell you what happened a year ago right now. I'm the Recreation and Park Commissioner for the city of Los Angeles, and I went to Washington to ballyhoo our convention center. I dropped Mr. Hoover a note saying, 'I'm going to be in Washington,' and one of his agents called me up, out of the blue, and said, 'Well, Mr. Hoover would like to see you, Ed.' I made arrangements to take one of the heads of United Airlines with me, but at the last minute he got called away. So I called the agent, a very delightful man, and said, 'The other man can't come but I have a lovely young lady here, not my date or anything, but back here helping us and she'd just love to see Mr. Edgar Hoover.' And he said, 'Bring her along.' So she said, 'I'm going to take a postcard and ask Mr. Hoover for his autograph.' So we went and visited for a while and the little girl said, 'Mr. Hoover, could I have your autograph?' And he said, 'Wouldn't you rather have your picture taken with Ed Crowley and me?' The little girl about died. She's a lovely gal, Dory Merrill, she's a PR girl for the Ambassador, but I got a kick out of it. She was worried about asking for an autograph and he says, 'Why don't we have a picture taken?' I'm on his mailing list and I write once in a while and always say, 'I'll see you in La Jolla in the summer.'

"Now, the thing that hurt me about the whole affair—I got that kid [Allan Witwer] the job as manager of that hotel and then we couldn't fire him. He came up here one day and said, 'If you can me, I'm going to blast Mr. Hoover and tell that you're picking up his tab and all that.' Well, he was a guest of the Murchisons, nothing wrong, we didn't want anything, but there was a big scandal and that Anderson keeps pecking away at it. I sat and I talked to the kid and I said, 'Allan, who are you hurting? You're not hurting the Murchisons.' Look, Mr. Hoover is an institution. He hasn't done anything. We were all together at the Casa Mañana. He comes out, he comes to his home—it's the man's hotel. I'm not even sure he paid all his bills, I don't know. I imagine he did—the kid was the manager. But it wasn't one of those things. Edgar Hoover was our friend. I might have him in here [Town House] as my guest. I don't need anything in Washington. Those scandalmongers. It always hurts me when I read those articles about Mr. Hoover. He is such a down-to-earth, fine, warm man. I've been in Washington many times, but this last time is the only time that I said I'd like to see him. I know he's busy, there's just a line of people all day long. He hasn't got a chance. It's awful.

"Look at this picture. I go back there and a girl wants an autograph and he asks wouldn't you rather have your picture taken? He's a nice guy. He didn't have to call me. He's a hell of a guy. So what if Mr. Hoover comes out there for a week or two and he's his guest? I'm complimenting guys and gals all the time in the operation of the hotel."

Clint Murchison and Sid Richardson operated the Del Mar racetrack as a charity foundation, which George E. Allen characterized as a racket.

ALLEN: "It was a racket, if you want to know what it was. You see, they could go in and buy the track with their foundation, the Boys' Club deal, and there's no taxes. They would lend the money, then get it back, but, you see, they would then control the track. Sure the Boys' Clubs would get something, but it was a tax racket. One time they wanted to buy all the tracks in the United States. George Humphrey, who was Secretary of the Treasury, wouldn't let them do it."

It was an ambitious project.

ALLEN: "When a man has made a lot of money, when he's got nothing but money, he's got to think of things like that to do. Clint and Sid were each worth about half a billion dollars."

When I asked Don Smith about it, he said he had trouble trying to explain the operation to people.

SMITH: "The operating company that ran the racetrack was a regular organized California corporation operating for profit. That's what I had to keep explaining to people all the time. I never did explain it to everybody; they never could understand it. The Del Mar Turf Club was actually the operating company for Boys Incorporated, but we were a private corporation operating only for profit, just like any other business. The fact that we paid rent to Boys Incorporated was incidental to business. The amount of rent we paid was not the important thing. We were a separate corporation. And we operated that way, completely and very distinct from the charity. We had to. That's the way we were set up and that's the way—There were pretty smart people involved in this thing, they knew what the law was [laughs], and I worked like hell to make it work because I thought it was a great idea."

Marine General Howland "Howling Mad" Smith, the hero of Guadalcanal and a trustee of Boys Incorporated, was obviously one of those people who never understood Smith—or perhaps understood him too well. At any rate, he became disenchanted with the meager profits realized by the foundation and blasted the Texas oilmen in a news story. In response to the General's charges, Hoover gave an exclusive interview to the *Morning Telegraph:* "I know Clint Murchison quite well," he said, "and I think he would be the last person in the country to use such a plan as a clever tax or business subterfuge. In fact, I spoke to Murchison about ten years ago about devoting some time and help to youth work, and the charitable corporation of Del Mar is one of his answers. This work helps directly in making the nation sturdy, for communist penetration is currently directed mainly at labor organizations and youth organizations."

It must have come as a pleasant surprise to the oilmen that their little summer sojourn away from the Texas heat to the balmy shores of La Jolla was instrumental in the fight against Communism. They were under the impression that their front man, Senator Joe McCarthy, was carrying the ball on that project.

It was in the same interview that Hoover offered his now famous rationale for horse racing: "Actually, from a law-enforcement standpoint, a well-conducted racetrack is a help to a community, if only for the reason that the people at the track are finding an outlet for their emotions, which if they weren't at the track, they might use for less laudable escapades."

In the old days, Hoover stayed at the Gulf Stream Hotel in Miami, which was owned by the family of G. David Schine, the once celebrated sidekick of Joe McCarthy and Roy Cohn. I don't know if they complimented him in Miami for the twelve to fourteen days he spent there every year at Christmastime, but he did enjoy a free ride at Harvey's in Washington, D.C. for the twenty-odd years that Julius Lulley owned it. The last waiter who attended him at Harvey's was William Holley. "I waited on Mr. Hoover from 1951 until, I guess, 1965," Holley told me. "When his other waiter left, they wanted to know who was going to take the responsibility of waiting on Mr. Hoover, and Mr. Lulley came up with the idea that I was the most capable. Mr. Lulley thought Mr. Hoover was a god. Mr. Hoover required a lot of care. If he didn't like something, he told you about it, but kind of kiddingly. I'd always have to bone his fish for him, and if there were any bones in it, he was going to have me locked up.

"They came around three or four times a week. Most times it was just the two of them, Mr. Hoover and Mr. Tolson. Very little company. There wouldn't be any spare chairs at the table. It was a table for four but I'd always take away the extra chairs so that nobody could sit down. Of course, the house took care of everything, except the tip, which they gave me in cash, ten percent. I signed all of his checks. He never saw a check. As long as Mr. Lulley was there, that was just written off. After Mr. Lulley died, his business manager operated it for a long time and that policy didn't change one bit. Then Jesse Brinkman bought it and they didn't go for all this freeloading stuff. I never did present him with a check, but they sent him a bill in the mail. His visits tapered off, and finally he just stopped coming completely. He's never been to the new location."

HOWARD: "Julius was a heavyset, tall, jolly man who was one of the greatest restaurateurs that ever lived. They had wonderful personnel and the atmosphere was beautiful and nobody had better get within three tables of Edgar Hoover that wasn't all right. His table was always reserved for him and nobody could sit there. The protection was on the moment he walked in. There couldn't be a noisy group of people or anybody inebriated—they would be shunted to the third floor. On the elevator. Edgar didn't like to drink in public. Usually at Harvey's he would have two or three or four miniatures before dinner as we sat there on an evening. The miniatures would be behind the napkin, and Clyde would pour one miniature and dispose of the bottle. He had a very good appetite in those days—I'm talking about the thirties and forties—a gourmet eater, and it better be right. And, of course, they didn't dare serve him anything that wasn't right. The food had to be served properly, cooked properly, and everything else had to be just so. If not, the waiter heard about it. I mean, if a glass of water wasn't in position or a napkin wasn't on the table, why the waiter got a going over. But the waiter, Shorty, who was a colored man, loved him. Edgar would threaten to send him to Siberia or someplace else, you know, but the waiter knew he loved to kid and laugh."

Hoover mellowed in his later years. Donald E. King, his waiter at the Del Charro in 1969 and 1970, never saw that side of Hoover.

KING: "Mr. Hoover and Mr. Tolson had dinner by the pool every night. They sort of sat in a corner with their backs to a wall, with a view that commanded the whole pool area. They were always alone. Nobody ever went near the table. Not even the busboys. He and Clyde came out at eight sharp and left around ten. They ate and then sat a while listening to the entertainment we had by the pool, a guitar player and singer. Mr. Hoover was not a hard person to wait on. Most of the time he had—they both did, he did all the ordering—prime rib, medium well, no potato, and a green salad with his own dressing, Milani 1890. He brought it the first night and we kept it there for him. Brought his own special kind of salt, too. On occasion he liked olive oil and vinegar, and it was a special kind of olive oil. Dessert was normally Crenshaw melon or pineapple sherbet. Once in a while they had steak, New York cut, and it was flown in special by a company in Los Angeles. Also the sherbet was flown in special by Carnation. He tipped fifteen percent, right down the line. He never complained about anything. I never took a piece of meat back, he never left a big piece indicating that it wasn't done right or something. I thoroughly enjoyed him.

"They are both great gentlemen. The first week he was there I was so impressed that I took my wife Barbara over to his table one night. And I was told nobody goes near the table—as I said, not even the busboys. I took Barb over and I said, 'Gentlemen, I realize I'm violating all security measures or whatever, but I like you two so much that I would like to present my wife, Barbara.' They both stood up and shook hands with her, and Clyde sat down because he wasn't well—excused himself and sat down—but Hoover stayed there standing all the time Barbara was there. He could probably have had me thrown in jail, you know, or whatever, but extremely nice. The next year, Barb and Leslie were both there, and I told Hoover and Tolson that they were there. I said, 'If you get a chance, would you mind stopping by and saying hello and meeting my daughter.' He said he'd be delighted. When they left, Clyde went right on over to the room, and Hoover came over to the table, shook hands with Barbara, told her how nice it is to see her again, and how nice it was to meet Leslie. Just a perfect, perfect gentleman. Right down the line."

Great Fun to Be With

There is no question that J. Edgar Hoover, the stern disciplinarian, was great fun to be with when he was relaxing. "He knew about conversation," actor Jimmy Stewart told me. "He knew about the— Sort of— He wasn't a shy introvert at all. He knew about all sorts of things. He liked to meet people, he liked to be with people, and I thought always that he was very easy to be with and it always surprised me. Every time I met him, no matter when it was, the first time I met him or the last time, it always surprised me that he was so easy to be with and so easy to talk to and—uh— he put everybody around him at ease [pause] I thought." (There was something about Hoover that made people want to make speeches about him.) "Yet—uh—I had a feeling that I was with a very strong, determined man, always," Stewart added gratuitously. "He knew the answers—as far as law enforcement was concerned, he knew the answers to most of the things that people would ask him, but he was always looking and always improving and always trying to better the agency. Of course, I mean, I'm completely biased in Mr. Hoover's favor. I think [pause] I think that what he did for his country was a monumental thing, and I hope that someone can come and take his place, because I think the country certainly needs it. There isn't any question about that, in my mind, and I just hope somebody turns up that can follow in his footsteps." Now, that's quite a mouthful for Jimmy Stewart.

WELK: "I called him in Washington one day and asked if he was free for lunch, and when he said yes I told him I had already invited the girls from my home state of North Dakota that worked for Senator Milton Young, and asked if it was okay and he said, 'Oh, certainly.' Mr. Hoover was very bright and told a lot of little stories and spoke a lot of wisdom, and later on the girls told me that was the highlight of their lifetime, they were so impressed with the man. That was in 1971, just a year before he passed on. I think I seldom went to Washington without giving him a ring, and a few times when we came I think we went up and said hello to him in his office, and then they showed us around in his office one time. And it's something that— Let me say, the feeling that I have when I meet big people like that is that I am a little bit timid about it. I'm a little back-

ward and I recognize how important they are to the nation and how valuable they are and I try not to take their time any more than I have to.

"I was on his mailing list and he sent me his magazine each month and
I read his writing and I bought everything he said. I was very strong in
his philosophies for America. I, of course, am that way about our country.
I feel that our country needs more men of his caliber. I think he was a
powerful man for America."

WILLIAM P. ROGERS, former Attorney General and Secretary of
State: "Edgar Hoover was a very genial man to be with and he liked to
tell stories and he told them very well. He told stories about the FBI when
you prompted him. We used to see him socially in Miami too, when
President Nixon was Vice President and I was Attorney General. We
used to go to Key Biscayne, and Edgar and Clyde Tolson used to stay at
the Gulf Stream in Miami. I remember Edgar's birthday—wasn't it January first? We'd have dinner, Clyde and Edgar and Mr. Nixon and myself.
Edgar and Mr. Nixon were good friends. Edgar used to come to the
President's home for dinner. Matter of fact, I think the last time that
Edgar was on *Air Force One* was the time that Mrs. Rogers and I were on
the plane too and President Nixon had a birthday party and a cake for
him on the plane. And there's some pictures of that occasion in the White
House. I think it was in January 1972, the year that he died."

ALLEN: "He'd discuss every case with you. Tell you everything.
Hoover was a very outgoing fellow and he would never say, 'Don't quote
me.' Never. He didn't care what he said. He told you what he wanted to
tell you, and he never had any fear about it. He'd never hesitate to tell
you what he thought. He was absolutely fearless—there was no fear in
him."

LEROY: "The last time I saw Edgar we went to Washington to have
dinner with President Nixon, myself, my Kitty, and Irene Dunne. It was
a dinner for the President of Finland [on July 23, 1970]. I called Edgar
up from here and I said, 'Edgar, I'd like to spend a half hour with you.'
And he said, 'Well, you know, Mervyn, I'll keep a half hour open.' Well,
we were in his office two and a half hours with him and during that time
he was telling us about the Chappaquiddick case. Very, very interesting. I
can't tell you what he said, but you can bet that much of what he said
never came out in the press. He wasn't afraid to tell you things. He wasn't

afraid of anybody. You know, of course, he was no friend of the Kennedys —that you know."

Harry Duncan, a neighbor of Hoover's, was a close friend for many years: "We spent many, many very pleasant and wonderful years together. He was good at any kind of talk. He was the greatest guy there was for conversation. And he was quite a jokester and trickster. He got a big kick out of life and joking with people. He was a great practical joker. Everybody can say that for him. We used to have a friend by the name of Harry Viner. He was Jewish and owned a big laundry here. Harry had a funny way of talking, had a Jewish accent, and the Boss could imitate him pretty well. Of course, they were close friends. Whenever we were in Florida we had to go over to Harry's house for one meal, or we'd meet him down at Getty's, a restaurant down there where we ate occasionally."

Former Congressman Emanuel Celler remembers those days: "We were always puzzled as to how a friendship could exist between Hoover and Tolson and Harry Viner. Viner was a peculiar individual, a rough and tumble sort of man who pulled himself up by his bootstraps, an immigrant, who went into the laundry business in Washington and became wealthy. Viner was very uncouth and we never could understand the relationship between the two because they'd be together almost every night.

"Viner spoke with an accent and Hoover would imitate him—he would do both voices. He'd say, 'Harry, were you in Europe this summer?' Then he'd answer, 'Yes, I vas to Europe.' 'Did you go to Switzerland?' 'Yah.' 'How did you like Switzerland?' 'Vell, take away da Halps and vat've ya got to Svitzerlun?' 'Where else did you go in Europe?' 'How should I know where I goes, Rae [his wife], she buys the tickets.' That's the kind of guy he was."

The Band Arrived in a Hearse

There is no doubt in my mind that they truly admired and respected him. And perhaps even if they wanted to draw blood, they wouldn't know where to find it, at least not knowingly. Like most of us, Hoover had his friends compartmentalized. Many of them, including Stewart, LeRoy and Welk, never knew of his fondness for practical jokes.

HOLLEY: "One time Mr. Hoover had all the road signs changed going to Mr. Lulley's farm in Bowie. Got people mixed up on how to get there.

He was a great prankster. One time he dumped a basket of silver down the steps, and another time his other waiter, Shorty Clay, was going on a trip and Mr. Hoover called the police and had them stop him for fifteen minutes just to shake him up. Things of that sort."

MRS. FENNELL: "He was one of the world's worst teases. Oh, the sleepless nights I used to spend when he'd tell me that if I swallowed an orange seed a tree would grow out of my belly button. He played a lot of jokes on Julius Lulley. Once Julius was having a dinner party at his home which was to be catered by his restaurant. What he didn't know was that J. E. had the driveway blocked by special agents so the catering truck never arrived."

General Harry Vaughan was the White House's liaison with the FBI during the Truman Administration: "One day while I was having lunch with Hoover at Harvey's, I mentioned that I planned to spend the weekend at William Hellis's farm in New Jersey. Now Hellis was a Greek multi-millionaire who owned oil wells and a steamship company. He bought the Sinclair farm, a gorgeous place, worth millions, and he was a great friend of mine. Hoover said, 'Say, ask Bill to send me some of that pork sausage he makes over there, it's the best in the world.' When I mentioned that to Hellis as I was about to leave on Monday, he found he was temporarily out of sausage, so he said, 'We've got it on the hoof.' They got a little shoat, about eight weeks old, and put it in a crate.

"The pig didn't say a word all the way to the Justice Building, but the minute I got in the elevator, he said, 'Oink, oink,' and everybody was looking and wondering what the hell was the funny noise. When I got to Hoover's office, he was out, and his secretary and three or four of the girls said, 'Ain't he cute,' and 'Oh, let's see it,' and I said, 'Okay, I'll leave it with you.' They pulled a slat open and the pig got out and ran around the office, and, of course, the press gave me credit for going in and clowning and turning a pig loose in Hoover's office.

"Everybody got a big laugh out of it, including Hoover, who called me the next day to say that Lulley was going to raise it for him out there on his farm in Maryland. He said, 'When it weighs about a hundred pounds, we'll have a feast.' I forgot about it, and about a year and a half later, I was talking to him on the phone, and I said, 'What about that pig roast?' He said, 'We've lost it. She's turned out to be the finest brood sow. She had a brood of ten pigs last month, and Lulley says we'll kill her over his dead body. He's going to keep her.'

"Oh, about a week after I brought the shoat to his office, he sent me this book—I don't know what you call it, but they paste all the pages together and cut the center out to make a receptacle—a jack-in-the-box type of thing, and it had an imitation hotdog on a spring hidden inside and when you opened the book, the thing popped up. The title on the cover said, *How To Raise A Dog*, and inside it was inscribed in Hoover's writing, and it said: 'To my favorite General: May you be uplifted by this offspring of the pig you brought me,' and it was signed, J. Edgar Hoover."

HOWARD: "He was a great kidder and a man of great humor. He loved to play jokes on Lulley. If Julius was about to do anything that Edgar thought his wife—I think her name was Birdie—might object to, Edgar would make it a point to find out everything he had done and then write her a letter or send Birdie a photograph of him at a function that maybe she would have objected to. And it was always just a running gag to pull Julius's leg. He loved to go to Julius's farm out near Bowie. One time Julius had this beautiful barbecue at his farm, and the band arrived in a hearse. Edgar had hired the hearse, and his agents down the road had taken the musicians out of their cars and loaded them into the hearse. And this big hearse pulled up in front of all the guests and the band got out of it. Anything for a laugh. I often wondered how he could afford to do it on his salary, but to him it was worth fifty bucks or whatever it cost to get that much of a laugh.

"He enjoyed a good joke more than anything in the world, and by that I mean if you tried to play a joke on him, look out, because about fourteen other jokes are going to be played on you. One time my friend and I got a piece of Stork Club paper and just put our fingerprints on it without using any lampblack or ink, folded the envelope, mailed it to him special delivery, and two days later a man knocked at our apartment with a complete rundown on both of us. But that's the only joke I ever played on him. I didn't fool with Edgar that way. I was afraid of him. Well, I respected him, let's put it that way, and the man had so many serious things on his mind.

"Did you know that Edgar loved the Stork Club? Sherman Billingsley was a very good friend of his because Sherman was a real tough man from Oklahoma, but Sherman was honest and fair. I knew Sherman in Prohibition times when he had all his speakeasies, even when he had 51½ East Fifty-first Street, which was a speakeasy with slot machines on the second floor. His suppliers were the top people in the rackets, like Owney Madden, Maxie Gordon, Frank Costello, Longie Zwillman, Little Augie, Big Frenchy—he knew them all. But his downfall was fighting the unions. He would not have a union man in his place, and that's what finally broke him."

ALLEN: "Walter Winchell introduced Hoover to Billingsley. Hoover was crazy about Winchell. Don't forget, Winchell did a hell of a job for Hoover, if you get down to it. He really helped Hoover's image with his radio show and newspaper column. I heard Hoover in the Stork Club one night tell one of the toughest guys in the country that as long as he stayed out of Edgar's bailiwick, he'd stay out of his. I won't tell you who it was, except that he was a Mafia boy who always went to the barbershop in the Waldorf."

The only story that anyone ever told me about Hoover that had the remotest connection with straight sex came from Allen: "There's a funny story he used to tell on himself about the time he went to a Bar Association meeting out in El Paso. Frank Murphy was Attorney General then and if you remember, it was Murphy's sister who said, 'He looks more like Jesus Christ every day.' Murphy was a very sanctimonious Catholic. It so happened that there was a madam over in Juarez who was one of Hoover's informers, and so when he and Clyde got in that first evening, they went over to check with her on some information. Of course, the girls in the house saw them. The next night, after Murphy gave his speech, he told Hoover, 'I've heard all about this slum section in Juarez, I'd like to see it.' So as they were driving around, they came by that madam's house and one of the gals looked into the car and said, 'Hey, you back here again tonight?' Hoover said Murphy damn near fired him."

Just Part of the Service

If his friends are overly protective about his reputation, he on the other hand was a very thoughtful friend. And if at times he used the Bureau as a private catering service to facilitate his consideration, it was perfectly understandable. He was the patriarch. He had given birth to his organization, had nurtured it, defended it, watched over it like a brood hen. No one, not the press or any of his friends or superiors (at least in protocol), ever gave it a second thought.

HOWARD: "I'd like to show you several ashtrays that we have as a memento from him, where after visiting our home, all of a sudden a month later these two ashtrays arrived and in each corner was a fingerprint of ours and with our name, birthdate, everything in the center and signed by him personally. And when our two boys were born, he sent an FBI agent out and had their toe prints put on little gold coins and inscribed them on the back with his name."

SMITH: "My association with him was friendly, but as I've said, I left him alone. I didn't want to bother him unless it was important. Once I had to get to Rome on urgent family business and I turned to him. I got an emergency call at three in the morning. So there I was in La Jolla, wondering how in the hell I would get to Rome. I had no passport, no plane reservation, no plans, nothing. So I paced the floor for about two hours and my wife walked behind me with a pot of coffee, and I was drinking cup after cup until finally at about five-thirty, the only thing I could think of was to call Hoover's office. They gave me Helen Gandy, his secretary, and she turned me over to a real nice guy who promised to get back to me after I told him my problem. Well, he was back in no time and he said, 'You're all set at the Ambassador Hotel in Rome and we're working on your passport. If I can get some answers now, it will save time when you get to New York.'

"FBI men from the New York office met me at the airport, and after I changed my clothes, they had a nurse there to give me a shot, and a photographer to take my picture for the passport. This was on a Saturday, and they're closed on Saturday. They took me over to Rockefeller Center and the guy on the elevator said, 'It's closed,' and the FBI guy said, 'Just let us off at the floor, will you.' [Laughs.] So he did. A fellow sitting back there with his little thing gave me a passport, and they got me on a plane. I was in Rome within forty-eight hours after I got that call in La Jolla.

"When I landed in Rome, their man, he was the legal attaché at the embassy, met me at the plane. Lucky, because God they were stacked up. Miles. It was Easter Sunday at that—1958. A little gal came out— 'Mr. Smeeth, Mr. Smeeth'—and then I saw a fellow walking right behind her, and I said, 'Yes,' and she said, 'There's a man in there waiting for you,' and I said [laughs], 'I think he's right behind you.' And she looked around and that's who it was, and he said, 'Come on,' and we went inside and he said, 'Can I see your bag here?' And I had a great big thing and I put it up there and he said, 'Okay.' Of course, he spoke Italian fluently, and the guy went over it and I got through customs in two minutes. Without his help, I'd have been there another two hours. I've since traveled all over the world, and I've had FBI men meet me at airports, and they always were very kind and thoughtful, and, I might add, very efficient."

STEWART: "After we finished *The F.B.I. Story* and it was in release for some time, I remember my wife and our four children and me were going to take a trip to Europe, sort of a sightseeing trip. Three or four days before we left on the trip, I got a call from Mr. Hoover, and he said, 'I understand you're going to Europe with your kids,' and I said yes, and he said, 'Well, every once in a while one of my men will come up to you and just check if everything is all right.' And this is what happened. And I thought it was a very nice thing for him to do. There was no— There was no big falderol about it, but as we'd land in Spain or Italy or someplace, a man would just come up to me, just out of the crowd, and say, 'The Boss asked me to just check with you and see if everything is going all right,' and would hand me a card and would say, 'If you need us any time, why here's where we are.' And it—and I must say it was a very pleasant, nice feeling. It was such a nice, considerate thing for Mr. Hoover to do."

LEROY: "I was operated on at Mayo's, and every morning after my operation there was a guy who walked in, looked in my room, and said, 'Good morning, Mr. LeRoy, how are you?' And I said, 'I'm fine.' I thought it was one of the guys from the hospital. About after four days of this, when the fellow came in again and said, 'Mr. LeRoy, how do you feel?' I said, 'I feel fine, but let me ask you a question: What do you do here in the hospital?' He smiled and said, 'I have to tell you. Mr. Hoover asked me to check on you every day to see how you were.' That's the kind of man J. Edgar Hoover was. When I went around the world with my wife, he had people check me and see if I was all right, was all taken care of. Edgar just wanted to be sure that I was okay. Not every place but a lot of places, and it was a thrill for me to have a man walk up and say, 'Mr. Hoover wants to know how you are.'"

"A Sense of History"

His thoughtfulness also involved many personal acts. He wrote letters, remembered birthdays, and was always accessible to those he liked.

EFREM ZIMBALIST, JR., movie actor and star of the FBI television series: "Our friendship consisted of meetings once or twice a year and a rather large correspondence over the years. He was very sweet. I received a little decoration from the Army, and I went to Washington to receive it at the Pentagon. My father went with me, and it was very sweet of Hoover to come. It was his own idea completely. And when something would happen, a degree that I received, in these situations there was always a note or telegram from him, which was so thoughtful. It brought you up short, really. You wondered how, with all he had to do, he could think of little things like that. I remember when my stepmother died a number of years ago, while the show was on, and it was a very sad time, as that always is, and when we came out of the church in Philadelphia, there were two agents there who said if there was any way they could be of help, you know. They've always had that attitude, they're very kind.

"He wrote often but his letters were very short. I'd get mad sometimes when people would attack him, and I'd write him: 'That so-and-so, I'd like to get my hands on him.' And always his reply was 'Dear Efrem, Thank you so much for your kind sentiments. I greatly appreciate them,' or something like that, but never more. Never any emotionalism of any kind and never any self-pity, even in the last years when he was being attacked by everybody and told to resign and all this kind of thing.

"My daughter came with me in 1972, that last year, and he was so sweet to her. He had his picture taken with her and he was just lovely, courtly, and sweet with her. She came out of there with her head spinning. There was something tremendously impressive about seeing him in his office. It gave you a sense of history, really. You would wait in the outer office there and he had this marvelous old colored man [Sam Noisette] who would take you in. You'd go through his office and into the small office in back, and it was always— He'd come around the desk to the door and it was like meeting history. The only other man that ever gave me that sense of history was Sam Rayburn talking about a previous Speaker like Clay, you felt they were almost contemporaries. There weren't that many. About four or five before him, and he'd say, 'Clay was a good man, but'—this or the other thing, as though they were almost on an equal footing. Well, Hoover, because he had fifty years there, had that same intimacy with the greats of the past."

As best as I could determine, Hoover had no political ambition.

ALLEN: "You know, I've read where Hoover was supposed to have had

Presidential ambitions at one time, but that was all nonsense. He had not the slightest interest in politics."

LeRoy: "Edgar gave me a farewell party at his house, honoring me and the cast of *The F.B.I. Story,* and I stood up and I said, 'Edgar'—I was making a toast to him, we had about forty people there in his home—'you're such a great man and these are all your friends here and I can't tell you how happy I was that you let me make *The F.B.I. Story.*' And I said, 'There's one thing I'd like to know, Edgar. You're not a Democrat and you're not a Republican, you're really a man of the people. Why don't you run for President?' And as quick as a flash, he said, 'Mervyn, I'll run for nothing where you have to make a deal.'"

Nor did he have any business ambition.

LeRoy: "He was offered the job of the Hays Office one time, two hundred thousand dollars a year, and all expenses, and his answer was 'I'm dedicated to the FBI.' I was asked to speak to him about it. He turned it down flat. And he turned down General Motors, too."

Allen: "I was at La Jolla with Hoover one day when Howard Hughes came to the Del Charro and tried to hire him. Offered to let him write his own ticket, just anything in the world. This was around 1955, before Hughes went into seclusion. He phoned and made an appointment to see Hoover. He and Clyde were staying in a bungalow—they had the nicest bungalow there. I talked to him right after his meeting with Hughes and he told me everything they talked about. Hughes wanted him to represent him in Washington. To be his contact man, lobbyist, so to speak. You see, Hughes was a nutty fellow to begin with. He said, 'You name the price and I'll pay you anything you like, give you a lifetime contract—any amount of money.' Hoover said, 'I appreciate your offer but I'm not interested in any job.' But the thing that tickled Hoover was that when Hughes first came in, he looked all around and said, 'Is this place bugged?' And Hoover said, 'Oh, no, there's no bugs.'

"When you think of it, though, you can see that Hoover would have been a great lobbyist. The greatest. He was very popular on the Hill. And this is the thing about Hoover—and this is just an assumption—I think most people were frightened of Hoover. They thought he had a dossier on everybody and so they were scared. I think that was one of his strengths. That's a great source of power, but I'll say this—I'll guarantee you that under no amount of money would he have used it. But a lot of people have a guilty conscience."

"Equal but Subordinate"

I suppose that in the course of my research I heard just about every malicious story ever invented about Hoover and Tolson and their potential for a homosexual marriage. Everything from "J. Edna" to "Mother Tolson." One high Washington official told me that he had it on good authority, anonymous, of course, that Hoover got off a train early one morning and embraced his young white chauffeur (his chauffeurs were always black) who was waiting for him at the station. I never believed any of the stories, and I'm only repeating this one because the subject cannot be ignored entirely.

ALLEN: "Tolson was sort of Hoover's alter ego. He almost ran the FBI. He's not only a brain, but the most unselfish man that ever lived. He let Hoover take all the bows, all the credit. He was a great administrator, worked all the budget stuff, and could speak for Hoover on anything. You can't take it much further than that. They were very, very close because he needed Clyde so much. He couldn't have done the things he did without Clyde. He discussed every decision with Clyde. Clyde had as much to do with running the FBI as Hoover did. And he is such a sweetheart. Quiet, unassuming. Hoover would say, 'My God, shut up, Junior, you're putting my ears out.' Clyde would say, 'Aah.' Paid no attention to him whatsoever. Why, if Hoover was alive today and Clyde hadn't had his stroke, and you wanted to know about the situation in, say, Guatemala, call Clyde. He'd give it to you quicker than Hoover. And he wasn't jealous of Hoover, either. He never let anybody know how much he helped Hoover."

This contemporary version of Damon and Pythias intrigued me and I pursued it with others I interviewed. Former Assistant to the Director William C. Sullivan thought Tolson was a "man of unbelievable narrowness, provincial and reactionary. He was sort of a watchdog for the Director, but I found nothing about him that would put him in the category of being a brain. The brains behind the budget for many, many years was John P. Mohr. Tolson had to lean on him for his computations." Former Assistant Director Robert Wick called Tolson the "best detail man I have ever known. He had a photographic memory. He could look at a memorandum and spot something wrong in one second. He was so good at this sort of detail." Wick agreed that Hoover never made an important decision without consulting Tolson, and that Tolson actually knew more about what was going on in the Bureau than Hoover did. "Tolson could decide many things on his own. Most of the time, of course, they talked it over."

For at least twelve years, Charles Spencer, a former San Diego bookmaker, occupied box 218A directly in front of Hoover's table at the Del Mar Turf Club. They talked frequently, exchanging racing information, both at the track and at the Hotel Del Charro. I asked him whether he ever saw any evidence of a homosexual relationship between the two men.

SPENCER: "Oh, Christ, I heard rumors about them a thousand times. All around, every place, and I think it's just the result of people unable to believe that two men could be as dedicated to their country as those two were. It wasn't just speculation and it was worse than rumors. It had to be developed by jealous and envious people that were out to do somebody in. Their demeanor was always flawless. Very businesslike. The best way I can put it is that Clyde Tolson was the Associate Director of the FBI. He lived twenty-four hours of every day, seven days a week for the full year as Associate Director of the FBI. It was a Director and Associate Director relationship. The conversation was seventy-five percent Hoover and twenty-five percent Tolson. Wherever they were, whether at the track, by the pool, or in their apartment, Clyde Tolson was Associate Director, and believe me, nobody ever saw anything different. Sure, they were good friends, and Tolson was his equal—but subordinate, if you know what I mean."

Perhaps one way to judge Tolson's importance is to look at what happened when he was disabled by a series of strokes beginning in the early 1960s. It was around this time that Hoover grew increasingly cantankerous. There was a long series of classic boners that were uncharacteristic of Hoover's cool performance in prior years. Accusations and recriminations were tossed to the media like raw meat to hungry wolves. I don't mean to make too much of this, but perhaps it's true that Tolson had a stabilizing effect on the Director, and when Hoover lost that rudder at a time when he needed it most, the frenetic sixties, things got out of hand. As we shall see later in this book, Hoover had no one else to turn to when the crunch came. Tolson seemed to be the only one who didn't want to replace the Boss, who had no other interest except to serve him. Others in the FBI hierarchy, men like Cartha "Deke" DeLoach and William C. Sullivan, were engaged in palace intrigue bids for his throne.

Hoover's reliance on Tolson was so crucial, according to Hoover's chauffeur, James E. Crawford, that Tolson came to work even when he was ill.

CRAWFORD: "A lot of times Mr. Tolson would call up and say he couldn't go in because he didn't feel too good, and Mr. Hoover would say, 'Ah, come on, get out of bed, come to the office. You might feel better.'"

It is quite possible that although Tolson survived him in death, Hoover never survived that first stroke that disabled his lifelong alter ego.

The First Black Special Agent

James E. Crawford retired from the FBI on January 31, 1972, after serving thirty-seven years as Hoover's chauffeur and personal handyman. He was one of the first Negroes—he resents being called black: "When I was coming up, you called me black, you was asking to fight"—to become a special agent. Following his retirement, he continued doing chores at Hoover's home, and at the time of this interview in June 1974 he was performing the same services for Clyde Tolson, who was living in Hoover's home. Crawford's wife, Dorothea, who accompanied him to my Washington hotel room for the interview, occasionally joins in the conversation.

CRAWFORD: "Mr. Hoover called me the night before he died. He had bought some roses from Jackson and Perkins and he had called me that night to come out and give him a hand on helping him plant them, because he and I both were crazy about roses, and I told him I'd be there about eight-thirty in the morning. And I got there and didn't hear him or anything. So the housekeeper, Annie Fields, waited until around nine or nine-thirty, and she came out in the yard—I was out there unpacking the roses—and told me that she hadn't heard Mr. Hoover this morning. So I said, 'I better go up and see what's wrong with him.' So I went upstairs, and there he was lying on the floor right by the bed. I touched his hand and it was cold. Of course, I got horrified and I called Annie to come up there, and my brother-in-law, who was chauffeuring for him at the time, and they came up but they didn't touch him.

"Oh, good God Almighty, I think it took me two weeks to get over it. I was expecting the man to come down in the yard at any moment and then you go up there and you find him dead on the floor—what do you do but just get a terrible shock? The first thing I did was call Mr. Tolson's apartment and he had left but he had forgotten something and he came back for it and that's when the telephone was ringing. I told him he had better come on over here."

Why don't we start at the beginning. You first went to work for the Bureau in 1934.

CRAWFORD: "March the twenty-six. I was hired by Mr. Tolson. I worked in the warehouse for a couple of paydays and then I was called to headquarters and worked in Mr. Tolson's office as a messenger. That's when I met Sam Noisette, Worthington Smith, and some of the other fellows who worked in the front office. All I had been all of my life was a truckdriver, a worker out in yards, or building curbstones or something like that. After a while I started chauffeuring for Mr. Tolson. At that time he was living at the Westchester, an apartment house on Cathedral Avenue near Massachusetts Avenue. Even in those days, that would still be in 1934, Mr. Tolson was Mr. Hoover's top man. The staff was small and if anybody got in trouble or anything went wrong, then you had to go see Mr. Tolson, because Mr. Hoover didn't take up his time seeing employees who had gotten into hot water.

"They both had chauffeurs in those days because Mr. Hoover lived southeast and Mr. Tolson lived way out here in the other end of town. Sometimes Mr. Hoover would take Mr. Tolson home, which made me happy. Then when Mr. Hoover's chauffeur died the next year, I went to drive for him and that lasted until I retired in 1972."

Was Mr. Hoover's car bulletproof in those days?

CRAWFORD: "Not at that time. He got a bulletproof car in about 1937, I believe. It was a Pierce Arrow. He kept that car a long time. I drove it all the time we had it. It caught fire one day by a hotel just standing still in the street. I'm standing on the corner, waiting for him to come out of the hotel, and the car caught on fire, nobody in it at all. And the glass in the doors was about an inch and a half thick and you couldn't keep it from rattling. Oh, good God, it rattled. A set of brakes went about a hundred miles. Tires wore out quite fast, and the mileage, goodness. It had a heavy duty engine and the body was an ambulance chassis so it could hold all that excess weight."

DOROTHEA CRAWFORD: "Tell him how upset everybody would get if it wouldn't be right for him the next morning. Everybody, the whole crew of them, would be so nervous that the car wouldn't be right or have a rattle in it."

CRAWFORD: "If the car wouldn't start or was running raggedy, then of course they'd have all the guys who were taking care of the car and they would get in a dither, you know about what the Boss is gonna say. The garage that took care of the car used to be on Twentieth Street, but as the years went on the cars would change. We had a Buick one time, I think, that wasn't worth a quarter, and then I think we had a Chrysler too one time that didn't stand up. I can't remember the years that these were now, but from then on I know they got Cadillacs and they were pretty good. By then we were getting a new car every year, but I don't know whether the old cars were traded in or shipped to some other office."

Why did he need a bulletproof car?

CRAWFORD: "He was getting so many threatening letters, but Mr. Hoover didn't get shook up as much as most people around him. They'd tell him to be careful and they'd go out of their way to make sure things were secure. But he was a fearless man. For example, we used to leave his home, go by and pick up Mr. Tolson—that's after Mr. Hoover's mother died [in 1938] and he moved to Rock Creek Park. And we would come down Massachusetts Avenue, down through Rock Creek Park into Virginia Avenue, and down Virginia Avenue, and I would let them off around Fifteenth Street—Fifteenth and Virginia—and they would walk about six or seven blocks. And they did that every morning if it was not raining, or it was not threatening rain. Mr. Tolson wasn't a great walker."

"He Was Crazy About Those Dogs"

Would he engage in conversation in the limousine?

CRAWFORD: "There was a partition behind the driver's seat. So you couldn't hear what they said in the back. In the first cars we had, the partition would not come down. They had a microphone in the back and a speaker up front, and he would tell you where he wanted to go through this speaker. But as the cars got better and newer, the window would go up and down, so he would put the window down and tell you, then he'd put it up. Now sometimes if there was nobody, he'd leave the window down and we'd talk about different things, you know. There wasn't a whole lot of talking he was going to do anyway. He would be very concerned and talking like if one of the pups got sick. He always would say, 'How's the pups?' or 'What is Cindy doing today?' or 'How's G-boy?' You see, I'd feed the dogs when I'd get there in the morning and I'd play with them, and make sure they got the food while I'm waiting for him. And we'd be out there in the yard, the dogs running around playing and digging up roses and things like that, and when he was by himself coming home he'd start asking about what did they do today. You know, those dogs had the whole run of the house and the whole run of the yard, but they never got out of there except when you took them out to the hospital or something.

"He was crazy about those dogs. When he'd come home those dogs could tell the sound of his car coming down the street and they'd go right through the house and stand at the front door until he put the key in and unlocked that door, then they'd be all over him. And he'd go hang his coat in the closet and come back and sit in his favorite chair and his bottom would no more than hit that chair until those dogs would be in his lap. The last G-boy—he had about three of them—died first after Mr. Hoover died, and Cindy—she was a cairn too—died about eight months later. G-boy was about eighteen years old, but Cindy was only eight or nine, but she grieved herself to death. That dog wouldn't eat. She would get there by the chair that Mr. Hoover used to sit in and lay there all day long. You could hardly get her to get up to go outdoors.

"When he was working in the house, up there in his library—he'd bring his work home and he'd be working on it all day Sunday—Cindy would be lying up there at the top of the steps where she could look through the glass and see who's coming to the door, and G-boy would be lying in front of the desk asleep. And anybody came up the walk, you'd know it because Cindy would start to bark."

Everything Had to Be Just Right

What was his routine like?

CRAWFORD: "Saturday morning, there probably would be Mr. Harry Duncan—he lived behind Mr. Hoover—Mr. Tolson, probably Mr. George Allen would meet at Mr. Hoover's house for breakfast, then they'd go to the races, wherever they are running: Bowie, Pimlico, Charlestown, Laurel, Havre de Grace—it's closed now. There is something going the year around. After the races, we'd go to Mr. Duncan's house for dinner. Then on Monday night, Mr. Duncan and Mr. Hoover would eat at Mr. Tolson's house, and that would be all for the three of them that week.

Then Mr. Tolson and Mr. Hoover would go down to Harvey's. That was mostly every night until the later years. After Mr. Lulley died, they would eat at Mr. Hoover's one night and Mr. Tolson's the next night. Whenever they went out to dinner, they usually would come out around nine o'clock, unless it was a banquet or some social affair, then it would be around midnight."

You worked long hours?

DOROTHEA CRAWFORD: "Well, everybody asks me how I have stood it. I don't know. I have gone through different stages. I've prayed, I took up hobbies, I involved myself in the children and all of their business. I tried working at churches. I took up everything to make myself—"

CRAWFORD: "Well, we had so many children that I just had to work to support them."

DOROTHEA CRAWFORD: "We have five children. My theory used to be, there is no way we can pry him away from his dedication so let's just leave it. At first I would think that maybe that it would be more important not to work and then demand help or some relief so you could have time with your children. Then after a while we got to thinking that there was no need for us to try to force it any further because it was hopeless because they were all dedicated. He was dedicated and they were saying he was doing a wonderful job and all like that, and I told the children, 'Your father is tired,' or 'Your father has to work long hours, so we'll make out among ourselves.' So we were very close. James worked fifteen hours a day, seven days a week. Holidays too."

What did you do on Sunday? Drive him to church?

CRAWFORD: "Sometimes we'd go to church. He didn't go to church too much. In the old days we used to go to the office on Sunday. I'd sit there and wait for him. Sam Noisette had to come down there too, and Worthington Smith. We'd have to come down there on Saturdays and Sundays. In those days we didn't get overtime. There was no such things as overtime. Later on we got paid eighty percent of it.

"Sunday was my day for gardening. When he was younger, he would help me on Sundays when he was home, both of us got out there together and we'd do his work together, and he could outwork me and I was a much younger man. Before we put the artificial grass in there, he had beautiful Merion bluegrass. And he was very particular about the lawn. He was particular about everything. It had to be just right. He and I got along beautifully. Now, I did what he wanted me to do. If he wanted the car there at eight o'clock or seven o'clock, I had it there about fifteen minutes before. He never had to wait for me, and that's all he asked.

"He put the Astroturf in after I had my first operation in 1968. I had a brain tumor. After I got ill there was nobody to take care of the lawn. They were reluctant about having anybody do anything for Mr. Hoover unless they knew them. They didn't trust outside people. Like if he was having something very special done, he would have me right there to watch them. Like if someone was painting the house, he'd send me back up there to see they did it right. If they were supposed to put on two coats, he wanted to make sure they put on two coats, and that they didn't goof off all day in the yard. If they worked inside, I'd stay right there in the room with them."

DOROTHEA CRAWFORD: "Tell him about the great big old fish pond in back."

CRAWFORD: "Oh, yes, we had a fish pond too. It held about three hundred gallons of water, but it was glass and it was built up off the ground. That was my job. All you got to do if the glass gets cloudy is get a piece of double-ought steel wool and wipe the glass off. Your arm will go down that far [indicating his shoulder]."

DOROTHEA CRAWFORD: "James knows how to do everything."

CRAWFORD: "In the wintertime I would take the fish and bring them in the house, where we had two aquariums. It was very nice in the summer. There was a patio around the fish pool, and he had a chaise lounge where he'd lay out there in the sun. He liked to take the sun. But he didn't stay long. The flies were heavy and it was so hot down there. He used to sit on the back porch, which is a huge screened porch, wide and long, that was very comfortable. It was just like a regular living room, had everything out there."

Would you get the evening off when he dined at home?

CRAWFORD: "No, because Mr. Tolson usually went home with him, so while they were eating, I ate my dinner in the kitchen, and when they'd get through, then I would take him home. He tried to eat around seven. They'd walk in and have a cocktail first. I would build a fire in the fireplace and Annie would fix dinner. Sometimes the little log wouldn't even burn out before they were through and ready to go to bed. They would eat in about twenty minutes."

"He'd Look for You to Thank Him"

How did you become a special agent?

CRAWFORD: "It was in 1943 and I think it was during the time when the NAACP was pressuring the Bureau because they didn't have any Negro agents. I always thought, by us being in the Bureau, and had been there some time, that he was kind enough to say, 'Well, we're going to appoint some of you fellows we got around here.' And when I got the letter, I like to fell out. You see, he would write you—like every time your promotion came up—he would write you a letter to say that you got an ingrade coming up or you was being skipped over a grade, being promoted to another grade.

"One time I was supposed to get this award and the secretary forgot to send it out and he asked me that night, he said, 'Crawford, did you get a letter from me?' I said, 'No, sir.' He said, 'You didn't?' I said, 'No.' He said, 'Well, I wrote you a letter.' I know when we got to the office that morning, someone was standing down there waiting for me to come in to give it to me. Anything he did for you, he'd look for you to thank him. So when I got the letter appointing me a special agent, I could have dropped dead because I had no idea, and I was with him all day long.

"'Here's something for you,' he said and he handed me the letter. He was ready to go, so I couldn't stand there and read it. I put it on the seat and as soon as I dropped him off at the hotel, I tore it open and was I surprised. I had to go home and tell my folks all about it. When I came back to pick him up, I thanked him very much, told him I certainly would do my best to keep up the image of the FBI. Then a couple days later I went to Quantico for the training."

DOROTHEA CRAWFORD: "You stayed by yourself down there that time because you were the only black man."

CRAWFORD: "I stayed by myself, yes. But it was nice."

How would you assess your years with Mr. Hoover?

CRAWFORD: "I always had great respect for him. I worked hard and I didn't have much of an outside life, but I have no regrets. I could have thrown my younger life away and wouldn't have a dime now, wouldn't have anything. I'd be on Social Security or welfare. My feeling is if you get anything in this world, you've got to work for it. I don't believe nobody is going to hand you anything on a silver platter. I just don't believe that. Thank goodness I had sense enough then to know that I had to work in case I did get old. I didn't want to be like my father was, elderly man with no kind of job and expect for his children, his sons, to go to work and help take care of him. I didn't want that."

A Grand Tour of 4936 Thirtieth Place

Anthony Calomaris was only twenty-one when Hoover died, but his memories of his next-door neighbor go back to his early childhood.

CALOMARIS: "Mr. Hoover bought his house at 4936 Thirtieth Place in 1939, before the second story was finished. We purchased ours at 4950 Thirtieth Place in 1945. As you can see, the numbers skip, but we lived right next door, on the same side of the street, and our gardens were separated by an alley. My first introduction to Mr. Hoover was as a tot in a stroller. My mother would be leaving the house at eight-thirty, taking me for a stroll to my grandmother, at the same time Mr. Hoover left in the morning. He was always very friendly, and as I grew up we chatted whenever we met. All through my elementary and high school days, we'd both be leaving at the same time in the morning, and quite frequently I'd be coming home from a school function when he was returning, and so on those days we chatted coming and going.

"My brother's birthday and Mr. Hoover's were both on New Year's Day, and we always exchanged presents at Christmas. He was quite lavish with his gifts. He would send my mother roses or poinsettia centerpieces, and one time it was a preserve set with nuts. He knew I had a fondness for root beer when I was a teenager and he used to send me a case of it. Usually, though, it would be an autographed book that he'd send special delivery, and it was always some new book which he either had written or okayed for the FBI. He'd inscribe it 'Best wishes and Merry Christmas,' put in the year, and sign it 'J. Edgar Hoover.'

"The gifts that he was given on holidays were unbelievable. The flowers that were sent, the food, the candy, the presents—they were just showered on Mr. Hoover. I don't know where he ever found room for these things. I know that his two-car garage was filled to the top with everything you can imagine. If possible, though, if you gave him something, he'd have it out, which was marvelous. I think he cherished every gift he received. Yet —and I don't know if I should mention this but so many people do this—

you receive a great many gifts and, of course, you can't use them all, so you give them to someone else and the sentiment's still there. Why not?

"I remember one Christmas when he was snowed in, and his housekeeper was away, Mr. Hoover invited me over on Christmas Eve. I think he had returned early from his holiday in Florida because of some FBI business. My mother had sent over some Greek pastries, which he loved, and he had invited me when I brought them over. I stayed about an hour and we chatted about antiques and so forth. It was Christmas Eve and we couldn't stand to see him alone. We love Christmas—they call us little Macy's around here. We have a nine-and-a-half-foot tree in the living room which has a thousand Christmas balls on it. Mr. Hoover thought it was gorgeous. He didn't have a tree, but he put a wreath up every year and Crawford, who did everything for him, used to put lights around the columns of the portico in the front. One year someone stole them.

"Once I kidded him about his Christmas decorations. I said, 'The holiday season is coming and this year I'm going to beat you.' He always had his up first, and it was like a race. I said, 'I'm getting mine up the last day of November. Are you going to top that this year?' He laughed, and a little later he said, 'Well, it's that time of year when those marvelous pastries are made.' It was a subtle hint about my mother's pastries. He looked forward to them, especially the *teropittes*. He called them cheese puffs. We'd send over about twenty-five or thirty and he'd freeze them and ration them off. His housekeeper would prepare four a night as hors d'oeuvres, which we thought was a great compliment.

"Of course, he'd always write a thank-you note. He was quite formal that way, which was marvelous. I must have a hundred letters and cards from Mr. Hoover. His Christmas card never changed. A very distinguished card about three and a half by five, with the seal of the Federal Bureau of Investigation, and it said, 'The Season's Greetings and Best Wishes for a Happy New Year.' It was signed, of course, 'J. Edgar Hoover.' We had three mutual interests: antiques, gardening and the neighborhood. He always admired our gardenias and roses. One time he wrote me a letter just to say, 'Dear Anthony, I've been admiring your roses for some time now and you can certainly be proud of having taken care of them and brought them to such enormous size and beauty. Sincerely, J. Edgar Hoover.'

"We were both avid collectors of antiques. For years, he went to C. G. Sloan's auction house whenever they had estate sales, which was about four to six times a year, and the exhibitions would normally be Saturday,

Sunday and Monday, and he'd go the day before the exhibition opened. He'd walk around and mark the numbers he was interested in, and leave his bids with one of the executives who'd secretly bid for him. I usually bumped into him there on Fridays.

"He purchased what he wanted. It didn't always go with his décor, but it reflected Mr. Hoover's other side which the public never knew. He collected Chinese jade and ivory, and he knew what he wanted. Toward the last years of his life, he began to put some items of his own into the estate sales at C. G. Sloan. Once he walked through an exhibition, and when he gave his list of items to Mr. Evelyn, the vice president of C. G. Sloan, Mr. Evelyn was very amused and he said, 'But, Mr. Hoover, three of these items you own already.' Mr. Hoover had forgotten that he'd put them up for sale—you have to put them in two or three months ahead of time—and so he laughed, also amused that he liked them just as much the second time around.

"I don't know whether I should go into this, but a great many of Mr. Hoover's pieces have been auctioned off by Mr. Tolson. Apparently, Mr. Tolson decided not to keep these items after he inherited the house and its belongings. A good portion of Mr. Hoover's estate went on the auction block at Sloan, without using Mr. Hoover's name, of course, but I recognized the items. In fact, I purchased a few of them myself.

"I've never had much in common with Mr. Tolson. He's a cantankerous old man. And that's as polite as I can be about Mr. Tolson. He's a very sour type, quite possibly because he's in failing health. As long as I can remember, he seemed to be falling apart. He was younger than Mr. Hoover, but he looked so much older, acted so much older, talked so much older. He used a cane and would wobble. It was so unbelievable, because Mr. Hoover was so spry. I remember when Mr. Tolson was seriously ill a few years ago and Mr. Hoover brought him to his home when he was released from the hospital. He stayed about four weeks and Mr. Hoover's housekeeper, Annie Fields, took care of him all that time while he was bedridden. I asked Annie if he gave her a nice gratuity, and she said, 'Are you kidding? I got ten dollars for the month.' So he isn't exactly Generous George. He watches every penny. Who he's saving it for is beyond me. Mr. Tolson was in that house by eight o'clock the next morning after Mr. Hoover died. Another thing that's very funny is that he sold the first group of things before he was supposed to. He didn't realize you have to wait a certain amount of time after a death; apparently he wasn't up on the laws. Now he never goes out of that house.

"Annie Fields and James Crawford, who was Mr. Hoover's combination chauffeur, bodyguard and gardener, now take care of Mr. Tolson. They're marvelous, really unbelievable. I'm just so sorry that they weren't better taken care of by Mr. Hoover in his will after the amount of service they put in. It's the only fault I can find with Mr. Hoover. Mr. Tolson did not need what he inherited. He had more than enough, being a bachelor all those years.

"Those two people, Crawford and Fields, kept that house immaculate. Miss Fields lived in. She prepared his meals and did all his laundry. She swept the front every morning and afternoon. She was always there, *always*. She's not the kind of housekeeper who would gossip. She kept very quiet about Mr. Hoover, she'd never say a thing about him, good or bad. She was there at his beck and call, night and day. Any time she wasn't there, I would notice because you'd see Crawford's car parked out front. Mr. Hoover was never by himself, except for that one Christmas I told you about. There was always somebody with him. Annie wore a gray uniform and she'd answer the front door. That Christmas was the first time I ever saw him answer the front door. I remember he was in a white shirt and the sleeves were slightly rolled up and he still had his tie on. His hair was neatly combed, and he wore the usual bluish-black slacks along with the black belt with the big silver buckle.

"Crawford was an absolute jewel. He did so much for Mr. Hoover. Annie took care of the interior of that house, but the exterior was left to Crawford. Mr. Hoover's garden looked like *House and Garden*, that's the way Crawford kept it. I give Crawford credit because he was the only gardener there and that lawn was watered constantly. I would see him daily, practically, doing gardening. I remember as a child asking him if he was with the FBI too, and he had smiled and said yes. I never asked again, but even then it seemed kind of, you know, strange. I'd see Mr. Hoover point to where he wanted things planted and so forth. Crawford did all the pruning and all the exterior painting. He was constantly whitewashing the cinderblock wall. If Mr. Hoover saw a crack, a chip, peeling paint, rust, anything, it had to be fixed immediately. That's how Mr. Hoover was. Everything was that way. Crawford was always seeding and taking care of the lawn and plants. He had Kentucky bluegrass, which was beautiful until, unfortunately, somebody presented him with a gift of that awful Astroturf. It doesn't look like it used to anymore.

"The house is basically what we used to call Federal Colonial. It is red brick with cream trim and a gray slate roof with copper gutters. It has a center front door, and the two windows to the left as you face the house are the living-room windows, and the two to the right are in the kitchen. Either in 1961 or '62, Mr. Hoover had a small portico added to the front, and as you enter the house there is an entrance hall, a small foyer, and after about eight feet, there is a staircase leading to the second floor. At the foot of the stairs was a Chinese teakwood table with an insert marble clover top, which normally had a bronze statue on it. I won't enumerate all the items in the house, because you already have everything listed in the inventory to the will.* Also things moved around the house quite freely. The walls throughout the house were literally covered with just—oh, scads of etchings, lithographs, oil paintings, watercolors, photographs, art objects, which he changed all the time to please himself. I'm sure the walls could not accommodate all the things he owned. One time when he was having the wallpaper cleaned, he had photographs taken so that everything could be returned to its proper place. He had summer and winter oriental rugs which not only changed with the season but often from room to room.

"He had one picture in the foyer which never changed and that was the famous one of Lincoln with his son Todd reading a manuscript. The foyer was where he kept a recent photo of himself with the incumbent President. I remember seeing Eisenhower, Johnson and Nixon, but I don't recall ever seeing one of Kennedy. To the left was a small archway leading to the living room, but this was enough space to have two built-in curio cabinets, glassed-in niches, lighted, very attractive, showing off his exquisite collection of jade and ivory figurines. He was very proud of it. Another item he proudly displayed in the foyer was a small mother-of-pearl cross that was given to him by the Pope. There was a telephone in the foyer, and on the wall above it was an exquisite German painting on porcelain of a semi-nude in a carved gilt-leaf frame and mounted in glass, a shadowbox frame. It's been auctioned off by Mr. Tolson. Right to the left of the porcelain painting was the door leading down to the recreation room. On the wall down those steps was where he kept his gallery of famous nudes, including the elegant one of Marilyn Monroe.

"Now going up the staircase to the second floor, he had an oil painting of himself on the first landing, and at one time there was a bronze bust of himself on a post at the top of the stairs. But it was in two other spots in the house through the years. Things kept rotating. The staircase had a

* For a complete inventory of his personal estate, see Appendixes, pages 325–390.

Tabriz oriental rug, a bright red with shades of brown and gold, and on the walls going up the stairs and the long hallway upstairs, he had a marvelous collection of autographed letters and pictures and political cartoons, with black frames and white mats. They were set in a row the way you'd have them displayed in an art gallery, not too pleasingly arranged, unfortunately, that is, one against the other.

"The master bedroom had a fourposter bed with an arched top canopy. There's a window that overlooks the alley separating our gardens, and in front of it he had a four-fold Chinese screen. All the windows had venetian blinds and it was kind of amusing because the blinds were always open when he was gone but the minute he was home they were closed. You always knew when he was home. Of course, he had numerous threats on his life, and the venetian blinds along with the Chinese screen completely blanked that window—I doubt that it was from us."

Were there agents guarding him?

CALOMARIS: "Only when there were serious threats. I remember two occasions, one for about four months and the other for about two months, when I saw the cars parked at either end of the street. It was great. You could cancel your insurance when they were out there. On these two occasions Mr. Hoover didn't seem nervous or upset, but he must have been worried because he received over a thousand threatening letters that first time—I think it was in 1968—when they had those riots in Washington, and the second time was around the Christmas holiday in 1970. The agents were there all night, whenever he was home, but they left with him in the morning. He always sat in the right-hand corner of his limousine so you couldn't see him, and his hat would always be at the other end of the back rest. He would place it so that if you did recognize his car, you would see the hat through the small back window of the Cadillac, but you couldn't see him in the other corner.

"Upstairs there are three bedrooms and a bath which is at the front, in the center, just above the front door, and he had a lavender-blue light on at night. From the bathroom window, you can walk out on a small balcony over the portico. One of the bedrooms was used as a den, where he had hundreds of autographed books in vitrine bookcases. The other room was a guest bedroom but nobody ever used it except Mr. Tolson that one time. He had a larger balcony in the back, which was above the screened porch, and occasionally he would lie there in a chaise lounge, but normally he preferred the screened porch, which had rattan furniture with grass mats on the floor and an old-fashioned ceiling fan. I know that in the late spring and early summer he enjoyed having cocktails there in the evening.

"The dogs were always about. They were kept in the kitchen and the pantry when he was not at home, but when he was home, they had the run of the house. They were little monsters. He didn't seem to mind that. Noisy as could be, they barked at anything and everybody. Then, of course, if it was a nice day, they'd be out in the garden. He loved those dogs. There was an incident during World War Two which shows how much he thought of them. He had gone on a holiday and had left the dogs in the care of his housekeeper. About the third day out, he became worried about them—somehow he had a feeling that something was wrong. He had his secretary check the house and sure enough she found that the housekeeper had taken off and left the dogs alone without food or water. He had her tracked down and agents found her in South Carolina visiting a boy friend or relations, and she was fired. That's when Annie was hired.

"Back downstairs again, as you come in the foyer, the living room is to the left. One of the things prominently displayed in the living room was a large stereo, the kind that flashes lights as different notes are hit. It was a novelty back in the early sixties when it was given to him. Next to that was a table display of medals and awards, and in a corner next to it was an exquisite early-nineteenth-century ormolu clock on a pedestal.

"There was a fireplace—he dearly loved a fire—and flanking it were a pair of Chinese Chippendale gilt mirrors, and the mirrors themselves about two-thirds of the way down had a small shelf on which he'd have a figurine. There was an elephant footstool—it was a stuffed elephant's foot —to one side of the fireplace, but later on I noticed it was relegated to the recreation room with its mate—he had a pair. There was a French fire screen, the folding fan type, in ormolu, and a lovely pair of French chenets. There was a long sofa—toward the end he had a few of his pieces reupholstered—and the last time I saw the sofa it was covered in a nine-teen-fortyish-looking flower with big leaves, something like palm fronds, tropical looking—he did like warm weather. There was a Chinese screen partially covering the sliding glass doors leading out to his screened porch, and there was a Chinese screen in front of the bar, black lacquered mate-rial with red and green accent. The coffee table, I think, was a Chinese Chippendale. There were two easy chairs, traditional types, flanking the fireplace, and they were covered in an antique gold brocade. I almost forgot—above the fireplace was a Lucien Powell oil painting. He had a big thing about Lucien Powell—he had at least three of his paintings. Of course, there were lamps and tables and knickknacks and art objects and oriental rugs, far too numerous for me to remember.

"The recreation room was in the basement, and as you came down the stairs there was, as I mentioned, his collection of famous nudes. As you entered the room, the first thing you'd see was a fantastic collection of eight-by-ten black-and-white photographs in black frames, the kind you put your diploma in. There were pictures of practically everyone he ever met, all famous people, of course, and they were all autographed. I remember the one with Shirley Temple on his lap and he smiling angelically. All four walls were wallpapered, you could say, in photographs. If there was paint on the wall you couldn't see it. There was the pair of elephant footstools, and above the fireplace at one time was a stuffed animal head. The room was furnished with the usual assortment of discarded living-room furniture—when its appeal or condition would start to slip, it was relegated to the recreation room, and from there it usually wound up in the garage or the attic.

"The few times I was down there it was exceedingly damp and I dislike dampness, even at my tender age, and I didn't stay down there very long. I found it very gloomy and depressing even with the lights on. As I recall, there was a bar with a brass rail and there was a long sofa against the far wall, with a coffee table, and there were four lounge chairs placed about the room. It was the only room in which you could freely walk around. In other parts of the house, since it was not a large house, it was quite an obstacle course to walk around things. I wouldn't say the house was cluttered, but due to its size, and since everything seemed to be there, it did make things look crowded. By the way, at the foot of the stairs to the left are the maid's quarters, a living room and bedroom with a bath.

"Back upstairs again, as you enter the house, you can walk from the foyer down a corridor straight through the house without going into any room. The first door on your right is a closet, and the second is the pantry. The kitchen hasn't changed since the day the house was built, which was modern for that time. There were always newspapers on the floor because of the dogs. Crawford lavished attention on Mr. Hoover's pets.

"The dining room was almost square in dimension. There was a little hanging curio cabinet, I remember, with a collection of English basset hounds, little miniature porcelain dogs curled up, sitting, barking, lying down, rolling—very cute. There was a mahogany dining table, with eight chairs, and the table was always highly polished. I never saw a tablecloth; Annie always used mats. There was only one window—it overlooked the garden—and hanging from a chain was the emblem of the FBI in stained glass. About three feet underneath this was this huge fish tank with exotic tropical fish, and flanking this, and at the foot of it and around it, were, depending on the season, different types of plants and greenery, which always looked lush and green. The walls were a pale green, very soft on the eyes, very rich-looking, and everything just glowed. There was a sideboard at the far end on which he kept a pair of Waterford crystal candelabra, with black candles, always black candles. On the wall behind the sideboard was a mural of a landscape. On the other side was a short server with a fine display of silver pieces.

"Mr. Hoover had breakfast and dinner at the head of the table and with the two dogs at his feet eating from a plastic plate. I don't know how many oriental rugs they ruined with stains, but the last one was in shades of burgundy, cobalt blue and beige, an overall floral design. I think this pretty much covers the house."

According to the inventory, his household effects and jewelry have been appraised at about seventy thousand dollars, and the house at forty thousand. How accurate are these figures?

CALOMARIS: "In my opinion, the house is worth at least a hundred and sixty thousand dollars, and you can roughly double the estimate of his personal effects, and that would be conservative."

"He Just Wasn't the Least Boring"

Do you remember the time Nixon came to dinner?

CALOMARIS: "This was when they had a newspaper strike in Washington. It was one of the few dinner parties Mr. Hoover ever gave. That's the night I met President Nixon. There were a few photographers outside from the television stations and I remember Mr. Hoover had opened the door—he was in his white shirt and tie but without his jacket—and when he saw the photographers, he quickly slammed the door. You see, no one was supposed to know about it. It was kept quite secret. He was shocked that they had found out. When the door opened again for President Nixon to come out, Mr. Hoover was nowhere in sight.

"I'm an autograph fiend, and this time I was lucky because Mr. Nixon ended up giving me four autographs. He didn't seem to want to talk to the television people who were standing there, and when I gave him my writing pad, he just kept turning the pages and signing his name."

You obviously had a good relationship with Hoover. Would you say that his attitude or interests changed as he grew older?

CALOMARIS: "I don't think so. He was always courteous and kind. He seemed a very gentle man. He had a sweet voice, sort of like your uncle would sound if he was talking to you, very gentle, very kind. He wasn't a snob at all. He'd greet anyone who said hello. He didn't talk down to me or patronize me. He'd always smile, never had a harsh word, treated everyone with respect. I had some marvelous conversations with him. He just wasn't the least boring. We used to take long walks through the neighborhood on a Sunday and we'd talk about everything, except politics. He'd say, 'We all have our own views.' And kind of laugh it off. My memory of Mr. Hoover will always be of a friendly, reserved gentleman who took pride in his house, took pride in his possessions, and most of all took pride in his reputation, which was spotless, at least as far as I know, and as far as I'm concerned, it always will be."

Happily, the self-imposed limitations of so many of his confidants in his private life almost completely disappeared once I got into his public role. Time and again colleagues and others whom I had expected to be circumspect and superficial turned out to be just the opposite. I was indeed impressed by the candor of General Harry Vaughan, the fairness of Ramsey Clark, the revelations of William C. Sullivan, the expertise of Kenneth O'Donnell, the warmth of Tom Clark, the intimacy of Dave Powers, the acerbic language of William Hundley, the tender anecdotes of Patricia Collins, the metaphorical allusions of Doug Lea, the scholarship of Stephen Spingarn, the forthrightness of W. Mark Felt, John P. Mohr, Robert Wick, Emanuel Celler, Ken Clawson and so many others. However, there was the verbose righteousness of Roy Cohn, the Nixonian arrogance of Tom Charles Huston, and the studied obfuscations of career politicians like William P. Rogers, Richard Kleindienst and Lowell Weicker, men who have been so conditioned by their profession that they are programmed on some obscure wave length. Yet even there not all was lost. In their most guarded moments, they too had something unique to say about our illustrious and elusive subject and his institution. What follows, I hope, will be both instructive and pleasurable.

PART
II

PUBLIC
LIFE

Genesis of a Legend

J. Edgar Hoover was twenty-two when the war came in 1917, the year he first went to work for the Department of Justice, his only employer for the next fifty-five years. His very first assignment introduced him to subversion. The war had created a suspicion toward certain foreigners, then called enemy aliens. To handle the supposed threat the Attorney General created the War Emergency Division and placed John Lord O'Brien in charge. In a CBS-TV interview on the day of Hoover's death, O'Brien recalled that he'd hired him to review aliens who volunteered for military duty and wanted to become citizens. "I discovered he worked Sundays and nights, as I did myself," O'Brien said. "I promoted him several times, simply on merits, and at the end of the war, at the time of the Armistice, he told me he would like to continue in the permanent side of the Department of Justice, and I took that up personally with the new Attorney General, A. Mitchell Palmer, who had him transferred to the Bureau of Investigation."

The zeal that Hoover had displayed in rooting out alien spies, saboteurs and draft dodgers was soon directed at the "Red menace." This was at the end of Woodrow Wilson's second term, during the era of bombs and Bolshevism. As the new head of the Bureau's General Intelligence Division (GID), at the tender age of twenty-four, Hoover assembled a card file on 450,000 "radicals" and built his first network of informers—two tools he would use later against the Communist Party. He was, in the meantime, desperately trying to digest the voluminous writings of Marx, Engels,

Lenin and Trotsky, a spicy broth for the young debater from Central High. The perceptions of conspiracy he formed then would remain unchanged throughout his lifetime. He became convinced that radicals were psychologically twisted. His assignment was to determine the scope of the Communist plot in the United States and the means by which participants could be prosecuted. His brief, which received wide circulation in the press, charged that there was a massive conspiracy afoot to topple all non-Communist governments.

It was as a direct result of this report that Attorney General Palmer invoked the wartime Sedition Act, which launched the "Red raids" by authorizing special agents and the police to conduct massive dragnet arrests in thirty-three cities. People were yanked off the streets, out of stores and offices; homes were broken into without search warrants. Six thousand persons were jailed and detained for days, in most cases without filed charges. In later years Hoover would look back upon these raids with considerable distaste, but at the time his work was greatly admired by those who were in power.

When the Ohio gang took over in 1921, Hoover was promoted to Assistant Director, a post he held for three years while the Bureau became the most corrupt and incompetent agency in Washington. According to historian Alpheus T. Mason, it "had become a private secret service for corrupt forces within the Government." After Harding's death, President Coolidge forced the resignation of Attorney General Harry Micajah Daugherty and in his place appointed Harlan F. Stone, who was instructed to clean up the Bureau of Investigation.

After casting about for a young man of "uncommon ability and character," Stone called Hoover into his office and said, "I want you to take over as Acting Director of the Bureau of Investigation." But Hoover, who had agonized over its corruption for three years as Assistant Director, did not immediately leap at the opportunity. With poise and confidence, he reflected for a moment before answering. "I'll take the job, Mr. Stone," he said, "on certain conditions." Asked to explain, Hoover told Stone he would not tolerate any political meddling, and that he wanted sole control over merit promotions. This response delighted Stone. "I wouldn't give it to you under any other conditions," he replied. "That's all. Good day."

In the aftermath of the turmoil created by the Harding Administration, the Bureau of Investigation, as the FBI was known prior to 1935, sank slowly into obscurity. The political appointees of other administrations were gradually replaced by young lawyers and accountants who spent their time in such mundane activities as searching for concealed assets in bankruptcy cases and digging through accounting records for evidence of anti-trust violation. Special agents were not authorized to carry firearms and did not have the power of arrest. The Bureau's only contact with street crime was through the Dyer Act, which made it a federal offense to transport a stolen automobile across state lines. Whenever a fugitive was located, the special agent had to ask the local police or a United States marshal to make the arrest.

The Bureau slept through the violence of the Roaring Twenties. J. Edgar Hoover, who was working hard at regilding the Bureau's image, was under almost constant fire from a small group of senators and congressmen who accused him of having used eavesdropping methods and mail drops against them because they were critics of the Bureau. It was not until the Lindbergh baby was kidnaped in March 1932 that the nation became conscious of the large number of criminal gangs that were abducting citizens and fleeing to other jurisdictions to avoid capture. There were 282 kidnapings reported in 1931, and probably that many again had not been reported. This alarmed Congress enough for it to pass the Lindbergh Law, which made it a federal crime to send a ransom demand or a kidnaping threat through the mails. For the first time the federal government was authorized to act against crimes of violence committed in jurisdictions other than on government reservations.

This legislation literally marks the beginning of J. Edgar Hoover's rise from obscurity. Another significant event took place in Kansas City on June 17, 1933, when a special agent, three policemen, and a prisoner they were guarding were massacred by Pretty Boy Floyd and his gang of desperadoes. Elsewhere in the Midwest, two thousand hardened felons were pulling bank robberies at the rate of two a day. Gun battles were an almost daily news item. The headliners included Machine Gun Kelly, Baby Face Nelson, Alvin Karpis, Ma Barker and her sons, Clyde Barrow (of *Bonnie and Clyde*), and John Dillinger, who became Hoover's most important prize.

Companion bills to the Lindbergh Law enacted between 1932 and 1934 put the Bureau foursquare into the crime business. As a consequence, law enforcement underwent the most radical change in its history. By the spring of 1934, the special agent had local jurisdiction, directly or indirectly, in almost every kind of major crime of violence, making him a roving policeman with the power of arrest and the right to carry any kind of arms. The Lindbergh Law was amended to create a presumption of interstate transportation if the kidnap victim was not returned within a week. Almost overnight, Hoover had to change the Bureau from a purely investigative organization into a combative one. By the end of 1934, special agents had trapped and killed Dillinger, Nelson and Floyd. When Kelly was captured in Memphis, he called out, "Don't shoot, G-men," and the phrase was to become the symbol for aggressive law enforcement by clean-cut young men on a crusade against evil.

Within two years the crisis had passed, but Hoover's G-men had only begun to impress their image on the nation's consciousness. The exploitation that followed in newspapers, magazines, books, movies and on radio was more than a spontaneous phenomenon. In speeches and in writing, Hoover personally took after the "scum from the boiling pot of the underworld," the "public rats" and "craven beasts," along with the "venal politician" and crooked police and "sob-sister" parole boards and "sentimental yammerheads" who were soft on crime. When the name was changed to the Federal Bureau of Investigation in 1935, there were those in other agencies who objected to the change because it gave the impression that the FBI was the only federal bureau of investigation, whereas there were more than a dozen others. Thus was the beginning of the legend of Hoover's FBI.

"My Way or No Way"

Back in 1924, when the central office was on the third floor of a building on Vermont Avenue at K Street, the Bureau was such a small operation that Hoover actually worked as a bouncer for the Attorney General's office. Ugo Carusi, who was executive assistant for six attorneys general, from 1925 to 1945, recalled those days in an interview in June 1972.

CARUSI: "There were no more than half a dozen staff men. I can cite one experience that will give you an idea of the size of that agency.

"When I first went to the Justice Department, and of course it happened in later years too, there would be people who would come in the Attorney General's office, probably demented or troublesome, and I remember the Secret Service man at the White House often felt sorry for them, you know, when they tried to see President Coolidge, and instead of calling the white-coated gentlemen, he'd say, 'Go over and see Mr. Carusi,' and then he'd call me up and say, 'Try to talk to these people and get them to go back home.' Well, if they didn't go home after I promised to look into their situation, I'd pick up the intercommunicating gadget we had and I'd call Mr. Hoover, who came up himself to escort them away. He'd just say, 'You'd better come along with me,' and take them by the arm, just almost like an arresting officer, which, of course, he wasn't, because the Bureau didn't have that power then. He would escort them out and get rid of them for us, either by turning them over to the police or by sending them to the hospital for a mental examination."

Hoover was a young man of twenty-nine when Harlan Stone offered him the directorship. Do you believe the story that he stipulated certain conditions before accepting the promotion?

CARUSI: "Oh, yes. That was his make-up. I wasn't there when he said it, but knowing him as I knew him, I believe he would say exactly that. And I would expect Justice Stone, whom I knew, to say the opposite, that is to say, 'If you take this job, I want you to run it.' That's the way Stone would act. So I'm sure there was that understanding, that from the standpoint of Stone it would be a free hand, and from the standpoint of Hoover, 'It's my way or no way.' As I say, I knew both men and I know darn well that's about the way it would be."

So you had an opportunity to watch the Bureau's growth from ringside, so to speak?

CARUSI: "That's right. Of course, it got its big lunge in late 1933 and 1934 when the new legislation was passed giving them the right to carry arms and to make arrests. It was an outgrowth of the Lindbergh kidnaping and all that business about the desperadoes. That's what gave it its big impetus, I mean, gave it its wider authority."

Did Hoover push hard for the legislation? Did he go to the Hill and testify?

CARUSI: "Yes, he testified, but I wouldn't give him all the credit on that. It was a joint effort between him and Homer Cummings, who was Attorney General from 1933 to 1939. Cummings had a big conference on crime, and President Roosevelt attended one session and spoke. I wouldn't want to say that one did less than the other or did more than the other. They worked very closely together on it. Of course, Hoover certainly presented facts and also presented what he thought were good arguments in favor of various parts of the legislation, and in the way of organization, and Cummings accepted it. Cummings himself was pretty strong on law enforcement and on strengthening the FBI, and they worked together beautifully on that.

"From the standpoint of authority, I think the Bureau got its biggest growth during those six years with Cummings. I'm not talking about numbers of personnel or anything like that. I'm talking about the number of laws that came within its competence and the building of its reputation. Remember that was during the time they had so many gunfights with Dillinger and those other gangs. I was very close to that. In fact, I wound up in Chicago with the Attorney General the next morning after they shot Dillinger, and, of course, got firsthand reports from Mr. Purvis and everybody else as to what happened. There was considerable public pressure on Mr. Hoover in a sense that these guys were marauders around the countryside and had evaded capture for a while, but finally they were met up with and dispatched."

Why do you suppose Hoover disapproved of Melvin Purvis?

CARUSI: "Well, he wrote a book, of course, and Mr. Hoover always looked askance at agents who wrote books. They were usually self-laudatory beyond good taste. At any rate, the FBI attracted a lot of attention in those days. And I think from that point on, and that's been the secret of Hoover's success, or one of the secrets—there are a lot of them—but one of the things that enabled him to do all the things he wanted to do was the very fine rapport he had with Congress. I'm sure that it was the sensational work of the FBI in those years—let's say 1934 to 1939, up until the time the war broke out in Europe. During those years he was building by his efforts and by his record and by the agents' records and sacrifices, he was building a terrific case with Congress and they were helping him all they possibly could. I suppose some Congressmen thought it was good politics, but I think most of them thought it was the right thing to do, and that's where he got his big start. And having gotten that start and that backing from Congress, from then on they took him pretty much at his word when it came to appropriations or authority of that kind. That's why in later years they were still on his side to the extent that he was the only person that was voted a special act—well, as you know, whenever there were regular salary raises, his was always so much more than everybody else for the grade of his position."

Why was that?

CARUSI: "Well, they wanted to keep him there, I guess."

You don't think they were intimidated—perhaps they were afraid of the files?

CARUSI: "No, heavens no. I never saw any signs of those files. It may be that some on the Hill were investigated, if there was any complaint or any indication of violation of the law, and in that case there would be a file, but to say that he just built up files to hold over their heads, he had other things to do. I never saw any signs of those files. I never heard anyone say that those files were thrown up against him. That he was blackmailed by them."

Do you remember Palmer's "Red raids"?

CARUSI: "That was still a live subject when I first went there, and also when the war broke out and we had our alien-enemy business in 1941. Somebody researched it to make sure we didn't make the same mistakes, and so I got to know a little more about it then. As I remember it, Hoover was in charge of the General Intelligence Division; but he was just a kid, and he always insisted that he was only doing his job, that policy was made elsewhere, and I wouldn't challenge that, because I can't imagine policy being made by a fellow in his early twenties.

"Maybe that's why he was so strict on discipline. You have to remember that when he went in he replaced a guy who didn't have that discipline and he had no agency that was worth talking about. Hoover went in with the understanding that he was to rebuild it and clean it up. When you start out that way, it's not surprising that you continue that way because it worked, and he kept on building and building and never took a step backwards. And with that start, from behind the starting line, so to speak, he had something to prove and he proved it. So when people start picking it apart and saying that this particular disciplinary rule wasn't necessary and that one was frivolous—you know, what difference does the length of a fellow's hair make?—you can take each one of those apart, but when you put them together and just call it strict discipline and tight management, then that explains Hoover's FBI. It is this, I think, that goes to the heart of Hoover's so-called ego. If by ego you mean he was ambitious and he wanted to handle things himself in his office and he was looking for a good reputation for himself and his agency, he had plenty of that. That was his driving force."

Would you want someone else to exercise that much power?

CARUSI: "If he does it with judgment, sure. One of the things that has come under criticism is that the FBI was not under Civil Service. But Congress insisted on making it that way, and there have been attempts to change it, but if you ever ran a Civil Service outfit, or an outfit based on Civil Service, you'd understand."

But why would it be more important for the FBI than the Secret Service or any other government agency?

CARUSI: "I think it built up a reputation that in Congress's mind justified it. It's as simple as that. Whether it can maintain that reputation is another matter."

In terms of bureaucratic protocol, was the Commissioner of Internal Revenue superior in status to Hoover?

CARUSI: "Yes. In fact, on technical grounds, and the technical grounds being that he was a Presidential appointment. Mr. Hoover was appointed by the Attorney General, but in compliance with the new law, his successor was appointed by the President with the advice and consent of the Senate. But they didn't do that during his tenure, and they fixed his pension to be full salary, but that doesn't apply to his successor, and, as I say, his salary bounced up ahead of everybody in what you might call a comparable position. But, after all, there aren't many who spend fifty years on a job like that. You've got to remember that the IRS Commissioner is a Presidential appointment, so what you're talking about is possible political considerations. Now that the FBI is in the same category, unless the fellow they put in is completely apolitical and acquires that kind of a status in the public eye and in the Congressional eye, they'll make changes when there are changes in administrations. And, of course, the Congress wanted their finger in too, you know, on confirmation. So I think that could be a different ball game. Then you would get a closer parallel between the IRS and the FBI.

"The thing about Hoover is that he really loved that agency. I was present when an offer was made to him that would stagger the ordinary mortal and he said no on the first go-round, and that was at a time when he was only making nine thousand a year. He was really wedded to that job and he gave it all he had and he wouldn't brook any interference with it. He'd stand up for his agency like I never saw anybody else stand up and never passed the buck, never said, 'Well, it was one of my subordinates who made a mistake.' He'd just clam up, but later he would discipline that agent. He had great respect for the organization and I'm sure he felt that if he demeaned a member of it, he'd be demeaning the organization and demeaning himself, so he stuck up for it and I admired him for that.

"This may surprise you. I worked very closely with him for twenty years, and probably talked to him almost every day on official business and also on occasion went to a ball game with him, and if I wanted to say a mean thing about him or find an incident of which I highly disapproved, I wouldn't know where to find it. My experience with him has always been right up on a very pleasant and delightful and inspiring plane."

"A Very Astute Empire Builder"

Malachi Harney was a Treasury agent for forty years and at one time was an assistant to Elmer L. Irey, whom he calls "the greatest cop of the century."

HARNEY: "Irey was a good Christian who didn't cuss, but the air would be blue when the subject of the Lindbergh kidnaping case came up. I don't mean actually blue, but the feeling about it was most intense. And listen, this book, *The F.B.I. Story* by Don Whitehead, it is actually studied distortions."

In *The F.B.I. Story*, Whitehead wrote:

The investigation of the Lindbergh case was directed by the New Jersey State Police, who had primary responsibility. But it developed into a cooperative effort between the New Jersey State Police, the New York City Police and the FBI. The big break finally came on September 15, 1934—two years, six months and fourteen days after the kidnaping—when a motorist bought five gallons of gasoline at a filling station on the fringe of the Bronx and handed the attendant a ten-dollar gold certificate.

After giving the driver his change, the attendant wrote on the bill the license number of the car—4U-13-41. He didn't connect the driver with the Lindbergh kidnaping, but he was suspicious of the gold certificate because these notes had been called in by President Roosevelt in April, 1933, when the United States went off the gold standard.

Three days later, a teller at the Corn Exchange Bank and Trust Company spotted the bill as a Lindbergh ransom note. The FBI was notified and the bill was given to one of the FBI-State-City investigative teams organized to concentrate on the kidnaping. A check with the State Motor Vehicle License Bureau disclosed that the license number had been issued to a Bruno Richard Hauptmann, of 1279 East 22nd Street, the Bronx.

Hauptmann was arrested. A twenty-dollar gold ransom note was found in his pocket. Another $13,000 of the ransom money was discovered in his garage. Dr. Condon identified Hauptmann as the "John" to whom he paid the $50,000. Evidence piled up against the accused man. He was convicted after a sensational trial, and on April 3, 1936, Hauptmann was electrocuted for the murder of Charles A. Lindbergh, Jr.

As the reader will note, no mention is made of the work of Treasury agents. In his *New Yorker* profile, published twenty-one years before Whitehead's book, Jack Alexander took issue with this same problem:

The tourists [on a regular guided tour of the FBI facilities] . . . get the impression that the F.B.I. has been responsible for the solution of most of the recent major crimes. In dilating upon the Lindbergh case, for example, the tour leader tells how "we" solved it, and directs attention to a large map of New York City on which the G-men, using colored pins, kept a geographical record of the trail of spent ransom notes. No mention is made of the fact that the New York police kept a similar map, or of the fact that Treasury agents really set the trap which caught Hauptmann. Perhaps few of the tourists realize that the ransom packets as originally made up by J. P. Morgan & Co. contained no gold notes, and that it was only because the Treasury agents insisted that the packets were remade to include $35,000 worth of them. The passing of one of the gold notes at a filling station led directly to Hauptmann's arrest.

In fact, in a radio message, Lindbergh had promised the kidnaper that the bills would not be marked. Writing about that moment in *The Tax Dodgers*, Irey said he "told Lindbergh that every single bill should be listed and a record kept of the serial numbers. Lindbergh argued stubbornly against it; he did not want to break his promise. It seemed extraordinary ethics to all of us." When Irey threatened to withdraw from the case, Lindbergh relented. At the time of the trial, Lindbergh told Irey, "If it had not been for you fellows being in the case, Hauptmann would not now be on trial and your organization deserves the full credit for his apprehension."

Has there always been jealousy between the Secret Service and the FBI?

HARNEY: "It's part of the bureaucracy. Briefly, the Secret Service, you might say, was the general service investigative outfit from the time of Lincoln, when it was originated. It was the only effective federal investigative outfit. Revenue was in and out of its own specialities, what with moonshining and stuff of that kind, and Customs had its own special laws, and so when it came to doing a job— Teddy Roosevelt used the Secret Service considerably to get some of these 'malefactors of great wealth,' as he used to say. And, of course, the Secret Service became very unpopular congressionally because it always involved some politicians, you see, and this was the great lesson that Hoover learned so well—that is, you have to have the political muscle and you have to have a defense against that congressman. This is imprinted in the whole history of the FBI. You have to defend yourself against these legislators, and it's really a work of art when you look back and see how admirably Hoover managed to control that situation.

"The simplest thing that he did—I'll make a little digression here—was in his appointment of agents. When he started out, he had a bunch of crooks and political hangers-on that he inherited from the Harding Administration. So now he's going to get a new outfit, and these fellows as they came along, some of us who thought we were pros at the time, laughed at these college boys a little bit because they were very amateurish, but they were intelligent, well-educated guys. And how did he recruit them? Well, he held his own entrance examinations, which he said were more rigid than the Civil Service examinations, and I think he was correct on that. He said his character investigations were certainly more searching, which they were. But he put a little gimmick to it. In those days eighteen hundred a year was a job, and a two hundred bonus was— oh, I mean, this was something. Hoover circulated around among congressional people the fact that there was an examination and that they ought to get bright guys to apply and use the same selective standards they would if they were recommending a boy to West Point or to Annapolis. This was a very astute pitch. Later when World War Two came on and he had to do a lot of recruiting, he also did it this same way.

"Anyway, we all had this battle, and Irey and Hoover were bitter enemies. Of the two, I always thought Irey was a gentleman and Hoover just simply an alley fighter—a good fighter, let's put it this way. But there was always a contest for this and that or for jurisdiction and so on. The Treasury wasn't satisfied with Civil Service investigations for its personnel, it didn't think they were rigid enough either, so as Irey's assistant for many years, I was in on a lot of that, especially during World War Two time, so it became a problem whether we would get information from the FBI.

"Whatever the FBI did in espionage, their intelligence was squirreled away down there on Pennsylvania Avenue and nobody had any access to it. In other words, millions and millions of dollars were spent getting very valuable information and except for Hoover's judgment on how it should be let out, the country was more or less helpless."

Didn't he trust you people?

HARNEY: "That's it. It would come to you as an administrator in the Treasury Department, for instance, that Source A says that Harry Dexter White is a member of the Communist spy apparatus, see? I was in a position to believe that when I got it, but the ordinary administrator getting hit with that would have to say, 'Well, show me. Give me a for instance, give me one witness.' 'We can't do that.'

"Now a big fight developed fairly late in the game between Hoover and the Secret Service. Up to this time the Secret Service had the authority to investigate its own business. That is, this investigative jurisdiction had been in our appropriation language for thirty years but had to be re-enacted every year. For some reason, they had not asked and didn't see fit to ask for substantive language. This is just a small incident, but I mean how does a guy acquire power? I'll tell you. Before Eisenhower told George Humphrey that he was going to be his Secretary of the Treasury, that word got out and Hoover met Humphrey in New York and arranged that the Secret Service would not have this investigative jurisdiction.

"On March sixteenth, 1951, I have the date right here, a bright young fellow from the Justice Department, who was representing the Deputy Attorney General, told congressmen, and I quote: 'I am here to voice the strongest possible objection to the enactment of that language. For many years appropriations for the activities of the Federal Bureau of Investigation have carried the language for the detection and prosecution of crimes against the United States. It is thus clear that the Federal Bureau of Investigation has exclusive jurisdiction over all acts involving violation of criminal laws of the United States except where the Congress has specifically otherwise assigned such jurisdiction.' Hoover has always put up the pose, 'Don't give me any more work, we can't take it on.' He didn't want a national police. Of course, he fought like a dog to maintain supremacy in the investigative field.

"That's the way he acquired power. And this is where the ordinary Civil Service administrator like myself catches it. It takes a year to educate a new cabinet member as to what the facts of life are, but a guy like Hoover can get to him in New York sixty days before he comes down on the job and work out some agreement as to giving away the Secret Service's authority in certain jurisdictions. This is part of the bureaucracy game, and it probably leaves you cold, but the only point I'm trying to make is that this man was a very astute empire builder."

The Director's Number One Ghost

Louis B. Nichols was the Director's first publicist and lobbyist, the person most responsible for the massive publicity campaign that transformed Hoover's G-men into household words. It was a triumph of virtue over evil. The G-men movies replaced the gangster movies, and the magazines, as one writer of the period observed, "bloomed with sagas of aggressive federal purity." Even children preferred the role of G-man to that of gangster.

The Bureau's Crime Records Division poured out an endless stream of magazine articles, mostly pulp, bylined by Hoover, which extolled the skill of the G-men and the futility of crime. There was a comic strip, "War on Crime," with continuity written by Rex Collier, a Washington newspaperman and friend of Hoover's, that was based on source material culled from FBI files. There were books and movies and radio shows—even business firms joined the crusade by marketing G-man pajamas and underwear for boys, and G-man badges, toy machine guns, revolvers, and handcuffs. But Hoover refused to let purveyors to the FBI advertise that fact. "We are in the midst of a crusade for law enforcement and it would be a mistake to cheapen it by any kind of commercialization" is the way the Director phrased it. As the symbol for the crusade, Hoover went on the lecture circuit. "My only ambition," he said, "is to be able to feel when I am through that I have made some small contribution to law enforcement." With a fondness for statistics and a talent for capsulizing his message, Hoover told audiences that someone was murdered in this country every forty-five minutes, a major crime was committed every twenty seconds, crime costs each American $120 a year, one out of every sixteen heads of families suffered loss of life or property each year, there were 3,500,000 active criminals in this country, and so on. Through the years, FBI statistics, now the official yardstick of the country's criminal condition, have not only reflected a steady increase in crime, but also a higher batting average for the Bureau, which, through the recovery of stolen goods (mostly automobiles), "always pays its way."

Hoover upbraided politicians for hampering policemen, policemen for taking graft, lawyers for aiding criminals, parole boards for being too lenient, and mothers for playing bridge when they ought to be watching their children. No phase of American life seemed to escape his paternal vigilance.

Lou Nichols was the man behind the scene. For many years he appeared to be Hoover's heir apparent, his Bureau importance rivaling that even of Tolson, but he never could achieve a social relationship with the Boss. Nichols began the interview by briefly outlining his FBI career:

NICHOLS: "I became interested in the FBI through two factors. One, Rex Collier was a young reporter for the Washington *Star* who covered the Justice Department. Rex and I were close personal friends when I was attending Washington University law school and working part time at the YMCA. He talked to me an awful lot about the Bureau and about Mr. Hoover, and at that time there was a radio program based upon some of the FBI activities, and I listened to that religiously every week. So after I graduated, I made an application and went through the six-week training course. I was appointed a special agent on July twenty-third, 1934, and my intentions then were of working for two or three years, saving my money, getting married, going back to my hometown of Kalamazoo, Michigan, and hanging out my shingle.

"Within three weeks after I was in training school, I had changed my mind completely. I became thoroughly sold on the Bureau, its mission, its objectives, and I made the determination that this was to be my career. I was transferred to Birmingham, then Atlanta, and in October 1935 I was assigned to the Washington Field Office. Early in 1936 I was transferred to Bureau headquarters as a supervisor in the old Research Division. That same year I attended the first school for special agents in charge, and before I had completed the course, I was designated SAC in Pittsburgh. Then before I could leave, two or three things happened that I had been handling, and Mr. Hoover called me in one day and said that there was a time when everybody had to look to the field for the future, but the Bureau was growing and there were opportunities for advancement at the seat of government. If I had no objection he would like to consider keeping me right there so I could keep on doing some of the things I was doing."

Were you then a ghostwriter for him?

NICHOLS: "Oh, I used to do things for Mr. Hoover, sure. But I don't care to—"

Did you have anything to do with his first book, Persons in Hiding, *published in 1938?*

NICHOLS: "No, I had nothing to do— Well, only to this extent: Courtney Ryley Cooper wrote that book. I did some of the research work and would prepare memoranda on certain aspects, certain chapters, and then Ryley would put it in his narrative form. And he, of course, was a very fine reporter himself, and he would go to the field and interview people and stuff like that. In 1938, I was put in charge of the Research Division, and then in '39 I was made an inspector and assigned as Mr. Tolson's assistant. In 1941, I became an assistant director, and ten years later Assistant to the Director. I acted for Mr. Hoover whenever he was out of the office or out of town. There are two assistants to the Director, and Mickey [D. Milton] Ladd was the other one. He handled the investigative stuff and I handled policy and administrative matters, plus the outside contacts and, well, the grief for the Bureau. You can't have an organization like the Bureau and not have grief from time to time. I continued in that position until I retired in 1957, at the age of fifty-two."

Why did you retire?

NICHOLS: "Well, two or three reasons. Basic reason, I had made the decision that I never wanted to be in the Bureau the day after Mr. Hoover left the Bureau. I had been trained for a period of ten years by him for the future, and having made that decision, I felt that I could have had anything I wanted in the Bureau, but I knew I could not continue the pace because I was working seven days and seven nights almost. And I neglected my family, and I'd had good offers from time to time, and finally I came to the conclusion that if I was a free agent, I should retire. So I went in and talked the matter over with Mr. Hoover, and left it solely up to him. I told him about the offers I had received, and it was Mr. Hoover who pretty much caused me to go with Mr. Lewis Rosenstiel at Schenley Industries—I had turned Mr. Rosenstiel down five times— because Mr. Hoover thought that would be a greater challenge [laughs] and it would be financially remunerating."

What were some of the things you did to enhance the Bureau's image?

NICHOLS: "For example, I worked up the radio program *This Is Your FBI* that had the top rating on ABC for about nine years. I helped organize it, helped get it started, and I reviewed the scripts."

Did you have anything to do with Don Whitehead's book The F.B.I. Story?

NICHOLS: "Sure. I got Don Whitehead to write that book."

It was your idea?

NICHOLS: "Sure."

Did the FBI supply him with research material?

NICHOLS: "Oh, very definitely, very definitely. We felt that the time had come to have a definitive story written on the Bureau, and I'd known Whitehead around town here and had followed him for a long period of time, and he, in my book, was one of the best reporters in the business. He was a two times Pulitzer Prize winner, and at that time he was the Washington bureau chief for the New York *Herald Tribune*. I talked to Mr. Hoover and he was very enthusiastic over it."

Did you work on the book?

NICHOLS: "No. Well, I worked on it by giving him source material. He would want to know about a situation and we would give him the source material."

How would he know the situation existed unless you told him about it?

NICHOLS: "Well, I'd tell him about a lot of these situations."

Did you edit the book?

NICHOLS: "No, I did not. Oh, I reviewed the book, the manuscript as it went along, but I did not— No, no, you don't edit Don Whitehead."

But wouldn't this be like the radio or TV shows—you'd have the last say on it, wouldn't you?

NICHOLS: "Well, I had a lot of say on it, and the way we'd handle that, if I saw something that I thought gave an erroneous impression or maybe wasn't one hundred percent accurate, I would point that out to Don, and matters of opinion where he was expressing an opinion or a conclusion, well, that's his business. We never injected ourselves into that. We were concerned primarily with facts."

"It Was a Beautiful Story"

I asked Mervyn LeRoy, who directed and produced the film version of *The F.B.I. Story*, which starred Jimmy Stewart, whether it was possible that the public got the FBI's authorized version of itself in the movie and in the television series with Efrem Zimbalist, Jr.

LEROY: "I could have had that series beyond a doubt. I turned it down. I could have made millions. I said, 'I don't want to do it. I made *The F.B.I. Story,* that's enough.' Now I'm kicking myself. Edgar offered it to me. Edgar was very close to Jack Warner too, but not as close as he was to me, which I can prove by the letters he wrote to me. I don't think anybody's got as many letters from Edgar as I have.

"Here's something I've never told anybody. Everybody on that picture (*The F.B.I. Story*), from the carpenters and electricians right to the top, everybody, had to be okayed by the FBI. I did one scene, the one where he has his first meeting with the men, and after I shot the picture, they discovered that one extra shouldn't have been in there. I don't know why. So we had to shoot the scene over. I had two FBI men with me all the time, for research purposes so that we did things right. He and his men controlled the movie."

Why would you let him do that?

LEROY: "Because I had to. Well, I wanted to, anyway. I wanted it to be just as perfect as it could be. We never had a bad review on *The F.B.I. Story* of any kind. Don't forget, I got Edgar in that picture. We went to Washington, to his office, and I said, 'Look, we're all set, let me shoot this. If you don't like it—' He said, 'I told you, I don't want to do it.' I said, 'I don't care what you told me. You are the FBI and you gotta be in this picture.' He said, 'All right, but I'm not going to speak.' I said, 'You don't have to speak. You're writing at your desk and I'm going to bring in Clyde and he comes in and hands you something and you okay it and he goes out.'"

Does Clyde speak?

LEROY [laughs]: "No. No one does. There's narration over it, if you remember the movie. And he did it. Now the first time I brought the print of *The F.B.I. Story* to Washington to run for Mr. Hoover, we ran it at night, about eight o'clock. He took me in the projection room and he had about twenty men in there who I'd never seen, all FBI men, and I was never so nervous in my whole life. I perspired, because I was back in the last row alone working the fade, you know, working the sound to make sure the sound was right, and I sweated all through the picture. I perspired like you've never seen. I was soaking wet. And for this reason, they didn't laugh in the right places, they didn't seem to show any emotion, including Mr. Hoover and Mr. Tolson and Deke DeLoach and everybody that were in there. So when the lights went up, I was absolutely worn out. And Edgar stood up and he motioned for me to come over to him and he put his arms around me and he said, 'Mervyn, that's one of the greatest jobs I've ever seen,' and they all started to applaud. I guess they were all waiting to see how he liked it. [Chuckles.] But they were so crazy about it, and I cried. I was really so moved that I cried. But I mean working this hard and trying to do something that he would like. Because you're doing a man's life and you're—and he could have said, 'Scrap it!' [Laughs.] Then I guess I would have had a heart attack. Of course, I was pretty sure he wasn't going to scrap it, because he had FBI men with me all the way through. I could have blamed them for a little bit of it, you know. Well, it was a beautiful story, it was the story of the FBI."

ZIMBALIST: "Every script was approved by them [the FBI] for, primarily, jurisdictional correctness and the fact that it was a literal case. We had some scripts that were dreamed up by our writers that they turned down because no such case by any stretch of the imagination had ever taken place. In the beginning, the episodes were based strictly on FBI cases that were dramatized and liberties taken. Later on the practice came to be somewhat different in that the writers would work with an FBI agent to produce a story that was close enough to something that had actually happened. When the agent was unable to restrain the writer and he came up with something that was totally unprecedented, then the FBI would refuse the script. Deke DeLoach was in charge of it for a long time, but it was Tolson who put the violence ban on us. There was one show, I think, where we had four deaths in it, and it was just when all the violence stuff was hitting the fan, and the story committee and all those people started to scream and point a couple of fingers at the FBI for having a show that, according to them, promoted violence. Tolson put out the order that there would be no more deaths—immortality. We didn't kill anybody, I think, the last two or three years."

Was everyone checked out by the FBI?

ZIMBALIST: "I can't say for sure, but from my knowledge, I know that everyone who played an agent was, and I know of some others who were as well. I know that Hoover's policy was that he didn't want any criminals or known Communists or subversives appearing on his show, and certainly not representing the Bureau as agents."

Dillinger and the Anonymous Purvis

Getting back to Nichols, I asked him why Hoover disliked Melvin Purvis, and pointed out that Purvis didn't fare much better in Whitehead's book.

NICHOLS: "He didn't care for him. You're right on that score. Purvis was doing a lot of freewheeling on his own and he was in water over his head. Sam Cowley was the guy who actually handled the Dillinger case and Purvis was a figurehead. As far as Whitehead's treatment of Purvis is concerned, it was not anything on my part. Don felt that the Dillinger case was very well known and he wanted to deal with some of the things that were not so well known. He didn't want to rehash things."

Yet the Dillinger case was a turning point in Hoover's career. He kept Dillinger's death mask in the anteroom next to his official office nearly forty years.

NICHOLS: "That period also included the Machine Gun Kelly case, the Bremer kidnaping case, the Karpis case, and that whole hoodlum era. It wasn't just Dillinger."

In his book *American Agent*, Melvin Purvis recalled what happened the night they killed Dillinger:

I stood with my cigar shaking in my mouth, a match in my hand ready to light it. My eyes ached from the strain. Finally, John Dillinger came out. On one side of him was Anna Sage [the "woman in red"]; on the other Polly Hamilton.

Dillinger was surrounded by women and children as the crowd moved onto the sidewalk. Suddenly, he turned his head and looked right at me. Apparently, he didn't recognize me. I struck the match and lit my cigar (that was the signal for the agents to close in).

Then, I waited for what seemed like an endless length of time, hoping against hope the crowd would disperse. As it reached the sidewalk, it did begin to separate. The number of patrons around Dillinger dwindled as he and the two women turned and walked up the street. . . .

I was about three feet to the left and a little behind him. I was very nervous. My voice was squeaky when I called out:

"Stick 'em up, John. You're surrounded."

Without turning, he drew his .38 automatic. He never got to fire it, though. Shot, he fell with his head in an alley beside the theatre. His gun was still in his right hand as he went down. I leaned over and took the gun. Then I called an ambulance. John Dillinger died on the way to the hospital.

In their biography, *Dillinger, a Short and Violent Life,* authors Robert Cromie and Joseph Pinkston described the event this way:

At 10:40, more than two hours after the full-scale vigil began, the main door of the Biograph was pushed open and the most wanted man in the United States sauntered out, a woman on each arm. Dillinger turned left toward Halsted Street, where Mrs. Sage had an apartment, and his complete lack of concern showed that he had no hint that his amazing luck was about to end in a blaze of gunfire.

As the three passed the doorway of the Goetz Country Club, a tavern just south of the Biograph, Dillinger stared incuriously at Purvis, who was standing in the doorway. A moment later, when the trio was opposite the National Tea Company store, Purvis tried to light a cigar—the prearranged signal for his men to close in—but his hands were trembling so violently that he failed to do so.

The intended sign was caught, however, and two or three of the watchers walked unhurriedly in behind the threesome. None of the government men spoke, but the man who was being followed suddenly sensed that the scene was playing wrong. Mrs. Sage had dropped behind the other two just before the action began. Polly Hamilton, seeing men with guns, dug her elbow into Dillinger's ribs as a warning, and at the same moment he broke into a run, just at the mouth of the alley, his right hand tugging frantically at his trouser pocket.

All over the street guns flashed into view—Purvis tore the buttons off his coat getting his out in a hurry—and the customary night noises were drowned by a rapid series of shots, Chicago's theme songs in the thirties. Four bullets struck Dillinger, one in the back of the neck, virtually at point-blank range. He was driven forward and down, landing on his face with his own gun still uncleared. Agent Charles Winstead is believed to have fired the fatal bullet. . . .

Sergeant Conroy rolled Dillinger onto his back and began searching him as Purvis knelt to inspect the gold ring Dillinger always wore and to remove the pistol, a .38 automatic with the safety still on, from the right-hand trouser pocket.

Then Purvis, who for almost five months had dedicated every waking hour—and probably some of his dreams—to the task of hunting down John Dillinger, sounded suddenly unsure of himself. He turned to a city policeman and asked, "What's the procedure now?"

Before including Hoover's version, it should be noted that Samuel Cowley was not at the Biograph on that historic night. He was waiting at the Chicago Field Office with an open wire to Hoover's home. Yet Purvis is not even mentioned in *Persons in Hiding*, much less given credit for what is unquestionably the FBI's most celebrated bust. Here's the way Hoover chose to tell the story in his book:

Months before, he [Sam Cowley] had been called away to take command of the Special Squad in our search for John Dillinger, mapping out the plans, making the arrangements and signing the contract with Anna Sage, the brothel keeper, who had delivered John Dillinger for a reward of money, and not immunity from deportation as she later asserted. Anna Sage sold out Dillinger for five thousand dollars, which was paid her. She was made no other offers of reward of any kind. It had been Sam who had commanded the field of officers on that night, when the Indiana bandit, living true to his real character of a sneak and a coward, had attempted to throw a woman in front of him to act as a barricade as he drew his gun in an effort to shoot down the three Special Agents who were closing in on him. The marksmanship displayed by these three men—none of whom, it may be surprising to know, ever have been publicly named—was little short of miraculous. Had they been less than expert, Dillinger might have still been alive and they might have been dead, for the bandit's body was all but concealed by the feminine form which he had seized with an outstretched arm and thrown before him.

It was Cowley's skillful selection of such men as these, his calmness and thoroughness of preparation, that brought about the elimination of Dillinger. It was due to his modesty that the general public did not know the true facts concerning the downfall of our most publicized ruffian of recent years.

Four months after Dillinger's demise, Cowley was killed in a gun battle with Baby Face Nelson. Hoover's version of Dillinger's cowardice is not substantiated by any official account. Purvis's name is not included in the index to *The F.B.I. Story*, but Don Whitehead does mention him briefly:

Despite the plastic surgery, the outlaw was identified beyond doubt [when he entered the theater]. Cowley called Hoover, who was pacing the library at his home in Washington. The decision was made to take Dillinger as he came out of the theater, rather than risk a gun battle inside the crowded show house.

When the trio emerged, by prearrangement Purvis lit a cigar. The trap began to close. Dillinger must have sensed that something was wrong. He glanced over his shoulder and saw an agent moving toward him. He darted toward an alley, clawing a pistol from his pants pocket. But before he could get his gun into action, three FBI agents fired five shots. Slugs tore into Dillinger's body and he pitched on his face. The chase was over.

The next day, Hoover wrote Cowley: "I wanted to write and to repeat to you my expressions of commendation and pleasure last evening upon the excellent results which you attained. . . ." As a reward, Hoover promoted Cowley to the full rank of inspector.

"The Kaiser's Mustache"

A year after the Dillinger episode, Melvin Purvis quit the Bureau. In his 1937 *New Yorker* profile of Hoover, Jack Alexander wrote,

Hoover encourages his men, especially those with families, to accept promising offers from the outside and sends them on their way with his benison. With one conspicuous exception, he is enthusiastic about his graduates. The exception is Melvin Purvis, who won nationwide publicity when he led the party that ambushed John Dillinger. Since leaving the F.B.I., Purvis has been boosting Post Toasties in advertisements as a prime aid in man-hunting. He is now busy organizing the youth of America, under the Post Toasties aegis, into the Melvin Purvis Law-and-Order Patrol, each member of which is a Secret Operator. Purvis's breakfast-food crusade against crime leaves the Director cold.

Alexander took note of Dillinger's death mask:

In the anteroom where visitors wait to be admitted to the Director's presence the most compelling decorative object is a startling white plaster facsimile of John Dillinger's death mask. It stares, empty-eyed, from under the glass of an exhibit case. There are other exhibit cases in the anteroom, but this one, like a prize scalp, is significantly located closest to the Director's office. Grouped about the mask are souvenirs of the memorable night when the spectacular outlaw was cornered and shot down. . . . There are the straw hat he was wearing, a wrinkled snapshot of a girl which was fished from his trousers pocket, and the silver-rimmed glasses he was wearing to heighten his disguise, one of the lens rims snapped by a bullet. There is a La Corona–Belvedere cigar he was carrying in his shirt pocket that summer night, still banded and wrapped in cellophane. . . . After the ordinary tourists have probed all the shivery possibilities of the anteroom, they are led through a series of other rooms in which are displayed an even greater variety of confiscated armament and forbidding mementos . . . and two more facsimiles of the Dillinger death mask. The mask apparently is a sort of Kaiser's mustache with the F.B.I.

NICHOLS: "Mr. Hoover was a very solid person, and he built the FBI on a solid basis, because the guy was thoroughly honorable. When he said something, people knew it was true."

But he knew how to portray an image, which was something you had a hand in.

NICHOLS: "Oh, I think there's a certain element of truth to that, and I think that he, on the whole, had a very friendly press. Now, in recent years, it has been a little different, but in those early years he had a friendly press. He lasted some fifty-odd years, so he must have been doing a lot of things right. He had a good organization, a good team, with a lot of dedicated guys, and you take all that brain power and put it together— But he's the one who set the standards, make no mistake about that. He was the taskmaster. But I never found him a hard man to work for. Some people say he was difficult. He had a standard of perfection and he expected everybody else to go up to his standards.

"He had a memory like an elephant. Something would come up—I can't recall any specific incident—and I'd check every place and I couldn't find it, and I'd go back to him and I'd say, 'Listen, I can't find this.' He'd say, 'Did you look so-and-so-and-so-and-so?' 'Yes, it's not there.' 'Well, then you ought to look at so-and-so.' I'd go back and there it was. That's happened countless times.

"He had no patience for an individual who made a mistake and then tried to alibi it. But if you made a mistake and when it was called to his attention you said, 'Listen, that was a stupid boner, wasn't it?' He'd say, 'It sure was. Just don't do it again.' He'd say nothing more about it. But if you tried to alibi your way out of it, he just wouldn't let you do it. I learned that very quickly. I'd beat him to the punch. The moment I made a mistake I'd go to him immediately and say, 'I pulled a stupid boner.' Why, he was immediately very sympathetic, and he would try to help extricate me. But, listen, the closer you were to him, the more severe he was."

Would that include his secretary, Helen Gandy?

NICHOLS: "Gandy was a tremendous asset to the organization. First of all, she'd been with him from the year one. She had a phenomenal way of getting along with people. She is a very sweet person, and she had a very keen perception, and her understanding of human nature is just uncanny. And she would translate all that into action when things would come up by a comment here and a comment there [laughs] to the Director. But she was under fire all the time, the same as I was. I used to catch the hell for the entire Bureau. If somebody needed to be laid out, Mr. Hoover would lay them out, and then he'd get it off his mind and off his chest and that's that, that's the end of it, then go on to something else. The next hour, he might be commending that person for a job well done."

"A Controversy with God"

Few men have observed the Director at work as closely and for as long a period of time as William C. Sullivan, who was the Bureau's number three man before he was forced to retire in October 1971. Sullivan spent twenty-eight of his thirty years with the Bureau in Washington, moving up through the ranks, from special agent to supervisor, unit chief, section chief, inspector, chief inspector, Assistant Director in Charge of Domestic Intelligence and Foreign Operations, and finally Assistant to the Director in Charge of All Investigations, Criminal and Security, and Foreign Operations. He had a long and distinguished career until, as he says, "I got into a controversy with God." Sullivan's iconoclasm is welcomed in these pages. His viewpoint may be biased, but then whose viewpoint is not?

SULLIVAN: "You want to write a book, and I want to get the facts across to the public. I'm not getting a dime out of it, and I don't want a dime out of it. I was offered five different contracts to write a book, and I turned them all down. I decided I didn't want to capitalize on my break with him. It went too deep and it meant too much to me. If you offered me money, I'd be insulted."

What was it like working with Hoover on a day-to-day basis?

SULLIVAN: "If he liked you, you could do no wrong; if he didn't like you, you could do no right. That's the way he thought, in terms of black and white. Professionally, he was a charmer. He'd charm anybody that came in there: ambassadors, admirals, generals. He could be all things to all people. If a liberal came in, the liberal would leave thinking that 'My God, Hoover is a real liberal!' If a John Bircher came in an hour later, he'd go out saying, 'I'm convinced that Hoover is a member of the John Birch Society at heart.' He was a brilliant chameleon. Make no mistake now. I'm not underestimating the man's mental capacity. He wasn't intellectual, or academic; he was suspicious of the academic community, of any intellectual

—Henry Steele Commager, Dr. Robert Maynard Hutchins—of any scholar. He disliked them instinctively. But he had a very cunning, crafty, shrewd mind and he could make fools out of some of these people that I alluded to, he could make fools out of some senators and congressmen. He'd wrap them right around his little finger. He was a master con man, let me put it that way. He was one of the greatest con men the country even produced, and that takes intelligence of a certain kind, an astuteness, a shrewdness.

"When a man went in to talk with him, he did all the talking because always he was conscious of his own limitations in the field of knowledge, and so he'd keep talking. He didn't want the man to ask him any questions, particularly if he was an educated man, because he might not know the answers and that would upset him terribly. He had to have the answers to all questions. So he'd keep talking right up until the last and then all of a sudden break off the interview and shake hands with the fellow and send him on his way. I've known some people who later said, 'Gee, you know, I wanted to ask him some questions but I never got a chance.'

"Oh, he was wonderful at small talk. And very engaging, you know, and very, very interesting, and every once in a while he'd get quite witty. One time years ago he sent me out to speak in the Midwest and he said, 'Now, we're under attack for tapping phones, and when you're called upon to speak at this conference, I want you to be extremely careful not to say anything that's going to cause us any trouble in the press.' I said, 'Mr. Hoover, the only thing I'll talk about if I'm called upon is the weather, the weather conditions.' And he looked at me and he said, 'Oh, no, no, no, don't talk about the weather conditions. They'll accuse us of having a tap on the Weather Bureau.' Now that was a clever response. He was very good at light talk."

A Gentleman of the Old School

Sullivan's comment reminded me of what Efrem Zimbalist, Jr., had told me about his first meeting with Hoover after he was selected to play the role of Inspector Erskine in the FBI television series.

ZIMBALIST: "Before we began filming the series in 1965, I went back to the Bureau for about a week's familiarization, which included interviews with the division heads, then down to Quantico at the Academy, and the last day was an interview with Hoover which lasted slightly over two hours and I don't recall his ever pausing in his conversation once. He just talked at breakneck speed on every subject imaginable, and with such a command of thought and language that there wasn't room to get in the amenities of conversation. When it was over, I looked at my watch, and I'd been in there two hours and four minutes. He was a great conversationalist, had a great sense of humor, and wide knowledge of every area of life, and he just chatted most charmingly and interestingly about every subject—he crossed decades and continents and everything else.

"He spoke with complete frankness, complete candor. Whatever came into his head, whether it was on a controversial subject or what, he said exactly what he felt, *exactly*, without hedging, without sweetening the pill or anything like that. If he didn't like somebody, he said it; if he did like them, he said that too. Just exactly what he thought. He was absolutely fearless. Which was so impressive to me because it was the first time I'd ever met him, and I would have expected him to be a little tentative in his conversation, but not at all.

"And, as you know, he was a formal man in the tradition of the old school of Washington politics. There was a formality to him, and when I came home two days later, I had a letter, my first of many letters from him, and it was 'Dear Efrem,' and he just alluded very briefly to the meeting and so forth, and then he signed it 'Edgar.' And we were on that basis ever after, which was surprising, considering the fact that he was essentially a formal man. His letters were always very terse, very laconic, to the point and nothing else, and you wouldn't expect that kind of informality from him."

Was the meeting a briefing?

ZIMBALIST: "Oh, no. This was in no sense that. It was just a pleasant conversation. He talked about everything except the FBI, as I recall. About Washington society and Hollywood and Shirley Temple and Khrushchev."

Can you recall what he said on any of these subjects? Why would he bring up Shirley Temple?

ZIMBALIST: "He had a picture of her there, and I think that may have been how it came up. He was very fond of Hollywood, of Hollywood people, and he'd had, I guess, pleasant experiences with them, and he liked that. About Khrushchev, he met him at a party and he started bragging that their agents would know everything the FBI had, and Hoover said,

'Well, we know exactly where every one of your agents are, don't make any mistake about that.'

"He was a gentleman of the old school. He had that marvelous slight Virginia accent—it was a gentility, really, that he had—and I enjoyed watching him talk because he had this little dialect, those little ways the Virginians have of saying words. Very charming. And, as I said, he spoke with complete candor. That's why he was such a Godsend in Washington, where everybody is creeping around and pussyfooting and foggybottoming and all that kind of thing, and Hoover was a breath of fresh air. He was a benevolent, in a sense, despot. I mean, he was the ruler of a very powerful arm of the government, and it takes a strong man to run an organization like that, and he was the *ideal*, he was the benevolent ruler. Absolute integrity. He was a man who had an honest power, who used it wisely, very wisely, and with restraint. He didn't want to build an empire. My personal opinion is that his attitude toward attorneys general—he was criticized for being uncavalier to an official who was over him—I think his attitude was that the FBI was a continuing body and an attorney general was a political appointee. He wasn't about to put the Bureau's destiny under somebody who was appointed because he helped somebody get elected. He saw that very clearly, I think, from the very beginning. I really think if history is fairly told in the years to come—which is a big question—I think his importance is going to be enormous in this country. He's going to rank as one of the great figures. But it depends on who writes the history and God knows what our future is going to be."

"An Institution Is the Lengthened Shadow of One Man"

Returning to Sullivan, I asked him if Hoover had any cultural interests.

SULLIVAN: "He was very conscious of the fact that he was not educated. He never read anything except the memos and investigative reports that passed over his desk. He had no interest in any kind of culture. He was not interested in plays, not interested in poetry, not interested in political science or history or biography. He never read anything that would broaden his mind or give depth to his thinking. He went into government out of high school and then went on to law school, and his whole background was narrow. He lived with his mother until she died, never traveled abroad, and I never knew him to have an intellectual or educated friend. Neither did Tolson. They had nothing in common with anybody who was cultured. They lived in their own strange little world."

Was there a time in your life when you admired Hoover and wanted to emulate him?

SULLIVAN: "When I was a starry-eyed young agent, I came off a farm and I had been teaching school for eight hundred dollars a year out in the country. I had hardly been forty miles away from home and I wound up in the halls of the Justice Department. I was all eyes. Then we were subjected to the terrific propaganda that the instructors gave out: 'This is the greatest organization ever devised by a human mind.' They kept quoting Emerson: 'An institution is the lengthened shadow of one man.' They hit us with that almost every day. They drilled that into us. I don't know whether you grew up on a farm or not, but when you grow up on a farm, you chop wood, you shovel manure, you milk cows in the subzero weather of the morning, you pitch hay, and you sort of get a grasp of realism. After about four or five weeks of this, I used to sit there and ask myself, 'How much of this is true and how much of it is fiction?'

"They laid it on so heavily. I'll never forget the first time he came in our class, because at heart I'm quite a liberal. I don't like anything dealing with regimentation or the military. I went out to get a drink of water and I saw men, agents, lined up along the walls, and I said to one, 'What's going on?' He said, 'You know from the schedule that the Director is due to speak in your class in the next five minutes. We're forming a guard for him along the corridors.' You know, I went back in my room and it just disgusted me, it really did. That type of thing I thought was very undemocratic. He came in, and to tell you the truth, I can't remember a thing he said. He didn't say anything that remained with me. He was an awful speaker. He sure could put you to sleep.

"I was told by a Bureau friend to keep my mouth shut in training and to not criticize Hoover or the Bureau, because there were spies in every classroom, made up mostly of Bureau clerks who had gone to night school for their law or accounting degree and were now going to become agents. They deliberately put them in every class to spy on the rest of us. A word to the wise was sufficient, and I kept my mouth shut. These guys would walk up, you know, but you could spot them, and, boy, I gave that type of person a wide berth, and everybody else did.

"Before I ever left training school, it was told to me by people who knew their way around the Bureau, and particularly by a couple of friends I had in the Bureau, 'Hoover is an egomaniac, and when you go out in the field be very careful. Don't write any letters criticizing the FBI, because he considers himself to be the FBI, and therefore you'd be criticizing him.'

"I went out in the field and worked with Charlie B. Winstead, the fellow who shot and killed John Dillinger, an old Texan, and we became fast friends. Charlie told me the same thing. He said, 'Bill, are you going to stay in the Bureau or are you just going to be here for the duration?' This was during the war and there were an awful lot of draft dodgers in the Bureau. There was a great exodus out of the Bureau when the war was over. I said, 'I'm going to stay.' Charlie said, 'Then remember we've got an unusual man heading the Bureau in J. Edgar Hoover.' And he took off on Hoover's ego, his conceit, his vanity, his love of receiving gifts, his penuriousness, and he said, 'Be extremely careful how you approach him. When you go back to Washington, if I was you, I'd never ask to see him, because you can't win. You go in and if he doesn't like you, if he doesn't like the suit or tie you're wearing, you're done. If he likes you and you make a good impression, it really doesn't mean a hell of a lot, because those bureaucrats back there are the ones who make the recommendations for pulling people in from the field and not Hoover, and they'll color things the way they want. So my advice is don't ever ask to see him.' And by God I didn't. I never did see Hoover until I was pulled back as a supervisor when I came back from Europe. I didn't go in to see him until he called me.

"Charlie said, 'Write on his birthday and at Christmas and every other day, always write flattering letters to him. You may not like this'—and I had never written a letter like that in my life and probably you never have even now—but he said, 'Let me tell you, if you don't do this when everyone else is doing it you're going to stand out like a sore thumb. It's up to you. If you want to progress in the Bureau, if you want a good assignment instead of being bounced around from one office to the other, you better do what the others do and write these flattering letters.'

"I followed his advice, and when I got back to the Bureau I discovered that Charlie was right. Everyone was writing him these damn flowery letters. He must have had file cabinet after file cabinet full of this stuff. I remember an assistant director called me one day. 'Say,' he said, 'the Boss just came back from the Appropriations Committee.' I said, 'Yes.' He said, 'You know,' and he mentioned a certain assistant director's name, 'he's got a flattering letter in, telling the Boss what a marvelous job he must have done up there on the Hill. I'm calling you because I'm writing one now, right now, and every assistant director is going to write him one. You better get yours in right away or you'll be the only one that didn't.'

"I stopped, no matter what it was, whether it was a hijacking case or a bank robbery, and dictated a flattering letter, and this is the way it went. He just loved to get these letters. You just couldn't praise him too much; you couldn't be too lavish in telling him what a great job he was doing for the country. Or praise him to his face. Tolson had a standard phrase that he used all the time: 'The Director will go down in history as the greatest man of the century.' And, of course, Hoover knew that Tolson was saying that all the time. It got to be a joke. I mean this wasn't all grim, there was a lot of damn in-fighting and a lot of controversy, and a lot of bloody encounters, but there was a lot of humor too.

"I remember the time McGovern criticized Hoover and said he ought to retire. That was in *Life* magazine. So orders went out for all officials of the Bureau to rally to the cause and to write critical letters to McGovern. Well, I didn't think it was a good idea and I said so in two or three places. I said McGovern would know right off that this was a command performance, that we'd been told to do this, and what good would the letters do? Well, it didn't matter. The Boss said these letters have got to be written, defending him and saying that he's got to go on for the sake of the country. Somehow this bothered me a little bit more than it should have and I delayed in writing my letter. Finally, I got a call from Tolson's office, asking if I had written the letter. I said no, I hadn't. 'Well,' this guy said, 'we expect you to write the letter. This is a test of loyalty.' So the test of loyalty boiled down to whether I was going to write a letter berating McGovern, whether I was going to give him hell or not. So I sat down and wrote a letter I thought I could live with. I used a lot of words but I didn't say much. I said, 'Nobody needs to defend Hoover, his record speaks for itself.' Well, that doesn't mean anything. And so on. I gave the letter to Jim Gale, one of my assistant directors, to mail. And damned if I didn't get another call from Tolson's office, wanting to know whether the letter had been mailed. I said yes and I was asked if I had mailed it myself, and I said I had given it to Jim Gale to mail. I'll be damned if he didn't call Gale to see if I had given him the letter and whether he had mailed it."

"Hoover Had a Thing About Dillinger"

I have more questions about Tolson, but first I'd like to back up and ask if Charlie Winstead ever told you why Hoover hated Purvis?

SULLIVAN: "Purvis was a publicity seeker just like Hoover, and Hoover wasn't going to put up with any agent being a publicity seeker. After all, he had the monopoly on publicity, and he wasn't about to put up with Purvis getting headlines, and this is what caused the rift between them. Then, good God, Purvis wrote a book. That was it.

"Hoover had a thing about Dillinger. If he were alive today and you went in to see him, he'd tell you about Dillinger. The older he got the more he talked about Dillinger, Ma Barker, Karpis, and all those old cases of the thirties. He would talk on and on about this stuff, which I guess is understandable, and is no criticism, but that's the way it was. He'd go on in great detail, over and over the same stuff, and one of our liaison men, who would take visitors in to meet Hoover, told me, 'Jeez, I wake up at night reciting what Hoover has said, because he says the same things over and over and over again.'

"Hoover, of course, was not a man who knew how to handle a gun. He wasn't that type. They set things up for him on some of those arrests in the old days so he'd get the publicity. One time they had a picture of him in the paper holding a machine gun, but that was phony. He never really arrested anybody."

What about Dillinger's death mask?

SULLIVAN: "That was so morbid that we used to get criticism. One time a doctor from Baltimore wrote in a very nice letter saying, 'I'm very interested in the FBI and have been a great supporter of you, Mr. Hoover, and the Bureau. I recently took a tour of the Bureau with some friends and may I make some suggestions?' He then proceeded to criticize the Dillinger mask and other exhibits. He said, 'I think it would be better for you and the public would be more than pleased if you got rid of them.' Gee, was Hoover mad. He was furious. He immediately said, 'Put him on the No Contact List!' You know, the Nixon White House got the idea for the Enemies List from us. This is true. For years we had this No Contact List which was made up of people Hoover disliked or people who criticized the Bureau, and we'd have no contact with them. Oh, some of the finest people in the country—scholars, writers, intellectuals—were on that list.

"Every once in a while, one of these people would be listed as a reference on an application for somebody, let's say, applying for a position at the White House, and we'd have to write a memorandum to Hoover and say, 'This man who is on the No Contact List is listed as a reference. What do you want us to do?'"

Did the FBI have special squads collecting information on celebrities?

SULLIVAN: "No. What was done—it was understood out in the field that Hoover wanted to get derogatory information on celebrities—and so agents in charge would be on the alert. Whenever they developed any derogatory information on celebrities, whether they were entertainers, intellectuals, politicians or educators, no matter who they were, they'd send that information in to Hoover. The Washington Field Office was a great source of information because of the nature of Washington, with all the congressmen and so forth, and so they'd just send it in to him. The first thing we did when anybody was elected to Congress was to run to the file and see what we had. We shouldn't even have a file on them, they're none of our business, but I don't know of any people being selected specifically to do that type of work."

Tolson Had a Grudge against Mankind

Now getting back to Tolson, I understand he was very sharp?

SULLIVAN: "In the beginning, yes. I'd say the last eight or nine years a big change came over Tolson. And in the last two or three years he didn't amount to anything. He just wasn't able to— He'd call me up and start saying something and all of a sudden he'd stop and say, 'What's the next word I want?' Maybe twice out of fifteen times I might guess the right word, and if I did, then he'd go on. If I didn't guess it, he'd get mad and slam the receiver. The poor old guy. He should have retired years ago and it would have saved us a lot of trouble. He got terribly sour. He seemed to have a grudge against mankind, against human beings, particularly agents. He used to make the charge, 'Agents are no damn good; all they do is work three hours a day,' and that's just not so. They used to tell the story at the Bureau— First let me explain that dismissal with prejudice makes it almost impossible for the discharged person to get another job, particularly in government. Hoover would use that pretty freely.

"As the story goes, and this was made up, not true, you understand, Tolson went in to see Hoover one day and said, 'Edgar, gee, I feel awful. I'm depressed and I'm melancholy and I think I'll just go home for the day and go to bed.' Hoover said, 'Clyde, don't do that. There's no need of you going home. Why don't you just go ahead and fire somebody? Just look down the list, pick out somebody, and fire him. You'll feel a lot better.' Tolson looked up and beamed. 'With prejudice?' he asked.

"There's another made-up story about Hoover buying a burial lot. One day he said to Tolson, 'Clyde, we're getting old and sooner or later we're going to die. I want you to go out and get two burial lots for us, side by side.' Hoover was a real miser and he said to Clyde, 'Don't sign anything. Let me know what they're going to cost before you firm things up.' A day or two later, Clyde came back and said, 'Edgar, I've got two burial lots just as you want, side by side, and they're going to cost the following,' whatever the figure was. Hoover said, 'Why, that's outrageous! That's far too much, far too much. I'm not going to pay that for a burial lot. Clyde, I'll tell you what you do. Go ahead and buy your own lot, and rent a vault for me for three days. I'll only be there three days.'

"After Hoover died, I remember talking about old times with one of the assistant directors, and I said, 'Hoover really thought that he was going to be in that new building.' Hoover had followed its construction very carefully and he was going to have a private elevator going up to his office, and I said, 'He really thought he was going to live and be in that new office over there.' And he said, 'How sure are you he's not going to be there?'

"A book could be made up of stories about Hoover and Tolson. Many of them would be absolutely true. Like the one about the wadcutters. First let me explain that a wadcutter is a bullet with a flat top—the lead is severed right at the casing, and it's used for target practice. There's enough lead for accuracy and it saves a lot of money. We've been using wadcutters ever since I entered the Bureau. This happened some years ago. John Mohr called me one day and he said, 'Say, at the executive conference, I'm going to bring up a subject and I wonder if you'd support me.' I said, 'I will, John, if I agree with it.' He explained that he wanted to give graduates of the FBI Academy a looseleaf notebook engraved with the FBI seal, their name, class, and the date of their graduation from the Academy. 'Everybody likes some little thing to take back home,' John said, 'and this will be good public relations. Also it's useful. I've researched it thoroughly and it will cost hardly anything if we buy them in large quantities.' I told him he could count on my support, and so at the conference, John said, 'I want to take up a subject matter,' and he explained about the notebooks.

"Tolson, negative as always, said, 'No, no, Mohr, I wouldn't be in favor of that. That's a bad idea. Suppose one of these graduates went sour and embarrassed the Bureau? He'd have in his possession this notebook binder with the seal of the FBI on it.' And again he said, 'That's a bad idea, Mohr." John, who has a quick temper and is very smart, started to get a little irritated. He said, 'Good God, Mr. Tolson, embarrass the Bureau with a looseleaf binder? We give every one of these men an official diploma with J. Edgar Hoover's signature on it. What could be more official than that? If we're going to be embarrassed by a man going sour, we're going to be embarrassed by this diploma, not by just an old looseleaf binder.' Well, Tolson saw that his argument didn't hold water, and he backed off. 'How much are they going to cost?' he asked. Mohr estimated about five hundred dollars for a three-year supply. 'No, no, no,' Tolson said, 'it's too much, too much.' By that time Mohr was really mad and he said, 'Damn it, Mr. Tolson, we shoot off more money than that in wad-cutters in one month at Quantico.' Now Tolson was also getting mad. 'Mohr,' he said, 'what are wadcutters?' Well, I thought I'd roll out of the chair. I wasn't supposed to laugh, I was supposed to look real grim, but I couldn't possibly look grim. I laughed like the devil. Anyhow, we lost. We didn't buy the notebook binders."

"Hoover and Tolson Were a Real Twosome"

"There never was a day that went by that we didn't laugh like the devil, once or twice a day. There was always something uproariously funny, you know. And generally it centered around Hoover and Tolson, some damn thing that they did or said, and we'd laugh and laugh and laugh. It wasn't altogether a grim business. But you had to be careful where you laughed. You could get transferred out of there in twenty-four hours.

"That reminds me of an incident at one of our annual liaison parties. Everybody was having a good time and one of the agents walked up to Tolson and put his hand on his shoulder, you know, in a joking manner, and he said, 'Clyde'—and, of course, you never called them by their first names—'Clyde, why in hell don't you people treat us men as men instead of boys all the time?' The next day he had a letter waiting for him in his office when he got in. He was transferred to the Washington Field Office. Busted right out of headquarters.

"Another time we were in conference and Hoover was down on Al Belmont, one of the finest men we ever had. Hoover was mad as hell at him. He'd get down on one person and then another, sometimes he wouldn't speak to you for five or six months, and everything would be done by memorandum. And this time it was Belmont. I think it was the time we couldn't catch the Communist fugitives. He just gave us hell, every one of us. We were seated around this big table in his office and he was just lashing out at all of us, and finally he turned and he said, 'Belmont, how many security cases are you investigating today?' Well, you never know, they change from day to day so quickly that you couldn't possibly know the answer. Belmont never hesitated. He said, 'Thirty-one thousand, two hundred and sixteen.' You know, that stopped Hoover. It kind of took him by surprise. He didn't speak for a moment or two, and shortly thereafter the conference broke up. On the way out—Belmont and I were always close friends—I said, 'Al, how in hell did you ever remember that number? You must have a phenomenal memory.' He looked at me. 'I didn't remember,' he said. 'I made that one up out of thin air. You didn't think for a moment, did you, that I was going to tell him that I didn't know the answer after him giving me hell all the time? I knew he wouldn't know the answer.'

"As you know, Hoover and Tolson were a real twosome. When Lee Boardman was made Assistant to the Director on the investigative side, he made a fatal mistake. I don't understand how a man who had been around the Bureau that many years could make this mistake. After he was in his new position a few weeks, he called Tolson one morning and said, 'Say, you folks got any luncheon commitment today?' Tolson said, 'Well, I'm having lunch with the Director.' 'Well,' Boardman said, 'I thought I'd join you, make it a threesome.' My God, what a fatal statement.

"I suppose because he was the number three man he thought he was in the inner family, but nobody ever got in that inner family—there was just two people living in that family. Within four or five weeks, Boardman got a letter advising him that his position was unnecessary and it was being dissolved. He was transferred as Special Agent in Charge of the Washington Field Office. There was no number three man for about eight or nine months. I think Boardman resigned and then Al Belmont was moved up to that spot. That number three man spot has been a hot seat. Many have left under a cloud."

Would Hoover use rough language when he was mad?

SULLIVAN: "Oh, sure. He could swear like a trooper. One of his favorite expressions was 'He's a thirteen-carat son of a bitch.' Why he'd even swear at Miss Gandy, his secretary, and he'd swear at different agents, which I don't criticize him for, but just keep the facts straight. He read the smut but I don't ever recall him using it in conversation. He'd use words like 'bastard' and 'no-good son of a bitch' or 'thirteen-carat son of a bitch' and words like that. And he'd use those very frequently. I've seen the man many times every day for years, but I don't recall any lewd or foul language."

Was the FBI a good organization?

SULLIVAN: "The men in the field—I have the highest regard for the average special agent. He is a fine human being, but he never knew what went on at headquarters, and to this day he might fight vigorously for the Bureau because he still doesn't know. That's no criticism of him. The strength of the FBI, and I'd like to make this point with you, was always in the special agent in the field offices. He is a good man. Most of them are selected by the men in the field. Applicants apply at field offices, where they are interviewed, and it is field supervisors who make recommendations to the Bureau. So, actually, they are hired out in the field, and they work in the field, and few ever get to know what goes on at headquarters. And what goes on there would make a hell of a story if the truth was ever told, and it wouldn't be a pleasant story."

"Hoover Was Always Hitting Us for Gifts"

Can you give me some specifics?

SULLIVAN: "Well, for example, Hoover was always hitting us for gifts, and we'd have to buy him extremely expensive gifts. His anniversary with the Justice Department, his anniversary with the Bureau, Thanksgiving Day, Christmas Day, his birthday, we were always pitching in on a collection for a gift. They handled it very cleverly. It would always come out of Tolson's office to us. For example, May tenth, 1971, I was told that he wanted a garbage masher. And I had to chase around to find one. It happens that I had a very close friend with Whirlpool out in Chicago, and I explained my problem to him. I said, 'Look, I don't want any unusual favor but do you ever sell any of these damn things for cost?' He said, 'Oh, yes, we do that all the time.' But 'hell,' he said, 'we'll give you one.' I said, 'No, no, absolutely not. I won't take anything like that, but if it's ethical and proper, I'll buy one from you for cost.' So we got him a garbage masher. Us Bureau officials paid for it out of our own pocket. It cost each of us about ten or fifteen dollars.

"We used to collect from the supervisors but they got very angry. One supervisor absolutely refused to contribute. He said, 'The only time you need to come to me for a collection is when you have to buy flowers for his funeral, but don't come for any other occasion.' We kicked in his share because they kept a count. For example, I used to have a hundred and thirty-three men working for me in the Domestic Intelligence Division, and if you took up a collection of two dollars each, they'd add it up and make damn sure it totaled two hundred and sixty-six dollars. So when somebody didn't contribute, then I would have to throw in extra money to have it come out even. Every year we had a whole series of anniversaries that required gifts, year after year after year, and now that Tolson has inherited everything, he's selling this stuff at auction for good money.

"He never bought a thing. Everything he had either belonged to the government or was given to him. The guy was a miser. He wouldn't spend a penny on anything. He put many thousands of dollars of that book *Masters of Deceit* into his own pocket, and so did Tolson, and so did Lou Nichols. They had absolutely no right to put this in their pockets because we wrote the book. I'm only talking now about *Masters of Deceit*, which was a best seller. I was in charge of the research to write that book. This meant that every day I had men and women doing research and submitting rough drafts to me. I started the whole thing when I recommended in a memorandum that we write a book on the subject of Communism. My idea was to give the proceeds to the Damon Runyon Fund or the American Heart Association. I never dreamed they were going to keep the money. When he agreed to the book, he said, 'Put all the men you need on it.' At one time I must have had eight people writing every day on the damn thing. It took months. It was a tremendous research job. We wrote what we thought was a good, solid, scholarly book, but Nichols, in particular, and Hoover, didn't like the quiet tone of the book. They wanted something that was jazzed up, more sensational. Nichols said, 'You can't sell any serious study like this.' I argued with him, and we had quite a session over it, but I lost. Nichols turned it over to a Ph.D. in the Crime Records Division, Fern Stukenbroeker, to jazz it up, put in what Nichols called anecdotal material, and it was jazzed up. If you read it now, you have to admit that it is a pretty light, frothy damn book.

"The FBI spent millions and millions of dollars on public relations. Reams of stuff came out of the Crime Records Division, which was really a propaganda mill set up by Nichols, and we used to have an inside joke in the FBI. Every time that Hoover received his paycheck, we said he ought to run over to Nichols and say, 'Here, Lou, I'm going to give you half of it because of the wonderful propaganda job you've done for me.'"

Masters of Deceit was published by Henry Holt and Company, which was owned by Clint Murchison. It sold 250,000 copies in hardback and two million in paperback. Holt also published Hoover's *A Study of Communism,* selling 125,000, for total earnings of close to $500,000. His last book, *On Communism,* published by Random House, sold around 40,000 copies. I asked Nichols if Hoover had kept the income from the sales of *Masters of Deceit.*

NICHOLS: "Uh [long pause], I don't know the specific details. I know that he gave me some money on it, but I swear to goodness, I just don't remember the amount. I don't want to give you a figure unless it's absolutely accurate."

Were you involved in the writing of the book?

NICHOLS: "Yes, I would say that I did a tremendous amount of work on it. Stukenbroeker did a lot of work on it too, but I did the finished writing with the help of another chap."

Did Stukenbroeker get any money?

NICHOLS: "No, he did not."

Did the money go to the J. Edgar Hoover Foundation or other charities?

NICHOLS: "No, but I do know that Mr. Hoover used a lot of money that nobody knew anything about for doing things for different people. Things have happened to a lot of people in the Bureau, and nobody knew about it, knew where the money was coming from. But I know where some of it was coming from and it was coming right out of Mr. Hoover's pocket. He was a very generous man."

"He Was Worth at Least a Cool Million"

SULLIVAN: "Hoover had a deal with Murchison where he invested in oil wells and if they hit oil, he got his share of the profits, but if they didn't hit oil, he didn't share in the costs. I was told that by somebody who handled his income tax returns.

"If anybody ever gets into it, I think he was worth at least a cool million when he died. He had extensive—unless they've gotten rid of them very surreptitiously—holdings in Center and Snyder, Texas, and Farmington, New Mexico. I don't know what they've done with this. There's a lot of hanky-panky that went on for years. This is all, at least subconsciously, a part of my break with him. One time he got into serious trouble on his income tax manipulations, and we had to send an accountant from New York, who unfortunately is dead now, to Houston, Texas, where apparently the operations existed. He told me afterward, 'Good God Almighty! If the truth was known, Hoover would be in serious trouble, he was in clear violation of the law, but I think I got the whole thing straightened out.' This man was supposed to be the best accountant in the Bureau—better than any we had in Washington. Apparently, he did straighten it out. But he did say that Hoover had done something that was a serious violation of the law.

"Why don't you ask Nichols about using his FBI contacts after he left the Bureau to get legislation put through that saved Lewis Rosenstiel and his Schenley Industries millions of tax dollars. Nichols was involved in all kinds of things along this line. He used all his FBI contacts and Hoover was furious, because when Nichols left he called for a list of Nichols' key contacts on the Hill and there was no such list. Nichols kept them to himself. Nichols used the Bureau to promote himself and get himself a big job with Schenley, and he has since made a fortune. If you don't believe me, go out and take a look at his farm in Virginia."

In March 1971, Nichols testified before the New York Joint Legislative Committee on Crime, which was probing the infiltration of legitimate business by organized crime, that he had made many close contacts in Congress during his years in the FBI, and that he used these contacts in 1958 to lobby through Congress an excise tax bill that saved Schenley $40 million or $50 million in taxes. Known as the Forand Bill, the legislation extended the storage period for liquor from eight to twenty years. It seems that at the outset of the Korean War, Lewis Rosenstiel had stepped up production of bonded whiskey because, as Nichols explained to the committee, "Everybody felt in 1950 that we were on the verge of World War III, and production would be shut off." Nichols admitted that he lobbied from a sick bed: "While I was recovering from a heart attack at the time, I did exercise my right of petition in discussing the merits of the bill. The great job of advocacy before the committee was performed by a colleague, Ralph Heymsfeld, now deceased. The company [Schenley] did have a service office in Washington. But any charge or suggestion that money was passed to obtain favorable votes is a lie." Not only did the Forand Bill save Schenley from bankruptcy, but the market value of its stock increased 67 percent.

SULLIVAN: "My God, the things that went on! I hope you'll pardon my bluntness, but after thirty years I happen to know a little bit of what went on.

"Take that right-wing Freedoms Foundation up at Valley Forge. This guy W. C. Sawyer, who was in charge of the awards, and Nichols would get together every so often and Nichols would say, 'Isn't it about time you gave the Boss a five-thousand-dollar award for his patriotism or outstanding work or some damn thing?' So five thousand dollars would come in to Hoover and it would get into the press that he had been given the George Washington Award and the money would go into his bank account. Nichols hit Sawyer twice for the award, so by the third time Sawyer was getting a little tired of this, but he gave Hoover another five thousand dollars. Then he went to Nichols and said, 'Now, look, we've given Mr. Hoover three five-thousand-dollar awards, and he's gotten a lot of publicity, and we're not overendowed, would you mind returning that last five thousand dollars back to us?' When the question was raised with Hoover, he said, in effect, 'Hell, no! They gave it to me and I'm going to keep it.' And he did.

"Then there's the J. Edgar Hoover Foundation that Nichols started. It's a joke. Nichols got Rosenstiel to kick in a whole lot of Schenley stock and the damn foundation never did anything. Like everything else, it was set up to glorify Hoover. Hoover ran the FBI to glorify himself, and the foundation likewise was set up to glorify Hoover."

The Boss Loves to Read Lurid Literature

What about Hoover's relationship with Tolson—any evidence of it being homosexual?

SULLIVAN: "That's a very delicate matter. All I can tell you is that it came up constantly and people from different parts of the country would write in and make charges. Rumors were always floating around the office, but I don't have any factual information."

Is it possible that Hoover was asexual?

SULLIVAN: "I don't know. I heard that he kept lurid literature of the most filthy kind in his desk. Naked women and lurid magazines that dealt with all sorts of abnormal sexual activities. I first learned about this when a friend of mine—this was years ago—and where the hell he got the key I don't know, but he had a key to Hoover's desk. One night he went in and opened it. Many of us had pass keys that opened doors to any of the rooms. He found all that junk in a bottom drawer and I believe him because he's an honorable person. He's long since retired, and I don't know that he ever told it to anybody else, because it never came back to me. The Bureau was rife with gossip. A secret police organization generates gossip. Now Mickey—Milton Ladd—who used to be Assistant Director of the Domestic Intelligence Division, and he later held the same position I held, number three man, told me himself that whenever he got hold of something that was sexy and juicy and lurid, he'd always send it to the Boss. He said, 'You know, the Boss loves to read that literature.' If it pertained to government officials, Hoover would then pass it around to the President, the Cabinet, the Attorney General—he loved to pass on this sexy stuff."

I've heard a great deal about Hoover's secretary, Miss Helen Gandy. What kind of a woman is she?

SULLIVAN: "I think that Helen Gandy is one of the most remarkable women that I've ever met. She was completely devoted to the Bureau. I'm not so sure she was as devoted to Hoover as some people think, but she was devoted to the Bureau. She came in as a young girl from New Jersey and was just a clerk and then, I think, a steno, and finally a secretary, a very capable woman, a very systematic woman, a woman, to my knowledge, of flawless character. I liked Miss Gandy very, very much. She ran that office with an iron hand, and she had a lot of power in the Bureau. She made more than one clerk an agent. If she thought that a person had the qualities to be an agent, she wasn't hesitant about going in and telling Hoover. He listened to her, but God he was mean to her. She probably would never admit this, but I can give you one example that I witnessed myself.

"I went in one morning. He had called me for something or other, and at the same time he had buzzed her. She came in and I knew she was upset. She was afraid of him, really afraid of him. And he said, 'Look at these files!' He had two files there. 'Didn't I tell you to have these on my desk the first thing this morning? Now, it's'—it was something like ten o'clock—'and they were just brought in to me a half hour ago.' He just berated her mercilessly, and she kept saying, 'Yes, sir . . . yes, sir.' At that time she had only been with him some fifty years, and he said, 'Don't ever let this happen again! And when I tell you to have a file on my desk first thing in the morning, I *want* it on my desk the first thing in the morning, and don't you *ever* have a file brought in later than what I tell you!' God, it was awful, and tears came to her eyes, and all she did was say, 'Yes, sir . . . yes, sir.' And he kept after her, and, finally, she just slowly turned and walked out. Then he turned to me, and his face was red and florid—you know, he was mad as hell—and he started talking to me about whatever it was we discussed that morning.

"He'd get mad at her over something and he'd say nasty things about her behind her back. You don't have to say those things, particularly about a woman that gave her whole life to him. God Almighty, she was there the first thing in the morning, and she was there the last thing at night, and she worked and worked. Let me tell you something, that woman was in there every Christmas handling all the toys that this fellow Louis Marx used to send down, the one Hoover claimed he didn't know, Ellsberg's father-in-law. Marx would send probably three or four hundred dollars worth of toys every Christmas, and then Hoover, you know, would send them to the children of his friends in Washington. Of course, Hoover and Tolson were vacationing in Florida Christmas week while Miss Gandy was in there working. I've been in there myself helping to handle a few of the parcels, moving them from one place to another, but most of the time the rest of us took leaves at Christmas, while Miss Gandy was in there working. I admire that woman even though she may dislike me for breaking with Hoover. I don't blame her for sticking by Hoover. I'd have done the same thing in her position. I'm still very fond of her.

"Talk about being cheap, though. Hoover wouldn't even buy Sam Noisette, who was with him forty years, a decent Christmas gift. He'd take some little gift that he'd received from somebody and have it rewrapped and he'd give it to Noisette for a Christmas gift. He used him and Crawford and the others just like slaves.

"But I've seen millions upon millions of public dollars squandered in the Bureau for nothing. I'll give you a small example. Every year he bought a new automobile that cost thirty thousand dollars, all armor-plated. Look at the good that would do in medical research. He kept two of the cars in Washington—they were always working on them—in case one wasn't running right. He kept one in Miami, one in New York and, as I remember, one in Los Angeles.

"Every time he went away on vacation, the boys would overhaul the cars. They were always breaking down, and whenever he went anywhere, like to the airport, for example, they'd take it out on test runs first to be sure everything was right. You see, one time when they were rushing him out to the airport—the car had just been overhauled—a radiator hose broke. Something was always going wrong. After that incident, they didn't take any more chances. They always had a backup car following that big limousine. If anything went wrong, why all they had to do was say, 'Mr. Hoover, just step into this car and we can go right on our way.'"

"We Buried Our Failures and Publicized Only Our Successes"

Was Hoover powerful, and if so, what was the source of his power?

SULLIVAN: "Oh, yes. He was very, very powerful, unbelievably powerful. We don't ever want another man in that position of power again. He was in there such a long time, and he gathered all the dirt that was present on people in high-ranking positions, all the irregularities, not necessarily sex alone, but financial irregularities or political chicanery. It doesn't have to be something of a sexual nature, although that would be included. He was a genius at implying that he knew all this information, and sometimes he didn't know as much as he implied, but it didn't matter. Once it reached them that this implication had been made, damn it, they had a guilty conscience, and they may have done something that even Hoover didn't know about, but they assumed that he did know. That placed him in a position of power, and they were all afraid to get rid of him. I know Nixon was actually afraid of him. Knowledge is powerful, and he had knowledge of the most damaging kind, knowledge of people's misbehavior.

"Next you have services. He was in a position to render all kinds of special services, simple things like meeting celebrities at the airport in Paris and getting them a discount at their hotel, or if their wives wanted to buy expensive items, take them shopping where they could get it at cost. He was rendering services all the time, every day of the year. One of the main reasons we opened up the office in Bern was to entertain his high-ranking friends who vacationed in Switzerland. That was why I opposed the expansion of the legal attaché program. I held the line on it as long as I could, and I raised so much hell, I was really rough on him, I really was mean, but there was three and a half million dollars going down the drain when it should have gone into medical research or public housing or into education. Our men were at the disposal of his friends all over the world. It was a terrible squandering of public money.

"Put services alongside of knowledge, not as important as knowledge, but extremely important. There is another form of service and that is the information given out of the files that was helpful to politicians. This doesn't mean derogatory information, but information that was helpful to politicians in their politicking, information given out of the files to high-ranking heads of corporations and things of that sort that really got industry solidly behind him. What he didn't have behind him was the intellectuals."

What about performance?

SULLIVAN: "We did a reasonably good job. I know the kind of work the other agencies do and we presented ourselves as the elite, as being almost superhuman. Well, if it was ever made public how many fugitives we never caught, that certainly would dull the edge of that argument. If it was ever made public how many bank robberies we never solved, that would dull the edge of that argument. Now, when I say that, I'm not saying that we didn't do a reasonably good job. The strength of the Bureau was always in the field offices, and I can't say enough fine things about the average special agent, who doesn't know anything at all about what you and I are talking about. Whenever possible, we buried our failures and publicized only our successes, and, hell, anybody can look gigantic if they can get away with doing this."

Promoting the American Way of Life

The Freedoms Foundation was conceived by advertising executive Don Belding to perpetuate the American Way of Life. It achieves this lofty credo by evaluating the Americanism of prominent Americans. This endeavor consumes nearly all of the million dollars the Foundation earns each year from donations received from rich corporations. Awards are made to persons and organizations which contribute "toward the understanding and propagation of the American Way of Life," as defined by the foundation. For example, the foundation's "principal award"—the George Washington Award—went to John Wayne in 1974 for his record "America, Why I Love Her," which expressed "proud and unabashed patriotism." In 1968, when Deke DeLoach was Hoover's number three man, he received an award for these lines: "America and her Flag have been slandered for fighting for freedom abroad. . . . She is being rebuked for protecting her law-abiding citizens. . . . She is being censured for her refusal to become a welfare state, and few are openly defending her."

Although the foundation has attracted a sizable number of superpatriots and reactionaries, it is quick to dispute charges that it is devoted to right-wing causes. In his book on foundations, *The Money Givers*, Joseph C. Goulden listed some of its officials and benefactors: Kenneth D. Wells, a former "labor management man for Union Oil Company of California"; Edward F. Hutton, a "New York stockbroker and longtime patron of rightist causes (during the 1930s he financed the American Liberty League and the Crusaders, formed to fight President Roosevelt and the New Deal)"; W. C. (Tom) Sawyer, "who ran the Americanism program of the American Legion"; Charles R. Hook, "chairman of Armco Steel and a sponsor of the Birchite Manion Forum"; Mrs. J. Howard Pew, "wife of the Sun Oil president, whose foundation is a generous supporter"; retired Admiral Felix B. Stump, "headline orator for the Christian Anti-Communist Crusade"; Dean Clarence A. Manion, "member of the national council of the John Birch Society, adviser to the Rev. Billy Hargis' Christian Crusade, and founder of the Manion Forum"; Mrs. James B. Patton, former "president-general of the Daughters of the American Revolution"; Howard (Bo) Callaway, "an avowed segregationist who managed to get to the right of even Lester Maddox in a Georgia gubernatorial race"; Associate Justice Tom P. Brady of the Mississippi Supreme Court, who, "in a book called *Black Monday*, wrote that Negroes are 'inherently inferior' to whites and that the U.S. Supreme Court's 1954 decision on school segregation was 'unconstitutional' and part of a communist conspiracy."

When the J. Edgar Hoover Foundation was incorporated on June 10, 1965, by Louis B. Nichols, the purpose stated in its charter was "to safeguard the heritage and freedom of the United States of America and to promote good citizenship through the appreciation of its form of government and to perpetuate the ideas and purposes to which the Honorable J. Edgar Hoover has dedicated his life." The foundation was to "combat communism or any other ideology or doctrine which shall be opposed to the principles set forth in the Constitution . . . or the rule of law."

The charter stipulated that the thoughts of the Director were to be propagated in the following manner: "conduct education programs; organize study groups; give lectures; establish scholarships and endow chairs . . .

[and] circulate magazines and books and pamphlets." However, until the passage of the Tax Reform Act of 1969, which requires that foundations distribute all net income on a current basis, the contributions of the J. Edgar Hoover Foundation were limited to token grants to the Freedoms Foundation, which set aside one room in its American Freedoms Center as a J. Edgar Hoover Library on Communism and Totalitarianism. The library, which the Freedoms Foundation says contains "one of the largest collections on these subjects available to the public," was described by Goulden as a "mishmash of volumes obtainable from any serious public library, many of them hand-me-downs from the American Legion library in Indianapolis."

The expenditures of the J. Edgar Hoover Foundation for the years 1965 through 1968 totaled $11,125. Except for $1,500 donated to three FBI clerical employees to assist them in continuing their education, all expenditures went for books or various services performed by the Freedoms Foundation. The reason given by Nichols for the low expenditures was that the foundation's income was nominal until after 1969. Lewis Rosenstiel's major contribution—securities with a market value estimated at over a million—was made in 1968, but no income was realized from it until 1969.

Walter Winchell was the first to report the existence of the J. Edgar Hoover Foundation, but it was Maxine Cheshire who first revealed the names of the major contributors. "I was really way up there on the list after that story," Maxine told me. "I can still call people all over the country and say, 'Remember me? I'm the person who did the Hoover Foundation story,' and they will go stand on street corners at two o'clock in the morning. I can call county sheriffs, I can call police lieutenants, and say, 'I'm the person who exposed the Hoover Foundation,' and they'll just do anything I want them to do. All I have to do is ask. I made the top of the Hit Parade for a long time with Mr. Hoover after that one."

"Oh, let me tell you about that gal," Nichols exploded when I mentioned Maxine Cheshire's name.

NICHOLS: "It so happened that I was with Mr. Rosenstiel on his boat in Florida. Mr. Rosenstiel had strange work habits, and the two of us would prepare the budgets for Schenley Industries, and we spent, oh, about two weeks on his boat working on this. One day the marine operator put through a call to me on the boat, and it was Maxine Cheshire, and I think this was a Friday. She asked me a little bit about the Foundation. I answered and I told her I would be back in Washington on Monday and would be very happy to talk to her, that this was very unsatisfactory to carry on a conversation on the radiotelephone because the static made the reception bad. She said, 'Fine, I will not do anything until Monday.' On Sunday she came out with the story. The story intimated that Mr. Hoover was in league with the underworld. She had picked up the [Hank] Messick stuff about Mr. Rosenstiel and Meyer Lansky and people like that, and she related that to Mr. Rosenstiel and Mr. Rosenstiel to the underworld, and then, ipso facto, Mr. Hoover was related to the underworld."

In all fairness to Maxine Cheshire, there is no sinister connotation in her story. She did observe, however, that "Whisky tycoon Rosenstiel has been described as a 'father figure' to Roy Cohn," and that "Cohn refers to Rosenstiel as 'Commander in Chief.'" The two "routinely salute each other on sight." Whatever that's supposed to mean.

Before accepting money from Rosenstiel, did Hoover have him checked out?

NICHOLS: "As a matter of fact, we checked Mr. Rosenstiel out before I went with him. Yes, sir. I hope you give me credit for a little more sense. Let me give you the background of the foundation. Mr. Hoover celebrated his fortieth anniversary as Director of the Bureau in 1964. I had been thinking for a long time that something should be done in a big way to perpetuate the ideals to which Mr. Hoover had dedicated his life. So I had talked to, oh, two or three people. I talked to Mr. Rosenstiel about it, and he was heartily in accord. He thought that Mr. Hoover was worthy of something significant."

Were Hoover and Rosenstiel friends?

NICHOLS: "No, the only time Mr. Hoover has ever seen Mr. Rosenstiel was on occasions when he was with me. I took him by Mr. Hoover's office a couple of times, but they never had dinner together or anything like that. And so I went in to see Mr. Hoover and I told him that I wanted to organize a J. Edgar Hoover Foundation and its sole objective would be to promote citizenship, patriotism, the American way of life, the American heritage, and, I slipped in at the end, the perpetuation of the ideals to which he'd dedicated his life's work. Had I mentioned that first, he would have vetoed that right off the reel."

Why?

NICHOLS: "Contrary to a lot that has been in print, Mr. Hoover was a very modest man. He almost had an inferiority complex. He was a very selfless man, but when he had a job to do, nothing was going to stand in his way, he's going to do it. And he's going to be aggressive and use whatever aggression is necessary to accomplish it, but as far as anything inuring to him, the guy had a sense of humility that you don't find in many men, and had I told him what my real purpose was at the very outset, he would have said no, and that's why I gave it to him as a sugar-coated pill.

"At the time, I didn't know how much money would be involved, but I told him that I thought Mr. Rosenstiel would contribute to it. He didn't want any fund-raising campaigns. He told me that specifically, and I said, 'Well, there won't be any organized fund-raising campaign, but we'll see what we can do.' So we incorporated the foundation under the D.C. law as a non-profit corporation, and Mr. Rosenstiel made a fifty-thousand-dollar contribution to it. His was the first contribution, and then I contributed some Schenley stock worth in the neighborhood of twenty-two thousand dollars. William G. Simon [former Agent in Charge of the Los Angeles Field Office] came in with five thousand dollars. Roy Cohn had an organization that George Sokolsky started, the American Jewish League Against Communism, and they gave five hundred dollars. There were a few other small contributions. Then in 1968 Mr. Rosenstiel had a family foundation which he decided to liquidate, and he gave, oh, something like twelve and a half million dollars to the University of Miami for their school of oceanic research. Then he gave, oh, several million dollars to Brandeis University; he gave two or three million dollars to the Cardinal Spellman Trust Foundation, and I just can't begin to recall all the beneficiaries, although at one time I had the accountants make a tabulation, and they figured he had given out something like fifty-four million dollars in that short period, which I used in that statement before the New York legislative committee.

"I happened to be in Washington—I kept my home down here—and I had stayed over because Manny Celler, who was a friend of Rosenstiel's, and had been a friend of mine over the years—Manny was the Bureau's great defender in the late thirties and early forties, and it wasn't until recent years that he became a little critical, but that I think was all political and not what was in his heart—at any rate, Manny was having his eightieth birthday dinner, so Mr. Rosenstiel came down for it. He called me and I went over to his hotel and out of the blue, he said, 'I'd like to see your friend Mr. Hoover.' I said, 'What do you want to see him about?' 'Well,' he said, 'I want to give you a million dollars for the foundation and I want to tell him about it.' I called over there and Mr. Hoover saw us.

Mr. Rosenstiel told him that as a result of personal regard for Mr. Hoover and of his regard for me, he was thoroughly enthusiastic about the concept of the foundation and he wanted to make his contribution. And he did. And that's that."

I thought he contributed a million and a half.

NICHOLS: "Well, that could be misleading, because your annual reports are based on the market value of your assets, and Mr. Rosenstiel made a contribution of a million dollars, face value, of Glen Alden bonds, which later increased in value. The initial fifty thousand dollars in Schenley stock became worth something like two hundred and thirty thousand dollars when we tendered them for Glen Alden bonds. These are the accurate figures."

What charities has the foundation supported?

NICHOLS: "We're very proud of what we do. For example, last year [1973] we contributed twenty-five scholarships to social science teachers from the D.C. school system and the Washington area for a three-week seminar at Freedoms Foundation on the meaning of our liberties. That was twelve thousand, five hundred dollars. We contributed twenty-five hundred dollars for the support of the J. Edgar Hoover Library at Freedoms Foundation, another twenty-five hundred dollars for periodicals, books and stuff like that, and we contributed five thousand dollars to Freedoms Foundation for their overall administration."

I repeated Sullivan's charge that Nichols had arranged with Freedoms Foundation to give Hoover three $5,000 awards and then when Hoover was asked to return the money after the third award, he refused.

NICHOLS: "The Freedoms Foundation gave Mr. Hoover, as I recall, two awards, and I had nothing to do with either one of them. They came from Freedoms Foundation before I had any connection with it, and I do recall that sometime after the second award—it was not contemporaneous with the second award, but Ken Wells, who was then the president of Freedoms Foundation, made an approach, and I cannot remember whether it was direct or whether it was through somebody else, to solicit a contribution from Mr. Hoover. But I know that Freedoms Foundation story pretty well and everything Mr. Hoover did with it."

Did they get a contribution from Mr. Hoover?

NICHOLS: "I don't think so. No, they didn't. They didn't."

How does this differ from what Sullivan said?

NICHOLS: "Well, it's a figment of his imagination to a certain extent. Now it is true that the J. Edgar Hoover Foundation has made good contributions to Freedoms Foundation."

But that's not Hoover doing it?

NICHOLS: "No, no."

And he did turn them down?

NICHOLS: "Well, I don't think he turned them down. I don't think— He just never did anything about it. Well, I guess, it's tantamount to the same thing."

According to the 1969 tax law, foundations now have to contribute all of their income. Were you doing this prior to 1969?

NICHOLS: "Oh, yes. Oh, yes. One year we contributed more than our income. I think that at the present time, and I don't want to be held to this because memory is fleeting and fanciful, but we are about ten percent over the requirement. We contributed five thousand dollars to the American Bar Association's Fund for Public Education, to be used by the section on criminal law, of which I was chairman and one of the movers and organizers, to be used in the implementation of ABA standards for the administration of criminal justice."

What was Hoover's interest in the foundation?

NICHOLS: "He had no interest and involvement whatsoever. And he didn't leave any money to it. Incidentally, he did leave his favorite ring to my son. This year the foundation purchased Mr. Hoover's personal library from Mr. Tolson for forty-five hundred dollars and we contributed it to the FBI Academy at Quantico. It is about fifteen hundred volumes, with many first editions and autographed copies. I just couldn't bring myself to seeing that ever go on the market and be split up.

"We also made a contribution of ten thousand dollars to the Boys' Clubs of America; fifteen thousand dollars to the National College of District Attorneys; five thousand dollars to the National College of Defense Lawyers for the J. Edgar Hoover lectures on the protection of innocence; five thousand dollars to Southeastern University to be used as scholarship awards for needy FBI clerical employees who wanted to become special agents; twenty-five hundred dollars to the Boy Scouts of America. The year Mr. Hoover died we contributed five thousand dollars for the exhibit case at the National Presbyterian Church, which has a few of the President's and a lot of Mr. Hoover's sayings, and we contributed thirty-six hundred dollars to the Scripps Clinic and Research Foundation for a fellowship for one of the doctors they were bringing in to train.

"Our income in 1973 was about ninety-one thousand dollars and except for insurance and stuff like that, the only expense we have is for a young lawyer who up until a year ago, we paid his office six hundred dollars a year to handle all the clerical records, and this year we're raising him to a thousand dollars a year. That's the only outlay, and for many years I paid for everything myself."

Have you talked to Tolson about any contribution?

NICHOLS: "No, I have not, and I don't think I will. Now that's Mr. Tolson's money and what he does with it is his business. I would hope that he would think of the foundation, but I wouldn't presume to ask him."

Playing It by the Book

There was a time, many decades before Watergate, when the press portrayed General Harry Vaughan as the most corrupt politician in American politics. Thanks to the inquisition of Joe McCarthy, Vaughan became the most celebrated influence peddler in the world, the man behind the so-called home freezer rip-off that shook the Truman Administration to its foundation. How innocent we were then. McCarthy ruined a lot of careers, but luckily he didn't make a dent in Vaughan's. I was looking forward to meeting this formidable man, but when the General walked into the Mayflower's Rib Room I found myself shaking the hand of a spry little man with an anxious smile. He had come to talk to me about J. Edgar Hoover, whom he had worked with during the time he was Truman's top military aide.

I interviewed the General in June 1972, before Truman's death, and a year or so before Merle Miller published *Plain Speaking* and told us what President Truman thought about in those days. I think Miller missed a bet in not getting to Vaughan, who probably knows more about Truman than any man alive. Their friendship goes back to 1918 and the Missouri National Guard. They were both in the Field Artillery, Truman in the

129th and Vaughan in the 130th, part of the 35th Infantry Division. They went overseas together and both returned as captains. For twenty years they went to summer camp at Fort Riley every summer. In 1940, shortly after he became Truman's secretary, Vaughan was called to active duty, but after an airplane accident in Australia in 1943 he returned to Washington as the Army's liaison officer for the Truman Committee. Then when Truman was elected Vice President, Vaughan became his military aide, a job he held throughout Truman's Presidency.

VAUGHAN: "Harry Truman's way of running a staff was of the military. He divided up the work and assigned each staff member certain responsibilities. I had everything that had to do with the Army, everything that had to do with veterans, and everything that had to do with the FBI. About a week after Harry Truman became President, Matt Connelly [the President's appointments secretary] called me and said, 'The boss wants to see you in his office, right now.' So I went in, and there was J. Edgar Hoover. The boss said, 'Sit down,' and I sat down and they finished what they were talking about. Then the President said, 'Harry, I called you over here because I want to start off on the right foot with Mr. Hoover and I want things to work smoothly between this office and his. Anything that I have to give to Mr. Hoover, that I want for his eyes, that I want to get his attention, I'll give it to you and you'll go over and put it in his hand.' And he said, 'Mr. Hoover, when you have anything that you think I should know about, you give it to Harry and tell him that you want me to see it and he'll hand it to me within an hour. That's the way we're going to operate.'

"We did exactly that for eight years. Every report that Hoover made to the White House came across my desk. He'd have a little note up top calling attention to pages and paragraphs he wanted emphasized, but I read all these reports, and if I thought there was something the President should read, I called his attention to it. Otherwise, it went into the files for information.

"Hoover and I shook hands that day and my first impression was that he was a very serious man, and I've never had occasion to change that opinion. I accepted the commission and I said, 'Mr. Hoover, I'll try to cooperate one hundred percent with your office,' and he said, 'I certainly will, General,' and in no time at all we were on a first name basis. Well, actually, it took about a year of talking across the desk before one day he said, 'No, Harry, I don't think we ought to do it that way. It ought to be done like this.' He was the first to establish the basis. I have found Hoover to be one of the finest public servants that I ever knew. Sure, he was dictatorial to the men in his department, but he worked perfectly with me, we were always on a friendly basis. He never told me he'd do something that he didn't do, and if I asked for something and he decided it wasn't possible, he'd say, 'Harry, I can't do that. There's a reason,' and it was usually pretty logical. We couldn't have worked any smoother if I'd have been Tolson. One thing about Hoover, I think that in every case you could depend on Hoover playing it by the book.

"At the time of our first meeting, Hoover gave me very specific instructions on how to get to his office. He said, 'There's going to be a lot of talk, you coming to my office, my coming to your office. When you come over here, I advise you to come in on Pennsylvania, get on the elevator, go to the seventh floor, walk around to the other bank of elevators, go down to the third floor, walk around to this bank of elevators, come up to the fifth floor, and come into my office. You and I have legitimate things to talk about. It's the President's business, it's my business, it's your business, it's nobody else's business. Now a lot of the press are outside of your office and they'd notice if I came over there.' "

In other words, he never came to your office.

VAUGHAN: "That's right. If I had said, 'Now, the President has directed me to tell you so and so, how about coming over to my office,' I think maybe he'd have done it. It might have hurt the hell out of him but—"

Would it have ruined the relationship?

VAUGHAN: "I don't think it would have helped it a hell of a lot, and I didn't give much of a damn about it. We had a good arrangement. The minute I got to Hoover's office, that nice Negro fellow [Sam Noisette] would say, 'Come on in, General, you can go right in.' Oh, on occasion, I might have waited two or three minutes, but usually I went right in. Our meetings were strictly business, no social talk, just two members of a staff that were anxious to cooperate, and I found Hoover that way all the time."

Why did Truman bypass the Attorney General in his dealings with Hoover?

VAUGHAN: "Theoretically, the Attorney General is over the FBI, but in practice the FBI is an independent agency. The reason was that Hoover was such a dynamic personality. By 1945 Hoover had already established his position in terms of power and importance. I don't think there was any doubt about it."

Was it because of the files?

VAUGHAN: "The files, of course, were important. They were a tool."

Were they intimidating?

VAUGHAN: "To certain people. I'm sure there was a hell of a lot in there about me, but it didn't concern me a damn bit. I'm sure they made some of the bastards on the Hill walk more carefully. They never bothered Truman. When he had occasion to disagree with Hoover, and strongly, he didn't hesitate to do it."

Could you describe an incident?

VAUGHAN: "Sure. Hoover was so successful with the FBI nationally that he wanted to take over foreign duties. He wanted to expand the FBI to foreign activities. Truman created the Central Intelligence Agency to great protest from Hoover, who wanted to take it over as an auxiliary of his organization. Truman said no. I heard him say that one man shouldn't operate both, 'he gets too big for his britches.' He said, 'Hoover's got plenty to do, he's done a great job, he'll continue to do a great job in the United States as the FBI, but the CIA is a separate organization and should be under different auspices.' Hoover was very provoked by that, and he tried to argue with the President, giving his pitch about his organization, that it was operating smoothly, that it could be expanded more easily than starting a new organization. Truman never refused to listen to an argument, but once he made up his mind, that was it. He said no, and when Hoover persisted, he said, 'You're getting out of bounds.' I think Hoover was smart enough to agree to it. He didn't like it, because he had great ideas about his international importance. He was an egotistic little guy, there's no doubt about that. He thought nobody could be as right as Hoover on any particular subject, which was a difficult thing to combat."

What kind of Attorney General was Tom Clark?

VAUGHAN: "I think he was a very good one. Let me tell you why he left the Supreme Court. That might indicate to you the kind of man he is. He made a deal with President Johnson. Johnson wanted a vacancy on the Supreme Court so he could appoint a Negro, which would give him some prestige in the Fourth Ward or something. So Tom Clark created a vacancy by resigning from the court so they could appoint Thurgood Marshall. And the deal was that Johnson would appoint his son Ramsey Attorney General."

Didn't Hoover ride rough-shod over him?

VAUGHAN: "I don't know if you could say that he rode rough-shod, but Tom Clark didn't tell Hoover what to do. He didn't mess with him at all. He let Hoover run his own show. At least, that's my opinion. Actually, I don't think Harry Truman would have appointed Tom Attorney General if he hadn't had his arm twisted by Sam Rayburn and Tom Connally from Texas. You know these Texans, oh how they stick together."

In *Plain Speaking*, Merle Miller quotes Truman as saying that "Tom Clark was my biggest mistake. No question about it." When asked to explain this remark, Truman said, "That damn fool from Texas that I first made Attorney General and then put on the Supreme Court. I don't know what got into me. He was no damn good as Attorney General, and on the Supreme Court . . . it doesn't seem possible, but he's been even worse. He hasn't made one right decision that I can think of. . . . It isn't so much that he's a bad man. It's just that he's such a dumb son of a bitch. He's about the dumbest man I think I've ever run across. . . . As I say, I never will know what got into me when I made that appointment, and I'm sorry as I can be for doing it."

At the time of Truman's comment to Miller in 1962, Tom Clark was still on the Supreme Court. And, of course, Harry Vaughan had no idea that Truman had made that statement at the time I interviewed him in 1972—*Plain Speaking* was not published until late 1973.

In his biography, former Attorney General Francis Biddle recalled that he had invited Hoover's confidence, "and before long, lunching alone with me in a room adjoining my office, he began to reciprocate by sharing some of his extraordinary broad knowledge of the intimate details of what my associates in the Cabinet did and said, of their likes and dislikes, their weaknesses and their associations. Edgar was not above relishing a story derogatory to an occupant of one of the seats of the mighty, particularly if the little great man was pompous or stuffy. And I confess that, within limits, I enjoyed hearing it. His reading of human nature was shrewd, if perhaps colored with the eye of an observer to whom the less admirable aspects of behavior were being constantly revealed."

I asked Vaughan whether Hoover had provided Truman with similar reports?

VAUGHAN: "When we went in, the FBI had about a dozen phone taps on various people in Washington, and they used to give me a report on the phone conversations. For example, they had one on Tommy Corcoran, you know, Tommy the Cork, who was sort of a lawyer here who was on Roosevelt's kitchen cabinet. He's a big wheeler-dealer, and for some reason Roosevelt was a little suspicious of him and had the FBI put a tap on him. When these reports started coming in, I said, 'What the hell is this?' and they said, 'This is a wiretap on so-and-so,' and I said, 'Who ordered it?' and they said, 'Oh, that's been going on for six months, three months,' or what have you. I told the President, 'I'm getting these reports. I read them over and it's the most dull, deadly stuff—Mrs. Corcoran calls up the grocer and orders this, she calls her hairdresser.' 'Well, I don't give a goddamn whether Mrs. Corcoran gets her hair fixed or don't get her hair fixed,' Harry told me. 'What the hell is that crap?' I said, 'That's a wiretap.' He said, 'Cut them all off. Tell the FBI we haven't got any time for that kind of shit.' "

In *Plain Speaking*, Miller offered this quote from Truman on Hoover: "One time they brought me a lot of stuff about his personal life, and I told them I didn't give a damn about that. That wasn't my business. It was what he did *while* he was at work that was my business."

I telephoned the General after I read that and he was completely surprised because he had no knowledge of it. Then I asked him a question that I've asked most interviewees:

Do you think Hoover and Tolson were homosexuals?

VAUGHAN: "Oh, no!"

What makes you so positive?

VAUGHAN: "Well, because he was a red-blooded, virile individual. I can imagine that I might be in a job like that, having an old college classmate of mine associated with me, and we'd be living together. In fact, one time I heard a member of the press say that the reason that Harry Truman and his staff spent two weeks down at Key West without their wives was because 'most of those bastards are homosexuals.' "

Did Truman ever bring it up?

VAUGHAN: "I know Truman never considered that aspect of Hoover. As

I recall, he wanted to see Hoover about something one time, and I said, 'We're going to this party this evening and probably Hoover will be there.' Truman said, 'Oh, no, he never goes to parties. I think that guy, in a sense, must be anti-social, but when you think of some of the hostesses in Washington and the social obligations that you're liable to get tied up in, I don't blame a guy for being anti-social.'"

I must say I've read some bad things about you, General.

VAUGHAN: "There's a type of reporter and writer that never want to be hampered by facts. They rise above principle, you know. There was one book that amused me because it said that I was a regular customer at an after-hours bottle club in Washington. And I told Harry Truman about it and he laughed. He said, 'The idea of you being accused of being a drinker—hell, you don't drink enough to remember the taste in between times.' You know, if I could handle liquor the way Harry Truman does, I'd use more of it because my doctor, General Wallace Graham, tells me I ought to take a big stiff highball at five o'clock every afternoon; it could be beneficial to me. Truman takes a big stiff drink of bourbon and little shot of water after he gets his pajamas on, before he gets into bed. He's asleep in ninety seconds. If I did that, I wouldn't close my eyes till morning.

"Which reminds me, I'll bet in my lifetime I've played four thousand hours of poker with Harry Truman. But there was never a poker game in the White House while Truman was President. We played on the *Williamsburg* and every day during our two-week stays in Key West. We'd play poker after Truman finished his nap at two o'clock in the afternoon. We'd play from two until six, then we'd have dinner, and then we'd play from seven until midnight. There would be Clark Clifford, Admirals Dennison and Leahy, Fred Vinson, the Chief Justice, General Landry and George Allen, who Truman appointed to the Reconstruction Finance Corporation. Allen didn't realize it was a job you had to work at. When he found out there was work connected with it, he didn't stay long. He's allergic to work. But everybody likes George Allen. He's jovial, a very personable guy."

Were you referring to Washington Confidential *by Jack Lait and Lee Mortimer?*

VAUGHAN: "Yeah, that's the book. They also said I was hobnobbing around with gangsters. [Laughs.] Frank Costello and I were in business together. Why, I wouldn't have known that bastard if he had come in and bit me. My friend William Rogers, you know, who was with Brownell, and is now Nixon's Secretary of State, well, he and Joe McCarthy were buddies. He was counsel for the committee that was supposed to be carving me up in small pieces, supposed to be investigating the five-percenters. That was in 1948. The Senator who was chairman was in his dotage, and so Joe McCarthy and Karl Mundt ran the committee, and the Democrats on the committee didn't even come to the meetings, you see. When I appeared, there were only three Republicans up there to give me hell: McCarthy, Mundt and Margaret Chase Smith, who was friendly with McCarthy in those days. Rogers' associate counsel was Bobby Kennedy. It was just witch-hunting and trying to discredit me to such an extent that Truman would have to fire me, so it would be embarrassing to Truman.

"The morning I was to go before the committee, I walked into Harry Truman's office, and I said, 'Boss, you know the tranquillity of your administration is a hell of a lot more important than whether I'm on active duty or not. If I retired it would take the heat off.' Oh, God, he got red in the face. He stood up and came around the desk and put his arm around my shoulder. He said, 'Listen here, you and I came into the White House on the same day and we're going out on the same day. Don't ever let me hear any more of this horseshit about you retiring. These people don't give a damn about you. They're trying to embarrass me. You go up and tell those bastards to kiss your ass.' These are his exact words. Now that is what I call Social Security, when the boss talks to you like that.

"You see, Truman didn't ask for executive privilege or any immunity for any of his staff. If they wanted to call them, they could call them. So I went up and that was the time that Joe McCarthy had that alleged letter and he said, 'What is your connection, General, with Frank Costello?' 'Why,' I said, 'I don't know a thing about him. Who is he?' 'Oh,' he says, 'a big New York gangster.' I said, 'I never saw him in my life. I wouldn't know him if he came in here.' 'Well,' he said, 'that's not what this letter says.' 'Well,' I said, 'who wrote that letter?' 'Oh, no, that's confidential.' 'Well,' I said, 'may I see the letter?' 'That's confidential.' And that's the way it went. He could have been holding a laundry list, for all I know."

Was the letter included in the exhibits?

VAUGHAN: "Oh, no. Nobody ever saw it. 'It's confidential,' he said. 'I can't show it to anybody.' And, of course, he accomplished what he wanted. He got headlines in the press and the headlines said I was connected with Costello and in the story it said that I denied it, but then you know a hundred people read the headlines for one person who reads the story. But that's an occupational hazard in politics."

You don't look very sinister to me.

VAUGHAN: "I've always been too lazy."

The Home Freezers Caper

What was Hoover's reaction to your problems with Joe McCarthy and the home freezers?

VAUGHAN: "I never discussed it with him. I purposely avoided the subject because I didn't want to embarrass him to the extent he might feel called upon to express himself, which would get him in dutch with McCarthy. Say what you will about that son of a bitch McCarthy, he had plenty of power up on the Hill because most of those other senators were scared to death of him.

"I'm sure Hoover appreciated that it [the freezer episode] was petty larceny. If a man [who gave the freezers] had been paying off for favors received or favors that he hoped to receive or something— But he just sent out about half a dozen freezers to people that he had met in Washington and liked. The main idea was to send one to Mrs. Truman, who had gone back to Independence with Margaret in the summer of 1945, the way they had done the ten previous summers when Mr. Truman was in the Senate, to spend June and July and August back home. And this year, instead of being a senator's wife, she was the First Lady, and all the neighbors and their friends on the farms in Jackson County wanted to show their appreciation and so they brought her chickens and sausage and fresh vegetables and fruit, and they had an ordinary family-sized refrigerator, and pretty soon the damn thing was busting out at the seams. The fruit was spoiling and she was having to throw it away. She didn't want to hurt anybody's feelings so she called me up at the White House and said, 'Is there any place where I can get a home freezer?' They hadn't been making any during the war, and I said, 'I don't think you can, but there's something you could do right out there without any help. The Coca-Cola company is getting away from those big ice chests'—if you'll remember, they had those big ice chests full of cold water and a couple of blocks of ice and you'd go in and roll your sleeve up to your shoulder and dive in to grab a Coke— 'and they are putting in these automatic dispensers.' I said, 'I'm sure the Coca-Cola people in Kansas City has got many of those big antiques in their warehouse and they'd give you one with the greatest of pleasure, and you can set it out on the big back porch outside your kitchen and every day or so put in a two-hundred-pound block of ice and it will keep all the perishables people can send you.' 'Oh,' she said, 'that's a brilliant idea!'

"Well, in my office, while I was having this phone conversation, was a friend of mine from Milwaukee who was in the advertising business, and he went on back to Milwaukee that night and going through Chicago he called on a mutual friend of ours by the name of Dave Bennett and just casually mentioned Mrs. Truman's situation, and he said, 'You know what, there's a fellow up in Milwaukee that's going into the manufacture of home freezers, and I was in his warehouse last week and he's got forty or fifty experimental models sitting on the floor and I'm sure he'd be glad to send one to Mrs. Truman.' Dave Bennett said, 'That's fine. If you find that he's got any surplus, you have him send one to Mrs. Truman, you send one to Harry Vaughan, you send one to Fred Vinson and John Snyder, and you send one to the White House secretaries' lunch room. Then send me the bill.' I didn't know anything about it. Bennett was a very eccentric sort of millionaire. He owned a company that supplied material to perfume makers, essential oils and other ingredients used in the manufacture of perfume. The United States government needs a little perfuming sometimes, but I don't think they buy it.

"The freezers were all sent and about a week later we took off for the Potsdam Conference. Well, this thing arrived at my house and my wife didn't know anything about it. She thought maybe I had ordered it and so —we had a freezer, we didn't need one—she said, 'Just set it out there in the garage.' A week went by and she didn't get a bill, and she wrote to the address on the shipping tag, asking that they please send her a bill if I had ordered the thing. They wrote back and said, 'That was paid for by Mr. Bennett of Chicago.' And that was the sum total of the whole damn business—the freezer episode. The damn thing was an experimental model and it broke down the first time I put it in operation out there in the garage. I tried to get a repair piece and finally had to have it made. It cost me seventy-five dollars to keep it running for four or five months. I finally got rid of it. I had to pay ten dollars to have it hauled away. It should have gone to the Smithsonian Institute.

"If Harry Truman had received five percent of what George Allen and his friends spent on Ike's Gettysburg farm, by God he'd have been impeached. And some dope who never did a nickel's worth of business with the government gave Mrs. Truman and me home freezers and I'll bet you I got ten million lines of copy on it. That stupid little story went all over the world. Mrs. Truman was very much provoked. She said, 'I'd already taken your advice and called the Coca-Cola people and they'd sent me a big ice chest about the size of a piano crate and it would hold all the vegetables in Jackson County. I didn't need the thing at all, but here it arrived.'

"If Harry Truman hadn't been able to sell his farm—he and his brother owned a six-hundred-acre farm in Jackson County—at considerable profit for real estate development, he would have been damn near on relief, because when he first got out of the White House there was no Presidential pension, there was even no allowance for him to have an office. He hired an office and two secretaries down in the Federal Reserve Building in Kansas City and he had a hell of a time paying for it because he didn't have a nickel.

"You know this book he wrote, his memoirs, he got six hundred thousand dollars for that and the government took three hundred and seventy-five thousand of it in taxes. And Eisenhower was President then and didn't move a finger to help Truman. Four years before, when Eisenhower came out with his book, Truman instructed the Internal Revenue Service to consider that as capital investment because, he said, 'General Eisenhower is not an author by trade,' and Ike saved four hundred and fifty thousand of his six hundred thousand. Ike was a great man in many ways but he was pretty vindictive. The first time he came to Kansas City as President, Truman called up the penthouse and said to the aide that answered the phone, 'This is Harry Truman. I want to welcome the President to Kansas City,' and this aide said, 'Just a minute, Mr. Truman,' and he came back in a minute and said, 'I'm sorry, Mr. Truman, the President is too busy to see you, to talk to you.' If any of Truman's aides had done that to Herbert Hoover, we'd have gotten shot.

"I'm prejudiced about the matter and everybody knows I am, but I think Harry Truman was the only President we've had, in the last fifty years anyway, who never got a nickel out of the office, and if he had, I'd have been in a position to know it. He was offered money through me on a dozen occasions. I remember one fellow who gave me five thousand in cash during the 1948 convention, and he said, 'I want you to give this personally to Harry Truman. I want Harry Truman to have it.' When I showed Harry these five one-thousand-dollar bills, he said, 'You write him a letter and thank him and say in the letter that you turned the money over to Bill Boyle,' who was the National Democratic chairman. I gave Bill Boyle the money and we both wrote to this fellow to thank him for his contribution to the campaign. That guy could have gotten mad at somebody and said, 'Why, I slipped Harry Truman five thousand dollars under the table and he never said a word about it in his tax return.' All that stuff, you know. You can't take a chance on those kind of spooks.

"Conflict of interest is a very lucrative situation that was invented and developed and practiced by the legislative branch, but is very heinous if discovered in the executive branch. That's what's known as a horse from a different garage. Oh, the fringe benefits congressmen get. Oh, brother. We had a guy out in Missouri that was pretty famous in his time, but he was old-fashioned, he had to use a horse and a gun. His name was Jesse James.

"I never got one nickel. When we bought this house we live in now, we sold the one we first built when we came up in 1940, and in 1950 we bought this one, and there was a difference of ten thousand between what we sold the old one for and what we paid for this one, and when we were negotiating the papers, my wife said, 'If I could just find some of the money you got credit for stealing, we wouldn't have to borrow ten thousand from the Acacia Life Insurance Company.'"

The Red Menace Revisited

Along with the Presidency, Harry Truman inherited the Red-hunting factions that permeated Congress in the turbulent years of his administration. One of the men who tried to relieve the pressures generated by this hysteria was Stephen Spingarn, a former counterintelligence expert with considerable expertise in espionage, a field pre-empted by Hoover's FBI.

SPINGARN: "I was in the Treasury before the war, and afterward I came back as assistant general counsel and legislative counsel, and I was counsel for the Secret Service. At this point, the Department of Justice proposed an internal security bill, and this came out of the FBI, as all the internal security bills did, you see, and it was a typical cop's bill—they paint the barn to cover the knothole. You know the sort of thing, a big loose bill that throws grapples out in every direction. Among other things, it legalized wiretapping but without any safeguards. Believe it or not, I was in favor of legalized wiretapping on the specific written permission in individual cases—the Attorney General plus a court order—but this they didn't want. It also required anybody who had been trained or indoctrinated in foreign intelligence operations to register with the Department of Justice. This would have covered me, any CIC [Counter Intelligence Corps] agent or any scholar who had studied foreign intelligence work. What they were trying to get was the delayed operation agent, the man who is sent over here, the Russian agent, who spends years establishing his cover before he goes into operation. So they wanted a hook to hang him with. So the hook they thought of was to force anyone who knew anything about intelligence work to register. You see, if you didn't register, you could be charged with criminal penalties. Their scheme would cover thousands of people who were innocent on the hope they would pick up a few delayed agents. And there were other things like that in this bill.

"So I sat down and wrote a letter for the Secretary of the Treasury's signature, criticizing the bill, and recommending various amendments and restrictions to cut the bill down to proper size. The letter was approved by the Bureau of the Budget, and the Justice Department was advised that their bill, if amended as recommended by the Treasury, would be in accord with the President's program. In no time, an FBI lawyer, a brash young man named Mike Horan, came over to Treasury to ask us to withdraw our recommendations and let the bill go through. It was nonsensical, you see, and of course we refused to do it.

"A little while later, I was invited to go over to the White House. First, however, I had been detailed over there to write the President's civil rights program in 1948, and then his legislative program. They asked me to come over permanently, and Clark Clifford wanted me to be his assistant. So Clifford asked me if I had any skeletons in my closet, and I said not that I could think of, unless you regarded the fact that my father had been president of the NAACP as a skeleton, and he said no, he didn't think so. Then he said, 'By the way, the FBI doesn't like you. Do you know why that is?' And I said, 'Yes. It has nothing to do with my security, which is impeccable, but I've had frequent controversies with them.' I mentioned the FBI's internal security bill and the fact that I had been on the working committee of the President's commission that wrote the loyalty program, and we had given the FBI a hard time on that one too. We had tried to get Hoover to come before the commission and testify on what the big problem was, how serious it was, and he wouldn't do it. Instead he sent one of his assistants to give us a big snow job full of generalities and few facts. So I had written a questionnaire for this FBI man that was rather pointed and sharp.

"I explained all this to Clifford and he decided that it didn't make any difference. So I went over there for a year as his assistant, and when he left—he was special counsel to the President—to go into private practice, Charlie Murphy, who had been instrumental in bringing me over there, moved into his slot and I moved into Charlie's, which was administrative assistant to the President. I was also the legislative counsel of the White House, the key man on loyalty and security. I was regarded as the White House expert in this field. My qualifications stemmed from the fact that I had been legal counsel to the Secret Service, and that in World War Two I had commanded a counterintelligence outfit overseas for several years that captured five hundred and twenty-five spies."

Would you say that Truman's loyalty program gave impetus to the Mundt-Nixon bill, later the McCarran Act?

SPINGARN: "That's a complex question. Let me give you some background. Remember there had been some rather loose security in the thirties and early forties, and in the war, of course, we'd been the allies of the Soviet. I'd say until 1947, when ADA [Americans for Democratic Action] was established, it was liberal doctrine in the United States that a Communist was only a left-wing liberal and that you could do business with him, and they were therefore in all the liberal organizations, you see. The ADA said, 'We will not knowingly admit Communists or Fascists to our counsels and we will throw them out if we find them there.' This was the first time that had ever been done by liberals in the United States. So all liberals in the thirties, you might say, who had been active in liberal causes, had had some association with Communists. So what happened later was that McCarthy could therefore pin some Communist label on almost any liberal. And the result was that he smeared a great many people on that basis, wholly—I mean these were good patriotic Americans who were no more Communists than you or I are. They wanted change and the Communists always gave lip service to the most liberal causes. It was true they never tried them out in their own country, but they were very strong for them here. I must say this: There were Communists and there were some spies, but they were a very small group. They were the ones who should have been detected, not by the House Un-American Activities Committee procedures but by counterespionage, by the FBI working clandestinely.

"Now, when the war was over, certain revelations came to light from disclosures by Elizabeth Bentley and Whittaker Chambers. They had been Communist agents, and their stories made good copy. Bentley, if you'll recall, was involved with several spy rings that siphoned out thousands and thousands of government documents during the war without the FBI ever suspecting a soul. In August 1945—that was after her lover, Jacob Golos, a top Soviet NKVD agent, had died in her arms—she went to the FBI office in New Haven, went in cold, and told her story to two agents. It took her two or three months to convince them. Then, within days, the FBI got out a huge report, maybe two hundred pages long, and sent it to the White House, the Treasury, every place where any of the people she mentioned worked in the government. From that time on, all hell broke loose. The reports kept getting bigger and bigger. They were eighty percent Bentley's stuff plus whatever they could pick up by independent investigation, which was very little, of no value particularly, all it did was confirm that Bentley was telling them many truths—that the Silvermasters did live at that address, that they did have a photographic lab in the basement and stuff like that, corroborative detail. But, you see, of the whole Silvermaster crowd, not one was ever convicted. They all got away with it. It was pure inefficiency, a rotten, lousy, bumbling operation by the FBI. Later, of course, there was a big foul-up in the Judith Coplon case. She too got off because they wiretapped her and her lawyer, stuff like that, which they had no right to do.

"At about the same time, the famous case of the Soviet spy code clerk, Igor Gouzenko, broke in Canada.* He also had picked up his papers and rushed to the Canadian police with his story. This had considerable shock value. In addition, there were several peripheral cases of the so-called fellow-traveler type thing that the House Un-American Activities Committee was agitating, and the House Civil Service Committee held hearings in 1946, and they came in with a report deploring government security as lax and recommended that something be done about this terrible Communist situation.

"This put the finger on President Truman. He had to do something. That's when he created the President's Temporary Commission on Employee Loyalty, an interdepartmental commission composed of Army, Navy, State, Treasury, Justice and the Civil Service Commission. I was on the working committee that wrote the program. The main purpose of it

* Gouzenko, a code clerk at the Soviet Embassy in Canada, went to the Canadian police and exposed a large Soviet spy ring in Canada.

was to stave off Congressional pressures, and because there were, in fact, some security problems. The program provided that all government employees would have to be screened for loyalty and security by the loyalty boards set up in the various agencies. It was not as good a program as I would have liked to see, but it was a lot better than it might have been.

"In March 1947, by executive order, the President created the Employee Loyalty Program. It set up what Truman and his entourage regarded as a useless and enormous edifice which was going to do more harm than good, and it was probably unconstitutional to boot. Meanwhile, the House Un-American Activities Committee, of which Nixon was a star member, loved this stuff. They blew it up. It made them heroes. And they even took an old tired-out ass-end-of-history picture involving Alger Hiss and made a national sensation out of it. Although it had been over for years, you see. That was pretty good work. So there were many factors here. The fact that the Cold War was developing. What had been a warm friendship, an allied victory together, was now developing into a cold war. Stalin was as suspicious of us as we were of him. He wanted to dominate Europe, and we were giving him trouble, weren't we, coming up with ideas like the Marshall Plan and all that stuff.

"And don't forget J. Edgar Hoover. He was right in the thick of it. He had made his big mark on the kidnaping and bank robbery bit, but that was over with. Now he had turned to the Red menace. He did a piss-poor job on counterespionage, one of the poorest, in my opinion. I have written in my mind a little playlet. Hoover was always saying that the Communists were the most dangerous when they were underground, you see, so the membership of the Communist party, which at its peak in the mid-thirties was around a hundred thousand, had declined to about ten thousand by 1950. But Hoover kept saying it was more and more dangerous because it was going underground. Now based on that, I wrote a little play in my head in which Hoover is testifying at the House appropriations hearing and an FBI man rushes in and hands him a note. Hoover looks gravely at the note, turns to the committee, and says, 'A very serious blow. The last member of the Communist Party has just died and the Party has gone completely underground and is now more dangerous than ever.' [Laughs.] Hoover's preoccupation with the Communist menace was based partly, I think, on a sincere belief, because he was a hard-liner on that, and partly on the fact that it was his meal ticket—his was the only appropriation that ever went through Congress not only without a nickel getting cut but with them urging more money on him."

Nixon Is "Going to Be a Good Man for Us"

Bradshaw Mintener, a longtime friend of Hoover's, remembers the Director's maiden appearance before the House Un-American Activities Committee.

MINTENER: "I can't remember the exact time, but I went to see Mr. Hoover one day and he said, 'This is a big day for me.' I said, 'Why?' He said, 'I'm going to make my first public statement on Communism before the House Un-American Activities Committee. Would you like to go over with me?' 'Oh,' I said, 'that would be great.' So I went over with him. I think J. Parnell Thomas, who was later discredited, was the chairman*— I'm not quite sure of that. I don't think it was Martin Dies; it was after that. Sitting at the left, as you faced the committee, on the left end, was Richard Nixon, and he asked Hoover several questions, good questions, and I said, 'Who's that young man?' He said, 'That's the new Congressman from California.' 'Oh,' I said, 'he's the one that did what he did to my Yale classmate and best friend, Jerry Voorhis, whom during the campaign he called a Communist and he faked pictures on him, and so forth.' Hoover said, 'I know all about that, but, so far as law enforcement is concerned, he looks to me as though he's going to be a good man for us.' Period. That was it. He finished and we went back to the FBI office. He felt very good about the speech and the reaction to it."

Using Scare Tactics to Blow Up His Appropriations

SPINGARN: "By the time the McCarran Internal Security Act came along in 1950, the situation was so screwy it's almost impossible to understand it without having lived through it. I mean you could have called a piece of toilet paper an anti-Communist measure and passed it through Congress. All you had to do was put the Red label on it and immediately it was like —law. But when I went to the White House in 1948, the Mundt-Nixon bill was racing through Congress at an enormous clip. The President wanted to do what he could to stop this outrageous bill, and everything that has happened since has shown what a fraud and a farce it was, you see, because the main provision of the McCarran Act was taken from the Mundt-Nixon bill. It set up the Subversive Activities Control Board and

---

* Thomas, who was the chairman during the hearing in question, later served time in federal prison for operating a kickback racket with his office payroll.

THE DIRECTOR

all that business of registering Communist-front organizations and Communist organizations and so forth. The SACB sat there for some twenty years doing nothing and it was finally abolished. It was worse than useless because it created the impression that something was being done when in fact this was mere façade.* They ruined a lot of careers, my friend, for absolutely nothing.

"The Mundt-Nixon bill suffered several reversals, but that didn't deter hard-liners like Richard Nixon, Karl Mundt, Homer Ferguson and Pat McCarran. It was perfectly apparent to me that you couldn't beat something with nothing. I therefore recommended to the President that he have an internal security legislative program of his own and I prepared it. It was sent to Congress by him on August 8, 1950. It attracted all the attention of a willow rippling in the wind. It just was too late to stop McCarran, who was the same kind of animal as Nixon and Mundt, although he was a Democrat—a likable old scoundrel, but a scoundrel.

"All four Congressional leaders—Alben Barkley, John McCormack, Scott Lucas and Sam Rayburn—recommended to the President that he *not* veto the bill. Truman not only vetoed it, but he did something unique in the history of vetoes. He attached a personal message on top of the veto message to every member, saying that this was a very important matter and he urged them personally to read that veto message, but it was too late for that too.

"Back in August, after the President's legislative alternative drew a dud, it was suggested that a statement of support from Hoover would give the President's recommendations a big boost. On August twenty-second I wrote Hoover to the effect that his public support 'might contribute notably to unsnarling the unholy mess which has developed with respect to all this internal security legislation.' My thesis was that the McCarran Act would actually hurt security by lumping a lot of patriotic Americans with a few genuine subversives. It would completely blur the picture. You know, if you protect your diamonds and your toothbrushes with the same degree of zeal, you lose fewer toothbrushes but more diamonds."

What was Hoover's response?

SPINGARN: "The Director chose to remain silent. There was no endorsement and no response. Nothing at all. Of course, you see, I had attacked

* Born on September 23, 1950, the Subversive Activities Control Board was legally buried on June 30, 1973. It cost taxpayers about $10,000,000 to keep its five board members going these many years, and in all that time they registered only one group, the Communist Party, USA, and never a single Communist.

him in June that year for a statement in *U.S. News and World Report,* where he had puffed up the dangers of the Communist fifth column. That made me mad because I thought it was a lot of crap. There was no suggestion in anything Hoover said that we were beating the Communists or that we were even hurting CPUSA. His contention was that they were getting more and more dangerous. In my opinion, he was using scare tactics entirely as a drum to beat in order to blow up his importance and appropriation, which was his perennial obsession."

What if Truman had personally made the request?

SPINGARN: "I don't think it would have made a damn bit of difference. Hoover did his thing without too much concern for anybody. In other words, he wasn't taking orders from Truman or anybody else, least of all the Attorney General of the United States."

"Not One Proven Case of Japanese Espionage"

Tom C. Clark was not aware that Truman thought he was a "dumb son of a bitch" when I saw him in his Supreme Court office in June 1972. He had many good things to say about the former President, and I doubt that the knowledge would have changed anything. The fact that Hoover had called his son Ramsey a "jellyfish" and the worst Attorney General in his experience had no visible effect on his reflections on the Director.

CLARK: "I entered the Department of Justice in 1937. I was then in War Risk Insurance, and the FBI had to deal with insurance that was affected by the first war. Cases in which soldiers sued the government. I defended those cases and in 1940 I came into the Trust Division, at about the time I became the head of the Anti-Trust Division on the West Coast."

Were you on the West Coast when the Japanese camps were set up?

CLARK: "I was in charge of that."

Is it true that Hoover was against placing American-born Japanese in camps?

CLARK: "He never expressed himself that way to me, but he may have been. I worked with General DeWitt, who was in charge of the Western Defense Command. I was his civilian coordinator, so he and I would run around and pick out sites for these camps. At first the idea was to have a curfew. However, public opinion began to get so bad that after three or four months DeWitt put in removal orders, so then the Congress organized the War Relocation Authority. When it became effective, Milton Eisenhower took over the whole thing. That was, I'd say, about April 1942. I served from December 1941 until then.

"The way we handled it—they were housed in the same neighborhoods, sort of like ghettos are in big cities—we had the Census Bureau come out there. The census was just taken the year before, 1940, and we got them some space there in a hotel. They brought all their raw papers out there, and they drew up maps of how many people of Japanese descent were in the various blocks. Then the Army Engineers would build a camp, like the Santa Anita racing stables, then whenever the apartments were ready, we would create a zone and say, 'Everybody in this zone report to such and such a processing station,' as we called it. Then they would put signs up in the area and put dodgers on all the doors and grounds so everybody would know about it. The Japanese people would come in and turn in their radios and electronic stuff. We tried to do it with as little dislocation as possible, but it was a very frustrating job."

Did you honestly believe they constituted a danger to the war effort?

CLARK: "I think most of the heat came from economic problems. You see, the Japanese had been for many years second-class citizens even though they were born in the United States. In California they couldn't own land, they couldn't lease land—they had all kinds of statutes that were unconstitutional but no one ever brought them up. So the Japs would go to places like reservoirs where they had a dam and down below the dam would be rocks or rocky soil, or go into freight yards where they might have expanses of land around, or they might go under high tension terminals of electricity. Those were places where the soil was poor and nobody wanted it. They'd go in and get the rocks out and start tilling it just like your wife might till a rose, and before long it was a beautiful place. The greatest tillers ever in the world.

"So the people would get jealous. Next door the grass was mighty green and it used to be pretty bad. We used to go down there in the valley and you'd see the Japs going out early in the morning, it would just barely be light, and coming back after dark. They'd be out in the fields all day. Hard workers. So I think it was largely along that line. Somewhat like the problem with the blacks in the South, it had just been building up that way for a long, long time. Then I think there were some people who got somewhat frantic. I used to get telegrams and telephone calls: 'Last night I saw someone signaling from down in Long Beach,' or somewhere. So you'd check with them and it would be, 'I saw a window shade go up and down.' In the end there was not one proven case of Japanese espionage."

In the first seventy-two hours of the war, FBI agents in the United States, Hawaii, Alaska and Puerto Rico arrested 3,846 Japanese, German and Italian enemy aliens without publicity or violence—a sharp contrast to the mass roundups of World War I. But then a plan was formulated to move some 120,000 Japanese-Americans to relocation centers. On December 10, 1941, after attending a meeting in the office of Secretary of the Treasury Henry Morgenthau, Hoover expressed his opposition in a memorandum to Attorney General Francis Biddle:

. . . The Secretary stated that he had been in communication with his representatives in San Francisco and as a result had ascertained that the task which they were carrying on [freezing Japanese assets and businesses] was an enormous one and that he believed more drastic measures should be taken in order to adequately cover and complete it. The Secretary then put in a call to Mr. X, one of his representatives in San Francisco, and this conversation was heard by all in the Secretary's office. . . . It was the opinion of Mr. X that there should be a round-up of the Japanese in San Francisco, Los Angeles, and in the bay cities of San Francisco, as well as in certain sections of the San Joaquin Valley. . . . The Secretary inquired of me as to whether this could be done. . . .

I suggested to Secretary Morgenthau that he call you by phone. I told the Secretary that I felt that you would be reluctant to approve any such program unless there were sufficient facts upon which to justify the cases of the persons arrested, as I believed you would be opposed to any "drag-net" or "round-up" procedure. I pointed out to the Secretary that in the arrests which had already been made of the Japanese, German, and Italian alien enemies, factual cases had had to be prepared on each one of them prior to their arrests and that these had to be approved by the Attorney General, and that of course citizens of the United States were not being included in any arrests, as the authority to make arrests was limited to alien enemies and unless there were specific actions upon which criminal complaints could be filed, you had not approved the arresting of any citizens of the United States.

The Secretary then called you . . . and you were in accord that the matter should be further considered and that certainly no action should be taken last night of the character recommended by the Treasury Agents in San Francisco. . . .

In a later memo to Biddle, Hoover again expressed his disapproval:

The necessity for mass evacuation is based primarily upon public and political pressure rather than on factual data. Public hysteria and, in some instances, the comments of the press, and radio announcers, have resulted in a tremendous amount of pressure being brought to bear on Governor Olson and Earl Warren, Attorney General of the State, and on the military authorities. It is interesting to observe that little mention has been made of the mass evacuation of enemy aliens.

Most of the Communist Cases "Were Somewhat Squeezed Oranges"

CLARK: "From there I went to the War Profits and Anti-Trust Division in Washington, and the FBI would run cases down for me that were originally investigated by Mr. Truman's committee, which was investigating defense plants. So I became acquainted with Mr. Hoover in that capacity, and later I became head of Anti-Trust, in March of 1943, and in October I became head of the Criminal Division. The Attorney General claims the privilege of transferring systems from one division to another, and Anti-Trust was somewhat of a squeezed orange at that time because of the war effort. Congress passed an act that permitted me or any liberalizer to suspend anti-trust cases if they interfered with the war effort. So Mr. Biddle was reorganizing the Criminal Division and he asked me to go over there and run it. Well, the Criminal Division, I suppose, is closer to Mr. Hoover than any other division, and I was head of it until I became Attorney General in 1945."

Was your relationship with Hoover friendly?

CLARK: "We had dinner together many times. Most of the time when I went with him it would be to Harvey's. He was out to our house two or three times. Hoover was not one to go out much socially, but we'd meet at rare intervals at somebody's place in the evening. But nearly all the contacts I had with Mr. Hoover were either in my office or his. When I was an assistant it would be mostly in his. After I became Attorney General [from 1945 to 1949], they were practically all in my office."

Would Hoover deal directly with the White House?

CLARK: "He wouldn't go through me but he had a man over there. I'm not sure but I think he had one there in Roosevelt's time. The idea was that if any problems came up on matters that Hoover was handling that involved the White House or what he thought of some national program or that had national aspects, why he'd send copies of memoranda to the President—usually the President sent it on over to me. Of course, I already had a copy but I got so many copies that I couldn't read them all—it would have taken twenty-four hours a day. I had my assistant read all mine and he'd give me what he thought I should see, what was important enough for me to see."

Did Hoover ever supply you with dossiers on cabinet members?

CLARK: "If you mean by dossier a report on one person, no, he never did. Many times in reports he might have a paragraph or two— He didn't like Mr. Morgenthau, for example, and he might take a dig at him, or he might indicate there were queers in the State Department, but as far as having a dossier that was devoted to one person, I never saw one of those in my life, on any person."

I understand President Johnson received some.

CLARK: "I rather think, knowing Hoover as I do, that he wouldn't do that unless someone indicated that it might be helpful."

Did you have to approve all wiretaps and bugs used in internal security cases in those days?

CLARK: "That started during the time of Mr. Cummings. He made arrangements with the telephone company that they could put in a tap on a phone. That was just before we went into the war, about 1937 or '38, along in there. But there was a Supreme Court case outlawing evidence obtained by a wiretap, so we would not use any evidence we got on a wiretap in a prosecution. Then when Mr. Murphy succeeded Cummings, I suppose that they continued that arrangement and then during the war I know that Mr. Roosevelt arranged to continue the operation with Mr. Biddle. When I came in, Mr. Hoover asked me to write a letter which he had drafted to the White House asking them to continue the arrangement, which I did. The arrangement was that he would make taps that didn't have to be used as evidence—say it was internal security and things of that kind. It was largely up to Mr. Hoover as to whether he thought there was a necessity for it.

"But I used to get queried by so many Congressmen when I'd come up on the Hill and appear before a committee, and they'd ask whether so-and-so's phone was tapped, that I turned all of mine over to Mr. Ford, who was my assistant. And I told him I didn't want to know who was tapped and who wasn't tapped. I was Attorney General for about four years and after Mr. Ford took over, I didn't know anything about the taps. When I first came in I asked for a list of the taps because I wanted to see what was going on, but Hoover increased these when he increased his Communist program. I don't think there were any more than there are now.

"After the war Mr. Hoover started what you might call his Communist program. As you know, Mr. Roosevelt was one who worked with the Russians in the war and he had a pretty close arrangement with them. And Mr. Hoover had an idea that the Communists were pretty strong. I rather thought that he overexaggerated it, which I used to tell him all the time, but he developed—at about the time the Iron Curtain got started, I'd say along about 1946—he began developing that subversive section that he had and spending considerable of his money on subversive activities. I don't know just what percent he spent, but I'd say compared to other specific programs it was large. Then he accentuated it from time to time and it grew into its height soon after I came here to the Court [in 1949]. During all that time that he was developing it, I got hundreds of memoranda, which I had my assistant screen. You see, Hoover was one that always wanted to put everybody on notice, so he'd send you a memorandum and they'd all be on your regular FBI onionskin form."

Was he sincere in his belief that Communism was a threat to the freedom of this country?

CLARK: "He was sold on it. He was a very sincere man. If he decided that something was bad, he got after it. I used to laugh with him about it. As a matter of fact, this club in New York—Saints and Sinners—had a program one time that I was on. They had a skit and an actor played Mr. Hoover's part. He and I were in my office and looking around, under my desk and stuff like that, to see if there were any Communists hiding. It was sort of a reflection of an attitude many people had towards Mr. Hoover's activities in the Communist field, and it was highly exaggerated. He admitted himself that only about one percent of these people were really bad, but in public I think he said ten percent. You have to remember that it was a small group that overthrew the Russian government, was his attitude. But most of the cases we had I thought were somewhat squeezed oranges. I didn't think there was much to them. And while some of these people often talked in terms of overthrow, they didn't have the means or the capacity at all to bring it about. I prosecuted the [Eugene] Dennis case [the top eleven members of the domestic Communist Party] and we won it, and we had some secondary cases, but I didn't think they were really such strong cases. Then it gradually petered out after McCarthy's time."

Was he tenacious in seeking prosecution in certain cases—for example the Judith Coplon case?

CLARK: "Well, no. He'd send you the memos. Of course, many times those matters would be returned to U.S. attorneys. We have ninety-three of them. If it was a national case like Dennis, he'd probably take it up with the Attorney General, but most of the time he'd take it up with the assistant who handled that particular business. They might take it up with the Attorney General, but ordinarily the Attorney General would never even hear about it unless they got into trouble."

Since he was so quick to censure his own men, do you think he was ever censured by an Attorney General when the FBI goofed as they did in the Coplon case?

CLARK: "I doubt it. It happened to me in the *Amerasia* case when I was an assistant. The FBI went over here and went into Harvard Hall without any warrants at all and cased this apartment. I didn't know a thing about it until after I filed the case and the people filed a motion to quash all this evidence on the grounds that they'd gotten it without any search warrant. So then the FBI told me about it and we dismissed the case."

Would you send a letter of censure or ignore it?

CLARK: "I don't remember sending any letter of censure. I used to kid with him about it. I thought he was a little off base on this Communist thing. I don't know what other attorneys general did. I rather think though that beginning perhaps in the thirties Hoover had pretty clear sailing. He was told by Mr. Stone in 1924 that he would have free wheeling, and I think it would be fair to say he had free wheeling for the rest of his life.

"He was pretty powerful in 1937 when I came in. He occupied a high position with governmental people and I think he had all the federal backing then that he had later. He had his vintage bullet-proof car and stuff like that. He gave me his bullet-proof car when I became Attorney General. We had an old car then. As you know, we couldn't get cars during the war. I think he had that car ten years before he told me I could have it. It had big windows, steel around the inside lining, had a telephone, but the only trouble was that it was so damn heavy the motor was too light to carry it around and it would break down a lot. I used it for two or three years, and he got himself a new one."

Do you think he thought he needed that kind of protection?

CLARK: "I never talked to him about it. I don't know how he felt about it. I don't think he did. Hoover went around a lot, and in the time I've known him he had a chauffeur. The only time I ever saw him using the car was coming to work and going home. Oh, once or twice we went out to Laurel to a horse race. It was very seldom that I'd be able to go with him. He went to the races quite a bit. I rather think he had agents watching him the whole time. Everywhere I went, they always had two FBI men."

I've been told that Tolson knew more about the operation of the Bureau than Hoover did, that he was the brains behind Hoover's success.

CLARK: "I doubt it. He had a succession of top people. I don't know of anybody who was able to surround himself with such capable people as Edgar Hoover. Top-notch staff. In fact, all the time I was down there, which was about twelve years altogether, I never met an FBI man who wasn't well above average. They were outstanding. I don't know how he did it—attracted people. I don't know whether he did it, or whether he had somebody else do it, but he had a knack for selecting the best ones."

We know that Hoover was up to date on technology, but do you think he matured intellectually? Weren't his views of the radicals of the twenties similar to his views of the Panthers and New Left of today?

CLARK: "His philosophy was different from those people. The end justified the means to him. He thought that the Black Panthers was an organization that was inimicable to the peace and security of the United States and it wouldn't hurt him any, he would have no compunction about tapping their wires or anything else to catch them. He excused himself on the ground that he was in the end effecting a good result."

I asked the same question of Ramsey Clark.
RAMSEY CLARK: "That's very hard to say. There were changes, and the changes may indicate that he didn't grow. For instance, he opposed wire-

tapping for many years. If I had to guess—and this is one of those things you can never really know—I would guess that an ideology overcame a professional investigative judgment, and that's what caused him to turn to favor the use of wiretaps. Or if not to favor them in any strongly affirmative sense, at least to concede their value. That would probably indicate a lack of growth, a firming of the hardening of an ideology that was in a sense disabling from a professional investigator's standpoint. You don't really think of Mr. Hoover as a man of intellectual interests. I don't really think of him as a book reader or an historian. He was interested in anecdotes and personalities, but his intellectual interests, in my experience with him, were quite limited."

I was referring particularly to his attitude toward radical movements. Do you think he ever appreciated the importance of social protest in a democracy, or did he always view it as a disease of some kind?

RAMSEY CLARK: "My guess would be that however he may have disapproved it, he understood the protest of the teens and the twenties because those were the years that his personal viewpoints were crystallizing, but he really could not understand, or even try to understand, the later incidents."

The Use of Hyperbole

Coming back to Tom Clark, I asked him whether Hoover had engaged in hyperbole when he said, and I quote, that the "Black Panther Party, without question, represents the greatest threat to the internal security of the country."

CLARK: "Of course, he had practice in doing that. Quite often, I think, although I never talked to him about it, he would pick out particular programs that he thought would help him in getting appropriations. For example, on the Dyer Act [automobile theft across state lines], I'm satisfied from the way the statistics worked that it was a statistical business for him and he worked very closely with local police and whenever the local police picked up a car they turned it over to the FBI. Then he'd report it on his chart, and when he went up to Congress he'd say we recovered so many automobiles worth so many millions of dollars in order to justify his appropriations. I've been up to the Appropriations Committee with him several times and he always had some gimmick. It was always closed doors, and he'd always have an investigation he was working on that would be some fantastic thing. Most of the time no prosecution ever came of it."

FBI statistics claim they get a ninety-seven percent conviction rate.

CLARK: "I expect that's true. But the reason they have the ninety-seven percent is because their cases are so strong—you get a picture of someone robbing a bank, you can't lose. Quite a few of their cases were turned over to them on a silver platter. That's where the friction between the local constabulary and the FBI exists. You'll hear it if you can find somebody who'll talk. They claim that Hoover steals their thunder, that they really uncover something but he announces it.

"On all his prosecutions, Hoover would make a statement, and I used to tell him, 'You may affect this prosecution, be careful what you say. Somebody might claim that you said something that was inflammatory.' Sometimes he would have one of his assistants or the Assistant Attorney General make a statement. Usually, if you remember the format, it would say, 'Attorney General Clark says this—' and then right under it would be 'Hoover.' They might as well not have mentioned me at all."

What about the prosecutor's discretion? In the Harrisburg case,* for example, do you think Hoover forced the Department into prosecuting against its better judgment?

CLARK: "I'd say that more than likely Hoover never said a word to those people handling the prosecution. But I think he'd reached the stage in his power that he didn't need to say anything. Coming from the FBI, it would be couched in terms that you'd know what the FBI wanted, the direction it was taking. The wording of the memorandum would leave you without any doubt as to how he felt, the way he'd characterize these people. He'd say they were dangerous this, that and the other thing. Anything but harmless. He'd almost put you in a spot where if you didn't prosecute, you'd be a first-class idiot. Hoover had a knack of always putting himself in such a position that he'd be protected and the other guy would not be. And sometimes I'd get a memorandum from him that would say he had sent one previously and nothing had happened, and he wanted me to check into it. He had a rather good ticker system for keeping up with those things, but I rather doubt that he called up whoever the prose-

* The prosecution of Fathers Daniel J. and Philip F. Berrigan and five others for allegedly plotting to kidnap Henry Kissinger.

cutor was and told him to get that thing up. He just didn't operate that way. He had much more finesse.

"His expression of 'jellyfish' wasn't that Ramsey was wobbly at all but that he wouldn't prosecute in certain cases, that he'd take a strong position and would turn down a prosecution at the outset. Sometimes a fellow looks guilty but you just can't prove it by running around like a bull in a china closet and trying to prosecute. It's a whole lot better for a prosecutor to exercise discretion and say, 'Well, I'm going to give him the benefit of the doubt. I'm not going to prosecute.' I'm satisfied that Hoover, like all prosecutors, picked out some cases that had some lure and some front-page stories on them, and I'm sure that not all of them were prosecutable.

"Hoover was critical of most attorneys general. He didn't like Frank Murphy at all. He was the only Attorney General I ever knew who got Hoover to go places with him. He knew that Hoover was a bit of an attraction. Hoover told me one time that they were having a parade at some military installation out West, and through some mistake, someone turned on the sprinkler system, and Murphy had on a white suit and he just looked like he'd been in a bathtub by the time they could get it turned off. Hoover used to criticize Biddle all the time when I was the assistant, very bitterly. I don't think he ever held out on anybody. He told everybody what he thought. He didn't like Biddle's prosecutive policy. He thought he was too soft."

If you were going to sum it up, what would you say were the sources of Hoover's power?

CLARK: "I think his power sprang from the efficient, dedicated way in which he, twenty-four hours a day, carried out his responsibilities. And I think you can get to the point in the minds of people who know you where you can do no wrong. When you have so many rights, people get to the point where if the name Hoover is connected with it, that's it. So I rather think that from the very inception of it, he had a pretty wise attitude. Mr. Stone and he built the agency by the selection of top-notch people and he built an esprit de corps, gave them something to shoot at, an idealism, a hard-working, dedicated person. Incorruptible. In that way he built up his strength, and then eventually you can get so much power that no one will go against you. That's about the way it is, I think. I don't think there was any deceit on his part, that he would talk to people and try to conspire and do those things. He would take each case as it came along and do the best possible job he could on it. He was very efficient and he was surrounded by dedicated people, and as a consequence the resulting product was usually high class."

"The Top Bureaucratic Operation in the World"

At the time that I interviewed Patricia Collins in June 1972, she had worked as a lawyer for fourteen attorneys general. The first time she was introduced to Robert Kennedy, she told him that he was nine years old when she first came to the Department. "He was bowled over," she recalled, "and forever after when he used to see me, he'd say, 'You know, this is Miss Collins. She came here when I was nine years old.' So we got to be great friends, and, oh, he was such a great friend to me when my late husband [Salvatore Andretta] was very, very ill."

COLLINS: "I came to the Department in 1935, when Homer Cummings was Attorney General. Mr. Cummings was a mighty figure. He really was a gigantic man."

You mean he was the star, not Hoover?

COLLINS: "Yes, you bet. And a real influence. Many times people ask me, you know, who the best Attorney General was, and they used to ask my husband this over and over again because he had seen so many of them. And for a man with legal competence, vision, imagination and stature, I don't think we've had any Attorney General who really reached Homer Cummings. Homer Cummings was responsible for the revision of the Criminal Code, he was responsible for the revision of the Civil Code. Now these things were done actually under the aegis of the Supreme Court, but it was Homer Cummings who got them started. He initiated the Code of Criminal Laws that was passed in the 1930s which gave the FBI authority to use guns and all that sort of thing. He had such vision. He set up the statute, or he was the inspiration for the statute that authorized interstate agreements between states and the federal government with respect to criminal prosecutions."

Was anything done in the area of civil rights?

COLLINS: "Not civil rights. That was a newer concept. That came later. But so much that needed to be done was done in a framed legal fashion by Homer Cummings. He was a giant of a man, he really was."

Then you had Frank Murphy?

COLLINS: "We can forget him. They got rid of him—shot him up to the Supreme Court to get him out of here, I guess. I don't know what that deal was. He was just a nonentity as far as this department was concerned. He was here very briefly and all he did was make himself unpopular. I can't point to anything Frank Murphy did. I guess he was here about a year. They had a story about Frank Murphy and his secretary, Lady Baumgartner, I think it was, and she was actually a nice gal, but she used to watch him like a hawk. The chauffeurs used to have a story that when he went out in the car, he would get down in the back of the car so she couldn't see him until he got out of her sight."

What about Herbert Brownell?

COLLINS: "I think he was a good Attorney General. He's a good lawyer. Of course, he's not the least bit outgoing; nobody in the Department knew him, but that's just the way he was."

He hasn't changed. He still refuses to talk.

COLLINS: "Herb was the kind who wouldn't talk to anybody when he was Attorney General. He's the man behind the throne, always, and he always wants to stay behind and not let anybody know he's there, but he wants to pull the strings. He's very warm and affectionate and outgoing with people he knows well, but he doesn't want any part of telling his story to anybody. He'll never write a biography. He's a private, very private, person.

"A whole group of American Bar Association people went over on the *Queen Mary* with him, all the way to England, and he and Mrs. Brownell never came out of their cabin, because he didn't want to have his coattails pulled by all those lawyers, and they stayed in their cabin the whole time. That's just his personality.

"Now Bill Rogers would be more likely to talk, although he's pretty guarded too. Of course, Bill's had a lot more public experience than Herb has. And he and Hoover were very compatible, which was the one circumstance in the entire history of Hoover, practically, that he got along with an Attorney General."

When do you think Hoover began dealing directly with the White House?

COLLINS: "I think the end run around the Attorney General to the

White House began in the Truman Administration. There was much closer liaison between Roosevelt and Cummings and Jackson and Biddle, so that things came to this department, hand-written notes from the President to the Attorney General. How it developed later, I don't know. I think Tom Clark was perhaps intimidated by Hoover. I don't think he and Hoover were ever on a very even conversing basis.

"And, Tom, as you know, is a very gregarious person. My own feeling is that Tom was happy to get off the Supreme Court. I think the sepulchral atmosphere over there got to him. When Tom was in the AG's office, it was a very, very active place. He was making speeches all the time, people were sitting out there in droves waiting to see Tom Clark. I was in the office directly across the way then, and I used to write speeches now and again and do various things that we had to do to keep it running. Suddenly Tom Clark goes over to the Supreme Court, he gets in an office, he's got a couple of people in the outer office, and nobody ever sees him. They say that when the phone rang, he'd grab it and say, 'Hello.' He was dying to talk to somebody."

From your experience, how would you describe the Bureau's relationship with the Department?

COLLINS: "Mr. Hoover's emphasis was always that he was not making policy and if there was ever an area in which he could decline to comment or to respond on the basis of substance, he would do so. He would always remind the Department that the Bureau was an investigative agency. Well, he ran the FBI as the top bureaucratic operation in the world. He made his own rules and abided by them. He did not permit any interference with them, and you just couldn't get anything out of him. You could batter him with memoranda all you wanted to, and he would furnish just exactly what he was going to furnish, an investigative report, period.

"I used to see him regularly when I was on Francis Biddle's staff during the war. He had to come through my office to get to Biddle. I had the best title I've ever had then. I was Assistant to the Executive Assistant to the Attorney General. I worked on the legal aspect of making recommendations to the Attorney General or briefing things that were brought to him for decision, developing opinions for him to sign—that sort of thing. I was there all through the trial of the German saboteurs. That trial was held in this department, over in the FBI section, and the legal military staff used to come in every day after they had had a session over in the FBI, and often Hoover came along. Of course, he was coming in and out all the time during that trial to confer with the Attorney General. So that was my first knowledge of him, and he was always very pleasant, but never broke down at all to any small talk at that time. He was very formal.

"Throughout the war, he was constantly sending over 'I think you ought to know' type of memoranda. Mr. Biddle used to take some of them seriously and lot of them he'd take with a grain of salt. I always had great admiration for Biddle and I never felt that he got the credit really that was due him for the protection that he gave civil rights, because if we had been stimulated to the point that Mr. Hoover would have liked us to be stimulated to, we'd have been in a lot more trouble with civil rights during the war."

Didn't Hoover oppose putting American-born Japanese in camps?

COLLINS: "He was not opposed to picking them up though, as far as I know. I don't know whether he was for the concentration camps, as they called them, or not. At any rate, it was a Presidential directive."

Did you enjoy the time Robert Kennedy was Attorney General?

COLLINS: "Oh, very much. I was just fond of Bob. He was great. He was, he really was a good Attorney General. If you'd go to some people around here, they'd tell you that we never had an Attorney General who had the close personal relationship he had with the staff. He always said he'd been here himself, he'd been an attorney down in the Criminal Division, and nobody had ever paid any darn attention to him, and he was going to fix that. So he was around the halls and talking to people, asking, 'What's your beef?' and all that kind of stuff. He was a hard worker, and could he delegate authority! I remember one time when they were going down to Alabama and Harold Reis, who was in this office, had been working with Bob on a lot of stuff, and before he went home one night, he stuck his head in— It was informal, you know, the people that knew Bob would stick their heads in the door without being announced, and Bob was usually in there with his sleeves rolled up. So Harold stuck his head in the door to say he was going home, and Bob was just at that point saying to Lou Oberdorfer, 'You're going to go on the plane,' and going around the room saying that to others, getting this bunch down to Alabama, and when Harold stuck his head in the door, he said, 'And you're going on the plane.' Harold never got home to get a toothbrush even. He was down there before he knew it. He could sure delegate, you bet. He used to say to my husband, 'Now, Sal—' And he'd just as soon say to him, 'You goddamn Guinea son of a bitch, you're gonna do this, aren't you?'

"But Bob was crazy about Sal, and Sal had a kind of thing where it was like father and son, in a way. Bob would say, 'Now, Sal, you're going to do that for me, aren't you?' Sal would say, 'I'll try to.' 'You're going to do it, aren't you?' 'What day?' 'What time?' Bob used to have his staff out there at Hickory Hill for lunch. At least once a month they'd go out there. He'd ask Angie Novello, his secretary, 'How many people are coming to lunch today?' And Angie would say how many, and he'd say, 'Well, tell them we're going to the house.' And they'd go out and sit around the pool and have hamburgers and hot dogs and chocolate ice cream with chocolate sauce on top of it with devil's food cake. But they'd sit around and talk about their business out there."

Some say he was cold?

COLLINS: "He wasn't. He was warm. Everybody talks about those hard blue steely eyes he had, but, honestly, you could bring a tear to his eyes. He would ask me about Sal when Sal was sick, he was so upset about Sal, and he'd come up to me and he'd say, 'How's Sal?' just as though it was a relative of his. After Sal died, I went over to the Hill on a reorganization plan. It was government operations, and he was on a subcommittee—he was a senator then—of some kind, and it was the first time he had seen me in the business world after Sal died. Well, he was late coming in, the chairman was already seated, but somehow or other, he just caught me in the audience. He walked right around the end of the bench and everybody was trying to stop him, you know, wherever he walked people were trying to stop him, and he made a beeline for me to tell me he was glad to see me out. And that's all he did, he went right back up. Now you know there was no coldness in that—that was warm.

"I used to go out to the Christmas party at his home even after Sal died. Ethel used to have those big Christmas parties, and anybody who had been on the staff, anybody he had known like that, as I was, he would always give me a big kiss and a hug. Anybody he knew and was fond of, believe me, he was warm.

"Ethel had a great case on Sal. She was very fond of Sal and she used to write him these cute little notes, bringing her ideas to him on little memos, and she'd sign them on the bottom with a heart with an arrow going through it. I saved those notes, they were so cute.

"When any Attorney General first comes in, there are all kinds of arrangements to be made. Not only education in terms of policy aspects in big cases and all that sort of thing, but just information on how you run the Department—what the papers are, what you have to do with the Civil Service Commission, what you have to do in terms of appropriation bills, and how much money you have to spend—and that was always Sal's job. Well, of course, when Bob came in, Ethel had all these ideas about redecorating the dining room and all the offices—she wanted to paint everything off-white. And she wanted new china for the staff luncheons. Well, everything Jackie had in the White House, Ethel wanted here, right away.

"Half the time Bob would say to Sal, 'Don't do it, Sal. Just listen to her, but don't do it. She's extravagant.' Bob was tight with a buck, just as tight as he could be, but with Ethel money was going out of style as far as she was concerned. One day she told Sal, 'Oh, I was over in the State Department. They've got the most wonderful reception room up there—oh, those gorgeous reception rooms. Couldn't we put another story on the Department of Justice and put some in?' She was that wild. She wasn't too serious about that but she was always telling Sal something that needed to be done, so one day she decided that we ought to have an outdoor arrangement for the personnel to eat out in our court at lunchtime so they could enjoy the sunshine. She got Sal to put in parasols and tables, and also a snack bar out there. It became known as Sal's Pizzeria. Then she had music piped in from twelve to two every day, and it nearly drove the attorneys crazy before it was stopped."

Do you agree with Hoover's comment that Bobby was the second-worst Attorney General he ever worked for?

COLLINS: "No. It was just because Hoover took a dislike to him—and I'm not sure that Hoover took a dislike to him from the beginning, although the beginning may have gone back further than I think. I know that when Bob started the idea of a police council of civilians—something like that—boy, Hoover really blew his top on that. I don't think he ever got over it. The boy Attorney General, you know. He just figured he was wet behind the ears."

Hoover thought that Ramsey Clark was the worst Attorney General. What are your feelings on that?

COLLINS: "Ramsey is a man of absolutely sterling integrity. He's a great, great guy. I'm terribly sorry that he went out of here with the reputation that he did. So many people you talk to say, 'Tom Clark's a great guy, but, boy, that son of his, that Ramsey, there's a—' Weak-kneed is what they considered him. Well, of course, it's just the opposite. Tom would play pussyfoot on things, Ramsey would not. The trouble with Ramsey is that he's a dreamer. There's not much give and take about him. He stands for what he stands on and he stands right there—"

That doesn't sound like Hoover's comment that "you never knew which way he was going to flop."

COLLINS: "But Hoover didn't look back to his principles. Ramsey had principles, and he may change his mind on things, but his principles really don't vary. He's very introspective. And most people found him very unable to delegate. He was just too hard a worker. He nearly killed himself; he was trying to read everything because he felt he was on the spot being Tom Clark's son and that sort of thing. He's a darn good lawyer."

When Johnson came in after the assassination, they say Hoover gave Bobby a hard time?

COLLINS: "Everything was tapering off very much. Bob got his wind up again when he went over to the Senate. But things had sloughed off here. My, he was a tragic guy."

What happened when Mitchell came in?

COLLINS: "Hoover liked Mitchell. I think they met man-to-man. They were just the same kind, actually. Hoover was a Republican from beginning to end, and I think he just got along better, he had more exchange with Republican attorneys general."

Did you know Hoover socially?

COLLINS: "During the Herb Brownell administration, we would have a big get-together once a year, a really elegant turnout, black tie. And a couple of times I drew Mr. Hoover as a dinner partner, and he was everything that you would ask of a gentleman, always very gallant. One time I remember he drew Simon Sobeloff's wife, Irene, who was very chic and such great fun when she was younger. She was able to kid people in a kind of poker-face way. She always used to take Edgar on, and we used to tease them considerably about how they were so stuck on each other. One night she took her shoes off and started singing 'Pistol Packin' Mama' for the entertainment of everybody, and Hoover joined with her. It was really quite a show. Oh, yes, he was always great fun when he was at these parties. I'm sure you've heard people say he was a great practical joker. I knew that more by reputation, and whenever I teased him about it he would reply to the effect, 'Well, certainly, and why not if you get fun out of it?'"

The Mafia Rears Its Ugly Head

Back in 1951 the hottest section in the Department of Justice was Internal Security. "It was like Organized Crime today," William Hundley, who worked for the section and is now a private attorney, recalled when I interviewed him in June 1972. "Everybody went into Internal Security, and I actually got put into what they called Smith Act cases. You might remember that we used to run around prosecuting all these Communists. They had already tried the Dennis case up in New York, the big landmark Communist case that Hoover really wanted prosecuted. After they won it, they decided to branch out and indict the leaders of the Communist Party in virtually every city in the United States. We had cooperation from the FBI that was unbelievable. They would assign an agent to every defendant and anything you wanted would be done. They made agents available, they made informants available, anything. They really wanted to win these cases.

"Hoover was always very ideological about the domestic Communist Party, and he was really gung-ho for that, he really put out. There was no question in his mind that Godless, atheistic, monolithic Communism was a threat. And, of course, they won a lot of cases, and then the Court got into the act and threw them all out. What it all added up to is hard to say. I would honestly think that the plusses were outweighed by the minuses. I mean, most of the American domestic Communists that I prosecuted—for Christ's sake, the only thing they ever threw was a pamphlet. Anyway, Internal Security started to die off. In 1958 I went over to be chief of the Organized Crime section—remember the Apalachin* meeting? When that hit there was only a couple of guys in the OC section clipping newspapers. There was absolutely nothing going on in the Justice Department. Apparently the Internal Revenue Service had done something back in the

* Seventy-five gangland leaders met at the palatial home of Joe Barbara in Apalachin, New York, on November 14, 1957.

Kefauver days, and Immigration, and they all got hit on the head, so nobody was doing anything. The Bureau certainly wasn't doing anything. It came as quite a shock to me. I had come out of Internal Security, where you had agents coming out of your ears, and get over into Organized Crime and you couldn't find an agent."

Why was Hoover opposed to organized crime investigation?

HUNDLEY: "Well, some of the agents would say— We got into this at the Princeton seminar on the FBI and nobody really came up with an answer. Everybody had different theories as to why the FBI really had to be brought into organized crime kicking and screaming. Some of the ex-agents felt that Hoover didn't, first of all, want to get into it because his statistics would go down. You know, the cases would be harder to make. Some of them said he didn't want to put his agents into a position where they could be corrupted, have them dealing with gamblers and hoods. Others said that he got himself locked in because he got in a big pissing match with Harry Anslinger over at Narcotics, who he didn't like, and Anslinger had the Mafia coming up out of the sewers the same way Hoover had the Communists coming up out of the sewers. So Hoover got himself locked in saying there was no Mafia. It was probably a combination of everything, but he just wasn't in it. There isn't any doubt, no matter what he said, he wasn't in it. He had no intelligence, he didn't know what the hell was going on."

Hoover's defense was that he didn't have the federal laws to fight organized crime until 1961.

HUNDLEY: "In a certain sense, there is some truth to that. But they always had an intelligence function over there, that's what they relied on, that's what they rely on now with all this peace stuff. It's inexcusable for them to say they couldn't have been using that function to at least be aware of what the hell is going on. I mean, how can you have the top investigative agency in the world and have all these top hoods meeting up in Apalachin and they didn't even know about it. Then you get into the idea that Hoover was a good bureaucrat. When he found out that Bob Kennedy was coming in and that he was kind of hot on this, he knew he had to do something."

What was Hoover's attitude on Valachi?

HUNDLEY: "Well, what happened on that—and there, I guess, is a good example of bureaucracy in action. There wasn't any question that the Bureau was interested in Valachi, really interested, because they were so far behind. And they came to me and they wanted Valachi, and we took him away from the Bureau of Narcotics and gave him to the FBI. The FBI did a pretty good job with him. They assigned really good agents, spent a lot of time developing this guy, and got a lot of intelligence information. Then when Valachi went before the McClellan Committee, and the thing started to bust out, then, of course, that's when you see J. Edgar Hoover as the complete bureaucrat. He came out and said he knew all this stuff before, never was interested in this guy—"

But wasn't he opposed to Valachi's testifying before the committee?

HUNDLEY: "Yes and no. I think that even that was a bit of an afterthought. Apparently, the Bureau was getting ready to put out their own version of Valachi. There was a lot of controversy within the Justice Department as to whether Valachi should testify before the McClellan Committee. The fact is that the committee found out about the guy and we put them off for a long time anyway, and we couldn't use him in any cases because his testimony was too dated and you couldn't corroborate it, so we really didn't have any choice. But it really wasn't until everything went sour that Hoover became the big anti-Valachi guy. Up until then, he was very high on him."

As I recall, when Bob Kennedy was counsel for the McClellan Committee, he complained vigorously that the FBI and the Justice Department were just shuffling papers back and forth and weren't doing anything about organized crime.

HUNDLEY: "Here's what happened. I was chief of the OC section under Rogers, and Courtney Evans was chief of the section over in the FBI, and he had a pretty good relationship with Bob. Whenever the FBI would tell Bob they couldn't do anything for the committee, they always used to say that it was the decision of the Justice Department—that's why I became the big son of a bitch. The first thing Bob did when he came in as Attorney General was to fire me. He said, 'Look, I've been too critical of you. I don't have anything personal against you, but nothing's been done down here and I'm going to bring in my own guy and you'll have to go.' If I'd had a job to go to, I'd have gone, but I was rather surprised, so I stayed on as a special assistant and had more fun than I ever did. I tried the Keogh and the Goldfine cases.

"Let me back up a bit here. In 1958, after Apalachin, Bill Rogers brought in Milton Wessel, a very bright guy, to head a special group to fight organized crime. Then all this in-fighting started and apparently Wessel really incurred the wrath of the Director, and he was shot down. Well, at the end of 1958, never officially, but through known agents and things like that, I found out that they'd started, on a very selective basis, to put bugs in. Apparently, the Bureau drew some distinction between bugs and wiretaps—only the Bureau could draw a distinction like this. For wiretaps, they always got the Attorney General's signature, bugs they didn't. It's pretty weird. Sometimes the bugs were put in the phone, if they could get them in, so they could pick up both ends. Now if you ever asked them officially, they'd say no, but believe me, I knew. They were doing some of it out in Chicago, in New York. I think somewhere internally a decision was made that organized crime was heating up and they didn't have any informants so they'd better do something to catch up, and that's what they started to do. When they learned that Bob was going to be Attorney General, they really spread out. That's when they started doing this bugging on a massive scale.

"I saw them start to operate in organized crime like they'd operated in internal security. Little things—you'd meet an agent out in the field, and I'd say, 'Where the hell were you last night?' And he'd say, 'Christ, I almost got caught climbing out of a goddamn window.' Putting a bug in, see. But down here in Washington, if you asked them officially, they always said no. And it wasn't a case of where they bragged about it or went out of their way to tell anybody what they were doing. Now, when it came to wiretaps, I knew in the internal security field that they went to the Attorney General and got his okay. Hoover didn't want to stick his neck out, so I just figured, well, look, Hoover's a smart guy, he's been around a long time, so I figured that when he started in 1958 that he got Bill Rogers to okay them in writing. But he never did. And then when Kennedy came in and he [Hoover] started enlarging, my guess was that he had gone to Bobby, that he had him sign every time he had a bug put in."

After Jack Got Shot, Bobby Was Sort of *Non Compos Mentis*

Not only did you know that they were bugging, you were seeing evidence of it. Weren't you getting information that they couldn't have gotten any other way?

HUNDLEY: "Well, yes, but that's a little more complex too. They sent

very little of the bug information over. Now and then they'd put something in a report, and for what it's worth, they would always try to disguise it so you wouldn't know. I guess if you've knocked around as long as
I have in Internal Security, well, I could spot it quicker than anybody
else, and I'd get a couple of them to cop out to me. I used to say to them,
'Don't send that shit over here. All you're going to do is screw up our
cases.' But it would never go beyond, any higher than that, as far as I
know. I don't paint myself as a hero. I didn't say, 'Look, you guys better
stop this.' I assumed all along that it was being okayed on a very high
level. In any event, it really wasn't until the Las Vegas skimming investigation came up, and they were trying to impress the Attorney General
with what a great job they were doing out there, and they sent a goddamn
report over that you couldn't miss it. It was all over it. And then there was
a big leak out there, and I swear to this day they sent the report over because they knew the casino owners had found the bug. Then the shit hit
the fan and they uncovered all the FBI bugs out there.

"This was after Jack Kennedy got shot, and Bobby Kennedy, although
he stayed on as Attorney General, was sort of *non compos mentis* until he
left the Department. After he became a senator, I got tipped off that
Hoover was trying to leak out the fact that Bobby authorized all the bugs.
He sent Deke DeLoach over to the *Evening Star*—Hoover was close to
the *Star*—to plant the story, but the editor insisted on attributing the story
to some official in the Bureau, which DeLoach wouldn't buy, so they back-
doored it. They got Congressman Gross in Iowa to write a letter and that's
how they got it out.

"I went over to the Senate to see Bobby when I got the tip, and I was
trying to tell him—first of all, I thought he knew—'Let's handle this the
best way we can. We'll take the position that it was sort of done in the nature of a security operation, we didn't use the evidence' and all those
things. And he said, 'Look'—and unless he was the greatest actor in history, he really got very upset. I liked Bobby Kennedy, but we weren't that
close. What the hell, he fired me once. And he said, 'You knew about it?
You knew and you didn't tell me?' And I leveled. I said, 'Bobby, I thought
you knew. I thought Hoover had your John Henry on every one of these
things.' And he said no. I came away convinced, and I'm convinced to this
day, that he didn't know. Now other people don't agree with me, but I
had this meeting and he convinced me. I was even saying, 'Look, Bobby,
even if you didn't know, I think it would be better if you said you did
know.' I'd rather go down in history as a guy who might have moved

around a little bit than as an idiot. I didn't say that to him, of course. And he said, 'How can I? I didn't know.'

"Now, when the thing blew, Hoover did everything he could to try to prove that Bobby did know. Christ, he came up with a memorandum that was written about twenty years ago—general authority. And then he got some affidavits from some agents about a meeting in Chicago and a meeting in New York where Hoover said they played these tapes for Bobby. I was at the Chicago meeting, and I don't want to knock the agents who submitted the affidavits, but it just didn't happen that way. We were having an organized crime meeting, and right in the middle of it Courtney Evans, who by then was the FBI liaison to the AG, brings in a recorder, puts it on a desk, and plays a tape. It was a tape of some Chicago hood complaining bitterly to a crooked police captain that since Kennedy had become Attorney General they couldn't fix cops anymore. It was a lot of play-up, obviously trying to impress the Attorney General. My immediate reaction was these guys have flipped their lids. This is unbelievable that they would play one of these damn illegal tapes for the Attorney General."

What did Kennedy say?

HUNDLEY: "He never said a word."

He couldn't have been that naïve.

HUNDLEY: "Think about it. If you didn't know, it could have been a local tape, it could have been a guy who had a thing wired on him. It could be anything."

Why do you think the relationship between Hoover and Bob Kennedy deteriorated to the point it did? It is my understanding that Kennedy consulted McClellan and Hoover before he accepted the Attorney Generalship, and they both advised him to take it.

HUNDLEY: "My guess is that Hoover liked Bobby at first. After all, Bobby worked on all this Communist stuff with McCarthy. I mean he had certain things going for him that Hoover would have liked. Hoover probably figured, Well, he's a gung-ho kid and his old man's an old buddy of mine and his brother's President. I can handle him. And I think it was more out of deference to Bobby's feeling about organized crime that Hoover started expanding his bugging program."

There are stories about Kennedy putting in a direct line to Hoover's

*office, and about his going over there in his shirtsleeves and sitting
on his desk. Once he supposedly caught the Director taking a nap.
Have you heard these stories?*

HUNDLEY: "Oh, sure. I was in Bobby's office once when he summoned
Hoover. I couldn't get over it. I was working on the Goldfine case,* which
involved a lot of politicians, and this was one of those cases where the Director was dragging his feet. I was telling Bobby about it and Bobby said
something like, 'I mentioned that to the Director,' or 'I mentioned that to
Edgar yesterday, and he has some explanation.' And then Bobby said, 'Do
you want me to get him over here so you can hear his explanation?' That
was too much, so I said yes. So he hit a goddamn buzzer and within sixty
seconds the Old Man came in with a red face, and he and Bobby jawed at
each other for about ten minutes. And Hoover kept looking at me. And he
went out, and it was amazing. I'll tell you one thing, he didn't give an
inch."

He had a good explanation then?

HUNDLEY: "I didn't think it was worth a shit, but I can't remember
what it was. And Bobby pushed him a little but he didn't back off. I became very fond of Bobby, but Bobby never moved Hoover that much, and
one thing you got to say about Hoover, he was tough. And he didn't back
down. He always stood his ground. I am convinced that the thing that
finally destroyed their relationship was that Bobby mentioned to too many
people who complained to him about Hoover that, 'Look, just wait,' and
we all got the message that they were going to retire him after Jack got reelected and Hoover hit seventy. And it got back to him."

Did they feel it was dangerous to fire him before the election?

HUNDLEY: "He had too many friends on the Hill, and he had done a
lot for the country; he was a pretty fine old man, but he'd just become too
difficult. He was almost seventy and it would be just terrible to fire him
when he was a couple years from there, and by a happy coincidence he
was going to be seventy after the election. And we'd retire him."

* Bernard Goldfine was the Boston industrialist accused of gifting Sherman Adams
and others to gain influence in the Eisenhower Administration.

"We Investigate and You Prosecute"

After more than two decades in government service, William P. Rogers
has returned to the practice of law in New York City. His spacious office
on the fifty-second floor of the Pan-Am Building, with its huge potted
plants and sweeping view of the skyline, befits a man of his prominence
and superlawyer stature. His wavy hair has now turned silver but his clear
blue eyes, shaded by thick golden eyebrows, belied his sixty-one years on
that July morning in 1974 when I sat across the desk from him to record
this interview.

ROGERS: "I first met Edgar Hoover when I became Deputy Attorney
General in 1953. My responsibility then, in a sense, was that of liaison
man between the lawyers in the Department of Justice and the FBI, so I
saw a great deal of him. He was cooperative with me, and with Herbert
Brownell, who was Attorney General before me—I was his deputy. Now,
Edgar Hoover was very conscious of his authority and didn't want anyone
to impinge on that authority, which was a good quality. It wasn't something people should criticize. For example, he felt that the investigation of
crimes over which he had jurisdiction should be conducted exclusively by
his people. He didn't want the lawyers to be involved in the investigation
—I'm speaking about the Department of Justice lawyers. He didn't want
any other department of government to get involved in those investigations. He insisted that the request for an investigation be made by those
authorized to do so and that he conduct the investigation. Now some people felt that he was difficult in that regard. My own view was that that
was sensible.

"One of the things that was interesting about him was that when Department lawyers put things on paper criticizing the FBI, he was apt to
take offense. He felt that probably it was being done for the record, someone was trying to make a record criticizing the FBI. When that happened, he would send back a long memorandum for the record too, and
what would happen quite often was a battle on paper between the lawyers
and the FBI. It was quite clear to me that the way to avoid that difficulty
was not to put it on paper, but to talk to the FBI first about it. And that
was the policy I followed. I said, 'I don't want anyone to be arguing with
Mr. Hoover or with any of the FBI agents on paper. If you have a prob-

lem, talk to them about it, and if you can't resolve it after sensible discussions, come to me and I'll talk to Edgar Hoover about it.' "

Of course, you did have a pretty big battle at one time, didn't you? Weren't you the first Attorney General to focus seriously on organized crime?

ROGERS: "I had been in Tom Dewey's office in New York when he was District Attorney, and I was Assistant District Attorney and prosecuted a lot of cases in New York City."

So you knew something about organized crime. After the Apalachin meeting, didn't you bring in Milton Wessel to head a special group to fight organized crime?

ROGERS: "That's right."

Wasn't there a power struggle between Hoover and Wessel?

ROGERS: "Well, we did have a problem there but that really was between Mr. Olney and Wessel and, as I remember it, Mr. Hoover, but that was all ironed out. By and large, we got along fine and—"

Didn't Hoover shoot Wessel down? Wasn't the special unit disbanded?

ROGERS: "Well, frankly, I've forgotten. I don't remember the details on that. But the Organized Crime section itself was very successful. Did William Hundley show you the report we had prepared of the achievements of the Organized Crime Division? If you go back and look at the accomplishments of those years, you'll find that almost every organized criminal mentioned during the Kefauver hearings was convicted by our office. I can name some of them: Artie Samish, Benny Binion, Frank Costello, two or three top people in the Mafia who were convicted for drug selling. Matter of fact, we put out a Blue Book in which we listed the accomplishments and the convictions that we obtained, and it really was a great record of achievement."

Hundley says the FBI had to be brought into organized crime kicking and screaming.

ROGERS: "That's correct. Mr. Hoover was opposed to it the way we went into it. As I say, he had a feeling that the lawyers in the Department should let the FBI know what it was they wanted investigated and the FBI would investigate it. Now that as a premise is sound, a perfectly sound proposition, but in order to make an attack on organized crime at the national level, you had to go beyond that. You had to have coordination of people in the Alcohol Tax, in Customs, the Treasury, et cetera, so you had to have a major national cooperative effort. And in order to do that we had to discuss it with the FBI, work out our plans, and so forth. Now at that time, as happens so often in government, there were some differences, but those differences never became serious, as far as I was concerned, with the FBI, or with Edgar Hoover. When we got to the point where there was a difference among our associates, then I would go over to see him or he'd come over to see me and we'd resolve it. And that's what happened."

Along the same line, Hundley says that the FBI began using bugs and wiretaps in organized crime cases the way they had in internal security. They made a distinction between a bug and a wiretap even when they placed the bug in a telephone.

ROGERS: "It's not a hard legal distinction to make. A tap, the word 'tap' is used when a telephone conversation is listened to without the knowledge of either party. There is a provision now that permits authorization with court approval, but at that time if there was an interception of a telephone conversation, without the knowledge of the parties, it was a violation of the law. It is not a violation of law to overhear a conversation or to record a conversation that's overheard or to listen in on a telephone conversation with the permission of one party. That's done in kidnaping cases all the time."

What about the planting of a bug?

ROGERS: "If it's a trespass, then that's a crime, but the overhearing itself is not a crime. For example, if instead of having your recording machine on the desk you had it concealed on your person it would not be a crime. Or if you have it on a chair in your office and I come in and talk to you and you've got a recording of what I said, that's not a crime."

What if the bug in the phone gets both sides of the conversation?

ROGERS: "Then it would be an interception. I'm really talking about what it was when I was Attorney General."

Did you authorize any wiretaps in organized crime cases?

ROGERS: "I never authorized any taps of that kind, nor did I have any information that they tapped wires contrary to my instructions. I don't believe it."

As far as you know, you never signed the authority for anything like that?

ROGERS: "No. That's my recollection."

I understand Hoover never made recommendations, but would only supply an investigative report, period.

ROGERS: "That's right. Now that demonstrates what I said earlier. He had certain policies that he followed, rigidly. Sometimes that annoyed people. It didn't annoy me, because most of the policies he followed were sound. He was not in the business of being a lawyer for the government; he was an investigator for the government. One reason he was so careful in not disclosing what was in the raw files of the FBI was that he recognized that a lot of the material was either of very little value or it would be unfair to the persons involved if the information was disclosed. His position was 'As investigators we collect all the information we can of any description that relates to the subject matter, and then that information is to be evaluated by the lawyers.' That's what the lawyers do, they evaluate that information and decide whether to present it to a grand jury or not. So he was rigid in that regard, because he said, 'We investigate and you prosecute. We will not evaluate. We will give you all the material, then you make the decision.' So he did not recommend prosecution or no prosecution, he did not attempt to pass judgment on the information that he passed on to us. And I think, on balance, that that was a very good policy."

"The Best and Happiest Years He Ever Had"

Would Hoover attend staff meetings?

ROGERS: "Yes, Mr. Brownell and I had him participating all the time. We had lunches about twice a week with all the people, the top assistants, and we ironed out our problems. As a matter of fact, Mr. Hoover often told me that those years, those eight years when Mr. Brownell and I were attorney generals were the best and happiest years he ever had. Those were great years. We had a department that was very well regarded, we had an outstanding team of people, and those were eight excellent years. And if you look back at some of the top people we had in the Department at that time, we had an extremely capable group of people. Warren Burger was there in the Civil Division and Simon Sobeloff from Baltimore, who became Chief Judge of the Fourth Circuit. We had usually an annual meeting of the top people and we'd go to some place like Quantico or Camp David and talk over our problems and work out our plans for the coming year, so they really were good years."

According to Pat Collins, the end run around the Attorney General to the White House began in the Truman Administration. Did that continue in your time?

ROGERS: "We never had any problem of that kind at all. Of course, President Eisenhower wouldn't have permitted it. In the case of President Eisenhower, when you were Attorney General and you had certain authority, he expected you to exercise that authority. And that included the FBI, that included Immigration, and that included the Prisons Bureau. That doesn't mean that if one of those men had a particular gripe that he wanted to make and he wanted to go directly to the President, the President wouldn't have seen him, but only in that event, never would he have had a liaison with a subordinate cutting out the boss. That would have been anathema to President Eisenhower. And to me.

"I remember an example of a case involving Sherman Adams. Sherman Adams and I were good friends and played golf together a lot, so this was not on an unfriendly basis at all. But it was after the problems in Central High School in Little Rock and some of the congressmen were dealing with Sherman Adams directly in connection with matters that I was involved in as Attorney General, and I got a call from Sherman Adams about it, suggesting what I should do and saying that he had been in touch with those people, and I said, 'Sherman, why don't you run this department?' And he said, 'What do you mean, Bill?' And I said, 'Well, you're doing my job now, and if you want to be Attorney General, come on over and take it.' And he said, 'Well, don't get mad at me.' I said, 'I'm not mad at you. I'm just saying the obvious and that is, if they want to give advice about how to run this job, have them come and see me, don't have them go to see you.' I said, 'Tell them to see me, otherwise I'm not going to do it.' He said, 'Well, okay, I understand.'

"Now Adams didn't do that very often, but this just happened. But what I mean is that President Eisenhower was the kind of a leader who selected people to do a job and he expected them to do it. He expected them to do the job in accordance with the plan that was in effect. In the case of the FBI, Mr. Hoover was part of the Justice Department and was subordinate to the Attorney General. Now President Eisenhower would have been very unhappy if the Attorney General or any cabinet officer was arrogant in the performance of those functions, but he expected them to carry out their duties.

"Quite often the President would be mad at something. He would be mad at a leak and he would call me and say, 'Please get Mr. Hoover to do the following,' and I would say either, 'I will, Mr. President,' or 'I don't think that's a good idea, Mr. President,' or 'That's not the jurisdiction of the FBI, Mr. President,' or whatever it was. But he asked me to do it, and I would call Edgar Hoover."

In his autobiography, Biddle wrote that Hoover gave him dossiers on cabinet members. Did he ever give you any?

Rogers: "No. I've heard all those stories about Edgar Hoover. None of these things ever happened when we were there."

President Johnson received some of these reports.

Rogers: "Well, if the President asked for it, he'd give it to him. I mean, the idea that Edgar Hoover was going around in a cheap fashion saying to cabinet officers, 'I want you to look at the dossier of some other cabinet officer,' I don't believe for a moment. I think that's bunk. It may be that somebody asked for it. You know, the Attorney General has the authority to get in your files, so if the Attorney General wants to get a file on some other cabinet officer, he can do it, but I don't believe the story that Edgar Hoover went around volunteering that kind of information."

I've been told by many people that Tolson was the brains behind Hoover. That if you wanted to know what was going on in the FBI, Tolson could tell you faster than Hoover could. Does that sound plausible to you?

Rogers: "Yes, I think so. I have no way of judging the last comment, because Hoover always seemed to me to have a very quick mind, but certainly Tolson did and Tolson was, I think, a very essential part of the success of the FBI, and I think he was invaluable to Hoover. In a sense, he was the chief of staff, if you want to put it in military terms, and he was very effective in carrying out orders, he is a man who has a grasp for details and he's a very good organizer."

What about Hoover's temperament? Did he have a short fuse?

ROGERS: "I never saw him get mad. I think like every red-blooded man he got mad, but in all the contacts I had with him he was very controlled. But I don't like to try to be a psychoanalyst. I really don't know. He would get mad at injustice, and he would get mad at stupidity, but I never saw anything in his make-up that suggested that his anger would supersede his judgment.

"Whether that happened later on, I have no way of knowing. You know, Edgar Hoover was proud of the FBI. And he had every reason to be proud of it. One of the things I think people misunderstand—fail to understand, is a better way to put it—about Mr. Hoover is that the FBI was his life—he wasn't married and he had no children and he had no family. The FBI—an organization consisting of men and women that Edgar felt responsible for and responsible to—was his life. The jealousy that he exhibited about the FBI from time to time was quite understandable. Some people fail to appreciate that because he was belligerent in his support of the organization. If an attack was made on the FBI which was unfair, he'd react very vigorously to that attack. If— A lot of times when you're in government an attack is made on you or your organization and you say, 'Oh, that's part of the game,' and relax.

"But that was not true in Mr. Hoover's case, for the reason I mentioned. And it interested me when on occasion somebody in Congress or somewhere else would make a speech attacking either Edgar Hoover or the FBI or pointing out some criticism, and Mr. Hoover would immediately send agents to the congressman's office, and the agents would say in effect, 'We've heard your speech and Mr. Hoover has asked us to come up and get a report on what you base that on,' and they'd have their books out. So the congressman would say, 'Well, I didn't have anything in particular, I was just making a general—' 'No, no,' they'd say, 'we want to get exactly what it was you had in mind.' Well, before they left, either the congressman had backed down completely or if he did have something of substance, then the FBI would follow it to its logical conclusion, and if the FBI was wrong, Edgar Hoover would do something about it. But if the FBI was not wrong, if the congressman was wrong, he'd go back on the floor of the House the next day and apologize."

Integrity Built from Scratch

As you know, some congressmen have charged in recent years that the FBI was tapping their telephones.

ROGERS: "I don't believe that it happened during my time in the Department of Justice. It is certain that a paranoia exists in Washington when people suspect that, but I think I would have known. I was in the Department eight years and if there were any taps of that kind, I think that somewhere along the line I would have found out about it. Now what happened after I left, I don't know, but there was no information, no rumors even, about it when I was there."

If you were to sum up his power, his sources of power, what would you say they were?

ROGERS: "First, he had an organization that had integrity which he himself built from scratch. Secondly, no matter what kind of an attack was made by whom, the public had confidence in the integrity of the FBI and in the integrity of J. Edgar Hoover. Now there is no single fact in American political life that gives a man greater power, in my opinion, than to have the public generally think he's an honest man and for the public to think his organization is an honest organization. So when an agent came to investigate and said, 'I'm an FBI agent,' and showed his shield, that person immediately said to himself, 'Here's an honest law enforcement officer who wants to question me.' Now that's a great source of power.

"Secondly, Hoover built an organization— I think it's well to keep in mind that it was a small organization, and it was small by design. Mr. Hoover could have expanded it many times if he had wanted to. He was able to, based on the public support he had, to gain great congressional support. The public respected him and his organization, and that reflected itself in the Congress. He had great congressional support.

"Thirdly, the policies that he maintained in the organization were sound policies, and the FBI was recognized probably as the outstanding investigative organization of its kind, ever. Not only in this country, but ever. I have no doubt that it is far superior to Scotland Yard or any other investigative organization that I know anything about. So for those reasons he became powerful but not because of an arrogance of power, not because he sought power. Had he sought power, he could have had a lot more. Well, he had a policy—put it that way—he had a policy that he did not want the organization to grow beyond a certain point. He often said that he had no desire to be an empire builder. Consequently, the organization remained relatively small.* If you contrast the size of the FBI with police departments in major cities, you'll see it's very small, much smaller than the police departments in New York or Chicago. Now, if Mr. Hoover had had any desire to be an empire builder, or had a power complex that is often ascribed to him by his opponents, he could have quadrupled the size of the FBI without any difficulty.

"Many times there was a demand on the part of either the executive branch or the legislative branch that the FBI be enlarged. Mr. Hoover always resisted. Often when there was a series of crimes that attracted national attention, the Congress would say, 'Let's turn the jurisdiction over to the FBI.' He resisted that. So on numerous occasions he had the opportunity to take over jurisdiction from state and local authorities, and had he done that, he could have increased the size of the FBI tremendously. He consistently resisted that. He told me time and time again, 'I have no desire to have a national police force. I think the function of the FBI should be limited, I think most of the responsibility for law enforcement in this country should remain with the states and localities, and I think that the role of the FBI should be limited in about the manner that it is today.'

"I can remember two or three cases where President Eisenhower said, 'Why don't we have the FBI get jurisdiction of that,' and I would talk to Edgar Hoover and he would say, 'No, I don't want to do that. I think that would be wrong. I don't want to build up a large national police force in this country.' If you look at the size of the FBI and the growth of the FBI as compared to other organizations, it's really amazing. Compare the growth of the FBI with the growth of any other organization in Washington, any department of government or any agency of government."

Do you think the files had anything to do with his power?

ROGERS: "No, I think that's an overpublicized concept. I don't know many persons who are fearful about disclosures of their files. You have fear of your FBI files? It never occurred to me. I can't think of anybody in my acquaintanceship who's been worried about his FBI file. Certainly the idea that Congress supported Hoover and the FBI so wholeheartedly was

* At the time of Hoover's death, the Bureau had approximately 8,000 special agents and 11,000 other employees.

because they feared disclosure of their files is nonsense. He got that support for the reasons I have mentioned.

I think it is well to keep in mind that in many cases when a person is employed in the federal government an investigation of that person is made by the FBI. That file is then made available to the appointing authorities, and, in the case of appointments requiring Senatorial confirmation, it is made available to the appropriate members of the committees of Congress. So that there is access by several people to some FBI files and undoubtedly, from time to time, things contained in those files through leaks or otherwise become public. But, traditionally, the FBI has been very careful to maintain the integrity of their files.

Was Hoover a political or non-political person?

ROGERS: "By and large, the conduct of his office was non-political. He was a political animal in the sense that he understood people and their motivations."

But did he play politics himself?

ROGERS: "No, I don't think so. Like every American, from time to time he expressed his views to people in private conversations, and occasionally those views were reflected in public print, but I think his activity was very limited."

But he knew how to play the bureaucrat game?

ROGERS: "Oh, yes. That's what I mean when I say he had good political instincts. He couldn't have lasted as long as he did and been as successful as he was unless he had good political instincts. Let me say this, he was an invaluable public servant. It's going to be a long time before we get that kind of man to do that kind of work as well as he did it over so many years. There are few people who come along in life who happen to fit perfectly into the niche they're placed in. He was one of those men. Frank Hogan in New York City was another one. People of that caliber are really of tremendous value to the system, to our society, and when I hear people now libel, slander, Edgar Hoover now that he's dead, it offends me."

There are critics who say, "Never another Hoover." Did he have a certain independence that others can't—or shouldn't—get today?

ROGERS: "Sure, sure."

Would the first Watergate investigation have been different if he had lived?

ROGERS: "I can't answer that. I really don't know. I don't want to— But let me answer your first question. Because of the integrity and confidence of his organization and the work he did, he had a guaranteed— No, he had a recognized and long-standing record of success which was so admired throughout the country that he had an independence and a power which resulted from those achievements, which is what you really want in the country."

Did Hoover exaggerate the Communist threat?

ROGERS: "No, I don't think so. And I think he can take certainly some credit for the lack of success of the Communist Party over the years in this country. I don't mean he was totally responsible for it. I also think that one of the remarkable things about America is that the Communist Party hasn't made greater gains here, particularly among the less privileged.

"To some extent I think there was a greater fear of the Communist Party than was justified, but that doesn't negate from the point I just made. One of the reasons I don't think the fear was justified was because the blacks in this country just didn't fall for it. Logically, they might well have. I mean, they were underprivileged, they did not have their constitutional rights, they were neglected and all the other things that would give rise to the feeling of 'Why don't we try something else?' Communism might seem to be a viable alternative from the standpoint of people in that position in our society. So to me the remarkable thing was that they did not. I have great respect for the blacks. They really love their country, you know, with all its faults, and even though they may feel from time to time that the country isn't treating them fairly."

The Old Man and the Kid

Few men in the last twenty years have accumulated more notoriety than Roy Cohn. There was a time when Cohn, Joe McCarthy and G. David Schine formed the most awesome triumvirate in Washington. Times have changed and some people now consider it poetic justice that in the last decade Cohn has probably spent more time in court as a defendant in criminal actions than as a trial lawyer defending clients. The man responsible for Cohn's legal nightmare—or, in his words, "vendetta"—is Robert Morgenthau, former United States Attorney for the Southern District of New York.

COHN: "The first time I met Edgar Hoover was in 1952, when I was in charge of this runaway federal grand jury up in the Southern District of New York, investigating the infiltration of a substantial number of American Communists into the Secretariat of the United Nations. The grand jury wanted to file a presentment, but the Department of Justice was trying to block it, and I was siding with the grand jury. The Department was putting pressure on me to kill the presentment because they thought it would hurt the Administration in the forthcoming election. I'm a Democrat but I didn't feel it would hurt anyone at all. I thought the only way you could get hurt is with coverups such as they had in the beginning—calling the Hiss case a red herring and things along those lines, as we see in Watergate today.

"In any event, I decided to get the advice of Mr. Hoover. I had received a number of letters from him about my work in the Julius and Ethel Rosenberg atom spy trial and the William Remington case, and in some other FBI-investigated cases I had handled, and they had been very cordial letters. So when I tried to arrange an appointment through channels, I got absolutely no place except reported back to my superiors in the Justice Department, who were all the more angry. Just as I was leaving my office in Washington one day, the phone rang, and when I picked it up, a woman said, 'Mr. Cohn, Mr. Hoover is calling.' Mr. Hoover came on the line and said, 'Roy, are you trying to see me?' I said, 'You're darn right I'm trying to see you. It's been rather difficult.' He said, 'Whenever you want to see me, you just pick up the phone and ask for me and you'll be able to see me.' I said, 'Well, when can I see you?' and he said, 'Come on over.'

"Within ten minutes I was seated across the desk from him. He told me in the course of that conversation to go right ahead, to stick to my guns and do what I thought was the right thing to do. If they fired me on account of it, let them do it. The Administration, he said, was on its last legs, and 'if they fire you, they'll make a hero out of you, and I will publicly back you up.' Of course, he was right, and a few weeks later I was hired by Senator Joe McCarthy as chief counsel for the Senate Permanent Investigations Subcommittee."

I'd like to back up a moment and ask you about the Rosenberg case. How do you feel about that case today?

COHN: "Well, all that's being said is being said by a very small vocal minority of badly misinformed people who are trying to make matinee television idols of a couple of convicted spies who were unanimously convicted by a jury, who had their convictions upheld by a hundred and twelve different judges—"

A hundred what?

COHN [voice rising]: "A hundred and twelve different judges to whom they applied, who had clemency denied by President Truman and President Eisenhower, and had about the most overwhelming set of evidence against them that has ever happened in any criminal case in history. But by a propaganda job being done by a vocal, emotional, same-old-story bleeding-heart minority today, they are trying to have the Rosenbergs portrayed as some kind of martyrs. They omit most of the basic facts and try to take advantage of a new generation which doesn't know what really went on. Among the basic facts they omit are such little details as the fact that Emanuel Bloch, Rosenberg's attorney, after the trial was over and the verdict was in, got up and thanked Judge Irving Kaufman for what Bloch described as a completely fair trial."

But haven't the critics charged that Bloch was wrong in not having the Rosenbergs take the Fifth Amendment?

COHN: "You're getting way off the subject, Mr. Demaris. I'm saying that one of the facts that is very relevant for the people to know is that when they put Bloch up, as they did in those two television spectaculars, as a hero pleading the innocence of the Rosenbergs and condemning the unfairness of the trial, they leave out the fact that Bloch is the one who got up and praised Judge Kaufman for a completely fair American trial. That's the first thing they leave out. The second thing they leave out is that all of this garbage that they talk about as new evidence today was presented by Morton Sobell in the form of a lengthy motion for a new trial based on this book *Invitation to an Inquest* by the [Walter and Miriam] Schneirs.

"The federal judge, Edward Weinfeld, of the Southern District of New York, one of the originators of the New Deal, whose political career was launched by Herbert Lehman and Franklin D. Roosevelt, is regarded as not only one of the ablest but as one of the most liberal jurists in the United States. In a scathing seventy-two-page opinion, he rejected every piece of so-called new evidence presented in behalf of the Rosenbergs and

Sobell and held that the evidence leading to the conviction was as strong and viable twenty years later as it was at the time. And this is another completely material fact which is concealed by these propagandists who want to do everything but bring out the truth. This is just an emotional byplay by a vocal minority trying to beat the drums for a propagandistic cause in view of the détente and things along those lines and just cover up the truth."

Tom Clark told me that most of the cases against domestic Communists when he was in the Department were "somewhat squeezed oranges," and Bill Hundley said that the only thing that the domestic Communists he prosecuted ever threw was a pamphlet. What are your feelings today on those times?

COHN: "Well, Justice Clark must have had breakfast with Ramsey before he gave that interview. As far as Hundley is concerned, that would really amaze me because anyone who knows anything about history knows two things: First of all, the domestic Communist movement is part of the international Communist movement, so you never view a local Communist movement as local because none of them are local. Their strength or their weakness depends upon the strength or weakness of the international movement of which directly or indirectly, loosely or tightly, they might be a part. Insofar as them being harmless people who just toss around pamphlets, let Mr. Hundley go around and talk to the hundreds of millions of people who live under Communist dictatorships throughout the world today, who have one newspaper, one radio station, no right to worship. Let him talk to some of the Jews who can't leave the Soviet Union and are being persecuted today. Let him look at some of these people who live under Communist dictatorship and then tell me, man-to-man, that all they are is a bunch of harmless people who throw around pamphlets."

In a New York Times Magazine *article, Tom Wicker wrote, and I quote: "Just recently, when FBI agents submitted affidavits bearing on the Roy Cohn trial directly to U.S. Attorney Robert M. Morgenthau, Hoover summarily transferred and suspended the agents. It has been charged that this was done out of Hoover's friendship with Cohn." What is your version of this story?*

COHN: "I know very little about it because it's nothing I ever discussed with Mr. Hoover. Morgenthau always specialized in using any investigative agency as a tool to do his personal political bidding, and to get after his own enemies. Well, he used three FBI agents in that regard in a case against me which in no way involved the FBI. He pulled them in from left field and made them sign affidavits without clearing them with their superiors, which is a grave violation of FBI discipline. This is the reason Mr. Hoover came down hard on the agents. As far as any significance to me or my case, it had absolutely none because, as a matter of fact, after these agents were transferred I was the one who had to subpoena them to get them back to New York to testify because they had evidence favorable to me to give. Two of the three testified as defense witnesses."

In his book, *John Edgar Hoover*, Hank Messick wrote:

Prior to his trial, Cohn secured an affidavit from an exconvict, Milton Pollack, which accused Morgenthau's office of offering him a pardon if he would in turn help Morgenthau "in inveigling Roy Cohn into some transaction that would result in his prosecution." Three special agents of the New York FBI office joined Morgenthau's staff in signing affidavits refuting Pollock's [sic] charges. The denials were filed with the court and, in due time, Cohn got copies. He turned his copies over to Nichols, who marched into the FBI office in Washington and demanded the three special agents be censured. John Edgar Hoover promptly complied. Each agent was given a letter of censure and thirty days to report to a new post—away from New York. Morgenthau was enraged and complained to the FBI. Hoover reacted again—the three agents were told they had only thirty-six hours to report to their new posts. What effect this demonstration of Cohn's influence had on prospective witnesses is not known.

I asked Louis Nichols about his recollection of the incident.

NICHOLS: "Here's what happened. Cohn told me— See, I testified on Roy's behalf in that case, and his defense lawyer has been kind enough to say that he thought my testimony was the one thing that brought about Roy's acquittal. And Roy got a raw deal in that case, I can tell you that without going into detail. Roy told me about the affidavits the agents signed and it didn't sound right to me. I said nothing to Roy at the time, but the more I thought about it, the more convinced I became that there was something fishy here. To begin with, a Bureau agent is supposed to state the facts and not become an advocate, and not express opinions, but to stick to the facts within his personal knowledge. So I called the Bureau and asked if they had seen these. They had no knowledge of them. So they checked into it, and I heard nothing more about it until I saw the story in the newspapers."

Did you go to Hoover's office and raise hell?

NICHOLS: "No, no. I called but I didn't talk to Hoover about it. I wouldn't do that to begin with, because that's not the way things are done. I just thought this sounded unusual to me, it represented a departure from policy as I knew it in the Bureau, and I felt duty bound to say something, and so I mentioned it. The next thing I heard was the story I read in the papers about Morgenthau spouting off and the transfer of the agents. That's the unvarnished truth of what happened there. That's all there was to it. The Bureau knew nothing about it, and my recollection is that the Agent in Charge in New York knew nothing about it. These guys were just tools of Morgenthau."

COHN: "I had no relationship with Mr. Hoover after my troubles with Morgenthau. There was an almost complete break-off of any contact between us very simply because I think we both understood that by virtue of his official position I would in no way want him to be embarrassed. In fact, he supplied some of the manpower in my first trial which did Morgenthau's bidding in the case against me, and I understood it, it's nothing I ever minded. And that was it. I saw nothing of him until my vindication. I just kept a million miles away from him. We would exchange Christmas greetings, I would always get a little something from him at Christmas even during this period, but I had absolutely no contact with him for a nine-year period.

"He was not a man you could approach on that basis. Most people who knew him had so much respect for his integrity that without a word ever being said, people who regarded themselves as his friends whenever embarrassing situations arose would just stay away from him and avoid the confrontation of his having to be the one to caution them to stay away."

You say your legal problems lasted nine years?

COHN: "He took a shot at me three times. Three different indictments, and, I think, a total of about twenty-six counts, every charge you can ever think of, one trial in 1964, one in 1969, one in 1971, and I was unanimously acquitted by juries on each and every charge, on every count. As the juries found, there was no basis for any of the charges."

Many have written that McCarthy had ready access to FBI files. What about the summary of FBI reports on individuals involved in the Fort

Monmouth case—that is, the Army-McCarthy hearings—how did you get hold of the FBI summary?

COHN: "Tom Wicker and others always get the idea that FBI reports figured in various of the McCarthy hearings because McCarthy and Hoover were close friends, and that Hoover was leaking documents and information to McCarthy, or to me, or to the committee. The answer is no, and the best way to illustrate it is by saying how that information came about. Here's how it worked. If Mr. Hoover has a report on a security risk or a loyalty risk—take Harry Dexter White—that doesn't stay sealed within the FBI. Mr. Hoover would disseminate copies of that to the White House, to the Treasury Department, to the Defense Department, to the National Security Council, to any place with which White was involved.

"The FBI stuff we got came from the various agencies to which it was disseminated, usually from people not on very high levels. Usually, it's the file clerk, or it's the sergeant who hates Commies, the sergeant who gets mad at the captain. Every single document we got, I can tell you the name of the person we got it from. In fact, a couple of months ago, I ran across the fellow who gave us most of the Fort Monmouth information. He's working for an advertising agency in New York now. He was in the Defense Department then. We got information on the Perez case from a general in the Army. All the FBI stuff we got, we got third-hand, either copied-over or synopsis reports from agencies. In all my entire period with the committee, we never got one single piece of paper directly or indirectly from Mr. Hoover, or the FBI, or with the FBI's knowledge or approval.

"Anyone who knows Mr. Hoover, knows that—forget integrity for now —Mr. Hoover was always much too careful to get involved in anything like that. Never would he dream of letting a copy of a document go to a Joe McCarthy or to anybody else. Mr. Hoover was much too careful a person and had his own guard up much too much ever to let anything like that happen. And, as I say, I'm not talking about his integrity, which was monumental; but, strictly speaking, his own self-protective device was so strong that he just didn't let himself get into these binds. That's why he lasted fifty years.

"His towering integrity has now emerged so strongly in the whole Watergate situation. It turns out that Mr. Hoover, who the liberals have spent all these years knocking and criticizing, was the one who quietly and quickly put the death knell on the Plumbers' plan and things like that. It really fascinates me to see how the liberals today are suddenly discovering that Mr. Hoover was a defender of civil rights and of people's rights rather than some kind of a police-state terrorist which they tried to portray him to be, and it's too bad he couldn't have gotten some of this recognition from them during his lifetime instead of now when his unsung acts have come to the fore in the Watergate situation."

"I've Got the Bums on the Run"

This interview was conducted on the back seat of a station wagon going to downtown New York City in late afternoon traffic. If Cohn was breathing I couldn't detect it. His eyes, hooded and flat, seemed unaware of the life and noise around him as the barrage of words flew from his almost motionless lips, bullets hitting my ears with perfectly equal emphasis, an unnerving performance. To break the tempo, I asked him if it were true that Hoover was "crazy" about Joe McCarthy, as Hoover's old crony George E. Allen had told me.

COHN: "Well, I think that's overstating it. I think he had a kind of— Didn't Mr. Hoover say it himself once: 'He's a Marine, he's Irish . . .'* That's about the way Mr. Hoover felt."

I've heard that Hoover used to give McCarthy hell for his drinking, for not doing his homework.

COHN: "I think that's substantially correct. Socially, by the way, they were both the same kind of people, they liked quietness. Almost never went to big parties. I don't think Mr. Hoover went to three Washington parties a year, and McCarthy wouldn't—he hated it. He hated anything where you had to put on a necktie and talk to some charming ladies on either side of you about the state of the United Nations or something like that. They were guys who would go much more for four or five friends getting together. Mr. Hoover used to love to come up and have Mrs. McCarthy, Jeannie, do the cooking. He used to come up with Tolson and there would be just four or five people and everybody could let—could exchange confidences and just sort of have a relaxed evening. Mr. Hoover

---

* In an interview in the San Diego *Evening Tribune*, Hoover said, "McCarthy is a former Marine. He was an amateur boxer. He's Irish. Combine those, and you're going to have a vigorous individual, who is not going to be pushed around. . . . I never knew Senator McCarthy until he came to the Senate. I've come to know him well, officially, and personally. I view him as a friend and believe he so views me."

had a very lively sense of humor. He was very sharp, nothing ever went over him, and there was nothing you could say in front of him that wouldn't come back and hit you ten years later. It always amazed me that a man as busy, with as many facts flowing through his mind, his retentiveness in later years for little things that happened was absolutely incredible."

What do you think happened to Hoover at the end?

COHN: "He probably started—his fuse started getting a little short. The intensity of the liberal attacks on him was so stepped up, and don't forget Hoover was a controlled outspoken person and he just stopped controlling his outspokenness, that's all. He was always outspoken. I mean, if he was sitting here with you and me, and we mentioned a person he didn't like, he'd say, 'That no-good so-and-so,' not using swear words but talk-tough words: 'I wouldn't trust that bum as far as you could throw this building,' or 'He's doublecrossed every friend he's ever had,' that sort of thing. The last words he spoke to me were about the liberal attack. 'I've got the bums on the run, and I'm staying right where I am,' he told me. Six days later he was dead."

"He Used the [Communist] Party as an Instrument"

Later I asked William C. Sullivan and John P. Mohr, who was the FBI's number four man for many years, about Hoover and McCarthy and Communism.

SULLIVAN: "We were the ones who made the McCarthy hearings possible. We fed McCarthy all the material that he was using."

Are you sure of that?

SULLIVAN: "I know what we were doing, I worked on it myself. At the same time, we were telling the public that we had nothing to do with it. I can't tell you specifically right now what we gave him, but we gave him an abundance of material. For example, McCarthy called in at the time he gave his speech in Wheeling, West Virginia, saying that there were Communists in the State Department, and I saw the memorandum that Hoover dictated on McCarthy's call. And he quoted McCarthy as saying, 'This caused headlines all over the country and I never expected it and now I need some evidence to back up my statement that there are [fifty-seven]* Communists in the State Department.' Well, so Hoover says, 'Review the files and get anything you can for him.' We didn't have enough evidence to show that there was a single Communist in the State Department, let alone [fifty-seven] cases."

Was Hoover sincere about the threat of the Communist Party?

SULLIVAN: "No, of course he wasn't sincere. He knew the Party didn't amount to a damn. But he used the Party as an instrument to get appropriations from Congress. Congressmen like John Rooney, for God's sake, did an enormous disservice to the country by eating out of Hoover's hand. He'd give him everything Hoover wanted. Everything for nothing. The Communist Party in this country has never amounted to anything since the late 1940s and yet it was built up as though the damn thing was a great threat to the country. It amounted to nothing."

MOHR: "As far as Communism is concerned, Hoover's view was the same on the day he died as it was back in the days of Palmer's Red menace. He was very consistent on that. Sullivan thought the Communist Party, USA, was no longer a threat, that we ought to forget about them. Personally, I think the Party was brought practically to its knees, but I don't think you should forget them any more than you'd forget anything that's a cancer or a sore on the country. I don't think you need to spend a great deal of time on them like we once did. Sullivan thought we ought to go out in the press and take credit for destroying the Party.

"One of the things that rankled Sullivan was that Hoover kept needling him about that speech at Williamsburg when he said that the Communist Party was practically defunct. Sure, it was a weak organization, but Hoover's contention was that, by God, with Communists you don't need to have a great big organization, that they're still a threat even when they're small, and that's true. They had a way of growing under certain conditions—at one time they reached close to two hundred thousand members in this country during the Depression."

* McCarthy launched his campaign of vilification at Wheeling on the evening of February 9, 1950, when he announced to a group of Republican ladies at a Lincoln's birthday dinner that "I have here in my hand fifty-seven cases of individuals who would appear to be either card-carrying members or certainly loyal to the Communist Party, but who nevertheless are still helping shape our foreign policy." When McCarthy repeated his charges on the floor of the Senate on February 20, the list of Communists had grown to eighty-one. It was clear from the debate that McCarthy had forgotten just how many suspects he had named at Wheeling.

"A Dossier on Every Member of Congress"

Until his re-election defeat in 1972, Emanuel Celler was chairman of the House Judiciary Committee, a position he had held for twenty-two of the forty years he served on the committee. When I interviewed Celler at his Park Avenue law offices in July 1974, he assured me that Hoover would not have altered the course of Watergate if he had lived.

CELLER: "I don't think there would have been any change at all in the whole business. Hoover naturally rolled with the punch, as it were, and he sought to placate every administration in which he served. Of course, there were occasions when he showed his independence, but in general, he acted more or less in accordance with the wishes of the administration."

What was the source of his alleged power then?

CELLER: "The source of his power derived from the fact that he was the head of an agency that in turn had tremendous power, power of surveillance, power of control over the lives and destinies of every man in the nation. He had a dossier on every member of Congress and every member of the Senate."

Were the members aware of it?

CELLER: "The members of the House certainly were. He had no right to have such dossiers. But he had them, no question about it."

You think he had special agents collecting that kind of information?

CELLER: "Well, he probably had a staff that clipped newspapers all the time, from all over the country, and the items were placed in the individual folder of anyone of any consequence or importance."

Would that explain why John Rooney's House Appropriations Committee gave him all the money he ever requested?

CELLER: "I wouldn't say that influenced John Rooney—Rooney and I were very close—but Hoover got almost anything he wanted from John Rooney by way of appropriations.

"Hoover was violently anti-Communist and he reaped the harvest of public good will during the McCarthy era when he tracked down all sorts of ultraliberals and those he felt were Commies or pseudo Commies; and, of course, that met with popular approval. I think he was sincere about it. He didn't want to do that just for the exercise of power. He believed there was evident danger, particularly in the McCarthy period; but remember back in the thirties, you know, Henry Ford and Father Coughlin were very stridently proclaiming against Communism and sought to find Communists in every nook and cranny."

Do you think the nation was in danger?

CELLER: "I don't think from hindsight that we were in danger, but from their point of view they felt we were in danger. I don't think Hoover ever changed his mind about that. I don't think he ever felt remorse about his going after an individual and persecuting him.

"In the Rosenberg case, I don't think the evidence was conclusive that they were guilty, and I don't think they should have been given the death penalty. I think the best that should have been done was to give them life sentences because there was some doubt there. And, of course, recent revelations seem to indicate that what was passed on to the Russians didn't amount to a hill of beans."

But, as you say, it is hindsight.

CELLER: "Of course, you must consider that this was all a reflection of that anti-Communist spirit that pervaded the country at that time, and undoubtedly had its effect upon Hoover himself, had its effect upon the jury, had an effect upon the judge."

What kind of man was J. Edgar Hoover?

CELLER: "He was a very pleasant man, very affable, very social-minded. You could talk to him and enjoy his conversation. He was very kindly disposed in his conversation, he never was violent in his talks. You could spend a pleasant evening with him. And yet I think that he felt that his job was a highly important one and that he wanted to track down thieves and crooks and those who were a possible menace to the security of the nation.

"He was very important to the nation when you consider what happened during his tenure of office, when you consider what happened to his counterpart in other countries, in Fascist Italy and Hitler's Germany, and considering the success that was attributed to those who were in the same position that Hoover was in this country, then you get that impression of his high degree of importance.

"He held in the palm of his hand the reputation of many people, and a good many of the members of the House and the Senate and the officials had a lot of skeletons in their closet. A lot of these men were not pure and righteous; they probably committed wrongs too, and it fed Hoover. It fed his tapping of their telephones and stuff like that. That's what made him so feared and made him loom large in the eyes of the public."

Do you sincerely believe that he tapped the phones of congressmen?

CELLER: "There's no question about it in my mind."

Wouldn't that be terribly dangerous?

CELLER: "There's no doubt about it being dangerous—it was illegal. He felt that the end justified the means. He felt that it was important that he do these things for the good of the country. And despite all that, I felt that he was a very nice fellow; our relations were very kindly all the time. Hoover was a good official but he went a little too far. That was the trouble with him, he reached out for a little more power than he was entitled to. But he was not a free agent. He never wanted to do anything contrary to the White House."

He gave Bobby Kennedy a lot of trouble.

CELLER: "Because Bobby Kennedy gave him a lot of trouble. They wanted to get rid of Hoover. But it was political dynamite to get rid of him and they didn't try it. They were afraid to let him go. They hated him, had no use for him at all. But Hoover never ran counter to what the President really wanted. I heard Johnson say one time that he wanted men around him who were loyal enough to kiss his ass in Macy's window and say it smelled like a rose. That's the way it goes usually in government."

"He's Got to Be Good"

In April 1971, at a time when the level of criticism against Hoover had reached perhaps the highest peak of his career, Congressman Hale Boggs, then House Majority Leader, accused the FBI of tapping the telephones of congressmen and senators. Boggs charged that the Bureau had adopted the "tactics of the Soviet Union and Hitler's Gestapo," and he concluded by asking for Hoover's resignation. This unprecedented state of affairs was underscored by the meager response of Boggs's colleagues to rush to the Director's defense. But one who did respond was Congressman Lawrence J. Hogan, a former special agent for ten years, who denounced Boggs's attack as a "red herring." Knowing by now pretty well how Hoover retaliated against his enemies, I asked Hogan how he responded to a friendly gesture.

HOGAN: "I defended the FBI because I know how zealous they are at protecting individual rights and liberties, and I know the individuals are the best we've got in America. And I got nothing to gain or lose. I don't need the FBI. I did it because I thought it was the right thing to do. Now, Tom Bishop [a special agent who worked in press relations]—I saw him at a banquet one night and he said, 'The Director is very grateful for the support that you've given him, the fact that you defended the FBI, and he's very grateful. Why don't you come down and see him sometime?' And I said, 'Oh, I don't have to do that, Tom. When I think the FBI is right, I'll defend them; when I don't, I won't defend them. I don't have to go down to see the Director to do that. I'm going to do it anyway.' And he said, 'Well, he'd really like to see you.' I said, 'Okay, I'll do it sometime.' Almost a year passed and I hadn't done anything about it and I saw Tom Bishop again at a banquet, and he said, 'You really ought to come down to see the Director.' So I said I'd do it.

"I made the appointment and then something more important to me came up and I had to cancel it. We set a new date and they were going crazy down there, they were saying, 'We want a firm date as to when he is going to come, and we hope he can come this time and not cancel it.' I didn't know why they were so upset, aside from the fact, you know, that when you go to see J. Edgar Hoover, you don't break appointments.

"So I called my wife, I think, the day before and asked her if she wanted to go, and she said she would, and then I had my secretary call Bishop, and that kind of threw him into a panic as to how many were going to be there. Well, we went down on the appointed day and we chatted and he expressed his thanks for my vigorous support of the FBI, and how everybody in the FBI was grateful that I was always ready to defend the FBI when it was unjustly criticized. I remember one thing he said when I commented that so much of the vicious criticism was so unwarranted, and he kind of brushed that aside, and he said, 'If some of these people stopped criticizing me, I'd be worried that somehow I wasn't doing my job right.' We chatted for five or ten minutes, then we had black-and-white and color pictures taken, and then he reached back and gave me this beautiful large plaque you see there on the wall, and I was completely astounded because I had not the slightest inkling that anything like this was in the works. Which explains why they were so anxious about knowing the date in advance. They made it special, with the FBI seal on it, and it reads, 'Presented to the Honorable Lawrence J. Hogan in gratitude for his outstanding support of law enforcement and the FBI. J. Edgar Hoover, March 14, 1972.' "

It was quite an elaborate compliment.

HOGAN: "I was impressed with the fact that he and the FBI would do that, because the FBI is really very special to me."

Has your FBI background been useful to you in your political career?

HOGAN: "Absolutely, absolutely. Probably one of the large factors in my getting elected was because the people were presold on the FBI. Here I've been out of the FBI since 1953, and every time I go make a speech someplace, somebody says, 'You spent ten years with the FBI.' I got three degrees, I've been a successful businessman, I've been in Congress four years, but the thing they always say is 'He's a former FBI agent.' That's one of the biggest things to my credit, and I'm sure that's because of the high regard people have for the FBI. And I know people voted for me for that reason, because they said, 'If he was in the FBI, I know he's honest, I know he's capable, and he's got to be good.' "

"Number Two to a Man Half His Age"

There is no official title to describe the White House duties of Dave Powers during the Kennedy Administration. He was the "sweet Mick" (Ken O'Donnell was the "terse Mick") who put John Kennedy to bed every night and got him up every morning. "I probably spent more time with John Kennedy while he was President for two years and ten months and two days than anyone else," Powers told me in June 1974 when I saw him at the Federal Record Center in Waltham, Massachusetts, which now temporarily houses the Kennedy papers.

POWERS: "Mr. Hoover had a meeting with the President on the first day of November [sic], because I went to mass with the President on All Saints' Day, which is November first, and I remember bringing—it was off the record—I remember bringing J. Edgar over to the White House. Let's see [hurriedly scans an appointment book], we had an off-record meeting on Vietnam October thirtieth—Rusk, McNamara, Harriman, McCone, Taylor, Forrestal. Then we went to Philadelphia for a fund-raiser. October thirty-first, the President signed the Mental Retardation Bill. Here it is! Thursday, October thirty-first, 1963: Lunch, off the record, with the Honorable J. Edgar Hoover."

Why would it be off the record?

POWERS: "Well, actually, we used to give the Washington *Post* and the *Star* a list of all the President's appointments, and this way, you see, it wouldn't be announced that he was meeting with those people."

Would you keep a record of it as far as his Administration was concerned?

POWERS: "Exactly. Ken O'Donnell and I had the job of keeping the President on time. Every minute of the President's day in the White House is accounted for in these books. Now, when the President would leave the White House, the Secret Service would have the detailed list of all his appointments, arrivals and departures."

Would President Kennedy tape some of his telephone conversations?

POWERS: "No. Well, for instance, when he was talking to Governor Barnett about Meredith going into Mississippi, he said, 'We are— I am taping this.' And the Governor said, 'So am I.'"

Why do you think Kennedy reappointed Hoover the moment he became President-elect?

POWERS: "Well, continuity in government—people were probably wondering about the difference between Kennedy and Eisenhower. The President knew that he could share in the experiences of both of these men [Dulles and Hoover], and he knew that they were honorable enough that if a month later, or a year later, he wanted them to leave, they would, but it was giving him an opportunity for a peaceful transition. I think maybe, I *know* that he had a real long meeting— The inauguration was January twentieth— Well, February twenty-third, his brother Bobby and J. Edgar came over about ten in the morning and stayed until eleven-thirty. It was a real, real long meeting. Now, a month later, and then each year after that, J. Edgar came over to attend the ceremony for the presentation of the Young American Medals for Bravery. He was very, very interested in that and he and the Attorney General and the President would be in the pictures with each of these boys and girls that had done something outstanding during the year and they'd be there with members of their family. And J. Edgar took great delight in this participation. It was always done in the Rose Garden.

"Now, I can remember several times when he came over on off-record meetings and I would meet him and bring him to what we called the Mansion, which is the living section of the White House. The President would have meetings up there rather than in his office if he wanted to meet somebody off record, so that they would not be spotted coming in or out by the press that hung outside the White House. Sometimes they'd come in the gate the tourists used on the public tours, and then be met there and escorted upstairs to the Mansion.

"J. Edgar was familiar with the fact that I was a baseball buff and we were walking over one time talking about memories and I remember saying to him, 'Well, there are only ten numbers, zero to nine, and the only thing that's important is the order you put them in.' I said, 'For instance, Ty Cobb has a lifetime average of three hundred and sixty-seven for twenty-four years. Now, I could not make a mistake on three-six-seven with these three numbers because no one would have batted seven-six-three and no one would have batted six-seven-three, so it had to be three-six-seven.' And, you know, we talked about these things, and it seemed to me that the President and Bobby had told him what a great memory that Dave Powers had. And we went along and he was asking about different things. I didn't know him that well, and I wanted him to be comfortable, and he was a nice man to meet. When he smiled, he had a charming manner."

Was he a little stiff?

POWERS: "Only the first time, then after that— I can remember meeting him maybe seven times in the White House. I'd say he had three off-record dinners. October thirty-first, 1963, he had a long lunch with the President and Bobby, and, as you know, three weeks later we went to Dallas. Their meetings, their luncheons were all awfully long when they had them."

Who initiated them?

POWERS: "I would say that the President did, but Ken O'Donnell could probably tell you more accurately. The President was great for this sort of thing. I know that the Director was not a cabinet member, but after the President had a few cabinet meetings, and all of his conversation would either be with Rusk or with McNamara while the other cabinet members just sat there, he realized that it was a ridiculous thing to call a group of men together when you're only talking to one or two, so then he set up these individual meetings whenever he wanted to know something specific about the different departments."

Why did the President feel he had to talk directly to Hoover when in fact his brother was Hoover's boss?

POWERS: "Well, he wanted this great balance. The President had a great understanding and he knew how tough it was for J. Edgar Hoover to feel that he was number two to a man half his age; the President cared about these things."

Would the President talk to you about these problems?

POWERS: "Well, you're not always talking about what the President said, you know what I mean? I'd be there when he'd be talking, like— The President hated to be alone, and when Jackie would be at the Cape in the summer with the children, especially the last summer of his life when Patrick was born and then later died, I had dinner with the President practically every night, and I'd be with him up until the time he went to bed. I'd be there when he'd be talking to these other men on the phone, and he might be talking to Bobby and say, 'Well, I talked to J. Edgar Hoover,' or he might be talking to Rusk and say, 'I talked to McNamara about it.' All of this sort of thing, see. But I was just there as a friend and it did not concern me unless the President wanted it to concern me, but I know how he cared about things like that, because he felt that the attorneys general up to that time had allowed J. Edgar Hoover to run the show. If the President felt you knew that much more about anything than he did, he wanted to talk to you about it. That's what made the man great.

"During those long summer evenings when Jackie was away, we'd have a second swim, and then he'd do his back exercises, and he'd insist that the help put his dinner on a hotplate, and so we'd both go into the White House kitchen and wait on ourselves. The President was a meat-and-po-tato man. He liked a daiquiri before dinner and then he got to like a little wine with his meal. Then we'd sit out on the Truman balcony and talk about political campaigns, and sometimes I'd tell him about the things I used to do when I was a kid, and he'd be greatly amused. He'd say, 'God, that must have been great!' And when we went back home, I'd show him the hills we'd coasted down or beaches we went to, and he'd say, 'God, that must have been great fun!' You see, his bringing-up was a little too fancy. He went to Choate and then Harvard and he never roughed it as much as he might have liked to.

"That last summer, we talked a lot about the coming election. In fact the last two days of his life, we actually were campaigning in Texas. It was one of the states he felt he could win. The weekend before, we had been campaigning in Florida. He spoke three times in Tampa and twice in Miami. But the thing that was so great, he'd be talking about past campaigns and, you know, I can remember one time he asked how a fellow was, his name was Matt Loftus, and he ran a tavern in Charlestown, and I happened to mention that he had had a heart attack. And we were in the pool and he picked up the phone and he said to the White House operator, 'Will you please get me Matt Loftus in Charlestown, Massachusetts.' When I think of it, the President loved the White House phones. I thought that what he would have missed most when he left there was the service of the White House phones. You'd give them a name and they'd come up with that person. And he loved that. And he talked to Matt that night, and that's what made him great, because he cared, and that's what we'd talk about those long evenings, about certain campaigns. When he had problems, he'd talk to someone who could solve them."

Would he watch television in the evening?

POWERS: "Saturday afternoon we'd watch the college football game and Sunday afternoon we'd watch the pro game, but he just wasn't someone who would have the TV on that much. The President was a nine-to-one man in the office. After his last morning appointment, we'd hit the pool, and then he'd put his robe on and go up to eat—he liked to take his lunch in bed. And if he took a bit of a snooze, fine, and then we'd have him back in the office until seven or seven-thirty. And he was a great tub man, even shaved sitting down in the tub, and we'd have papers for him to sign, and he'd have a board across the top, where he had his razor and mirror, and he'd sign the papers. He found a tub so relaxing."

It's my understanding that the word got to Hoover that he was going to get dumped after the 1964 election. Any truth to it?

POWERS: "The answer to that is that the word would not be 'dumped.' The President would never, never use that word. He would have been seventy years old and it would have been time for him to retire."

But he didn't want to retire. Wouldn't it have caused a conflict?

POWERS: "Not really, because— The President would have thought that 'conflict' was too strong a word. It would be a difference of opinion, he would have felt, which maybe requires a little more work, and maybe that could have been what he was talking to him about that three weeks before the assassination when he saw him. But the President never mentioned any of that to me."

"Only a Politician Hears the Nuance"

As President Kennedy's appointments secretary, Kenneth P. O'Donnell exercised far more influence than is normally associated with that position. Among his many duties was that of liaison with the FBI, but his relationship with the FBI went back to the time when Robert F. Kennedy was chief counsel for the McClellan Committee.

O'DONNELL: When I went to Washington in 1957, it was unknown to John Kennedy that I was coming. I went to Washington as assistant chief counsel—assistant to the chief counsel—of the McClellan Committee. Bobby Kennedy had, unknown to himself, fallen into the Dave Beck case, which evolved into the Jimmy Hoffa case, which evolved into organized crime, which eventually evolved into the biggest committee operation in the history of Washington. At the time Bobby called me, we had just taken over the state again. I'm a politician, happy with it. I did not want to go to Washington, but suddenly a case that had four people on it mushroomed into seventy-five people. The Senate suddenly appropriated all this money and Bobby wanted someone there he could be sure of, who would be his friend and watch things when he went away on trips. And that's how I got there. John Kennedy was the most surprised man in the world when he found out I was on the committee, because he didn't want me on the committee. He wanted me back in Massachusetts.

"We had a very frank discussion, he and Robert Kennedy and I. Of course, Bobby and I were close social and personal friends and I just felt he needed help. 'But,' John said, 'I need you in 1958.' He was coming up for re-election. 'You're going back to Massachusetts, and you're going to work on my campaign, right?' And I said, 'That's what I want to do, that's right.' And Bobby said, 'Right.' And that was it. So it was very clear that I was going to be there until the 1958 campaign and then after the 1958 campaign. He was running for President after 1956. We were all very clear on that. He had made his decision after the 1956 Presidential election, and that was going to be my job."

Was Hoover interested in what the McClellan Committee was doing in terms of labor unions and organized crime?

O'DONNELL: "Yes, we had a fellow who ultimately became my contact with the FBI when I went to the White House, and his name was Courtney Evans, who was assigned by the FBI as our liaison. If we wanted any name checks or anything else, his job was to report to Bobby but he really was reporting to me and I would report to Bobby, who was chief counsel.

"Now let me jump ahead to the day after the 1960 election. I had worked with John Kennedy all the time now, I traveled with him every day of his life. Bobby Kennedy was running the campaign at home; communications was Bobby Kennedy to me to him. And we just developed a relationship which is very strong on both sides. Until now I never got appointed in my life until this second, and I was never on a Kennedy payroll in my life. The election was over and I was sitting in a hotel room in The Yachtsman [in Hyannis Port] with my wife, and a man knocked on the door and said, 'My name is Peterson and I'm the head of the Secret Service detail and I've just talked to the President-elect and he said from now on I do everything with you, and I deal with you directly and not with him.' Which means absolutely nothing to me because I'm totally ignorant of the whole operation of the government anyway as far as the White House is concerned.

"I said, 'Well, I don't know what it means but fine. What do you want to talk to me about?' And he gives me the deployment of the agents and where they are, what they're doing and the whole setup for the security of the President-elect. And he said, 'He would like you to come over at three o'clock this afternoon to discuss the trip,' and I nod intelligently and say, 'Fine.' And the next knock on the door is Courtney Evans, who is the FBI liaison. He'd flown up that day and said, 'The Director has told me that he has talked to the President-elect and from now on I am to be the one—'

Now he and I had worked together on the committee, so I said, 'Fine.' I don't know what I'm going to do but at three o'clock I go over and he still doesn't say anything. He said, 'We're going to Florida. I think we deserve a few days off. You know, we've got to put this government together and I want to do it away from everybody. So you just take it over, that's your job now.' That's how I found out I was going to be in his Administration. To be perfectly honest with you, I wanted to go home. I don't think anybody knew what they were doing. It was a terrible campaign. But when somebody comes over and says, 'You're in charge of the Secret Service and the FBI,' all of a sudden you don't know what the heck they're even talking about, it comes as a little bit of a shock. My poor little wife, she didn't know what the hell— She wants me to come home, she hasn't seem me for three years, and his first order to me is 'Get the plane revved up, we're going to Florida. Just you and Dave Powers. I don't want anybody else.'

"Before we left for Palm Beach, the President made five appointments, again not to my knowledge. I became appointments secretary, Salinger was named press secretary, and Ted Sorensen was special counsel, and he reappointed Dulles to head the CIA and Hoover the FBI. That's the only appointments that were made at that time, and then we left for Florida."

In his book A Thousand Days *Arthur Schlesinger said that John Kennedy was advised by friends not to reappoint Hoover and Dulles, and then surprised everybody with the announcement.*

O'DONNELL: "No, he never discussed it with any of us, and I don't care what anybody says. I think he probably discussed it with Bobby, but I think he made up his mind that the victory was slender, that there should be some continuity in government, and as your first step to gain some confidence—we're not going to rock the boat at this moment. Remember, he didn't discuss many things with many people, you know. He made a lot of the decisions. But I know he wouldn't discuss it with Schlesinger or Sorensen in a million years. At that moment, he would not discuss it with me. Six months later, he'd discuss it with me, but at that moment, he wouldn't. Because I am what I think he thought was a very good politician, friend, and he knew I'd want to do the practical things that must be done in politics, but as far as discussing who's going to run the FBI or who's going to be chief of staff, he wouldn't think of talking to me about that—and rightfully."

When did he decide that Bobby would be Attorney General?

O'DONNELL: "Let's go to history, see, because it's so distorted. First, the New York *Times* ran a story which is true, that the Attorney General's job was offered to Abe Ribicoff. And Bill Lawrence was playing golf with Abe Ribicoff at the Palm Beach Golf Club, and he told Lawrence that he'd been offered the job and he was thinking about it, and Lawrence wrote it up in a front page story in the New York *Times*. And Ribicoff said, very practically and properly, 'As I see it, the biggest issue that's coming along in the next few years is civil rights, and I can't think of anything worse than an Irish Catholic President and a Jewish Attorney General telling those Southerners to put blacks in the schools. And I think I'm a lousy choice. I want to be in the cabinet but that's not the position I think I should be in to help the President, or help me either.' So Bobby was not his first choice for Attorney General.

"Bobby did not want to be Attorney General. Bobby and I spent days walking around Washington together. He really didn't know what to do. The President did not want him in the White House, because he felt he was going to have an ambivalence—a conflict really between what was his staff, which is me, and Bobby, and that the press is going to play on two sides. He called it the *éminence grise*—you know, somebody that you could go to besides the President. Well, he didn't want anybody to be President but him. So he didn't want anybody in the White House that was speaking with the authority of the President. When he spoke— Anything I said, I spoke for him. And that's the way he wanted it. And I didn't speak for him unless I knew what he wanted. We were so close that I could understand that, and he and I never had any quarrel in our life. Because he knew where he was going and I knew where he was going, and I knew his mind as well as he knew mine. He knows I'm not going to screw him. If I made a mistake, I made a mistake, we're not above that. That he'd understand, and he'd chew me out and that's it, but it's not something to hurt him.

"The President wanted Bobby with him because they loved each other as brothers, and Bobby's another that's never going to screw him. When you're running the Presidency of the United States, you'd like to have a guy around that at least when he says that two and two is four, he's not running out to the bank and chiseling on you. Whatever Bobby said, right or wrong or indifferent, was in John Kennedy's interest. That he understood. And when Abe turned it down, Bobby didn't want it, and he didn't want to give it to him, but he wanted Bobby in Washington. Well, Bobby was the best Attorney General we ever had, in my judgment. Bobby you could fight with, see. He knew what he didn't know, and the wonderful thing about the Kennedys is you could fight with them. They did not say they knew everything. They come on pretty strong, but you say, 'You're full of bull,' and they want to know why you said that: 'Why am I full of bull?' And I could say to John Kennedy, 'You're full of bull because of the following facts,' and the only reason he liked me was because he knew, no matter what he said, I'm not afraid to disagree with him, and after a decision is made I'm going to carry it out."

Before accepting the Attorney Generalship, didn't Bobby feel Hoover out on it?

O'DONNELL: "That is true. I was there. Well, to tell you the truth, I was walking around the building with him when he went up to see J. Edgar Hoover, and I think Bobby was more—less political than me, shall we say. Words meant a little more to me as a politician than they meant to him as a —so straightforward a guy as you can't believe. I got the words. He advised him to take it, but if I listened to the words carefully, he was hoping he wouldn't."

How did you arrive at that conclusion?

O'DONNELL: "Only a politician hears words, see, the nuance of a word. I said, 'Bobby, just tell me exactly what he said,' and he told me, and I knew Hoover wouldn't want him. He doesn't want the Attorney General to be more important than him. He's never had one. And he couldn't want Bobby to have it, he couldn't want that. But you can't say to the President's brother, 'Don't take the job,' because then Bobby would be alerted to it right away. But I said to him, 'He doesn't want you. Now you understand that?' But he wouldn't listen to me. I wanted him to run for the United States Senate, but he said, 'I'm running on my brother's name.' He'd have to be named first by the Governor to fill John's seat, which was not a problem, but he doesn't want to be named to anything.

"You've got to look at us going into the government, knowing nothing about the White House, knowing nothing about the powers available, knowing nothing about what they do, and all in love with the President ourselves. We don't want to hurt him. I go into what appears to be a very innocuous job, so nobody is going to complain about who is the appointments secretary, nobody is going to complain about Sorensen being a speech writer, but when you take your brother— And Bobby loved his brother so much that he didn't want to hurt him, see? And at the same time he knew that he was almost essential, that he had to be there. There is nothing that Bobby said that wasn't out to help the President and help the country.

"Of course, you may be getting some misguided information. Now we are sitting in a place where we get judgments from all over the government, from all over the country. Bobby doesn't have that. He's working with the Justice Department and he hears about judges and crimes, dealing with two committees in Congress on appropriations. But, I mean, I've got to sit there and pick up the telephone— There are ten cabinet officers and they've got ten problems, and on top of it all you've got the Soviet Union, you've got the crisis in Berlin, you've got Cuba, you've got the Chinese, you've got Latin America, you've got the Congress of the United States, the regulatory agencies. It isn't as easy— They keep thinking it's kind of easy and that's what Bobby and I used to argue about. I'd say, 'It isn't just that easy that you make one guy happy up in the Judiciary Department and anger fourteen guys somewhere else. I have to call every day, and they're calling your brother every day and yelling and screeching about a dam out in Idaho or something else. We got to take the whole thing and put it together; you don't have to do that.'

"You see, it goes like this. A senator says, 'I want Joe Blow to be the judge in the district.' All right. And Bobby has him checked out and says he's not qualified. And I'm saying, 'Who says so?' 'The American Bar Association.' 'So I didn't know they got elected. I thought *we* got elected.' Or appointing too many Democrats. I'd say, 'Well, Eisenhower appointed seventy-eight Republicans and two Democrats, but we're supposed to be fair though and be nice and even-handed and appoint fifty percent Republicans?' I said, 'No way!' I've got to deal with Bob Kerr, who's chairman of the Public Works Committee, chairman of the Appropriations Committee. Lyndon Johnson wants the judgeship in Texas and I got to live with him every day, the President has got to live with him every day, and what they do and what helps the Justice Department, really, that's a very minor part of our problem.

"For example, you've got George Smathers, say, and everybody's screeching because George Smathers votes against medical care for the aged. He told me two months ahead of time, he told the President. The bill lost by one vote, and the press all write a story and say, 'Well, here's the President's best friend.' He served in the House with him, he served in the Senate with him, they were great friends. He's still a good friend of mine. Bobby is screaming about it and the President said, 'Well, look, Bobby, *a* bill. He votes every time with us, and he's made a commitment to the AMA on this one and that's his business and not mine.' But we're just dealing with different worlds."

Bobby Had a Fetish on Organized Crime

When was the first time the President actually talked to Hoover?

O'DONNELL: "As I recall, he talked to Hoover in February [1961] for about an hour. It was just before the Bay of Pigs operation. I was in and out of it, but I didn't listen much. I knew about the Bay of Pigs, but the President didn't know I knew it. Bobby was present at the meeting. I would presume they were talking about the infiltration—you know, about which Cubans were Communists and which ones weren't. Miami has been flooded with Cubans. They all hate each other, so it isn't like saying which group is which group. I think they probably discussed what the FBI knew about who was in Miami. But the law distinctly says the FBI cannot go outside the United States. I took them with us on trips and they'd never been able to go on a Presidential trip before. I took an FBI agent with us on every trip because I'm trying to put the FBI and Secret Service together and make friends of them because they were at each other like this when I came in."

How did Courtney Evans work out as liaison?

O'DONNELL: "Let's put it like this. Every day Courtney Evans came over to see me. Every guy that goes in the government gets a name check, right? And his job was to deliver the checks and my job was to read the reports and report to the President before he made any appointments. If there was anything of any security nature that they were concerned about, Courtney Evans would bring it to me and I would give it to the President. But there was a direct line, Courtney Evans to me. That's because of the peculiar relationship. For the first time the Attorney General is the President's brother, and Bobby and I talked twelve times a day, so the reports that came to Bobby might be different than the reports that came to me because they think it's the same channel—and it was. It's a little confusing. But the Attorney General was in charge of the FBI when I was there. I was informed, and obviously if I wanted to call the Director I could call him, but I wouldn't call the Director. I'd call his boss, who was the Attorney General of the United States."

In other words, Courtney Evans was only a messenger?

O'DONNELL: "Well, we had a little special relationship with him. He'd deliver things that he thought I might have a little more knowledge on than maybe even the Attorney General might have, but he presumed I would then call Bobby, which I would do, and tell him what I knew in addition to what he knew, because the Secret Service obviously had some information and defense and intelligence agencies got some information also. The Attorney General, however, is a member of the National Security Council and so is privy to everything. As far as we were concerned, there just wasn't any conflict with the Bureau. Everything was available to us."

Then Hoover's access to the President was cut off?

O'DONNELL: "I'd say Mr. Hoover assumed that he was working for the Attorney General."

Was he unhappy?

O'DONNELL: "Very unhappy."

Did he complain about it?

O'DONNELL: "Never. I'll say this, the day they put a private line in—I know this for a fact—two members of the telephone company with an FBI agent present came into his office, which is the inner sanctum where nobody gets in, and they put a phone in just like that. And Hoover said, 'What's that?' And they said, 'The Attorney General would like a direct line to you.' And he said, 'Who authorized it?' And they said, 'The Attorney General.' And what do you say? Who do you call? In the old days, he might call Eisenhower, he might call Roosevelt—but who does he call now? The only guy he can call is me, right? And his answer is going to be loud and clear."

You mean no one could talk to the President without going through you?

O'DONNELL: "Nobody. Oh, it wouldn't be fair to say that. They could call Evelyn Lincoln, the President's secretary. But they would call me, whether it was Rusk or McNamara or anybody, it was just normal. I mean these were the channels you operate in, and the President operated in those channels. If they picked up the phone and called Mrs. Lincoln and said, 'I'd like to talk to the President,' they could get through. There was no problem with that, but they don't do well after they get there. Unless, of course, it's something very urgent."

One rumor that's been widely reported is that Bobby actually walked into Hoover's office one day when he was taking a nap.

O'DONNELL: "I wouldn't doubt it. And why not. I mean, it's like the President walking into my office. You're the boss, can't you walk into a guy's office? It just gets back to the crux of one thing—Bobby is the boss, and for the first time in Hoover's life he can't go over the boss's head."

Were you aware that Bobby was telling his people that Hoover wouldn't be around after 1964?

O'DONNELL: "Well, wouldn't he retire automatically at seventy? He'd have to submit his resignation, right? That's the law."

Would Bobby discuss his problems with the President?

O'DONNELL: "I'm not sure that Bobby had that many conversations with his brother, and I think if you want to go back a little bit, you'll find that we had a hell of a lot more problems than J. Edgar Hoover."

Bobby felt strongly about civil rights.

O'DONNELL: "That doesn't mean that's how his brother felt. Yes, Bobby was in it up to his eyeballs."

And organized crime?

O'DONNELL: "Organized crime, he's got a fetish on it. That does not say that his brother had one. His brother was spending his time saying, 'I hope the Russians don't hit us with nuclear weapons tomorrow morning.' Well, what the hell do you think you're thinking about every day when you walk in and you've got a cable that they broke through here or they're sending troops there, or there are missiles on their way to Cuba or Argentina might go Communist—you know, you've a few problems. Now Bobby, he's worried about his things, and his things he thinks are important to him, and when Walter Heller comes over, he's worried about the budget and economic recession, Arthur Goldberg is worried about a strike in the steel industry. And every one of these things can bring the government up or down or do something, right? So they all got their problems, and the fact that Bobby was his brother didn't mean that all he was thinking about was J. Edgar Hoover. He was so far down the list. I don't think the President and Bobby even discussed it, to be frank with you. Bobby took care of his own problems pretty good. He never went crying to anybody.

"Look, I think one of the greatest things that you've got to get—Bobby was my dearest, dearest friend, but this implication of Bobby's influence with his brother is rather overdone. This business about his being the number two guy. It probably started more trouble, but it was started by the press, not Bobby. It used to hurt Bobby. It killed Lyndon Johnson. It started the fight with Johnson and Bobby. But there was no number two man in Washington. There was only one number one man. Everybody else was second. Remember, Bobby was ten years younger than the President. So they didn't have that kind of relationship, and the President can't have a relationship; he's just too busy himself. Socially, Bobby had his friends, and the President had his. And ninety-nine percent of the time, I would be present when they met and it would be business, and he always called him Mr. President. I never heard Bobby call him Jack in my life after he was President.

"As far as Hoover is concerned, the President made the decision to keep him, and I don't know if Bobby had any influence on it or not. I think it made sense from the President's viewpoint. It would have been bad to retire Hoover, with the election being so close. It would have been a bad way to start off with the Southerners who were friendly with Hoover and some of the Congressmen who would have been concerned one way or another. Some fear him and some like him and we don't know which is which, but as far as what's going to happen when the President's reelected in 1964, there was no question in my mind that Mr. Hoover—that the law would not have been broken or changed or altered in any way whatsoever. He would have retired."

Would Kennedy have pushed the civil rights bill through the way Johnson did—was he that concerned about it?

O'DONNELL: "I think if history plays the game, he was much more concerned about it than Johnson ever was. I think if he had lived, you would have seen a filibuster, and this was why we were playing games with the tax bill, and this is where you get a confrontation with Bobby again—the tax bill and the civil rights bill. We wanted to get a tax bill first, as the President put it very succinctly, 'What good does it do a black to have his civil rights and no job?' All the economists in the country were saying, 'We need a tax cut to get this economy going again and to put people back to work.' And the first ones out of work when things get tough are the blacks. And he told Martin Luther King and a whole bunch of them, all the black leaders in the country, he brought them all into the White House, and he said, 'Boys, I know what you want, and you're going to get yelled at by your constituencies, and I'll take the rap for it. I just think the tax bill should come first. As soon as I get that off the hooks, then we'll go into civil rights, we'll have a filibuster, and I'm prepared to take the heat. And you can go out and tell everybody that it's me, that I'm doing it because I want the tax bill first. Now I think I'm right, I think my economists think I'm right, and it's going to put people to work. My brother doesn't think I'm right. He wants to go civil rights before the tax bill, and I think I'm going to do what I think is right.'

"And if you want to go back to Lyndon Johnson, that's one of the great things of all time. Lyndon didn't become a lover of the blacks overnight, you know. If you want to look at his record in the United States Senate, it wasn't very good. And John Kennedy was sincere about the black thing and he wanted to do it, he was going to do it. But he had a five-vote majority. You know, we were walking on tenterhooks all the time, and when you got into a controversial area you had a hell of a time. What people forget is that the tax bill we gave up under Lyndon Johnson is what we tried to get. And the civil rights bill passed because he went to them and said, 'Lookit, I'm the first Southerner in history and you can't do this to me. You'll never get another Southern President as long as you live if you filibuster this bill.' And they passed it. I think Kennedy would have had the fight of his life on it."

Johnson was a better arm twister?

O'DONNELL: "No! John Kennedy had more influence in Congress than Lyndon ever had. They don't even *like* him. You know where they all get mixed up? The only thing that Johnson ever passed— In 1966, he passed a heck of a program. Well, you know what happened in 1964, don't you? They elected eighty new Democrats, that's a switch of one hundred and sixty votes. You could be against motherhood and get a bill through if any Democrat wanted it. Now in 1966 he gets belted and things are right back to where Kennedy was. In 1967 and 1968 they couldn't pass anything. That's when Lyndon started to screech and scream at the Congress, but actually they just went back to where they normally are, which is about a five-to-ten vote edge one way or the other."

"Twenty-six Pages That Said Two Pages' Worth of Information"

To get back to Hoover, what kind of reports did you get from Courtney Evans?

O'DONNELL: "They irritated me because they were twenty-six pages that said two pages' worth of information. They would go around and say, 'Did you ever see Ken O'Donnell have a drink?' The guy says, 'Yes.' 'Well, who was he drinking with?' And he names seven guys, and they go to those seven guys and say, 'Did you ever see him have a drink?' By the time you end up, the guy is an alcoholic. So I called Courtney in and I said, 'Courtney, my friend, if you want to write down on one page, "I think Ken O'Donnell is an alcoholic," write it down. Don't bore me with seven pages of people saying you had a drink or your neighbors hate you or you parked the car across a guy's driveway. I'm not interested in that. Is he a security risk to the United States of America? We'll decide whether he's equipped to handle the job, not you. But if you say he's an alcoholic, then we'll check out and find out if he is, medically. I don't want to hear every rumor or every gossip that's running around town. Fifty people hate everybody in the world, for cripesake. Your next-door neighbors all hate you. I don't want any more of that. I want a two-page memorandum with a conclusion.' Well, the FBI won't make any conclusions. He said, 'We don't do that. We just give you the information,' and I said, 'Well, then don't give me a lot of information about that. Just say, "The guy takes a drink, period." I don't want to know what his neighbors think about him. I'm not interested. It's just a bore. I'm a busy fellow.'"

Did they use wiretaps for their information?

O'DONNELL: "Never. You get— They probably, I think, listen in to the foreign powers on occasion. But you know that. It says, 'A very qualified source says that the Russian Ambassador was seen with so-and-so at such-and-such a place. Thought you might like to know.' But President Kennedy didn't like that stuff. He didn't like to hear about their sex life, he didn't want to hear whether they drank, he didn't want to hear anything personal about anybody. When I objected to the reports, I went to him and said, 'This is what I'm going to say to Courtney Evans.' I said, 'I don't know whether it comes from Hoover or who it comes from, but when I say it, I want him to know I'm saying it for you. I'm not that important.'

He said, 'You know me. I don't want any part of that stuff. I don't want to hear about it. I'd like to see the report they've got on *me*.' We wanted the FBI to report facts. I wanted to know where a guy was born and where he worked, whether he was in a mental institution, or if he's a homosexual—say it, but prove it. Why is he? With whom? Where? And where's the police record? Prove it to me.

"For example, this kid lost a job because they said he was convicted for larceny, and his family was broken up over it. His mother came to me in tears one day and she said, 'He's only eighteen and he's trying to get a job with the post office. Can you help him?' So I called up and they said he's a criminal. 'The FBI report says so.' 'So send the report over.' I get the report, I call the FBI, I say, 'Courtney, I want you to go to the police station in Alexandria, Virginia, and get the blotter and I want to see it.' You want to know what the kid did? He was out with a girl one day and they went skinny-dipping and they jumped over a guy's fence into his pool and they opened his place and drank two bottles of Coke. Now, you mean this kid can never got a job again for the whole rest of his life? I said, 'You gotta be kidding. And you send me a report like that?' Well, the kid's working for the post office right at this moment, but this is what your problems are with these people. You have to interpret it yourself."

That reminds me of the report on the ambassador who was caught in a lady's boudoir by the husband as he was trying to exit through a window.

O'DONNELL [laughs]: "Well, it's public so I will say it. Courtney Evans came to me three times, one after the other—I'll capsule it—and said, 'Have you read the report on the ambassador?' And I said, 'Yes, and what else have you got?' And we don't discuss it any further. Courtney is a regular guy and he knows he's doing an onerous chore. He came back the next day and said, 'I've talked to the Director and the Director says, "Are you sure you've read it?"' And I said, 'If I said I read it, I'm sure I've read it.' He came back the third day and said, 'Has the President read it?' And I said, 'Yes, the President has read it.' He said, 'What did he say?' 'He said that from now on he's going to hire faster ambassadors.' I never got another report on that again about anybody. He got appointed the next day. You know, I said, 'Are you making a point somewhere along the line here that an ambassador may not have an affair with a girl? Should that preclude him from being ambassador?' I don't quite understand that."

Did President Kennedy think that Hoover was doing a good job?

O'DONNELL: "I think he thought the FBI was doing a good job. I think he honestly believed that. Mr. Hoover's views of the world and his were slightly different and I think the President thought that the history, that considering the problems, that Hoover had done a pretty good job with the FBI, but he thought his time had come and gone."

Do you mean in terms of the Communist threat?

O'DONNELL: "Once a month, Mr. Hoover used to deliver a report on the status of the Communist Party in the United States, which if I've ever seen ridiculous documents that probably is number one. The President thought Communism internally certainly was not a threat to the United States of America. I looked it up in the book—I don't know anything about Communism, or the Communist Party, to be frank with you, except what I read and what I got from the FBI—but I open up the book and I look at Massachusetts and they name the three top Communists and I wouldn't have difficulty finding them. That's the only state I knew, because they all had filed on the ballot and run for statewide office because they were legally allowed to run in the Commonwealth of Massachusetts, and I don't need fifty FBI agents to find them out, because their office is right across from me in the Park Square Building in Boston, and it says Communist Party of America. I told the President I thought we might be wasting an awful lot of money chasing things that we could look up in the newspapers."

Tom Clark thinks that a lot of the Communist cases were squeezed oranges.

O'DONNELL: "I couldn't agree more. I think when you took those who were trying to get our nuclear technological stuff, they're spies. That's different from the domestic Communist Party, which was a political apparatus, and there were awfully few of them. I think Mr. Hoover's time had come and gone, that's all."

"Hoover Went Directly to Johnson"

And Bobby Kennedy would see that he retired after 1964?

O'DONNELL: "I think the President probably more than Bobby. He was more of an historian, number one. And number two, I think he knew the depths of the problems facing the country. I don't think he needed any advice from Bobby, nor would Bobby take it upon himself to give him any. I think Bobby perhaps got along with Hoover better than the President did."

How were the meetings between the President and Hoover arranged?

O'DONNELL: "I think you'll find that all those meetings—there were five of them, except for one luncheon that I know of—were also attended by the Attorney General, who set them up in the first place. To my knowledge, the President had him to lunch once at the request of the Attorney General. And Bobby was there, and I was there for about half of it. Then he came over once for the presentation of a Freedom Medal and they talked for four or five minutes, and then he came over once in October, just before the assassination, which had nothing to do with Texas. They discussed civil rights."

Did they discuss integrating the FBI?

O'DONNELL: "I know Bobby discussed it and I know that the President discussed it with Mr. Hoover, and I think all of us discussed it with the Bureau at almost every level. If you want to look at the FBI, basically they're mostly Irish Catholics who were recruited because they knew they wouldn't be Communists because of their religion. They went out to Irish Catholic colleges—the Holy Crosses and the Fordhams and the Notre Dames—and recruited until it was replete with them. And Southerners. They've changed. That was the basis of Hoover's situation, and Bobby was the first one that really noticed it. I had noticed it but I hadn't thought much about it.

"We saw a problem coming in civil rights and we saw also the possibility that the Communists might attempt to infiltrate the black movement, and a lot of other people might too, and how do you police Harlem with a white guy who is a spy? They send an FBI guy down in a Brooks Brothers suit and a snap brim hat. He couldn't catch cold in Harlem. Ridiculous. Bobby was leaning on him, and he was succeeding too—would have succeeded—but this is the only thing really that could have been a problem.

"When Johnson became President—I was there for one year with Johnson—I said immediately, 'I'm no longer the liaison with the FBI. You can go through Walter Jenkins or whoever you choose but not me anymore. I don't want any part of them.' Every day they came over and they brought these reports—there's page one, page four, eleven, sixteen, seventeen, eighteen, nineteen, twenty. Now I've got to sign off on those papers like I read them. In case anything goes wrong, they say, 'Well, Ken O'Donnell had the papers and he read them and he said they were all right.' So I said, 'I don't sign anything I don't read.' And that was the end of it. Bobby was still Attorney General at the time, but the game was all over then. Hoover went directly to Johnson. Courtney Evans was dismissed as liaison, and the next day a guy named Deke DeLoach, who is now security officer for Pepsi-Cola, which is owned by Donald Kendall, who is Nixon's best friend—I never had anything to do with them again from that minute on, but I know they just went directly to Johnson through DeLoach, who's a Georgian; and his brother, who was a friend of Walter Jenkins, is an FBI agent in Texas. Of course, they were enthralled with my decision. The Bobby Baker case was hot on the griddle at that time, so I think he just didn't want me to see it and I didn't want to see it, so we had a mutual separation.

"I'll tell you, my only relationship and the only discussion I ever had with Johnson on anything dealing with the FBI was that I suggested he ought to talk to Hoover to keep him happy. And he said, 'That's a great idea. I'm going to have lunch with him.' That would be in January of 1964, and he said, 'You know, I've lived on the same street with him for forty years and we walked our dogs together.' That was the first time I even knew they knew each other.

"What they exchanged for information, I'm presuming, based on what I read in the FBI reports, they wanted titillating bits that one might want to hear about—who went out with who, and who was doing what to who— but it would come from Hoover directly.

There is a story that Johnson agreed to make Ramsey Clark Attorney General if his father resigned from the Supreme Court. The reason was that Johnson wanted to appoint a black to the court.

O'DONNELL: "That's not the reason. Johnson didn't want Nick Katzenbach, who succeeded Bobby as Attorney General when he went to the Senate, because they were so close that Johnson thought that Bobby was being both a senator and Attorney General. So he shifted Katzenbach to the State Department and asked me to recommend five names for the job, but I didn't give him any, because I knew they would be the ones he didn't appoint. What happened is that Tom Clark made the proposition to Johnson, but the appointment of Thurgood Marshall was an afterthought. It was just that Johnson didn't want Bobby to have any inputs at Justice."

To digress a moment, is it true that Johnson held meetings in the bathroom while responding to a call of nature?

O'DONNELL: "Well, Johnson was a gentleman, but he had some failings. [Laughs.] I remember one such conference with Douglas Dillon, this very erudite Harvard guy, and I was there myself. Not long afterward, Dillon resigned, but I don't know how much influence that particular incident had on his decision."

Is it fair to say that you don't seem too impressed with Hoover?

O'DONNELL: "I went to Washington unimpressed with J. Edgar Hoover, and I was not disillusioned."

"We Held No Secrets Back"

Robert E. Wick, who once headed the Bureau's Crime Records Division, succeeding Lou Nichols and Deke DeLoach in that position, told me that the FBI had "no such thing as a public-relations section or anything of that nature." As assistant director of the Crime Records Division, it was his "responsibility," he said, "to maintain the various FBI publications and to answer questions from the press so that the information that the public has a right to know was given out to the public, and we held no secrets back. I followed the policy of Nichols and DeLoach, of absolute forthrightness with the press. Mr. Hoover insisted on that and that's what we did. I'd tell Mr. Hoover the full facts and then we'd decide what we could say and what we couldn't say, what could be printed or broadcast and what couldn't be. My policy was, We're all going to the same place, so give the man the full benefit of the doubt."

Was Hoover an effective speaker?

WICK: "Oh, yes, indeed, indeed. This is why I— Many times I'd have newsmen say to me, 'I want an interview with Mr. Hoover.' Well, I'd try to get it and yet I realized this was sort of walking on eggs here because once you open the floodgates and let one news media man have an interview with Mr. Hoover, then the other man can say, 'Well, look, I've got as much right as Joe over here, so why can't I come in?' It would create considerable problems, and yet I wanted to have— Somebody would come out with a scurrilous article about Mr. Hoover that absolutely was not true, irrespective of what it was, and that would cause me to seethe quite a bit. I know it did Nichols too. And we had to try to counter these things some way and I think the best way to counter it was with the truth, always. Well, the best way to get the truth is to let the man himself talk to the man. Then that brings the problem again, you see? You let one man in, you should let others in. Because Mr. Hoover could express himself very well."

But he never held press conferences?

WICK: "He did one time against our best judgment. I remember the time he let all those women come in—it was November 18, 1964—against my judgment, against DeLoach's, but he said no, he was going to see all those women. It just so happened that they weren't the big top reporters, but he saw them and they asked him all sorts of questions. And from that meeting came the comment that Mr. Hoover made that Martin Luther King was 'the most notorious liar in the country.' And that was reported, and of course Mr. Hoover had reference to the fact that Martin Luther King had charged in a speech that all FBI agents down South were Southerners and biased and so on, and this is just not the fact."

Since his comment came shortly after the announcement that King had won the Nobel Peace Prize, don't you think the timing was unfortunate?

WICK: "Well, we— Indeed it was. Mr. Hoover should not have said that. It was ill-advised."

Do you think that his age had something to do with it?

WICK: "Well, it could have. Let's see, he was seventy at that time. I think it may have. Once he said it, he had to stick by it, and he did."

My impression of Hoover is that of a man who says precisely what he wants to say when he wants to say it.

WICK: "That's right. In that particular instance, I was there, I remember, sitting here and he was sitting there, and the girls, about fourteen of them, sitting around, and he was talking about Martin Luther King, and he said, 'And another thing, he's the most notorious liar in the country.' Then he talked about various other things, peculiarities he had, the way

King was attacking the Bureau, and finally one girl said, 'May we quote you?' and he said, 'Yes, go ahead,' and Deke said, 'Well, Mr. Hoover, you just said so-and-so,' and he said, 'That's all right. You can use that as a quote.'"

Didn't he also accuse King of being a degenerate?

WICK: "Well, I don't think he publicly said that. I don't believe he did. I think he was probably quoted as saying that because that was some of the conversation within that same conference. In fact, he said a great number of other things in that conference that he asked them not to— Sort of off the record and so forth."

It was reported that when Hoover and King met in the Director's office some two weeks later, Hoover confronted him with tape recordings of his sexual activities, and suggested that he tone down his criticism of the FBI.

WICK: "Deke DeLoach and I took Mr. Martin Luther King and two, three of his associates into Mr. Hoover's office, and that's the time—"

Did you stay in?

WICK: "I think Deke stayed in and I stayed out with one of the other aides with him. And we had many TV cameras and so on there. Although the agreement inside was to the effect that, well, Mr. Hoover told him, 'You can say anything you want to, it's up to you, but I don't want a press conference.' Well, Mr. King, of course, walked right out and took a piece of paper out of his pocket and announced that this was what they had discussed. It had been prepared ahead of time."

Did Hoover confront King with tape recordings of his sexual activities?

WICK: "That's not the fact."

I would appreciate hearing your version.

WICK: "I don't know. I wasn't there at the time, so I don't know what they discussed."

Are you aware of a story by Richard Harwood in the Washington Post *to the effect that certain newsmen were offered transcripts of these tape recordings?*

WICK: "I don't know. They may have been. Dick Harwood, by the way, is a very honorable man and a good reporter, a topnotcher. He's honest and— Mr. Hoover didn't— He thought the *Post* gave him a bad time."

"He Deliberately Set Out to Get Martin King"

The transcripts in question were the result of electronic surveillance (bugs) initiated by Hoover to determine if Martin Luther King was being influenced by Communist agents. Whereas the wiretaps authorized by Robert Kennedy were restricted to King's offices and perhaps his home, the bugs were installed in various hotel rooms and recorded some of the "goings on" Hoover would later refer to in a speech at Loyola University in Chicago when he spoke of "zealots or pressure groups" that were "spearheaded at times by Communists and moral degenerates."

The authority for the bugs, Hoover would assert years later, was based on a memorandum signed in 1954 by then Attorney General Herbert Brownell which, according to Hoover, gave the FBI general authority to bug in cases involving "internal security and the national safety" without getting the case-by-case approval of the Attorney General. As to the wiretaps, the authority dated back to a letter written by President Franklin D. Roosevelt in 1940 which gave the Attorney General the right to authorize wiretaps in writing on a case-by-case basis when the national security was involved.

From the first days of Kennedy's Attorney Generalship, Hoover bombarded him with memoranda linking King with "two hardcore, controlled Communists," one of whom Hoover believed to have direct links to a Soviet "apparatus." In Hoover's strongly stated opinion, these men were seeking to gain control over King, and hence over the Southern Christian Leadership Conference and, to a large extent, the civil rights movement.

Kennedyites have charged that the FBI violated its own rule against evaluating data in memoranda, and Burke Marshall, Kennedy's Assistant Attorney General for Civil Rights, said, "I think the FBI and Mr. Hoover deliberately set out to get Martin King." There is no question that the Kennedy Administration regarded Hoover's allegations as potentially dangerous. President Kennedy personally tried to persuade King to dissociate himself from the accused men, and when that effort failed, the Attorney General had no alternative but to authorize the wiretap.

Whether the wiretaps, or bugs, for that matter, were justified is not the important question. The fact remains that they are open-ended and undiscriminating in their collection of "evidence." Whatever the original rationale for the electronic devices, once installed they hear everything within range, and the tape recorders retain it all, whether or not it has anything to do with the allegations in question. In fact, King's alleged Communist friends were not subjected to similar surveillance, and the FBI never even attempted to prove the charges against them.

What remains is the ominous by-product that made it possible for Hoover to charge King with "moral turpitude," which, however deplorable, is not a crime, much less one within the FBI's competence. But to distribute confidential information about anyone under investigation is a clear violation of law. It was a federal crime in 1964 and 1965 to disclose the results of a wiretap.

The editor of the Washington *Post*, Benjamin Bradlee, told me that he refused to see the transcripts because he thought they were "offensive." I asked if he knew who had seen them.

BRADLEE: "They showed them to plenty of people. They showed them to Gene Patterson when he was editor of the Atlanta *Constitution*. But I'm sure that they were not printable, I mean, I have the substance of them; they had to do with his sexual exploits and they were— DeLoach told me about them and—"

How would he go about telling you that?

BRADLEE: "Well, by— Hell, he brought it up. He said, 'We have,' or 'There are,' I don't know. But he described the tapes, and the one that I particularly remember was King watching the televised funeral of Kennedy in some hotel room, I don't remember which, and he made some reference to the sexual habits of the President and Mrs. Kennedy."

And DeLoach would be peddling this?

BRADLEE: "Peddling smeddling. They were trying to discredit King."

I asked Jack Anderson if he thought Hoover had tried to intimidate King with the tape recordings.

ANDERSON: "He did have tape recordings on King, but I would think that if King called Hoover's bluff, how could he put it out? I know Hoover operated in far more subtle ways, but he certainly was capable of blackmail. In fact, he did it all the time, but it was implied blackmail. He would let senators know that he had picked up some information on them and he'd give it to them as an act of great charity, thereby doing them a favor but at the same time letting them know that he had the information."

But how would you know that's true?

ANDERSON: "People tell me things. They know I'm not going to use names. Yes, I've had people tell me that this has happened to them, and I have the impression that it's frequent. When I was friendly with Hoover, I personally was able to get files, any files I requested. I got involved in a libel suit once when Hoover was courting me—and when you get in a libel suit you fight with everything you've got—and I just called and said, 'Do you have a file on this guy?' They brought out the file, laid it out, and I went through the whole thing. It was extremely helpful, I might add."

Did the FBI ever offer you any of the evidence on King?

ANDERSON: "It was never offered to me but I did get it from unauthorized sources. I published one quote from an FBI document that had been sent over to the White House about an incident with a woman. I interviewed the woman in the case before I published it."

As assistant to the Director in charge of all investigative matters, DeLoach was then the number three man in the Bureau. The number four man was John P. Mohr, who held a similar title on the administrative side. My question as to whether he was aware that De Loach was involved in passing this kind of information to newsmen evoked a laugh.

MOHR: "I wouldn't think DeLoach would do anything dirty like that, do you? [Laughs.] I always thought DeLoach was a real upright young man."

He wouldn't, you mean, unless Hoover told him to?

MOHR: "I don't know whether [laughing] Hoover would have to tell him. Did you ever read any of the transcript? If not, why don't you ask DeLoach."

SULLIVAN: "DeLoach was the one who carried the ball for Hoover on King. Hoover knew all about it. DeLoach passed it up on the Hill. He took tapes and played them before some of the congressmen and senators."

This was all Sullivan could remember about the incident, but a few months after the interview, a former FBI official told the New York *Times* that Hoover had ordered Sullivan to send a copy of one of the tapes to Mrs. Coretta King to "frighten" her husband into halting his criticism of the Bureau. In an effort to mail the package so that it would not be traced to the FBI, Sullivan had it mailed from Tampa, Florida.

According to Efrem Zimbalist, Hoover did confront King with the evidence.

ZIMBALIST: "In my first meeting with Hoover, he alluded to Martin Luther King. As I say, he was just skipping over various topics of conversation when he landed on him. And he said, 'I don't like the man. I've said so publicly and I had him up here for forty-five minutes and told him so privately. I don't think he's a good man.' On to the next thing. Just like that. I mean, he stopped in his flight just to make that point. I think there was an unsavory background to Martin Luther King that he knew of and I think he resented this adulation of—"

Wasn't he being puritanical? Even if the allegation that King had sex with a white woman was true, what business was it of the FBI?

ZIMBALIST: "Whatever. Martin Luther King also made the mistake of suggesting that Hoover resign, and Hoover made that very clear to him in forty-five minutes, that if he didn't shut his mouth up, you know, that he'd be in real trouble. And he never opened his mouth about him again. Whatever he knew about him shut him up, because King was very vocal about Hoover at that time, saying that he should step down and so forth. And Hoover just read him off, whatever it was."

Recalling that meeting in an interview six years later, Hoover said,

I got a wire from the Reverend Doctor King in New York. He was getting ready to get the Nobel Prize—he was the last one in the world who should ever have received it. He wired asking to see me. I held him in complete contempt because of the things he said and because of his conduct. First I felt I shouldn't see him, but then I thought he might become a martyr if I didn't. King was very suave and smooth. He sat right there where you're sitting and said he never criticized the FBI. I said, "Mr. King"—I never called him reverend— "stop right there. You're lying." He then pulled out a press release that he said he intended to give to the press. I said, "Don't show it to me or read it to me." I couldn't understand how he could have prepared a press release even before we met. Then he asked if I'd go out to have a photograph taken with him. I said I certainly would mind. And I said, "If you ever say anything that's a lie again, I'll brand you a liar again." Strange to say, he never attacked the Bureau again for as long as he lived.*

* Published in *Time*, December 14, 1970. The meeting between Hoover and King occurred December 1, 1964.

"He Wanted to Smear the American Negro"

SULLIVAN: "Hoover had some damn thing in mind where he wanted to smear the American Negro as being pro-Communist. In the early 1960s, he raised hell because he requested evidence showing the extent of the infiltration of the Communist Party by the Negro. Well, hell, the Negro never infiltrated the Communist Party; the Party was almost free of Negroes. Then when we came up with an honest report, he was furious. He wouldn't speak to me for about three or four months, but I stuck by the facts.

"I made a test case in the late 1950s and tried to get a black into the FBI as a special agent, and he was turned down. His mother currently works over at Internal Revenue Service. I always wanted to get Negroes into the Bureau. My God, down South they used to hire them in the police departments and we were refusing to hire them. I didn't like that. I didn't like the refusal of the Bureau to hire Jews and after quite a struggle I did finally manage to get a young Jewish man into the Bureau, and he's still in. So I was always sort of an off-beat person and accused of being a troublemaker.

"For example, on October twelfth, 1970, I gave a speech before UPI editors in Williamsburg. I was part of a panel with President Brewster of Yale and John Kilpatrick, the columnist. We each gave a little talk and then the panel session opened and I got a question: 'Isn't it true that the Communist Party is responsible for racial riots and all the academic violence and upheaval?' I said, 'No, it's absolutely untrue. The Party is weak and is incapable of doing any such thing. We'd have the racial riots if the Communist Party had never existed, because the problem is indigenous to this country.' When I got back to Washington, all hell broke loose. There was a note for me to see Tolson, a note for me to see Hoover, and Hoover was furious. He said, 'Why did you give that answer?' And I said, 'Because it's the truth and you know it's the truth.' I put this in a letter to him later on, and I further told him that if I had to go out and see the American public, I wasn't going to give any more speeches for the Bureau. I had three scheduled and I told him, 'You better assign them to somebody else.' So he assigned them to former Assistant Director Thomas Bishop."

"Ten Nays and One Aye, and the Ayes Have It"

Coming back to Robert Wick, I asked him about the internal operation of the FBI at the staff level.

WICK: "Many times we'd have an executive conference. All the assistant directors and the assistants to the Director would sit there and discuss a matter, and we'd take a vote on some of these things. It often reminded me of Abe Lincoln: Ten nays and one aye, and the ayes have it. Tolson would say, 'This is what the Boss wants. If the Boss wants that, that's what he's going to get. The Boss thinks we ought to do it this way and that's the way we're going to do it. Now fix it up, get a memo so it reads that way. I'll tell the Boss,' and so forth. But in retrospect, as I look back on it now, ninety-nine times out of a hundred, the Boss was right because he had been talking to someone else, or Mr. Tolson had, about some matters that maybe we didn't know about."

What qualities did Hoover look for in executives?

WICK: "I think primarily that increment is very hard to pin down. I'd say dedication, excellent work within your own sphere."

Would being articulate help?

WICK: "Oh, yes. One must obviously be an articulate craftsman, because all the FBI is, and all it ever was, is an investigative agency. It investigates violations of the law. That's all it is, a fact-finding, fact-gathering, reporting agency. You've got to get the facts and then they must be reported. Certainly the meticulous care with which this is accomplished is a factor in an agent's progress in the Bureau. As Mr. Hoover said back when he became Director, a man's progress in the Bureau would be based directly, at least as long as he was Director, on merit, on his ability to get the job done. All right, that's what Mr. Hoover recognized. Mr. Tolson too. You don't make mistakes."

And if you made mistakes, was he shy about chewing you out?

WICK: "Oh, indeed not, because you knew what your job was, if you missed, you should be genuine enough to admit it."

How would Hoover go about it?

WICK: "He'd say, 'We cannot do this again.' 'It is not good for the Bureau.' That type of thing. 'Why did you do it?' 'You should get a letter of censure for acting in an ungentlemanly manner.' If you got a letter of censure, you might be held up on a raise, you could be docked in salary, all types of things; but it was understood that these were the conditions—there's no Civil Service in the FBI—and if you didn't like it, you could get out. We recognized that, but we also recognized that he was absolutely fair, eminently fair. When he had the facts, he would be absolutely fair, but he was very dispassionate about things. He'd weigh all the facts, then make up his mind, and stick to it. He was very honest, very candid about things."

What was the organizational setup?

WICK: "There was a director, Mr. Hoover; an associate director, Mr. Tolson; two assistants to the Director, who worked through Mr. Tolson, or directly with the Director, and these two men supervised the ten assistant directors who were in charge of the ten divisions—that is, Identification, Training, Administrative, Files and Communications, Domestic Intelligence, General Investigative, Laboratory, Crime Records, Special Investigative, Inspection. There are now, I think, thirteen divisions."

Would Mr. Hoover attend staff meetings?

WICK: "Sometimes he would. Often in what they called executive meetings he wouldn't be there."

How would an executive meeting differ from another type of meeting?

WICK: "When Mr. Hoover did not attend our meetings, one of the assistant directors would prepare an executive memo for the Director telling him what was discussed and what decisions were made and make recommendations as to what should be done."

Were you allowed to make inputs?

WICK: "Oh, absolutely. Any man could. I'd write memos to— Well, I'd go through channels, of course, but I'd write a memo from Wick to Tolson or someone else."

You were there when Bob Kennedy was Attorney General. What went wrong, why did their relationship go off the rail?

WICK: "I believe that Bobby Kennedy didn't have as good a grasp of the investigative technique or investigative know-how as he thought he had. He seemed to believe that 'Here's the result we want, now go and get it.' Mr. Hoover's view was 'I don't care what the result is. If there's a statute on the books, the FBI's job is to investigate that in a forthright, honest, expert way. And if the facts point one way, that's the way it will be, and we present our facts as discovered, as detected, as dug up, to the United States Attorney for prosecutive opinion. We don't care where the facts lie.'"

What happened when Bobby tried to get the FBI into organized crime?

WICK: "As far as our jurisdiction would allow, we were in organized crime. Mr. Hoover's judgment always was that we should never exceed the authority given us by the Congress of the United States, and he never did. When Congress gave us the authority in 1961, the Omnibus Crime Bill, we got into it more deeply."

Did Hoover want the bill? Did he testify in favor of it?

WICK: "Oh, he wanted it. I don't remember if he testified, but he'd talk to the senators and House leaders on the phone many times. And he felt no hesitation to express his views. He had many friends on the Hill. If he had been opposed to it, I think he could have affected its passage. He definitely was in favor of the FBI moving into the area of organized crime. There's no question about it. But, he said, you have to have the jurisdiction to do it."

Wasn't he opposed to Milton Wessel's group when they tried to investigate the Apalachin meeting?

WICK: "What they wanted to do was to have FBI agents and attorneys hired by the Department of Justice conduct investigations, and here you were having a group of attorneys not qualified as investigators conducting investigations and evaluating information prior to adjudication and all that sort of thing, and Mr. Hoover didn't go for that. He thought that was the improper use of the investigative function because if you investigate the matter then you should turn the results over for prosecution, not for public hearings of some sort. He felt quite strongly about that."

What do you think about the remark that it took an Attorney General with a brother in the White House to get Hoover into organized crime?

WICK: "Who is the chief law enforcement officer of the United States —the head of the FBI or the Attorney General? Was it up to Mr. Hoover to decide what laws we need and what we should do about it? You see, in most cases it is a local matter. In other words, what you had was a tremendous rivalry between Mafia gangs which manifested itself by murder. You had gambling, garbage collection, loan sharking, corrupt labor unions—Now, is that a proper function of the FBI? Where does local jurisdiction end? What is the county prosecutor for? What is the state police for, the local police chief—why do they exist? Mr. Hoover's viewpoint was that if you were to take the FBI and superimpose an investigative function right into every gang murder that occurs, every bombing of a laundry, say, or a dry-cleaning establishment that doesn't pay protection to the gang, then you are taking from the local police authority the incentive to investigate the case, or from the local prosecutor the incentive to prosecute it. You're superimposing one law enforcement agency right on top of another. Is this in the best interest of the American people? You're creating a national police force. How do you write your law so that a gang war in New York State is interstate because Joe lives out in Newark?

"Now, the FBI moved into the Las Vegas skimming and all that sort of thing. Hell, there was surveillances on airplanes going into the Bahamas, and all this money on these guys. Hell, I was in on all of it. So it wasn't Mr. Hoover's view that the FBI shouldn't have any jurisdiction. His view was that if we do have the jurisdiction, it better be clearly defined and it's up to the Congress to establish the FBI's jurisdiction, but not to the point where you kill off and completely stifle the local law enforcement authorities."

SULLIVAN: "Hoover refused to tackle organized crime until we wrote a monograph that demonstrated clearly that organized crime existed. There was the Apalachin meeting, and the FBI didn't even know it. We had to learn it from the local police. The Attorney General wasn't moving against it either. Bill Rogers got going on it after Apalachin—how could he avoid it?—but it was actually Bobby Kennedy who really put the great stress on it. He gave it the big push. I know because I was in charge of the operation. The man who did more than anybody else in the Bureau to break up organized crime once we got going into it was Jim Gale, Assistant Director of the Special Investigative Division handling organized crime. Gale is an extraordinarily intelligent, able man and he was one of my assistant directors when I was the number three man. Gale got the job done through sheer intelligence and imagination and drive."

What were your feelings about Bob Kennedy?

WICK: "I liked him. I used to go over and see him every once in a while. Ed Guthman [Bob's press secretary] is a very good friend of mine. Ed and I had the same type of job, you know, and so I'd confer with Ed on giving press releases, and then Cliff Sessions was over there too for a while, and, actually, I knew all those men and dealt with them over at the Attorney General's office. I'd get to see the Attorney General every once in a while on matters, but most of the time I'd deal directly with the press guys."

In *We Band of Brothers,* a book about those years, Ed Guthman wrote,

I came to the Justice Department with considerable respect for the FBI and a good deal of regard for Hoover. My opinion was formed not so much by what I had read as by observing the FBI in action, for during the fourteen years I was a reporter in Seattle I had worked closely many times with Hoover's men. But like many persons who come from civilian life to the Justice Department thinking nothing but the best about the FBI, seeing Hoover at close range was a revealing and ultimately embittering experience. . . . One evening after Bob had been elected Senator, he had dinner with Burke Marshall, Louis Oberdorfer and me. Hoover's name came up in conversation, and in the discussion that followed we concluded that the most scathing thing we could say about him was that after working at the top level in the Department of Justice we could no longer believe him.

When I asked Guthman about this quote, he urged me "to talk to people who not only were top people, but who had various positions—you get the Congressional Directories out of any library. You just go back through the Justice Department and I don't care what administration, you're going to find people who came to Washington thinking very highly of the FBI and came away with their feelings very badly reversed, and because of what they saw and what they knew of that operation. It isn't that we were prejudiced. Most of us didn't come there with any preconceived—if it was preconceived, it was very favorable—and what we saw and what we participated in turned us. And that's where you got to look."

Civil Rights Is a Gray Area

Another bone of contention with Bob Kennedy was the area of civil rights.

WICK: "Of course, that civil rights area is a very gray area as to just what is civil rights. You had no clear-cut court decision, and you don't just march in and start arresting people for not integrating schools or what. Now, the FBI had to work with the local sheriffs, with the constituted authorities throughout the South. I don't know of any instance where the FBI had to be forced into an investigation. I know the FBI investigated many police departments when there was an allegation of violation of civil rights. For instance, in the Philadelphia, Mississippi, case, Joe Sullivan handled the investigation of the three civil rights workers who were murdered. He's absolutely the best there is. If I ever did anything wrong, the last man in this world I'd want after me would be Joe Sullivan. He went right in there and presented facts to the United States Attorney sufficient to get indictments against various Southern police officers.

"I was sent down to investigate the Mack Charles Parker case that involved a police officer and several so-called rednecks who hauled this black out of jail, bumped him on the head, took him out of town, shot him, and threw him over into the Pearl River down at Bogalusa, Mississippi. We solved it, but we didn't get them indicted. We had the facts but a Southern jury just wouldn't indict these people. Well, this is the problem. You had to feel your way along."

How did the Director feel about enforcing civil rights?

WICK: "He felt that if the law is on the books, we're going to enforce it. He didn't drag any heels, he kept pushing, pushing, pushing to get it done, but he recognized that you've still got to live with these places. You've got an office in Savannah, you've got one in Jackson, Mississippi— we established that one in July 1964—"

It is my understanding that President Johnson had to force the Director to go down there personally to open that office in Jackson, which has been described as the spiritual capital of white supremacy.

WICK: "Well, he did. That was the day that this Lemuel Penn was killed. We had a strong resident agency there, but I think that President Johnson had to make a gesture, a means of dramatizing the need for greater law enforcement on the part of the FBI on civil rights matters in that area of Mississippi. I remember now. Your version of it is correct. He did ask him. I remember talking to the President the day Mr. Hoover opened the Jackson office. Deke DeLoach was down there with Mr. Hoover and I think Mr. Tolson was with him too, and two or three men from the Crime Records Division, and I was in charge of the office back here. Penn was a Washington schoolteacher who was in training down there when he was shot on the highway in the early morning hours, and I was in the office when the President called and wanted to know if we were in it, and I was smart enough to say, 'Yes, sir.' So I ordered a full field investigation on the basis of an interstate angle, although that was a local murder. But there were his civil rights and maybe a car angle or something. Anyway, we entered that case and solved it.

"Then I had the problem of getting hold of Mr. Hoover, who was coming back on an airplane, I think it was *Air Force Two*, and I couldn't get hold of him. I got a message to him there but he was airborne before I could get to him. I wanted to fill him in on it because the very second he landed—I think he landed in Baltimore—the reporters hit him, but luckily we got it to him before he talked to the reporters. He told them we were conducting a full investigation of the matter. But we just got by on a squeak on that one."

I didn't know you couldn't communicate with Air Force Two.

WICK: "I couldn't get hold of Bill Moyers, the President's press secretary, and I talked to a girl in the office and somebody in the situation room, and got word onto the plane that I wanted to have Mr. Hoover call me right away. Finally, I got somebody at the airport to pass on the information."

Wouldn't you say that Hoover and Johnson were pretty close?

WICK: "They had mutual respect for each other. They dined together and they talked together. Mr. Hoover would call him and ask his judgment on things, and the President called him many times just to ask him what he thought about something."

Did Johnson consult him about the consular treaty with the Soviet Union?

WICK: "That was a big flap at that time. The idea was whether it would be harder to surveil all the Communists coming over if they opened consular offices in various places. I imagine they talked about that, but I don't really know. Mr. Hoover never discussed it with me."

Hoover went against the President's wishes in that instance. In fact, he testified publicly against ratification even though everybody in the Johnson Administration was for it, including the Attorney General. How do you explain it?

WICK: "Well, if he believed strongly that this was the way to protect the country, then this was what he had to do. He felt he owed it to whoever in the scheme of things was in power to give them his best judgment, and he did, without any qualms."

In conclusion, I'd like to ask you about William Sullivan. What kind of an FBI man was he?

WICK: "He's a very fine man and knows more about Communism than anybody in this world. Yes, and he could express himself. You could sit in a meeting with Bill Sullivan and listen to him discuss matters of domestic intelligence for two solid hours and you wouldn't know that the time had gone by; you'd think you'd been in there ten minutes. He was an excellent teacher, and a very good man indeed."

SULLIVAN: "We never enforced the civil rights law, because Hoover was opposed to the whole civil rights program. Bobby Kennedy came in and started putting the pressure on it, and then we kind of had to change our ways, but for years we completely ignored the violation of civil rights on the part of Southern law enforcement. There are several reasons for this. Number one, Hoover wasn't in favor of civil rights; number two, if you went after the sheriffs and if you went after the other men, then they wouldn't cooperate with you on bank robberies, on stolen automobiles, they wouldn't cooperate with you on all the other crimes that the FBI handled, and so you'd be left without support from the whole Southern police force; number three, there was his support in Congress. His strength was with the ultraconservatives, with the Southern and Northern conservatives, conservatives wherever they were; and if he went ahead and started to barge into the civil rights field, he'd lose his support in Congress."

President Kennedy Told Martin King in the Rose Garden That His Phone Was Tapped

Sullivan's harsh judgment of Hoover's attitude toward civil rights is shared by Charles Morgan, Jr., a man whose life's work has placed him at the opposite end of the FBI's legal spectrum. Morgan is a Southerner who has been a civil liberties lawyer most of his life. He opened the American Civil Liberties Union Southern Office in Atlanta in 1964, and his accomplishments are indeed impressive. He won the Muhammad Ali case, and his landmark cases include the Reynolds vs. Sims case, which took twelve years before the Supreme Court handed down its one-man, one-vote ruling; and his victory in the Hadnott vs. Amos case made it possible for black candidates to be placed on Greene County, Alabama, ballots—the county probate judge was held in contempt of the U.S. Supreme Court. When I interviewed him in October 1974, Morgan was the head of the National Office of the American Civil Liberties Union in Washington, D.C. I asked him if he thought Hoover was personally opposed to civil rights.

MORGAN: "Yes. Sure he was. What the hell did he have over there as a black agent? He had a chauffeur, didn't he? That was his black contingent, as I recall it, in the whole Bureau up until the early 1960s. Being involved in civil rights work in the South, I heard an awful lot about Hoover over the years. One of the things I always found of interest was that although the authorization on the Martin King tap came from the Attorney General, Robert Kennedy, his brother, the President of the United States, told Martin in the White House Rose Garden that his phone was being tapped, not to use it on anything he wanted to talk about, and the reason it was tapped was because Hoover was going to attempt to use that information, not information off the wiretap, but Hoover had alleged there was a conscious agent of Soviet conspiracy involved in the civil rights movement. The political problem was that Hoover would say that and thereby defeat the Civil Rights Act, which eventually passed in 1964.

"Oh yes, Hoover was opposed to civil rights. He got along, played toady and footsie with the Southerners, and the white Southerners in Congress, the same as his agents did with the police in the South. I'm not saying that they were bigots. I'm not going into that. I'm just telling you the way the FBI worked in the South was to cooperate with the local police on every kind of case, whether it was bank robbery or civil rights."

You know this from personal experience?

MORGAN: "I practiced law seventeen years in the South, nine years in private practice and eight years with ACLU. One of the great problems that developed during those years was how in the world do you get the FBI to get the confidence of the black community, and would it be entitled to it if it had it? The answer to that is 'Of course not,' because by the nature of the role they had in the South, they could not. You can't expect an FBI agent who's working every day with the police chief, or the local policeman, to start investigating that policeman when somebody makes an allegation that they've been beaten up in a jail, or slugged by a policeman at a demonstration, because they're just not capable of it. I couldn't do it. I'd do anything for a friend except prosecute him. I don't think folks are inclined to do that.

"Hoover was a skillful bureaucrat and a person who called Martin King a liar when he won the Nobel Peace Prize. The civil rights movement knew early on that Mr. Hoover was listening to them. There wasn't any question about that."

King made a mistake when he charged that certain FBI agents were Southerners when they were, in fact, Northerners.

MORGAN: "He may have been wrong on the fact of the place of birth of those agents, but he was not wrong on the thrust of what he said. A great number of people in the North think that because somebody is born in South Boston and becomes an FBI agent and moves to Albany, Georgia, that he is a Northerner with different predilections from Southerners. As a white Southerner, I know that most Northerners who came South became two hundred percent Southerner in those years. Just because a person's born someplace else doesn't mean that he's not the biggest Confederate battleflag-carrier 'Dixie'-hummer in the United States of America."

Fine, but when you play that kind of a game with a man like Hoover, you'd better be square on your facts.

MORGAN: "I understand that. I always am, but I'm saying that as far as the employment records— Of course, he wouldn't have the birthplace— that would have been what King was told. Still, the thrust of King's remarks was true: The FBI was not enforcing civil rights equally in the South."

The FBI Was in Charge of Investigations That Were Convenient to Mr. Hoover

Hoover's defense was that he didn't have jurisdiction until the Civil Rights Act was passed in 1964. Also, the FBI is not a police agency.

MORGAN: "Just a moment. Under title eighteen, sections two forty-one, two forty-two and two forty-three, the FBI has had jurisdiction since Reconstruction over civil rights violations. I know the FBI was not in existence in Reconstruction, but the law was, and the law was there through-out Hoover's career, and he didn't enforce it. Hoover said the FBI wasn't a police agency, and I would agree with that, except that when a fellow comes out of a bank looking like John Dillinger or Jesse James, shooting off to the sky, and jumps in his automobile, the FBI agent jumps in his automobile and gives chase. He does whatever he has to do to make the arrest, including shooting him down. But if it's a civil rights violation, which is also a criminal offense under the laws of the United States, the same FBI agent would take notes. The Federal Bureau of Investigation is charged with the duty of enforcing *all* federal criminal laws that other agencies don't take precedence over, whether it's bank robbery, auto thefts or civil rights.

"Let me read section two forty-two: 'Whoever under color of any laws, statute, ordinance, regulation'—color of law means a policeman, sheriff, deputy sheriff, whoever it is—'willfully subjects any inhabitant of any state, territory or district to the deprivation of any rights, privileges or immunities, secured or protected by the constitutional laws of the United States, or to different punishments, pains or penalties because of such inhabitant being an alien or by reason of his color or race, that are prescribed for the punishment of citizens, he shall be fined not more than one thousand dollars or imprisoned for not more than a year, or both, but if death results, shall be subject to imprisonment for any term of years or for life.' There is absolutely no question today or at any other time in our history but that this falls within the ambit of the FBI.

"Under Hoover, the FBI looked upon itself as an agency that was in charge of investigations that were convenient—I mean, whatever was convenient to Mr. Hoover in the justification of his jurisdiction was exactly the way he went. He would say one day, 'We are not a police agency.' The next day, for a bank robbery, kidnaping or auto theft, he would be a police agency. When it came to the Mafia or narcotics, 'We're not a police agency. We have to rely on the local police, we have to do this and that and everything right down the line.' That's all well and good, but what happens when the local police beat up or deprive their citizens of their constitutional rights, or kill them? There ain't nobody else but Mr. Hoover. But he wasn't there until he was forced to be there, and he was forced to be there by Robert Kennedy in 1964. It started in Mississippi when three kids wound up in an earth dam. And they did their job again in other cases under *these* statutes. That jurisdiction didn't just crop up one day, it was there forever under Hoover."

The Urgent Birth of a Jellyfish

J. Edgar Hoover hated the Washington *Post,* and yet in 1970 he gave it one of its major exclusive stories. The reporter involved, Ken W. Clawson, who covered the Department of Justice for the *Post,* later joined the Nixon Administration as Director of Communications. During an interview in June 1972, Clawson described how he got his exclusive story.

CLAWSON: "On Monday morning [November 16, 1970], I had just left my home for the Washington *Post* when my wife received a telephone call from the FBI. I still don't know who called, but the guy said to my wife, 'We'll send a car out to get Mr. Clawson immediately,' and my wife said, 'You can't because he's already left for the office.' I got into the *Post* about ten that morning and there were about eight messages to call the FBI immediately. I called and Harold Leinbaugh of the FBI said, 'The old man will see you if you can get here in ten minutes, and if you want, we'll send a car after you.' I refused the car and I got over there in ten minutes, by God, and I walked onto the fifth floor and Leinbaugh grabbed me by the arm and hustled me into Hoover's office, and on the way he said to me, 'You'll have about twenty-five minutes with the Director.' I said, 'Fine.'"

Did you have any particular subject you wanted to discuss?

CLAWSON: "Well, no, except that Sunday, the day before, Ramsey Clark's book [*Crime in America*] had come out, and I had read the news stories and the reviews on it, and so I was familiar with that. I said the reviews of the Ramsey Clark book came out yesterday and they were very detrimental to you, and I asked if there was anything he wanted to tell me about it?"

In his book, Ramsey Clark said that the FBI suffered from "the excessive domination of a single person, J. Edgar Hoover, and his self-centered concern for his reputation and that of the FBI." He faulted the Bureau for its late entry in the field of organized crime, but he praised its methodology and imperviousness to politics.

Had Hoover read any of the reviews?

CLAWSON: "Hell, yes, he saw everything within a matter of minutes.

He knew exactly what I was talking about. I had the lead of the story in the first ten minutes: 'J. Edgar Hoover yesterday called former Attorney General Ramsey Clark a "jellyfish" and the worst Attorney General he has encountered in forty-five years as director of the Federal Bureau of Investigation.' The story also revealed for the first time the reason Hoover wouldn't talk to Bobby Kennedy the last six months he was in office. He said Kennedy was exerting great pressure on him to hire Negro agents and he just wasn't about to lower the standards of the FBI for any ethnic group."

In the story, Clawson quotes Hoover as saying, "If ever there was a worse Attorney General [than Kennedy] it was Ramsey Clark. You never knew which way he was going to flop on an issue." Until "Bobby Kennedy came along," he had never had any trouble with attorneys general. In comparison, Attorney General John N. Mitchell was an "honest, sincere and very human man." Hoover added, "There has never been an Attorney General for whom I've had higher regard."

CLAWSON: "It's a long goddamn story, close to seventy column inches of type. I had asked him questions specifically on Clark, and then on his own volition he spun out the Kennedy business right on the heels of the Clark business. And with that I knew that we were solid. Anything else from that point would be downhill. But here's the interesting thing about it. When you've interviewed a lot of people, you know within the first five minutes whether you're on the same wave length, whether you're going to do business with that guy, and we did. It was apparent to both of us, I think, that we could talk with one another. The interview took off . . . and it lasted and lasted and lasted, and I think I got out of there about one o'clock in the afternoon.

"When I came out of there, the agents out in the hall were amazed. They said, 'You've almost done the unprecedented thing of having the Director voluntarily skip his lunch.' They said, 'We don't think he's done that in years.'"

How did he appear to you?

CLAWSON: "I came out of there well convinced that the Director not only was not senile, as so often inferred, but he was one of the most vigorous and active minds I had ever dealt with, period. You know, over a two-hour period, if a man is senile it would seem to me that it would have to come out. Well, it didn't. If a person is vulnerable, he has to slip, and he never slipped. I came out of there completely convinced that he had the total capabilities to run that agency."

Who ended the interview?

CLAWSON: "I did, as a matter of fact. I was exhausted—two hours of taking notes. And I said, 'Sir, I've taken up a great deal more of your time than you had agreed to.' I said it two or three times, and the earlier times, he said, 'No, no. Let's go on.' And then I finally said that I was getting writer's cramp from taking these notes, and the third time I said it, he said, 'All right, it's been very enjoyable.'

"By the way, after this interview appeared, all those seventy publications that were waiting in line for years to interview him just descended on the FBI with the worst language you've ever heard in your life, and especially those conservative publications that had always supported him. And of course we were overjoyed at having this exclusive story."

That was quite a scoop. Were your stories about the FBI or the White House ever critical?

CLAWSON: "Oh, sure. I'm the author of the Daniel Schorr story about his being investigated by the FBI on request from the White House."

Then how do you explain your job with the White House?

CLAWSON: "To join a President who asked me to go to work for him. I have now on my wall at the White House an autographed picture of J. Edgar Hoover which he gave me a couple of weeks after the story."

He liked your story?

CLAWSON: "Right. And there aren't too many of those around. But later he got mad at me. This was right at the beginning of a series of errors that he made. Not that the interview was an error, but right on the heels of this interview, and by that I mean during December and January and February of '71, he made several classic boners. The Berrigan–Henry Kissinger kidnap thing was done during that period, special agent Jack Shaw in New York was banished to Butte, Montana, because of a college term paper he wrote that was critical of Hoover. Later, of course, there was William C. Sullivan, which was an exclusive story of mine too, by the way."

Sullivan Was Conceived by Hoover

In his front page story, dated October 2, 1971, Clawson wrote that Sullivan was "forced to retire after a series of policy disputes" with Hoover. "While Sullivan, 59, was on sick leave yesterday, his name was removed from his office door and the locks changed. Sullivan, once thought to be a likely successor to Hoover, 76, was not officially informed. The FBI . . . said that Sullivan had voluntarily retired, effective next week. . . . Sources close to the situation called the FBI explanation 'a lie of the highest Hooverian order.' . . . Sullivan's ouster was foreshadowed about six weeks ago when Hoover appointed W. Mark Felt into a newly created No. 3 post above Sullivan." Clawson said that "Sullivan's progressive attitude and efforts to modernize the FBI were making Hoover furious." According to Clawson, Sullivan, who was the only top FBI executive in recent years that "Hoover addressed by his first name," had been a "favorite of Hoover's for years because of his intellectual approach to his duties."

"That was his forte and also his downfall," an FBI source told Clawson. "He gained a broader perspective and with it came a more progressive attitude. I'm not saying everything he wanted to do was great; it wasn't. The point is, he wanted to change things; he wondered out loud why we did things the way we did; why it couldn't be done with more effective results. In the FBI, that is like pouring gasoline over your own head. The Director is the only one with a match."

CLAWSON: "Now, on the basis of my relationship with Sullivan—who I thought was the best FBI administrator I'd ever seen—it's one thing to call Hoover senile and quite another to say that his opinions and beliefs and techniques were frozen in old-time concrete, which was Sullivan's allegation, and which I think was an accurate judgment. Because Bill Sullivan more than anybody else was a product of the FBI. His whole life was spent in the FBI. And Bill Sullivan did what a loyal, conscientious FBI agent would do, and he knew that in a lot of techniques, especially on domestic subversion, they were out of date. Bill tried his damnedest as the actual number two man of the FBI, that's what he was, he was really number two, because by then Tolson was pretty much out of it. He tried internally to the best of his ability to get the Old Man's opinions out of concrete, to make him a little more flexible, because it was a different time and a different set of circumstances. But he made the major bureaucratic mistake, in that he said, 'Either you accept some of my ideas or I'm getting out.' Well, before he could bat his eye, he was out. So Sullivan in one way was loyal and smart, and in another way he made a bureaucratic blunder. You just don't challenge the Director unless you got the horses.

"Sullivan was only one of many guys that Hoover brought along to the number two position and then ultimately fired them. Deke DeLoach is an example of a guy who got out before he was fired. But they all suffered from the same malaise—they were all basically of the FBI mold. Hoover had conceived them, he'd brought them up, he'd matured them, he'd promoted them to that number two spot—and then it would happen, and it happened in various ways to each of them. Courtney Evans, for example, fell in love with the Kennedys. He was never number two but he was in a key spot as Hoover's liaison with Bobby Kennedy and the White House. But when you're dealing with guys like Bobby Kennedy, this kind of goes to your head. You get to go to Hickory Hill, you cook your hot dogs and play touch football. So Courtney fell in love with the Kennedys and Hoover got rid of him. Quinn Tamn was one of Hoover's favorites, and all of a sudden he committed the worst kind of heresy—he questioned some axioms and automatically became a bad guy. Deke DeLoach fell in with the Johnson people too deeply, the same sin Evans committed. It's tough to have to straddle that line. And the minute that Hoover realized that DeLoach was straddling a little more toward Johnson than toward Hoover, he was dead.

"To illustrate this point, Sullivan and I used to have lunch together a lot, and he would pick—I never was able to pick—a restaurant where he was confident nobody would see him. That was even true when Hoover still thought I was the greatest reporter alive—it still was not safe for Sullivan to be seen with me. All of that material in my stories that is attributed to other sources comes from Bill Sullivan. I felt sorry for him. He was convinced, and this is interesting because the man spent his whole life in the FBI, he was convinced that his phone was tapped. So I would call his house and say, 'Do you know who's calling?' and he would say, 'Yes, I'll call you back from a phone booth.' Then he would go to a phone booth and call me back. That was incredible to me as a reporter because here's the number two man of the FBI I'm talking to. Now, I don't know if the goddamn phone was tapped or not, I don't think so, but *he* thought it was. The fact that he thought so was just incredible."

SULLIVAN: "Oh, my God, I don't remember ever giving Ken Clawson one story. The one story he got from me wasn't on the FBI. He called me the day after I had my final session with Hoover. He said, 'The Washington *Post* will give you the front page for four days if you write a series of articles on the Bureau and your break with Hoover.' I said, 'Ken, thank you very much, but I'm not interested in writing articles, I'm not interested in writing books, I'm not interested in writing lectures, but I thank you very much for remembering me.' Then he came out with an article on me, but I didn't know he was going to print it. Mind you, I have high regard for Ken Clawson, he was a very gentlemanly fellow with me, and I have no criticism of him, but I just got to stick to the facts. I don't remember giving him material for his critical articles on the Bureau.

"It's true that it wasn't safe for me to be seen with anybody in the press. But the restaurant was the Lincoln down there on E Street, about a block from the Bureau, and there are always Bureau men in there, so there was nothing supersecret about it. I'd stop and chat with them at their table or they'd come by my table, although I never introduced them to Clawson. So while it was a little out of the way, it wasn't a secret meeting. This was lunch, not dinner. I was never in his home, and he's never been in mine. There was always a third party with us, Harold Leinbaugh, who asked me to have lunch with Clawson as a personal favor to him. Clawson brought him over to the White House later on.

"That business about my phone being tapped, that happened only once. This was the first week after I left the Bureau and I happened to know that my phone was tapped. So when he called me one day, I said, 'Give me your number and I'll call you from a phone booth.' This never happened when I was in the FBI, because my phone wasn't tapped then. Being in the Bureau as long as I had, I had sources of information in every part of it, and it was impossible for them to tap my phone without my knowing it, and it was impossible for them to tap it after I left without my being told about it. Now during the last few weeks I was in the Bureau, they covered the switchboard on me, my sources told me that, and they had one of my secretaries spying on me, listening to any conversation I had on the phone and so on, but my phone wasn't tapped.

"Let me make one thing clear. My retirement was not a bureaucratic blunder. I elected to oppose Hoover, and it stemmed partly from the October twelfth, 1970, incident in Williamsburg, where I said that the Communist Party was not behind the black movement, but actually it went back beyond that. As far back as the late 1950s when I tried to get black agents in the Bureau, and I did manage to get one Jewish fellow in. There are many facets to anything as fundamental as this. I opposed Hoover on many things, so that my break with him had been coming on for a number of years."

"A Colossal Ego"

You were a troublemaker and yet you became the number three man. How was it possible?

SULLIVAN: "Because I was able to glorify Hoover, to put it very bluntly. I had the capacity to glorify him through my work and that was the decisive factor. Let me explain this. The FBI was a great game, a game of playing up to the ego of Hoover, in writing him fancy letters, in praising him to the skies. Mark Felt, John Mohr, the Callahan who's there now, Eugene Walsh, Alex Rosen, and DeLoach—I could name all the rest. We all played up to the ego of Hoover, and that was the way to get along. If you didn't do that, you wouldn't last twenty-four hours. He was a man who had a colossal ego. Some used to say he was an egomaniac. Whether he was or not, I don't know, I'm not in a position to judge. But this is how we all got along with him. Everyone knows what he was, and no one had any affection for him, and he didn't have affection for anybody else—except maybe for Tolson. Now, I'm putting the facts right on the table. He didn't have affection for one single solitary human being around him, and not one single solitary human being around him had any affection for him.

"The reason I was made an assistant director was because Kennedy was elected President. Hoover was a brilliant politician. I mean, don't underestimate that guy, he was cunning and sly and crafty, and he was a real politician. So I was from Massachusetts, Kennedy was from Massachusetts, Kennedy disliked Hoover and he knew it, and Hoover thought it would be a good political move to appoint an Irishman from Massachusetts Assistant Director of the Domestic Intelligence Division, and this is right after Kennedy came in. That's how I happened to get my head above the branch, you see.

"Before my last promotion, back in 1968, I saw that the Bureau was disintegrating. That was when our boys were getting ambushed down there in Vietnam and getting killed right and left, and my friends in the military said it was due to lack of intelligence, they didn't have good intelligence. So I kicked it around with them and I said, 'Do you think that if we employed some of the techniques of the FBI to the operation in Vietnam that it would help some?' Well, they didn't know, but they thought it might be worth a try. And I said, 'Well, damn it, I'm going to go down and see what we can do about getting better intelligence to prevent these boys from getting ambushed.' I wrote Hoover to request military service and, in writing, he turned me down."

Even with these conflicts when DeLoach left in 1970 you got his job. I've been told that the reason you got the job was because of your loyalty, that you never opposed him until 1971.

SULLIVAN: "No, no, no, no. DeLoach and I were bitter enemies, and frankly, he appointed me in order to humiliate DeLoach, because the worst thing he could do to DeLoach was to appoint his number one enemy in that spot. By doing that, he degraded DeLoach, and DeLoach was furious to think that I took over after him, because DeLoach hated me with a passion. Let's get one thing straight: DeLoach left under a big cloud. He had opposed Hoover, quietly behind the scenes, unlike myself— I fight out in the open. Hoover distrusted DeLoach and he wanted to get rid of him; he was very anxious that DeLoach resign. DeLoach left under a cloud, this is the truth, and it can be established.

"Oh, I'll tell you, DeLoach was more than a wheeler-dealer. He had more irons in the fire than any ten men. I'm telling you, he was something. He was cutting Ramsey Clark's hide there with Johnson all the time. And not only Ramsey, but other people in Justice, including Nick Katzenbach, who was one of the finest men I've ever known, an extremely intelligent man, a man of real integrity. Katzenbach knew, I think, but he just ignored it.

I asked Mark Felt if DeLoach had bucked for the Directorship.

FELT: "I think DeLoach wanted very badly to be Director of the FBI and when Johnson was President, of course, he probably had an excellent chance for it, if and when Hoover had died. DeLoach had a lot of political clout; he was really the power behind the throne in the American Legion, and he had a lot of political clout out of Georgia, good strong Democrat and so forth. If DeLoach had felt that he had enough pull with Nixon to keep that job, he would have stayed, he wouldn't have left. Of course, I'm just theorizing."

What happened between Hoover and Sullivan?

MOHR: "He and Hoover got into what you call a rhubarb and Sullivan is hard-headed and it got down to the point where it was Hoover or Sullivan. That's what it amounted to. The rapport between Sullivan and Hoover was one of complete subordinate on Sullivan's part up until, I think, the fall of 1971. I can't remember exactly when but it was along about that period that the rapport started to weaken and it finally broke, and it broke completely as a result of his giving that stuff to Mardian.* But prior to that time, Bill Sullivan was most obsequious in his opinions and letters to Mr. Hoover. In no way would he oppose him."

What about Sullivan's speech at Williamsburg in 1970?

MOHR: "That wasn't fatal, that didn't become fatal with him, boy. It's true Hoover needled him about it and Sullivan kept saying he didn't, but by the same token, there was still a close rapport up until about the fall of 1971. Hoover was most concerned and considerate of Sullivan. When Sullivan was ill one time, Hoover sent him to Tucson, Arizona, to insure that he had the best possible doctors and everything else to recuperate. And that's the way it was, it was always that way."

I repeated this to Sullivan.

SULLIVAN: "Yes, that was a matter that I thanked him for in writing. I was putting in six and seven and eight hours of overtime a day in 1953 when Eisenhower came in. I was a pretty tough hombre in those days, but even my body couldn't stand that kind of stress. I'd get home at night so damn tired I couldn't eat anything and I'd just go to bed. That went on for months, until finally I came down with pneumonia. Then I had a secondary infection of some sort that they never quite identified until I got to Arizona. It was diagnosed as a fungus growth in the bronchial tubes caused by penicillin administered for the pneumonia. Hoover could have put me on sick leave, but he didn't, instead he sent me to Arizona, and it took eight months before my lungs healed. He was very helpful in that whole matter. Of course, as he told me, 'If you hadn't worked all that overtime you never would have been sick.' I guess he kind of figured the Bureau owed it to me, you see. Still he didn't have to do it, and it was mighty thoughtful.

"Now, let me tell you something about John Mohr. John and I went to

---

* Mohr is referring to the logs of the seventeen wiretaps. See Part III.

American University together. We were fraternity brothers and we played football on the same team—he was the fullback and I was the right half-back. We became fast friends, very close friends, and then when I entered the Bureau—he entered the Bureau in '39, I think, or '38, and I didn't get in until '41—he was always in my corner. Both of us are strong-minded and both of us can be kind of bullheaded and possessed of strong convictions, and so we would clash quite often officially, but never personally. I always had the highest respect for John Mohr. Now there are people who hate John Mohr like they hate me, because like me, he was controversial, and like me, he got into a lot of damn arguments, and like me, he stepped on an awful lot of toes. There are people who hate him with a passion, just as they do me. I was always in controversy and I was always stepping on people's toes.

"There is one thing John Mohr and I would disagree on. I think the truth should go out to the American public, no matter how ugly and no matter how unpleasant, if for no other reason than to prevent another J. Edgar Hoover from ever gaining that much power again, and abusing it the way he did. I think John has got the viewpoint—and I say this as his warm friend—the viewpoint that, 'Well, hell, let bygones be bygones.' John knows what he was as well as I do, and I had enough talks with John to know he shared my own views, but I don't think he'll say anything for the public. He'll tell you, 'Yeah, the Old Man was irascible. Yeah, the old fellow was irritable, he was small, he was petty.' He'll say the little things that won't do him a hell of a lot of harm, but I don't think he'll tell you the whole ugly truth on it."

I put the question to both Mohr and Felt.

MOHR: "I wouldn't have worked for Hoover thirty-three years if I didn't believe in him and believe in what he was trying to do. He was a hard taskmaster, no question about that. He was a stern, strict disciplinarian. However, that was one of the reasons I continued in the Bureau. If the Bureau had not had those strict rules, if he hadn't been that strict a disciplinarian, I would have gotten out because it would have become corrupt, like many police departments have become corrupt. He would discipline you for the most minor type of error and it really made an impression on you. He'd get mad as hell at me, but he wouldn't stay angry and keep me in the doghouse. He would do things that at the time he felt he had to do to discipline me, and he did! And it made an impression on me."

FELT: "Hoover was an extremely personable, charming individual, no question about it, but if he was mad, he could be extremely rough and extremely tough too. He could bawl you out very easily. His discipline was very tight and very severe. If he thought anybody did anything wrong, then some sort of disciplinary action had to be taken right away. This is where he gets the reputation of being a dictator, and in a sense, I guess, he was, but in a sense also, the best form of government would be a benevolent dictatorship—a firm, benevolent dictator. He was really sincerely trying to do what was best for the FBI, and for the country, but he just wouldn't tolerate any nonsense at all. I'm afraid he wasn't too sympathetic with imperfections.

"And don't let anybody kid you about Hoover being senile, either. He was sharp as a tack right up to the day he died. I talked to him every day, even on Sundays, and either personally or on the phone, and I didn't detect any changes at all in those last two or three years, and I did have very close contact with him. He was quick and alert, his foresight was excellent. He had a keen foresight, far better than the average. He would remember details. Now, they say that's a sign of old age—remembering things that happened thirty, forty years ago—but Hoover would tell you what was in a memorandum that went up there the day before, and you had better be very careful in dealing with him, because you couldn't say something today that was in any way even slightly contradictory to what you had said yesterday. It really kept you on your toes dealing with him."

MOHR: "He was functioning perfectly right to the end. He used to take home a couple of suitcases full of stuff over the weekends and work on it. Let me say this, if you had dinner at his house, you would never find a more charming host than Hoover. There would be no acrimony, there would be no conversation of anything that would, in any way, interfere with having a most pleasant sociable time with him. I had dinner with him a number of places and he was always a charming individual to be with. I've been out with him when he'd let his hair down, he'd drink with us and talk and have an enjoyable time. He never would go over the brink but he'd have a good time and you couldn't be more sociable than he was. He'd needle me, for instance, in a group after dinner but, you know, not in an offensive way. If something happened to be going at the time in the office, he'd give me a little needle. For example, one time he referred to me as— Let's see, what was it? I'm thinking about 'irritating bastard,' but that wasn't his word. He used to call Tolson bullheaded and he used to call me bullheaded, and he probably was right. I am bullheaded; I stick to what I believe is right. But when he would say, 'This is the way we're going to do it. That's it.' Then I'd do it. My thirty-three years went by fast. For the most part, they were real pleasant, happy years for me. I enjoyed going to work, and I worked every day, every Saturday. I worked many, many years of overtime and never got a penny for any of it. Didn't want any and never got any. And when he was out of town, he would make it a point to call in no matter where he was. He was a great man. I'll have to say that for him. He was a great man for the country and he was a great man for the FBI."

A Litany of Mistakes

SULLIVAN: "I can't say he was senile. He was shrewd and crafty and astute, but the problem was his ego. The older he got, the more conceited and vanity-stricken he became, and no one could flatter him too much. Why, you could say the most outlandish things to him from the standpoint of flattery and that was just what he wanted, and so he became more and more susceptible to all sorts of flattery the older he got, and the last five or six years, anybody who engaged in that game could wrap him around their finger, and did.

"Also his decisions were bad. Let me give you a few examples and you draw the conclusion. That TWA pilot who flew the hijacked plane to Italy—just the pilot and the hijacker. The pilot criticized us mildly for trying to prevent his taking off. He had a perfect right to his views, right or wrong. Hoover tried to get him fired. As a matter of fact, we conducted a very discreet investigation of the pilot to see if we could find something derogatory on him, and it seems to me we got some damn thing, not personal conduct, but something in the line of his flying ability, and Hoover tried hard to get him fired, went right to the head of the company."

Personally?

SULLIVAN: "No, no. He was pretty clever, he always had buffers. He went through the SAC, wherever the company's headquarters were located, and tried to get the pilot fired. TWA wouldn't fire him. Then he issued orders that no agent was to fly on any TWA plane. Good God, you can't get into some parts of the country unless you fly TWA, or you can't get in at the time you want to get in, and so we fought him over that for weeks and finally we backed him down and he rescinded the edict.

"Take another example. He decided that Xerox was not cooperating fully in the Ellsberg case. We were trying to find out how the Pentagon Papers got copied, which machine had been used, and so on—I don't remember all the technicalities. Xerox did everything it could to help us in that respect, but Hoover was convinced they were holding back, and so he issued orders to take out the Xerox machines and put in IBM machines in all fifty-nine offices. That would run into millions of dollars, and finally we were able to talk him out of that.

"The same thing happened in the case of special agent Jack Shaw, who was a fine, outstanding fellow, a captain in the Marines in Vietnam, a great war record, and a fine record with us, so fine that we sent him to John Jay College. And he defended us there, but he wrote a term paper in which he admitted, you know, that after all we weren't perfect, that we did have some shortcomings, and when the damn fools in the New York office sent their report to Hoover, he was irate, and he said, 'Get rid of him.' The whole thing was absolutely childish. They dug a copy of Shaw's term paper out of his wastepaper basket, but, you see, the Bureau was run by fear, and they were afraid, apparently, to hold on to it for fear Hoover would learn of it and then they'd all get their heads bashed in. Shaw's wife was dying of cancer and he had four small children, and he couldn't take the transfer to Butte. He asked that it be postponed, and Hoover said, 'No, transfer him anyhow.' He had no heart at all. Shaw later sued him and was awarded thirteen thousand dollars. His wife died and he had a very difficult period for a time."

Someone should have warned Shaw, as you were warned when you first went in, not to criticize Hoover or the FBI.

SULLIVAN: "I'm glad you brought that up. Actually, that's why I hesitated when you asked me if he was getting senile. I don't think that was the real problem. Actually, he was very consistent throughout the years. The things he hated, he hated all his life. He didn't vacillate any. He hated liberalism, he hated blacks, he hated Jews—he had this great long list of hates. Anybody that had any liberal views was persona non grata. He called them pseudo liberals, but he pronounced it 'swaydo.' It was always 'swaydo,' and nobody dared to correct his pronunciation. As far as he was concerned, there never was a real, genuine, sincere liberal or intellectual. They were all 'swaydo' this or 'swaydo' that."

The joy in the city room of the Washington *Post* over Clawson's exclusive interview did not carry over to the editorial page. In an editorial on

November 19, the *Post* said in part, "It seems as plain as can be, moreover, that it was not any softness about Ramsey Clark that stirred Mr. Hoover's enmity but rather the Attorney General's strength and firmness. For Ramsey Clark was the first Attorney General since Harlan Stone to lay down the law to the director of the FBI and to remind him that his bureau was a subordinate element in the Department of Justice. Mr. Hoover had become so accustomed to conducting the bureau as though it were an independent principality over which he exercised absolute sovereignty that he could brook no expression of authority from his superior. . . . As for Mr. Clark, he is quite tough enough and strong enough to take care of himself."

A Fatal Weakness in Leadership

In my interview with Ramsey Clark, I asked him about the relationship between Hoover and Kennedy.

CLARK: "It's essentially an interpretation of the men and their personalities and their motives. A clear factor must be Bob's emerging prominence as a crime fighter. The point of one of Mr. Hoover's shortcomings, I believe, was his jealousy of anyone who emerged with any degree of prominence in the field of law enforcement except himself, and I think his almost consistent history is one of keeping everybody else down. It's really a fatal weakness in leadership, because you need to do just the opposite, you need to bring them up. But Mr. Hoover's record, take with the chiefs of police, going back for many years, was to begin an attack of sorts on anyone who began to achieve national prominence. Well, Bob was coming on as a big crime fighter. People were talking about the Organized Crime section and he was going around the country making speeches and holding meetings and energizing other investigative agencies, and they were beginning to get some glory. This was a holy mission of sorts with him. He was just deadly serious about it and deadly effective. The Organized Crime section was going night and day. Subconsciously, or however, Mr. Hoover watched all that and it was getting into his bailiwick a little bit and he didn't like it. It stirred some jealousy.

"A major source of Mr. Hoover's power was knowledge, and, I think, in the early sixties he knew very little about organized crime, and his agents could tell him very little, and that's when they started putting in all these bugs. Soon Mr. Hoover was beginning to tell Bob Kennedy things he didn't know. You can build a reputation by just knowing a lot, particularly if you're in investigative activity. That's why when I called the Russian Embassy for this group of church people to see if I could get them to go over to Leningrad and monitor the Soviet trials of the Jewish people there, I knew that would go straight to the President, because I knew Hoover relishes little things like that. To a busy guy at the White House, that seems like 'Gee, those guys know everything, don't they? The FBI is really on top of things.' It's as simple as this, they got a wiretap on the residency and a grown man is sitting there listening so that when a call comes in he knows that's something Mr. Hoover would be interested in because everybody's learned of his idiosyncrasies in that Bureau and it gets up there. And sure enough, the White House was leaking like a sieve and so Jack Anderson had it in less than two months, but he misinterpreted it at first; he thought it was a tap on me, but of course it was a tap on the Russian Embassy. The point is that they deal in information.

"In early 1964, or late 1963, Mr. Hoover started going to a considerable degree directly to the White House, bypassing Bob. I think that's a lawless thing, terribly dangerous and cannot provide equal justice or even-handed law enforcement. The President is simply much too busy to get into those things, and the risks for political motivation or personality motivation are just enormous and terribly dangerous. The major conflict that was supposed to have arisen had to do with minority hiring. Bob wanted to get some black agents in there and Mr. Hoover took just a straight stand that he wouldn't compromise on personal standards.

"As far as the bugging controversy is concerned, I think the central truth is that if Bob had really known about it, Mr. Hoover wouldn't have been so secretive toward him and toward the Department of Justice. What you really find is a structuring of the thing in a way that protects the Bureau because that was the one thing he would always do was protect the Bureau first, and second try to accumulate enough authority to go ahead and do what he wanted to do."

Does it seem reasonable to you that Bob Kennedy was not aware of the FBI's bugging and wiretapping of organized crime? What about the meetings in Chicago and New York where the FBI actually played tapes for him? Wouldn't you have said "Where the hell did you get that?"

CLARK: "Well, there's several things going. First, we've known and assumed that many police departments are wiretapping extensively. Second, we know that the FBI has close needs, close relationships with them. You couldn't tell if it was consentual, where you had a guy wired and that wouldn't have required Attorney General approval at that time. Bob wasn't keenly aware really of civil liberties. He was keenly aware of organized crime and therefore he perhaps wasn't as sensitive as he should have been, but one thing you just don't do in the jungle of law enforcement, particularly when you're in a staff meeting and here are twenty-five guys, is say 'Well, who was your informer?' or 'Where did you get that information?' for a number of obvious reasons. I don't know what the context of the tape was, but I think you can be sure just from the nature of things that the Bureau wouldn't have said, 'A tap or a bug that we installed.'"

He Had Some Aberrations about Communism and Sex and King

Did Hoover ever fail to carry out an order?

CLARK: "Not as far as I know, and some were quite unpleasant to him. Like any other institution, if they didn't really believe in or empathize with an order, why the execution might be very poor, as in the Orangeburg massacre investigation. They might be very reluctant to do it. You would order them to do it and they would do it. That is, I would say that this looked like an important violation of federal law. I did those things with rare exceptions, in a personal communication rather than any formal thing. The formal ones— I suppose I turned down, I don't know how many, maybe forty, fifty wiretap requests. I would do those in writing because they were submitted in writing."

Who was your FBI liaison?

CLARK: "It was Deke DeLoach, but after Bob Kennedy's death I cut that off. I couldn't bear to do that anymore. We had a little episode there that I didn't like and I just lost confidence in DeLoach. We'd been searching for James Earl Ray, the assassin of Dr. King, and I had been in daily contact with them about it. I'd go over and see the evidence and hear what they had and they'd send me reports. This is unusual, because as a rule the Attorney General doesn't know what's going on in an investigation. They were showing me everything. In fact, if anything, they would show me too much, because they would be going down some blind roads and I'd worry for two days about whether a body they'd dug up on the beach in Puerto Vallarta was James Earl Ray or not. The fingers would be dehydrated and you couldn't get prints, so I'd be waiting around to hear about that sort of thing.

"The day of Bob Kennedy's funeral, I went up to St. Patrick's, and I had to get back down here early because we were having a ceremony in the courtyard of the Department of Justice that same afternoon for Bob. So I couldn't come down on that train. When I came out of the church, an agent said, 'Mr. Attorney General, Mr. DeLoach says that it's urgent that you call him immediately.' When I called him, he said that they had captured James Earl Ray in London and that he had tried to hold it up until after the funeral but he couldn't hold it up because Scotland Yard or somebody was saying, 'We can't do that,' and so they released the story apparently during the church service. I was a little puzzled by that. I had been told a day or two before that something might break and we'd heard about him trying to go to Rhodesia and we'd picked up something in Lisbon on him, and I was really concerned that he was going to get down to Rhodesia or someplace that we couldn't extradite him and there we'd be. But I got back to Washington and some of my people were really upset because they said there had been this long typed announcement of the arrest, that it had been laid on their desk either the night before or that morning—"

It sounds like they wanted to release it at that precise time.

CLARK: "I never have understood why. I mean, it's too bizarre for me to understand, but for some reason they decided they'd remind everybody the FBI was still on the job about that time of day and they did. I think I could have taken that. I mean, it's an idiosyncrasy and kind of a petty one, but the thing I couldn't take was that I believed that I'd been lied to, and you can't function that way. I'd been told with some elaboration that they'd tried to hold up and couldn't do it when in fact it had been just the opposite, that they had held up just to release it at that time. I called DeLoach in that afternoon and did what I don't do very often, that is, got upset and told him I didn't want to use him as a liaison with the Bureau because I didn't have confidence in him anymore, and that was the end of that.

"Actually, I hadn't been using him very extensively anyway. Even men like DeLoach were very careful about their outside relationships with the Director. The night Dr. King was assassinated, I decided to fly down there. I don't think I decided until after midnight, and I decided I wanted DeLoach with me so that I would have the very latest information available when I got there, because I knew the press and others would be all over me. Besides, by that time it was clear that there was a high potential for turbulence and rioting all over the country. So I told DeLoach that I wanted him to go with me and he said he couldn't unless the Director said it was all right. I said, 'I want you to go. You just tell the Director and you can get that straightened out.' In a little while he called back and said, 'Would you mind calling him?' So I called the Director about two o'clock in the morning, woke him up, and said I was going to fly down and I wanted to take DeLoach with me, and, of course, he said, 'Why, sure, go ahead.'"

Do you think Hoover confronted King with evidence of the tape recordings, or do you think he was too smart to place himself in that position?

CLARK: "Well, I think not only too smart, I just don't think he would do it."

Except that he hated King to an irrational degree.

CLARK: "He had some aberrations about people and things. He was very emotional about Communism and sex and King and these things, and he could have gotten carried away. But it obviously wasn't anything that was very specific or detailed, so it couldn't have been very much. Mr. Hoover was a religious man in his way and he equated Communism with sin. He just thought Communism was very evil."

Do you think there was a conscious effort to play up his role against all radicals? For example, his comment about the Black Panthers.

CLARK: "I think he had to have bad guys and he specialized not in creating them but in illuminating them, and the Panthers lent themselves to it. I think it was an absurd and outrageous exaggeration. There's nothing to support it, numberwise or conductwise or any other way. But Mr. Hoover was old-fashioned on race. There's just no use trying to ignore it, it's all through his character. I don't think he ever thought of himself as racist, but there were heavy strains of racism in his character. When you take his age and having been raised in a Southern city essentially, the District of Columbia, he just thought their place and role was different. Finally, after he came through all the metamorphosis of the 1960s, he was able to see revolutionary evil among them. Here's an illustration of the 'You'll be interested to know' type of memos I would get from Mr. Hoover: 'Communists are joining forces at every turn in treasonous coalition opposing our efforts in Vietnam, working with black power advocates to lay foundations for outright guerrilla warfare in the streets of our cities.' Well, that's designed to scare you, I guess. I turned it down. They had just all kinds of people they wanted to tap or bug and I turned them down consistently, and I haven't the slightest doubt— Oh, I shouldn't say the slightest doubt, but I have no real doubt that he obeyed all those orders with absolute fidelity. I don't think he put any of those taps on."

Johnson Enjoyed Having Him Around

It has been reported that when President Johnson was asked why he kept Hoover on, his response was that "I'd rather have him inside the tent pissing out than outside pissing in." Do you know whether he made that comment?

CLARK: "If he said that, he didn't really mean it. I think it's the kind of colorful thing he might say, but I think he kind of enjoyed having him around. He was always extremely cordial to Mr. Hoover, always anxious to have him involved. I wanted to kind of create a position upstairs for Mr. Hoover. I thought some kind of ombudsman role for a senior guy, some oversight of the CIA and FBI, but the purpose was to see if we couldn't move him out of the FBI before it got hurt too bad, because I thought there was pretty significant erosion of the quality of its performance and its personnel going on. But to a fellow like Lyndon Johnson— First of all, they were so close personally. They had lived across the street for twenty-odd years and the beagle was named J. Edgar, and the Johnson daughters felt he was a rich uncle or something. Not that they'd see him that much, but in the old days he'd occasionally come over for breakfast on Sunday. And then Mr. Johnson was young enough to have grown up in the Dillinger days, and he liked that sort of thing. I think he was really almost disqualified.

"Yet I think President Johnson showed that he could do more with Mr. Hoover than anybody who'd ever tried. Getting Mr. Hoover to go down to Jackson, Mississippi, to open that FBI office was quite a feat. I wouldn't have bet much on being able to talk him into doing it, but he did."

This brings up a real problem. People say, "Never again another J. Edgar Hoover," but what's the alternative?

CLARK: "First, he's an accident of history to a very considerable extent.

The probability of there being another J. Edgar Hoover is just very remote. The alternative, however, is to have public accountability. The FBI has not been publicly accountable and I think it needs an influx of manpower that will give it a much broader national experience, more different races and religions and viewpoints, an open performance. We've got to have a new sense of priorities there. Nobody, the public or the Attorney General, really has any sense of what the FBI's priorities are, primarily because the FBI doesn't really have priorities, and that's tragic. They need to begin a system of evaluation that would give them clearly focused priorities, and they need to focus and restrict their jurisdiction. Mr. Hoover was pretty good at that. If he'd been an empire builder, he could have built an empire. But he didn't really, not in comparison to what he could have."

What was it like dealing with him on a day-to-day basis?

CLARK: "It was difficult, frankly, in the last years. It was difficult to keep him on an issue and keep a focus on it until some agreement or decision could be made. He would tend to change the subject, to talk about other things, or to just kind of pre-empt the conversation. Usually I'd have three or four things I wanted to discuss with him and they would be tentative or preliminary to get his views and he would tend to talk about other things and frequently they'd be repetitious."

Was he being evasive?

CLARK: "No, I don't think so. It reminded me of some older relatives that I've had. As you get on in years, and particularly if you've had a rich experience, you tend to want to talk about things or relive things, and he would tell the same thing a number of times. In fact, it was hard for me to talk with him for thirty minutes without him bringing up Dr. King."

He had a thing about him, didn't he?

CLARK: "Yes, he did. It may have been this didn't happen with many people, but when he saw me, he would think of Dr. King. I don't think there were many occasions when he didn't start telling me something about him, and it would tend to be derogatory."

Was this before or after King's death?

CLARK: "Before and after. Mr. Hoover was a very direct man; at least, I always found him to be. He was quite candid in expressing his opinions if he expressed them at all."

Still you don't think he was being evasive when he changed the sub-ject?

CLARK: "It may be that he did it in a way that escaped my detection, but to me it really seemed to be more a person who was more used to talk-ing than listening, and more used to framing the subject than having someone else do it. I developed a practice of having him over to lunch every two or three weeks, just the two of us in my office. It would usually last an hour and a half, and I would find it would be right toward the end and I still hadn't gotten to the things I had wanted to discuss. So I'd have to just push it, say, 'Well, there are a few things I wanted to discuss with you.' Part of it too, I thought, was loneliness, really. I think he was a very lonely man and when he found someone to listen, he would just talk.

"He had some unusual ideas. He wouldn't have staff meetings in the FBI. He wouldn't have all his assistant directors meet and discuss things. It was run in what I would call an authoritarian manner. Now we were having staff meetings regularly and having everybody in—Prisons, Immi-gration, Legal Division, maybe a dozen outfits—but he never partici-pated in those. He came four or five times, but he'd talk about the things he wanted to talk about. It would tend not to be spontaneous and it wouldn't move. The meetings were quite unproductive. That's when I finally went to just the two of us.

"You see, he had all those associates down at the FBI and he really had a strong feeling that he shouldn't fraternize. One of the things I wanted to do—there were some things I wanted to do that I never did—was to have all the assistant directors to a lunch in my office. I did this at least once a week, selecting a different outfit each week, and I wanted to include the FBI, but it was obvious I wouldn't want to do it over his strenuous objections, because you'd defeat the very purpose. I wanted to get to know them better and to open it up a little so I could get to hear what they were thinking, what they were saying and doing, and give them some encouragement, but he just didn't think you should fraternize."

Would Tolson accompany him when he came to your office?

CLARK: "Only in the beginning. I always appreciated Clyde Tolson very much. But there were long periods there when Clyde couldn't come. I don't know the truth of the allegations and nobody would ever say, but Clyde had a stroke, I think, and it was pretty severe. He had a stroke in the night, and Mr. Hoover and his chauffeur—Clyde apparently called him—had to get him over to the hospital. They didn't want anybody to know it. I would ask him, 'How is Clyde?' but people in the Bureau wouldn't ask. I think Clyde had a series of strokes and I think he couldn't talk for a while. He was sick for months and months, I'd say in both 1967 and 1968, and of course I don't know anything about his condition after that time.

"I can remember the Director telling me at some length as if to justify—you see, he really needed Clyde because he didn't have any close relationship with anyone else—they were flying and the plane took a sudden drop and Mr. Hoover always wanted to think Clyde's condition had something to do with the change in pressure in the cabin. Mr. Hoover was a very lonely man. It was sad in a way. He had no close friends. His social contacts were just incredibly limited."

"A Sovereign Empire"

I was impressed and delighted with Ramsey Clark's candor and fairness, but William Sullivan saw it differently.

SULLIVAN: "Ramsey Clark would straddle the fence. For example, he knew that Hoover disliked him, he knew that Hoover would trip him up, and quite frequently, yet when Christmas came around he'd send Hoover a fine Christmas gift. To me, that's hypocritical. Sure, you have to work with him, but you don't have to send him Christmas gifts. You don't have to act as though everything was very, very cordial and pleasant. He knew that Hoover was knifing him in the back, but at Christmas along would come this fine gift. That's the kind of thing I don't approve of, among many others. It seems that even after he's dead, no one wants to take the chance of criticizing him for fear of some critical reaction to them. As a friend of mine said, 'Nobody dares criticize him, because they think he's going to rise from the dead.' None of the attorneys general had the guts to stand up to him and say, 'Look, you're working for the Justice Department; you're not running a sovereign empire.' None had the guts except Bobby Kennedy. You see the hypocrisy? John Mitchell was always running down Hoover and always criticizing him and was working to get rid of him. 'We're going to get rid of him,' he'd say. Yet when it goes on the record, he's like all the other hypocrites; he doesn't dare to criticize him. Mitchell adopted a con man approach with Hoover. He praised him and flattered him and jollied him and that's the way he tried to get along with Hoover, who dominated Mitchell.

"Kleindienst is another hypocrite, because he despised Hoover. He started a movement to get rid of Hoover. Kleindienst is the man behind the recommendation to get Hoover to testify before Congress on the operations of the Bureau. Hoover countered by saying that if he had to testify, he'd have to reveal all his sensitive wiretap coverage, and the Department of Justice dropped the whole issue.

Kleindienst complained to me that Hoover wouldn't cooperate. I was in Kleindienst's office one time when Hoover was on the phone and Kleindienst took the phone and started to make circular motions, and he leaned back in his chair and just grinned all over, you know, as if saying, 'Now this fellow is all wound up and off the beam.' He wasn't even listening to what Hoover was saying; he just kept the receiver going around and around, making a big joke out of it.

"They all wanted to get rid of Hoover: Mitchell, Kleindienst, Robert Mardian, the White House, including Nixon, but nobody had the guts to do it. And now that he's dead, they're still afraid of him. They think he's going to be resurrected from the dead. This is a phenomenon. Why should they have this tremendous fear of this man?"

The Attorney General Should Be a Politician

Richard G. Kleindienst holds the dubious distinction of being the first cabinet-level officer to be convicted in the Watergate scandal, and the second cabinet member ever to be convicted of misconduct in office. Although he lied several times to the Senate Judiciary Committee during his confirmation hearings, a felony, he was allowed to plead guilty to a misdemeanor—refusing "to answer questions" about the involvement of the White House in the settlement of an antitrust suit against ITT.

A protégé of Barry Goldwater, and a darling of the far right, Kleindienst first came to national attention as head of the "Arizona Mafia" that captured the Republican Presidential nomination for Goldwater in 1964. That same year Kleindienst lost his own Republican campaign for Governor of Arizona. He returned to his Phoenix law practice and quietly slipped back into obscurity. It was not until 1967, he told me in an interview on October 7, 1974, that he returned to the national arena.

KLEINDIENST: "President Nixon asked me to help him get delegates for his nomination. Then, in January of 1968, Mr. Mitchell became the general campaign chairman and I was designated the national director of field operations of the Nixon campaign and my responsibility again was in charge of the nationwide organization to get delegates for his nomination. As a result of that, I got to know Mr. Mitchell quite well. When Nixon was elected and he asked Mitchell to be the Attorney General, John Mitchell asked me if I'd be his deputy. I said yes, and here I am."

Do you think it's proper to make the office of Attorney General a reward for political work?

KLEINDIENST: "I think people who get in top policy positions of the United States government should be responsible to the general political forces of our country. Then I guess it depends on what you do once you get in the job. After I came in the Department of Justice, I thereafter never attended a partisan political meeting of any kind. I guess I wouldn't have become the Attorney General had I not had a political background. The only living I ever made for me and my family was as a lawyer; I made no money out of politics. It was quite a financial sacrifice for me and my family to be in the government. I had a very particular concept of the Department of Justice and tried to live up to it. But if you don't have people who come out of the political references of our country, again you frustrate the ability of the American people in their role as voters to bring about changes in policy in the executive branch of the government. The argument that you want to get some career person to be the Attorney General of the United States who's divorced from politics, I think is—I guess it has some appeal on the surface but if you examine it, it's rather specious and not very deep."

Did you enjoy those years?

KLEINDIENST: "The best years of my life were the four and a half years I was in the Department of Justice."

Did you enjoy working with Hoover? I know that Hoover said some good things about Mitchell, but I can't recall anything he said about you.

KLEINDIENST: "Well, every indication I got, both from him and people around him, was that he liked me. I always admired Mr. Hoover, you know, as a young man, and as I grew up and I was in politics. I've said so publicly many times. He was probably the finest lifetime career servant the government of the United States has ever had. I think it's very difficult to run an investigative federal agency for some fifty years with the even-handed balance that he did, without scandals and without having it be an instrument of partisan national politics. I think you do it as a result of your basic character and discipline, your ability to maintain discipline.

"When you are dealing with the sensitive investigation of federal crimes, you have got to maintain a discipline, because you cannot ever succumb to the temptation given by power to use information that you have for political purposes. That would be one of the great trespasses upon our political processes and freedom in this country. Secondly, you have to have agents trained so that information is used only for the purpose intended. One of the worst things that you can have, it seems to me, is the leaking of sensitive raw investigative material from the files of the FBI. You ought to read an FBI file sometime, because what it really is, depending upon the nature and the extent of the inquiry, is just a collection of statements by a lot of people. A lot of it can be hearsay, a lot of it can derive from prejudices or animus or hatred or vindictiveness, a lot of it can be speculation and guesswork. And the whole enforcement procedure in the federal government is predicated upon a very careful use of that kind of material.

"I always credited Mr. Hoover for being faithful in preserving the integrity of the files. The FBI did not prosecute people for crimes. It did not even make recommendations with respect to whether or not a person was prosecutable. I always said to myself, 'Well, that's correct.' The time when you get in trouble in the prosecution of your criminal laws is when the investigator makes a decision as to whether or not to prosecute, because sometimes because he's human, he gets a vested interest, you know, in terms of accomplishing his task. If he thinks somebody has done something wrong and works hard at it, he can become myopic in his vision and short-sighted and prejudiced and influenced by his own endeavors, and many times if that investigator then makes a decision to prosecute, you bring about a miscarriage of justice. Mr. Hoover was always satisfied to have his people get the facts and then turn those facts over to a career lawyer in one of the litigative divisions of the Department of Justice and then let them make the decision as to whether or not the case should proceed."

"Prosecution by Innuendo"

On November 27, 1970, Hoover told a Senate appropriations subcommittee that Fathers Daniel J. Berrigan and Philip F. Berrigan, who were serving federal prison sentences for destroying draft board records, and five others, including Sister Elizabeth McAlister, had plotted to kidnap Henry Kissinger in an attempt to force a halt to United States bombing in Southeast Asia, and "to blow up underground electrical conduits and steam pipes serving the Washington, D.C., area in order to disrupt federal government operations." The plotters would demand as ransom the release of all "political" prisoners in the United States.

This premature disclosure was followed by a barrage of criticism. There were charges that Hoover's remarks about the investigation before the indictments were returned had elevated the case into a test of his reputation. Liberals angrily charged the Director with "prosecution by innuendo." I asked Kleindienst whether Hoover had pushed for prosecution in the Berrigan case.

KLEINDIENST: "No. I think his testimony was an oversight on Mr. Hoover's part. I was responsible for the procedure by which the Berrigan prosecution came about. That kind of publicity is very bad when you have an ongoing, uncompleted investigation. It's prejudicial to those being investigated and it also makes the task of the investigative agency more difficult. When the investigation was completed, I got one of the top career professional lawyers in the Criminal Division [William S. Lynch] who had been in the Organized Crime section, one of the best career trial lawyers—he was a Catholic and a Democrat—and gave him the Berrigan file. And I said, 'I want you to be the chief prosecutor in this case, but I don't want the case prosecuted unless you take this whole file of information and determine independently yourself whether there is sufficient evidence to go forward with the case.' He studied it for a substantial period of time, but he was under no direction or compulsion from me. He came back some time later and said that in his opinion the case on the facts justified and warranted a prosecution of the Berrigans, and he said he'd be willing to undertake it and he did."

And Hoover was not pushing—

KLEINDIENST: "No, no. There was an investigation going on at that time, it continued after Mr. Hoover made his statement, and that is why, because of that publicity which emanated from Mr. Hoover's statement, that I asked Mr. Lynch to give an independent evaluation of the evidence. Having come to the conclusion that he did, I'd have to say to you that the case would have gone forward."

But you lost the case.

KLEINDIENST: "Well, it was a conspiracy case to begin with, and a conspiracy trial should always be one of the most difficult to prove. What you have in a conspiracy trial is proof, essentially, of what goes on in several people's minds with respect to their joint action and their intent to do something. If you make it easy to measure, you know, criminal intent in a person's mind, then you make it awfully easy to prove the commission of crimes that perhaps weren't committed. You will always find, therefore, that it is difficult to get a jury to bring in a verdict for you, just as a general principle, because to begin with, at the time of trial, the conspirators want to deny the conspiracy, they deny that they talked to each other in a manner that was in violation of the federal law. You're usually left to circumstantial evidence—circumstantial proof of what they really intended. I was not at all upset that we lost the Berrigan trial. I was, however, quite willing to have the case tried.

"The reason why is this: The trial of a case like that, provided you have sufficient evidence to go forward, also acts as a useful deterrent to—oh, kind of scatterbrained, harum-scarum conduct and activity like this on behalf of other persons. On the other side of the coin, let's say that the information we had with respect to this conspiracy—that is to say, the actual visit to the tunnels, the plans and the conspiracies to kidnap Kissinger and to blow up these tunnels—came to us, and then suppose a responsible officer in the Department of Justice said, 'Well, maybe they're going to do it and maybe they're not, but this is a very sensitive political issue, and if we prosecute them we're going to get a lot of political criticism, particularly from the young people and those who are sincerely opposed to the policies of the United States government with respect to the war.' So we decide not to prosecute. Then suppose the next week there is a bombing and twenty-five little secretaries get killed. Then they ask you, 'Why didn't you do something about it?' And you say, 'Well, we didn't really believe it, on the one hand, and number two, we didn't want to, and number three, it wouldn't be popular.' At that point, the whole enforcement function of an investigative agency, on the one hand, the FBI, and the Department of Justice to enforce the law, on the other, would just break down."

Was there an agent provocateur *involved?*

KLEINDIENST: "No, I think there was an informant."

Didn't he behave like an agent provocateur?

Kleindienst: "I don't think I understand what you mean."

The informant, Boyd F. Douglas, Jr., testified that in conversations with Father Philip Berrigan he was the one who first suggested they use a gun to kidnap Kissinger, and that he also offered to pay for the gun in conversations with Sister McAlister. Wouldn't that be entrapment?

Kleindienst: "I don't— My recollection of the specifics of the Berrigan case— I had an awful lot of things that I was involved in without following daily, you know, the specifics of the case. I don't believe that there was such but there might have been. I just wouldn't want to make a statement that would pretend to have that kind of precise knowledge on my part."

"Mitchell Doesn't Have Any Guts"

I asked William C. Sullivan whether Hoover had pushed for a prosecution on the Berrigan case.

Sullivan: "Of course he pushed on the Berrigan case. He pushed hard. If we had a case that we thought was a good case and the evidence was solid, we'd push it, we'd push it. We'd keep sending material over to the Department, just flooding them with material, to the point where, you know, if it was good evidence, they couldn't avoid it, they'd have to act on it. We wouldn't go over there and say, 'Look, we want you to prosecute this case.' We were more subtle than that. That would make us vulnerable. There was no bungling about it. We'd keep the pressure up, and we'd keep hammering away at them with evidence and asking for their evaluation: 'We want your decision on this matter.' We'd put them in a position where if they didn't prosecute, they'd be in trouble."

Did Mitchell censure Hoover for revealing the Berrigan investigation to the committee?

Sullivan: "No, he didn't have the guts. I tell you, Mitchell doesn't have any guts, I can tell you that much. In fact, Hoover was mad at Mitchell because the Department issued a press release on the Berrigans. Mitchell told me he was disgusted with Hoover. He said, 'I don't know what in hell Hoover is growling about, because I got him off the hook.' That was his exact phrase: 'I got him off the hook.' "

Did the FBI informant behave like an agent provocateur?

SULLIVAN: "To the best of my memory, we didn't suggest that he do any of those things. We didn't have to. These fellows were wild, you know. It was too bad. You don't want to get involved in entrapment, because you'll lose the case. And we didn't have to. It's too damn bad the Berrigans didn't stick to what they were trained for, clergymen. They were playing the game of romantic revolutionaries, but they didn't know what the hell they were doing. If Hoover hadn't come out when he did publicly on that matter, we may have made a case against them. They did talk about blowing up the tunnel there in Washington. Not that they would have done a hell of a lot of damage, but they would have gotten headlines. That's what they were after, headlines. They wouldn't have hurt anybody."

"Kick Him Upstairs?"

Returning to Kleindienst, I asked if he and Hoover saw eye to eye on law and order issues.

KLEINDIENST: "I remember [laughs] once during my confirmation hearings for Attorney General after Mr. Mitchell went to the re-election committee, I came back and there was a box on my desk and I opened it up and it was this little Latin-inscribed sign which said in effect, 'Don't let the bastards wear you down.' There was a note from Mr. Hoover which said, 'I saw this in a window at lunch and I thought you ought to have it.' He has written me many personal notes that were of a non-business basis. He was a very thoughtful man, you know. One of the funny anecdotes that he— One evening when a staff meeting was over, he was leaving and I was standing in the door, and he clapped me on the back and he said, 'Kleindienst, do you know why I like you?' I said, 'No, sir, Mr. Hoover. Why?' He said, 'Because you and I have the same enemies.' Well, everybody laughed at that, you know [laughs]. I didn't know whether we did or not."

He called you Kleindienst. Did you call him by his first or last name?

KLEINDIENST: "Oh, no. No, sir. He called me Kleindienst and I called him Mr. Hoover. I was a relatively young man to him, and I've always been taught to show respect to my elders, generally speaking, and I had a great personal specific reason to show my respect to Mr. Hoover. But he always, I think, essentially showed respect to me.

"I admired him, but I also felt this way about Mr. Hoover: When you have had a life of service with the accomplishments that he has had for some fifty years, and then as you get into the twilight days of your life and the end appears to be in sight and you're seventy-seven years of age, you can't be expected to have the same resilience and the same energy and the same attitudinal references that you had twenty years ago. I knew the time was approaching when Mr. Hoover had to leave. I think his age began to present some problems."

I don't quite understand—

KLEINDIENST: "Well, the older we get, the more rigid we get, the more—"

Was he getting rigid?

KLEINDIENST: "Yes, he was getting old. I think age has its effects in one way or another on all of us, particularly when you get in your late seventies, but these effects, in my opinion, were minimal. It did not interfere with his ability."

Was he getting senile?

KLEINDIENST: "Not in a marked degree. He was showing the effects of age, and I think he was becoming defensive as a result of his advanced years. I think he had a great desire to preserve the status role and image of himself and the Bureau, and as a consequence of that, might not have been as eager to launch out into new programs and experiments and ideas, but even by saying that, it did nothing, in my opinion, to appreciably or measurably interfere with the role, mission and function of the FBI. And I was always hopeful that Mr. Hoover would either have resigned or left the Bureau in such a way that his leaving would not detract from his significance and his service to this country and the role of the FBI. I think it's almost a blessing that he died in his sleep the way he did, or, you know, the rather abrupt circumstances, because that passing of his in a relatively peaceful way at that time in his life permitted, I think, a very thoughtful, considerate way for him to cease being the head of the FBI."

Wasn't the White House planning to get rid of him after the 1972 election?

KLEINDIENST: "I was involved in no understanding of that type. I think what I would have liked to see for Mr. Hoover was to have [pause] created for him some [long pause], by way of recognition, some role in the government by which he could have remained available as a counselor and adviser."

Kick him upstairs?

KLEINDIENST: "Yes, if you will. And in a manner that would have been satisfactory for him, bring in another younger, day-by-day head of the FBI. And I think that, if it had been handled correctly, could have been done."

Was Hoover political? For instance, did he play ball with the Administration?

KLEINDIENST [laughs]: "Well, to begin with, the head of the FBI, you know, works for the President of the United States. Right?"

Not the Attorney General?

KLEINDIENST: "The Attorney General works for the President. The FBI Director doesn't work for the Attorney General, he works for the President. The President puts in an Attorney General to help him administer the FBI. Career people generally respond to the overall broad policy directions of a new President, and Mr. Hoover, I think, lent himself to those broad policy changes in each administration. I don't think anybody would say that Mr. Hoover so ingratiated himself with a new administration that he was induced to do things that were contrary to the basic laws underpinning the function of the FBI."

"It Couldn't Happen Again"

As the fifth to be so named by Richard Nixon, William B. Saxbe took particular delight in being the Attorney General of the United States, a job he held for about a year. He said that he was in the process of changing the FBI. In what way? I asked.

SAXBE: "I don't know whether I'm changing it. I know what my concept of it is and I know how it is with the present setup. They are definitely part of the Justice Department. Their budget, their administration, all run through our system, and it's going to increase over the years. We're not making any radical changes, but there's no way they operate effectively outside of the Justice Department, nor should they, but they almost did for a number of years."

You mean there was an end run around the Attorney General?

SAXBE: "There was an end run, and a successful one, to the White House, to the Congress, and I would say a long way to the national police forces of the states and cities. They dealt directly with them."

Was it because of Hoover's prominence and his long tenure?

SAXBE: "I think that's part of it, but I also think there was a great desire for consistency, and as attorneys general came and left, you just couldn't have every Attorney General shaping the FBI to suit himself. I think Mr. Hoover recognized this and said, 'Well, we can't just bend with every wind that blows.' And I think we had an example of how that could happen after Hoover died. Gray was used, exploited. The FBI was demeaned by getting too close to political operations. My desire for the whole Justice Department is for a completely professional operation, and that means that we remove ourselves from politics over here just about as completely as we can for an appointive office. There's no one here making any political speeches, attending any political functions of any kind. And we are not involved in any political decisions. This makes my job easier in working with the FBI because I ask nothing from them any way politically oriented, and they know this now. It works both ways. I protect them from any political influence and they appreciate it, and it makes them more cooperative in working with this office."

How do you prevent the Director's job from becoming just another political appointment?

SAXBE: "Of course, Hoover was able to stop this by his prestige. We'll just have to wait and see; we can't forecast that. I hope that the precedent that I'm setting here in the year I've been here and the time I hope to be here is going to remain. I'm not at all sure it will. They could go right back and appoint one of the chairmen of one of the parties to be the Attorney General. I hope they don't. It's the only way you're going to retain objectivity and professionalism in the Department of Justice. If it doesn't work this way, you can expect an elective Attorney General, you can expect a continuing special prosecutor or whatever other extralegal agencies with the power to go to court and so on."

But Hoover had the power to go it alone—

SAXBE: "Well, it will never happen again, because he moved into a vacuum. There was no federal enforcement of any kind except for U.S. marshals when he came in. They had an embryonic FBI that, you know, wasn't exactly a pattern for— They were more like revenuers than they were like the FBI of today. So from that standpoint, it couldn't happen again. He moved into a vacuum and he pulled it together. It had been in existence long enough, however, that they knew what they wanted and they knew what they weren't getting, and that's why he did do this. And he was a genius in building a—its symbol. And he was able to use national publicity and it was used in a very helpful way in drawing attention to the FBI.

"You know, he had broad support across the country. During my reelection campaign, I suggested that Hoover should retire and I really stirred up a hornet's nest in Ohio during the campaign on this. Especially in Cincinnati. And I became aware of the cult that Hoover had built up and I backed away from it pretty fast. He was an institution. And I have found this to be true since I've been here. Every time I criticize Hoover or some of his actions, I receive a whole stack of canned editorials that come from little—Helena, Arkansas and Twin Falls, Idaho—papers that use canned editorials and somebody effectively circulates them. I don't think it's the Department, but they've got a very effective alumni association and they don't want any criticism of Hoover.

"But getting back to what I was saying, Hoover early realized that there were some areas that he didn't want to get involved in because they were nasty areas. The FBI always shied away from drug enforcement, and it's cost us. The FBI has a distaste for this kind of nasty business. You know, nobody wins in a drug bust. And they learned to use crime statistics early and they used them well. Mr. Hoover used Dyer Act* prosecutions very effectively for a long time. Now we're getting out of that business because we can't have thirty-five-thousand-dollar-a-year men chasing nineteen-year-old car thieves, nor can we have our federal penitentiaries filled with teen-age car thieves. I'm getting more and more U.S. attorneys to turn these over to local jurisdictions.

"The Congress is constantly trying to make more and more things a federal offense. They want to make dog fighting a federal offense now. Hoover didn't want to get into the ordinary day-to-day crime field, and he was correct in that. Not having known him, I can only look at the results of his work, and it's a pretty impressive outfit. And if he became overly

* Transporting stolen automobiles across state lines.

protective and overly involved in the last few years, I think you have to look at it in regard to the conditions and the attitudes of other people in this country during those years. I'm thinking about the New Left and what he considered the threat to our government. It's not an easy job to judge a dead man on his work. You have to take the physical evidence of the existence of the FBI and what it stands for and what he did with it. The abuses are relatively minor when you look at the whole picture."

PART
III

SECRET
LIFE

The Penultimate Straw

It will be a long, long time, if ever, before we know fully the complex role Hoover played in the Nixon years. Tom Charles Huston, the young man who conceived part of what John Mitchell would later characterize as White House "horrors," bluntly told me that Hoover was responsible for Watergate. Huston's bizarre rationale goes this way: If the Director had not opposed Huston's plan for illegal domestic intelligence activities, then Richard Nixon would never have had to give birth to its bastard offspring, the Plumbers, which he set up to do what Hoover would not. The link between the Plumbers and Watergate is G. Gordon Liddy, a Plumber, who devised the scheme to bug the Democratic National Committee. Huston reasons that Liddy would not have been in a position to do anything if Huston's own scheme had been adopted.

Since this convoluted interpretation of Watergate comes in the last chapter of Hoover's life, I decided to pursue it with both interviews and one final excursion into the fact and fiction of the written record. Quotations of White House transcripts and supporting evidence used throughout this section are from the published report of the Hearings before the Committee on the Judiciary, House of Representatives, Ninety-third Congress, Second Session, pursuant to House Resolution 803, a resolution authorizing and directing the Committee on the Judiciary to investigate whether sufficient grounds exist for the House of Representatives to exercise its constitutional power to impeach Richard M. Nixon, President of the United States of America, May–June 1974.

Hoover's first known involvement with the Nixon White House came about when William Beecher, the New York *Times* Pentagon correspondent, revealed part of the Nixon-Kissinger game plan for ending the war in Vietnam. Beecher's front-page story on May 9, 1969, began: "American B-52 bombers in recent weeks have raided several Vietcong and North Vietnamese supply dumps in Cambodia for the first time, according to Nixon administration sources, but Cambodia has not made any protest."

There was immediate denial by the Administration, yet over a period of fourteen months in 1969 and 1970 the United States conducted a total of 3,630 secret B-52 bombing sorties against Cambodia, with the apparent consent of Prince Sihanouk. Carried out under the code name "Operation Menu," the raids were kept secret from both the American people and Congress by clever double-entry bookkeeping which logged the bombings accurately for Pentagon records but disguised them as missions in South Vietnam for the rest of the nation.

In an internal memorandum written that same day, Hoover informed Tolson, Cartha (Deke) DeLoach, William C. Sullivan and Thomas Bishop that "Dr. Henry A. Kissinger, National Security Adviser to the President, called from Key Biscayne" to advise him of the *Times* story, "which is extraordinarily damaging and uses secret information." Kissinger said "to put whatever resources I need to find who did this," but "to do it discreetly, of course, but they would like to know where it came from because it is very damaging and potentially very dangerous."

The source of the leak was never found and apparently there was no awareness at the time of the investigation that the story had been published forty-eight hours previously in London after a British correspondent flying over Cambodian territory had seen bomb craters.

"Arrogant Harvard-type Kennedy Men"

Hoover's memo was time-stamped 10:35 A.M., and at 5:05 P.M. that same day Hoover issued another internal memorandum, which summarized his telephone report to Kissinger. After detailing background information on the author of the *Times* story, Hoover told Kissinger that

it is the conclusion of the contacts we have made that [the leak] could have come and probably did from a staff member of the National Security Council. I continued that Q [Beecher], while at undergraduate school . . . had a roommate who is now a staff member of the National Security Council. There is a strong possibility also that he may have gotten some of his information from the Southeast Asian Desk, Public Affairs Office of the Department of Defense, as the Public Affairs Office is constituted of employees who are pronounced anti-Nixon. I continued that Q frequents this office as well as the National Security Council, and the employees freely furnish him information inasmuch as they are largely Kennedy people and anti-Nixon. I said that also in the Systems Analysis Agency in the Pentagon, there are at least 110 of the 124 employees who are still McNamara people and express a very definite Kennedy philosophy.

I continued that this situation has made it very easy for Q to obtain information; however, the source we have been working through said it should not be ruled out that a staff member of the National Security Council who obviously was in a position to know the information contained in all three articles could have assisted Q. Dr. Kissinger said he has heard this as an allegation, too, but there is no proof; that he has heard it as a speculation. I said, of course, this is speculation all the way through tying it into this man N. . . . I said in regards to N we conducted an applicant investigation of him in 1962 and in February 1969 and the investigation reflected N* and other experts in his field are of the opinion that the United States leadership erred in the Vietnam commitment as we did not possess the interest or capabilities to obtain the original objectives. I said that in 1965 his name appeared on a list of individuals who responded to a request for a public hearing on Vietnam by agreeing to sponsor a national sit-in. I said the Royal Canadian Mounted Police in 1965 advised that N's name was on list of Americans who had reportedly received the *World Marxist Review Problems of Peace and Socialism,* a communist publication.

I continued that from another source it was indicated we should not overlook the Systems Analysis Agency in the Defense Department who had an employee named [deleted] and another named N currently employed as staff employee of the National Security Council. I said they are very close to each other and both are so-called arrogant harvard-type Kennedy men who would not hesitate to do anything to save their jobs. I said it was stated that N was particularly anxious to save [deleted]'s job with the Systems Analysis Agency. I said both men know Q and consider him a part of the Harvard clique, and, of course, of the Kennedy era and we should not ignore the possibility that N and/or [deleted] could be the source of the leak to Q.

I said that is as far as we have gotten so far. Dr. Kissinger said he appreciated this very much and he hoped I would follow it up as far as we can take it and they will destroy whoever did this if we can find him, no matter where he is. . . .

* At the request of the Department of Justice, the Judiciary Committee either omitted the names of the wiretapped individuals or substituted letter designations.

Hoover's memo is a Machiavellian masterpiece. Always the compleat bureaucrat, he knew all about Nixon's obsessive hatred for Kennedy and of his paranoia over the bureaucracy, and he did not hesitate to feed it, hinting along the way, and not too subtly at that, that he too resented the "so-called arrogant harvard-type Kennedy men" that were out en masse to subvert the new Administration.

A Divine Right to Eavesdrop

Nixon's reaction was electric. The very next day, following a meeting in the Oval Office with Hoover, Kissinger and Mitchell, Nixon authorized a specific wiretapping program to discover the source of the leak. Wiretaps were later ordered placed on thirteen government officials, including five of Kissinger's closest aides on the National Security Council staff: Morton H. Halperin, Winston Lord, Helmut Sonnenfeldt, Daniel I. Davidson and Anthony Lake. Also wiretaps were placed against four newsmen suspected of receiving leaked information: Marvin Kalb of CBS; Henry Brandon, Washington correspondent of the London *Sunday Times*; Hedrick Smith, diplomatic correspondent for the New York *Times*; and Beecher. That both Kalb and Brandon considered themselves close friends of Kissinger clearly indicates the degree of hysteria already infecting the White House.

The hook on which Nixon hung the wiretap order was "national security," but no one had ever defined exactly what that constituted. Other presidents, beginning with Roosevelt in 1940, had authorized FBI wiretaps on that basis. Although Roosevelt had limited his requests to "fifth columnist" alien groups, Truman had extended it to domestic subversives. In 1967, however, the Supreme Court ruled that wiretapping without a court order constituted unreasonable search and seizure, a violation of the Fourth Amendment. But this was not interpreted as a limitation of the President's constitutional power "to protect national-security information against foreign intelligence activities." Mitchell was a particularly aggressive exponent of the President's divine right to eavesdrop on any domestic group "which seeks to attack and subvert the government by unlawful means." It was not until the Keith decision on June 19, 1972, two days after the Watergate break-in, that the Supreme Court in a unanimous decision finally ruled that no domestic group or individual could be tapped without a warrant. Still left unresolved was the President's right to tap without a warrant in cases involving foreign intelli-

SECRET LIFE 249

gence, a loophole that affords broad latitudes of action to any secretive-minded President.

Having played this wiretap game many times before, Hoover insisted on getting written authorization from the Attorney General after receiving a White House directive for each of the seventeen wiretaps; but unlike other national security wiretaps, they were not entered in the FBI indices, and no copies were made of the files and logs, which were kept in the office of Assistant to the Director William C. Sullivan. This unorthodox procedure was requested by Colonel Alexander Haig, then an assistant to Kissinger, who submitted sixteen of the seventeen wiretap requests.

Yet in secret testimony before the Senate Foreign Relations Committee on July 23, 1974, released September 28, 1974, Kissinger placed the blame entirely on Hoover. "There was a discussion of specific individuals," he said, referring to the Oval Office meeting of May 10, "and Mr. Hoover suggested that four persons be put under surveillance in the first instance, three of them people on my staff considered security risks by Mr. Hoover. The fourth was a person the Director suspected of [deleted]." The three Kissinger staffers had been closely linked to the Kennedy Administration. "There is no doubt that some of my colleagues in the White House were very upset about the fact that I alone, of the senior officials in the White House, brought on my staff individuals who had been identified . . . with two of the previous administrations. There is also no doubt that the admiration of Mr. Hoover for the Kennedy family was very limited, that he had his views on that subject." Hoover, he said, would never have taken orders from him on who to wiretap, "especially as I believe I also fitted some of the categories he considered invidious, in one of the letters he wrote, as a Kennedy-type Harvard professor."

But the White House was also doing wiretapping of its own. One month after the first FBI taps were installed, John Ehrlichman, acting under specific direction from the President, authorized the White House's own security unit, then headed by John Caulfield, to install a wiretap on the home of Washington columnist Joseph Kraft after Hoover refused to do it.* It was Caulfield who allegedly wiretapped the house of a secretary in Senator Edward Kennedy's office who had been present at Chappaquid-dick the night Mary Jo Kopechne died. Caulfield would later monitor a

---

* In June 1969, on instructions from the White House, Hoover dispatched Sullivan to Paris with orders that he persuade the French police to institute full electronic surveillance on Kraft, who was interviewing North Vietnam representatives to the peace talks. The tapes were later shipped back to Washington in a diplomatic pouch.

Secret Service wiretap on Donald Nixon, the President's brother. In his testimony before the Watergate Committee, Ehrlichman acknowledged that he authorized wiretaps "from time to time."

The FBI did not uncover the leaks, nor did they stop. Disclosures of the Administration's position in arms limitation (SALT) talks with the Soviet Union, followed by the publication of the Pentagon Papers, led eventually to the creation of the Plumbers and the burglary at the Beverly Hills office of Daniel Ellsberg's psychiatrist on August 25, 1971. More on this later.

The seventeen wiretaps lasted for periods ranging from a month to twenty-one months. Originally initiated to discover leaks of classified material, the wiretaps were later used by the White House for purposes that now appear purely political. In fact, the taps on Anthony Lake, Morton Halperin and Daniel Davidson were continued long after they had left the National Security Council. For example, Halperin, one of the first whose home telephone was tapped, resigned in September 1969, but the tap, which was installed May 12 of that year, remained operative until February 10, 1971, the date Hoover discontinued all remaining taps. In the interim, Halperin was an adviser to Senator Edmund Muskie at a time when the Maine Senator was running ahead of Nixon in the polls. A total of twenty-seven summaries of the surveillance of Halperin's phone were sent to the White House during the period of the wiretap. In late 1969, Ellsberg was a guest at Halperin's home, and the wiretap evidence shows that his calls were duly recorded by the FBI. Later Halperin was a consultant to Ellsberg during the Pentagon Papers trial. Fifteen conversations between Ellsberg and Halperin were included in the wiretap data monitored by the FBI.

A Penchant for Ferreting Out Subversives

Meanwhile, behind the scenes in the top ranks of the FBI, a power struggle between Hoover and Sullivan was quietly reaching a climax. Sullivan, an assistant to the Director, with responsibility for all investigative and intelligence operations, domestic and foreign, was the Bureau's number three man. John P. Mohr, who held a similar title on the administrative side, was in the number four slot. At the height of the feud, Hoover suddenly promoted Chief Inspector W. Mark Felt to Deputy Associate Director, a newly created position directly under Tolson, which was interpreted as an effort on his part to insulate himself from Sullivan's abrasive challenge.

Sullivan took the big plunge in July 1971, when he allegedly approached Robert Mardian, an assistant attorney general with a penchant for ferreting out subversives. (He was sure he could tell a man's political bias from the length of his hair.) A golfing partner of Mitchell's and a close friend of Barry Goldwater's, Mardian rejuvenated the Internal Security Division, moribund since the last hurrah of Joe McCarthy. It was under Mardian's generalship that the forces for law and order conducted the largest dragnet operation in history during the May Day 1971 antiwar protest in Washington. Demonstrators and innocent bystanders alike, 13,400 to be exact, where scooped up in a four-day period and crammed into jails, with the overflow herded into a fenced-in practice football field near RFK Memorial Stadium. The niceties of constitutional protection were ignored, with the result that only a few were later convicted of anything.

Prior to his coming to the Justice Department, Mardian was general counsel under Secretary Robert Finch in the Department of Health, Education and Welfare. He helped draft the Administration's famous 1969 memo that effectively relaxed desegregation deadlines in Southern states. One former HEW lawyer told *Time* that Mardian "consistently tried to scuttle school desegregation guidelines." In defense of his tactics, Mardian candidly explained, "Look, you might as well recognize that you're in politics. There are two kinds of people in the world—winners and losers. I knew a loser once and he was a queer." ("That's a joke," he added.) Once established as head of ISD, Mardian and two top assistants, Kevin Maroney and Guy Goodwin, went on a subversive manhunt, weaving a whole string of conspiracy cases against antiwar radicals, most of which were ultimately lost in court on the basis of unsound prosecution evidence.

It was Sullivan, according to Mardian, who first approached him about the seventeen wiretaps. In an interview with FBI agents on May 10, 1973, Mardian said Sullivan contacted him "and told him that he was in trouble with the Director of the FBI and expected that he might in fact be fired. He did not explain why. He said that he had information that was 'out of channel,' that he wanted to turn over to the President of the United States. He said this was wiretap information and that, in his opinion, Mr. Hoover could not be entrusted with this wiretap information. Mr. Sullivan continued in conversation saying that Mr. Hoover had used wiretap information to blackmail other Presidents of the United States and

was afraid that he could blackmail Mr. Nixon with this information."
Mardian consulted Mitchell, who said "he would handle it." A short time
later Mardian was directed by John Ehrlichman to "fly immediately to the
White House in San Clemente." The "following morning after his arrival
in San Clemente, he went directly to the Western White House and
spoke with the President of the United States." Asked how the President
had reacted, Mardian said, "He directed me to obtain the reports from
Sullivan and deliver them to Mr. Ehrlichman."

Upon his return to Washington, Mardian said he "conveyed the President's message to Mr. Sullivan and asked him to supply all of the wiretap
material to him as soon as possible." Mardian said that Assistant Director
Charles Brennan "appeared in his office with an 'old beat up' satchel,"
olive drab in color, which "had William C. Sullivan's initials on it." Mardian then called the White House and was instructed to deliver the
satchel "to Dr. Kissinger and General Haig." Upon arriving at the White
House,

he went directly to Dr. Kissinger's office. Dr. Kissinger and General Haig were
present. He said he specifically remembered the incident because when he came
into the office, Dr. Kissinger addressed a remark which Mr. Mardian felt was
in extremely poor taste under the circumstances, to himself, Mr. Mardian, and
Dr. Kissinger's secretary. Dr. Kissinger said something to the effect, "Do you
have what I said on the phone," implying, according to Mardian, that Mardian
had results of a wiretap on Dr. Kissinger. Mr. Mardian said that he felt this
was in such poor taste that it did not require a reply. Dr. Kissinger also said
that he had been keeping logs for the time when he writes his memoirs, but
laughed and said he doesn't keep them any more. Mr. Mardian felt that this
was simply a jocular response, and there was no truth whatever in it nor was
there intended to be.

Mr. Mardian said that in Dr. Kissinger's and General Haig's presence he
opened the bag and removed a group of papers from the bag "clipped together"
with a sheet of paper on top which had the chronological listing of summaries of
wiretap information that had been previously furnished by the FBI to the
White House. He said that he and Dr. Kissinger checked by date and satisfied
themselves that Dr. Kissinger's material matched with the cover sheet which
Mr. Mardian was using. . . . . He said that after he and Dr. Kissinger and
General Haig were satisfied that the material in Dr. Kissinger's office matched
the itemized list, he walked into Mr. Haldeman's office . . . [and] he has
the distinct impression that he left the check list with Mr. Haldeman to check
against the summaries that Haldeman had in his possession in his own
office. . . . After Mr. Haldeman completed his check, Mr. Mardian said he re-

trieved the bag with all its contents and walked into the Oval Room of the White House and left the bag. He was specifically asked to whom he gave the bag. He said he preferred not to answer because of the President's order concerning employees talking about national security information.

At this point, the question logically arises as to whether the transfer of the wiretap material was not indeed an effort to hide the fact that Ellsberg had been overheard on Halperin's wiretap. In other words, the President wanted to keep it secret so as not to damage the government's upcoming trial against Daniel Ellsberg.

Playing a Dangerous Game

Nine months after Hoover's death, in February 1973, *Time* notified the White House that it was going to print the story about the seventeen wiretaps, which had been kept secret this whole time, apparently even from John Dean. In his testimony before the Watergate Committee, Dean said he made inquiries as to the source of the *Time* leak. "I called Mr. Mark Felt at the FBI to ask him first what the facts were, and second, how such a story could leak. Mr. Felt told me that it was true, that Mr. Sullivan knew all the facts and that he had no idea how it leaked.* I then called Mr. Sullivan and requested that he drop by my office, which he did. He explained that after much haggling, that the wiretaps were installed, but as I recall, Mr. Sullivan said they did not have the blessing of Director Hoover. Mr. Sullivan explained to me that all but one set of the logs had been destroyed and all the internal FBI records relating to the wiretaps, except one set, had been destroyed and all the material had been delivered to Mr. Mardian."

In response to a request from Senator Lowell Weicker that he elaborate on the nature of the interview with Sullivan, Dean said that Sullivan

recounted the fact that he had been involved in this and told me that he had at one point gotten the most trusted people in the Washington field office to undertake the function. That subsequently he had, when Director Hoover was trying to get copies of the logs, that he had told the Washington field office people to destroy all of the other logs so it ended up there was one set of logs and related memorandums that were in the custody of Sullivan, and there was some removal of these persons' instructions and I don't have all these details because Sullivan didn't give them to me, and gave them to Mardian, and Mar-

* Felt, who has since retired, was Associate Director, Tolson's old spot, under L. Patrick Gray and Clarence M. Kelley.

dian had possession of them apparently at the time he went to the west coast to
get instructions as to what he was to do with them. . . . At the time that the
Time magazine inquiry came in there was also an effort to determine how this
had leaked and that was very much a part of the conversation I had with
Sullivan as to how this could leak, and I recall discussing with Sullivan also
who else knew about this, and he told me that he thought that Hoover had
told and he mentioned the name of the person and I cannot recall it at this
time, and this person, in turn, had mentioned that he understood to Governor
Rockefeller and Governor Rockefeller in turn told Dr. Kissinger.

When Weicker pressed Dean on the point of Hoover's disapproval of
the wiretaps, Dean replied, "This is the impression I had. I had been told
sometime before after Mr. Mardian left the Department of Justice and
went to the reelection committee that something had to be done for Bill
Sullivan. Now he always worked on the assumption that I knew that
Sullivan had done some important thing for the White House."*

In an interview with FBI agents on May 11, 1973, John Mitchell said
that "sometime during the Spring or Summer of 1969 former FBI Director Hoover met with him and advised him that the FBI at that time had
some wiretap coverage on certain individuals specifically requested by the
White House." Although Mitchell's signature appears on all seventeen
wiretap authorizations, he has denied seeing or signing any of them.
Mitchell went on to state that the "reason Mr. Hoover came to him at
that time was because he, Hoover, was greatly concerned that such wiretaps were in effect and wanted Mitchell to informally intercede with the
White House in an effort to discontinue these wiretaps." Mitchell later
discussed the problem either with Haig or Kissinger at the White House
"and they (Mitchell, Haig and/or Kissinger) agreed that these wiretaps
could become 'explosive' and that this whole operation was a 'dangerous
game we were playing.'" Yet no action was taken.

The next time Mitchell

recalls hearing of this matter was during the period when former Assistant Director Sullivan was "on the skids" with Director Hoover and the FBI. The
closest he could place this time was approximately early Fall of 1971. He
vaguely remembers that Robert Mardian . . . contacted him, Mitchell, and at
this meeting told Mitchell that he had just recently learned from W. C.
Sullivan about the existence of wiretap coverage placed by the FBI at the re-

* Following Hoover's death, Sullivan came out of retirement to head the Justice
Department's Office of National Narcotics Intelligence, a job he held from August
1972 until June 1973.

quest of the White House on certain individuals. Mardian indicated to Mitchell that Sullivan was furious over the way he was being treated by the Director and that for this reason he disclosed the information concerning the wiretaps to Mardian. Sometime thereafter, Sullivan turned over to Mardian all correspondence relating to this wiretap coverage.

During approximately this same period, Mr. Hoover contacted Mitchell and advised him of the problems he was having with Sullivan and, in fact, showed Mitchell a lengthy letter he, Hoover, received from Sullivan in which Sullivan accused Hoover of running contrary to the President's wishes in many instances. Mitchell recalls telling Mr. Hoover that he had no choice but to get rid of Mr. Sullivan. At this point Mitchell described Mr. Sullivan as being "a little nuts." Mitchell recalls that after Mardian came to the Department of Justice as Assistant Attorney General in Charge of the Internal Security Division, Mr. Hoover became quite concerned over the fact that in many instances both Sullivan and his subordinate [deleted], were going directly to Mardian concerning cases being handled by the Domestic Intelligence Division and the Internal Security Division of the Department, which was an attempt, Mr. Hoover felt, to cut him off from access to these discussions. To the best of his recollection Mitchell stated that Mardian informed him, Mitchell, that he subsequently turned over all wiretap correspondence that he had received from Sullivan to Mr. John Ehrlichman of the White House. . . .

Concerning W. C. Sullivan, Mitchell related it was obvious he wanted the job of FBI Director since, on numerous occasions, Sullivan was in personal contact with various members of the White House staff and was always "name dropping and wheeling and dealing there."

A Dialogue on the Road to Götterdämmerung

On February 28, 1973, following his meeting with Sullivan concerning the *Time* leak, John Dean reported to the President. On this particular morning, Nixon is kindly disposed toward Hoover: "I have seen [Hoover] socially at least a hundred times. He and I were very close friends." "That's curious, the way the press just—" Dean interjects, but Nixon is anxious to make a point: "But, John—and that's the point: Hoover was my crony and friend. He was as close or closer to me than Johnson, actually, although Johnson used him more. But as for Pat Gray, Christ, I never saw him." Dean can appreciate the irony: "While it might have been, uh, a lot of blue chips to the late Director, I think we would have been a lot better off during this whole Watergate thing if he'd been alive, 'cause he knew how to handle that Bureau, knew how to keep them in bounds, uh, was a tough cookie."

"Well, if, if Hoover ever fought— He would have fought, that's the point," the President says, forgetting the long bill of particulars the White House, allegedly, had compiled against the Director. "He'd have fired a few people, or he'd have scared them to death. He's got files on everybody, God damn it." Dean laughs. "That's right," he says. "But now, at the present time," Nixon continues, "the Bureau is leaking like a sieve."

Later, of course, John Ehrlichman would paint a different picture of the Director. In an affidavit dated April 26, 1974, Ehrlichman said,

For some months prior to June, 1971, and virtually until his death, J. Edgar Hoover was the object of the President's criticism on a number of grounds: The FBI Director refused to enlist the Bureau in the Administration's efforts to suppress Narcotics Traffic; the President was known to feel that the FBI effort against domestic sabotage and violence was inadequate; a file containing a complete catalogue of problems, marked "The Company Director" exists in the possession of the Government. In late June and early July, the FBI effort in the Pentagon Papers case was the subject of Assistant Attorney General Mardian's strong criticism. On his assumption of responsibility in mid-July, Mr. Krogh joined in that criticism. During this period the Attorney General advised me, and I told the President, that Mr. Hoover had disciplined one of the FBI's top officials for ordering an FBI interview of Ellsberg's father-in-law. The disciplinary papers are known by me to be in the possession of the Government. It is against this background that the Young-Krogh unit [Plumbers] was established by the President and expressly given the job of investigating Ellsberg.

This is a replay of Huston's thesis that Hoover was responsible for Watergate.

The President's conversation with Dean on February 28 rambles all over the lot until finally the President zeroes in on Sullivan, which indicates that they have discussed him before. The following excerpts from the transcript will be amplified later by interviews with Sullivan, Felt, Mohr, Kleindienst and others.

"Yeah, I guess the Kennedy crowd is just laying in the bushes waiting to make their move," Nixon offers for an opener.* "Boy, it's a shocking

* The following transcript is from the House Judiciary Committee's version of the White House tapes.

thing. You know, we, we talk about Johnson using the FBI. Did your friends tell you, did your friends tell you whether—what Bobby did, or whether he [unintelligible]? Johnson believes that Bobby bugged him." Dean is willing to believe anything at this point. "I haven't heard but I wouldn't—" "Bobby was a ruthless little bastard," Nixon rushes on. "But the FBI does—they tell you that, uh, Sullivan told you that, the New Jersey thing. He did use a bug up there—just for intelligence work." Nixon is referring to the 1964 Democratic convention in Atlantic City. In the next breath, Nixon is commenting on Walter Jenkins, who was arrested for morals charges in the men's room of the YMCA during the 1964 campaign. President Johnson, says Nixon, "used Abe Fortas and Deke DeLoach backed up by, uh, some other people in the Bureau that were standing ready to go out and try to talk this doctor into examining Walter Jenkins to say the man had a brain tumor. He was very ill, that's why the erratic behavior. And this doctor wouldn't buy it."

The President wants to know what else Dean learned from Sullivan. "Well, I, you know, as I say, I haven't probed, uh, uh—" "Sullivan," Nixon prompts. "Sullivan to the depths on this because I—he's, he's one I want to treat at arm's length, till we make sure he is safe." "That's right," Nixon agrees. "But he has a world of information that, uh, may be available."

Nixon is anxious for Dean to tell him again what happened on the leaking of the seventeen wiretaps, and Dean repeats Sullivan's allegation that Hoover had told Patrick Coyne about it and he had told Rockefeller, who in turn had told Kissinger. "I have never run it any step beyond what Mr. Sullivan said there," Dean says, and then he goes on to say that when Hoover tried to reconstruct the records by going down to the Washington Field Office, he discovered that there was no evidence of the seventeen wiretaps. The records at the Department of Justice and the FBI showed "that no such, uh, surveillance was ever conducted." "Shocking," Nixon exclaims, but he's happy until Dean reminds him that Mark Felt is the only one left at the Bureau who could cause them trouble with the press on it. After discussing the pro and con of it, they both agreed that Felt would not "unwrap the whole thing" because, says Nixon, "everybody would treat him like a pariah . . . the informer is not wanted in our society."

The conversation rambles into other areas until Dean remembers another charge they can use against Johnson: "Kevin Phillips called Pat

Buchanan the other day with, with a, with a tidbit that, uh, Dick Whelan on the NSC staff had seen memoranda between the NSC and the FBI that the FBI had been instructed to put surveillance on Anna Chennault, the South Vietnamese Embassy and the Agnew plane, and this note also said that uh, Deke DeLoach was the operative FBI officer on this." But Nixon is still wondering why Hoover told Coyne about the wiretaps. "I don't have the foggiest," Dean says, but he assures Nixon that "we are stone-walling totally." "Oh, absolutely," Nixon agrees.

Referring to Lake and Halperin, Nixon tells Dean that "They're both bad. But the taps were, too. They never helped us. Just gobs and gobs of material: gossip and bull shitting." In fact, Nixon says, the tapping was "very unproductive. I've always known that. At least, I've never, it's never been useful in any operation I've ever conducted." Nixon then wants to know if Johnson bugged Goldwater, and Dean replies, "I don't know if he bugged him, but he did intelligence work up one side and down the other." "From the FBI?" Nixon wants to know. "From the FBI," Dean confirms. "Uh, just up one side and down the other on Goldwater."

On March 12, 1973, the President issued a policy statement that members of his staff would invoke executive privilege and not appear before the Senate Watergate Committee. However, the committee voted unanimously to "invite" Dean to testify. The next day, Dean and Nixon again took up the matter of introducing information damaging to Democrats, a diversion that apparently hinges entirely on Sullivan's willingness to expose past illegal practices of the FBI.

Nixon doesn't mince any words. "Did you kick a few butts around?" he asks Dean. "Apparently, you haven't been able to do anything on my project to take the offensive based on Sullivan." "But I have, sir," Dean assures him, and then goes on to explain that he's having a speech drafted for Goldwater that will ask why the committee is not looking into the practices of previous administrations. Also he was in the process of writing a letter to Senator Ervin saying, "This has come to my attention," and would then lay the whole thing out. Not only that, but Sullivan had sent him a note saying, "John, I am willing at any time to testify to what I know if you want me to." And, Dean points out, "it's a dynamite situation." But Dean cautions that the White House should stay out of it. Someone, Dean says, should sit down with Sullivan "and really take him over cross-examination of what he does know and, and how strong it is, what he can, can substantiate."

Nixon is distressed: "But John, who the hell could do it if you don't?" Dean agrees that's a problem. "Now, the other thing is," says Dean, "if we were going to use a tactic like this—let's say in the Gray hearings, where everything is cast that we're the political people and they're not— that Hoover was above reproach, which is just not accurate." "Bull shit," Nixon exclaims, "bull shit." Dean couldn't agree more: "Total bull shit. The, uh, the person who could, would destroy Hoover's image is going to be this man, Bill Sullivan. Uh, that's what's at stake there. Also, it's going to tarnish quite severely some of the FBI and a former President." "Fine," Nixon says.

Dean knows when he has a winning hand: "Uh, he's going to lay it out, and he, it's just all hell is going to break loose once he does it. It's going to change the atmosphere of the Gray hearings. It's going to change the whole atmosphere of the Watergate hearings." "How will it change, John?" "How will it change? Because it'll put them in context that, that, uh, a government institute was used in the past for the most flagrant political purposes." Now Nixon has his doubts: "How does it help us?" Dean is surprised: "How does it help us?" Nixon doesn't want to push too hard: "I'm being, I'm just being—" Dean doesn't give him a chance to finish his sentence: "Yeah, I appreciate what you are doing." "Red herring," Nixon volunteers, "is that what you mean?" Now that's something Nixon truly understands. Dean knows that: "Yes, it's a red herring. It's what the public already believes. It's just that people would just, I would say react, that, oh Christ, more of that stuff. Uh, they're all, you know, they're all bad down there. Because it's a one way street right now." Nixon still has doubts: "Do you think the press would use it? They may not play it?" Dean sticks to his guns: "It'd be difficult not to. Uh, it'd be difficult not to."

Being an expert in the game of quid pro quo, Nixon wants to know why Sullivan is willing to come to their rescue. "I think the quid pro quo with Sullivan is that he wants someday back in the Bureau very badly." "That's easy," Nixon says, "but do you think after he did this to the Bureau that they'd want him back?" Dean offers an alternative: "What Bill Sullivan desires in life is to set up a national, or domestic national, security intelligence system, a plan, a program. He says we're deficient. Uh, we've never been efficient since Hoover lost his guts several years ago. If you recall, he [Sullivan] and Tom Huston worked on it. Uh, Tom Huston had your instruction to go out and do it, then the whole thing just crumbled." Nixon is still not sure about Hoover: "Do you think Hoover would have cooperated?" Dean then suggests that they put Sullivan out in the CIA where he could study for a couple of years. "No problem with Sullivan," Nixon says. "We'll put him—I mean, he's a valuable man. Uh, now, would the FBI then turn on him, piss on him?" Dean thinks that a "lot of that would be lost in the shuffle of what he is laying out. I don't know if he's given me his best yet."

Nixon is persistent: "Why do you think he is now telling you this? Why is he doing this now?" Dean realizes that Nixon won't be satisfied until he hears a better explanation. "Well, the way it came out," he says, "is when I, when the *Time* magazine article broke on the fact that it charged that the White House had directed that newsmen and White House staff people be, uh, subject to some sort of surveillance for national security reasons [Dean knows the rules of the game], I called, in tracking down what had happened, I called Sullivan [who was then head of ONNI] and I said, 'Bill, you'd better come over and talk to me about that and tell me what you know.' I was calling him to really determine if *he* was a leak. That's one of the reasons. I was curious to know where this might have come from because he was the operative man at the Bureau at the time. He's the one who did it. Uh, he would not, you know, he came over and he was shocked and, uh, distraught, and, and the like [unintelligible] his own, uh, uh, his own [unintelligible] [laughs] frankly, uh, and then, and after going through his explanation of all what had happened, he started volunteering this other thing. He said, 'John, what, this is the only thing I can think of during this administration that has any taint of political use but it doesn't really bother me 'cause it was a national security purpose. These people worked—there was sensitive material that was getting out, was getting out to reporters.'"

Nixon is confused: "[Unintelligible] what we ordered?" "That's right." "Of course [unintelligible] the staff was involved in the God damned Vietnam War." "That's right." "That's what it was," Nixon reminds himself. A portion of the tape was deleted at "this point in time," and when it resumes Dean is saying, "But he said, 'John, what does bother me is that you all have been portrayed as politically using—" Nixon interrupts: "And never did." "And *we* never have," Dean says, obviously willing to take his share of the responsibility for something that happened when he was still at the Justice Department. "He said the Eisenhower Administration didn't either. The only—" Nixon again interrupts: "Never."

"—times that he can recall that there has been a real political use has been during Democratic tenure. I said, 'For example, Bill, what are you talking about?' Then he told me this example, of, of, uh, the Walter Jenkins affair, when DeLoach—" "Yeah." "—and, and Fortas, and—" "The Kennedys," Nixon exclaims, "the Kennedys used it, let me say, politically on that steel thing." "That's right." "That was not, that was not a national security, was it?" "No," Dean assures him. "Now I asked, uh, I asked *somebody* [meaning Sullivan] about that and they told me that what happened there is that, uh—they were being defensive of Kennedy, and so that person who would defend Kennedy necessarily—was saying that Kennedy had given Hoover orders and Hoover, being typical in this response, tried to get it yesterday as far as the answer for the President. And that's why he sent people out in the middle of the night and the blame really fell on Hoover." In his response Dean very cleverly substituted the word somebody for Sullivan—he was hardly in a position to impeach his star witness at this stage of the game.

As I read the transcript of this tape, I could visualize these two characters scratching their heads as they rummaged at the bottom of the barrel. "Does he know about the bugging of Martin Luther King?" Nixon wants to know. "Yep." "I wonder if he'd tell that, that would be good." "I think he would tell everything he knows." "You do?" "Uh huh. That's why I'm saying he is, he is, he is a trem—he's a bomb." Nixon wants it nailed down: "You really have to keep telling—" "Well, if that's, that's the, the real problem is, how it's structured, how can it be done. Uh, he sent me this note and I called up and I said, 'Bill, I appreciate getting that note very much,' I said, 'it takes a lot of guts to send a note like that to me.' And he said—I said, 'It's kind of a pleasure to see a man stand up, blowing a little smoke up him and the like.' Uh, he said, 'Well, John, I mean it. I am perfectly willing to do anything you want.' "

Dean goes into another long reiteration of Sullivan's assets to their cause. The problem is how to use the information. "I just have a feeling that it would be bad for one Bill Sullivan to quietly appear up on, uh, on some Senator's doorstep, and say, 'I've got some information you ought to have.' 'Well, where did you get it? Where—why are you up here?' 'The White House sent me.' "

They explore the various possibilities. They consider their Senate friends: James Eastland, Roman Hruska, who Nixon says "is the tiger on the Judiciary Committee on our side," and Edward Gurney, who Dean points out was "good during the ITT hearings." The problem, as Nixon sees it, is "would they go after the Bureau?" Dean introduces a subtlety: "They're not going after the Bureau. What they are doing is, they're taking the testimony of somebody [Sullivan] who is going after the Bureau." "Yeah, I know that," Nixon says, who knows from years of experience how sensitive a subject the Bureau is on the Hill. "They all look down the road and see what would be the result of what they are doing is, won't they?" Nixon wants to know. "I would think so. I mean, I'm just trying, how— Would they go after Johnson? Let's look at the distant future. Uh, look at the— How bad would it hurt the country, John, to have the FBI so terribly discredited?" Dean says that "maybe it's time to shake the FBI and rebuild it. I'm not so sure the FBI is everything it's cracked up to be. I, I'm convinced the FBI isn't everything the public thinks it is." Nixon agrees: "No." "I know quite well it isn't," Dean adds.

They pursue the subject of L. Patrick Gray's confirmation hearings before the Judiciary Committee and both conclude that the best thing would be to get him voted out of the committee "with a positive vote, uh, enough to get him out of committee, and then lock him at limbo there." Soon they are back with Sullivan and the problem of divorcing him from the White House. "The difficulty with the White House being involved," Nixon points out, "is that if we are involved in pissing on Johnson [unintelligible] that concerns me." Perhaps Sullivan could take the bomb to Richard Kleindienst. But if he takes it to Kleindienst, says Dean, "Kleindienst is going to say, 'Bill, just don't do it, because you are going to take DeLoach's name down with it, and DeLoach is a friend of ours.'" "Bull shit," Nixon says. Dean is quick to agree: "Something I have always questioned." "Nobody is a friend of ours," Nixon wants him to know. "Let's face it. Don't worry about that sort of thing." Of course, Dean didn't need Nixon to tell him that.

"Ninety Percent Baloney"

W. Mark Felt looks like central casting's idea of the typical FBI executive. He is tall, athletic, with handsome clean-cut features and a full head of silver gray hair. He is soft-spoken, extremely courteous, and very low key, exactly the kind of a man you would trust with the family's most sordid secret. But lately there has been speculation that he was "Deep Throat," the code name Washington *Post* reporters Carl Bernstein and Bob Woodward used in their book, *All the President's Men*, to protect the secret FBI source who helped them unravel the Watergate scandal. Felt denied it when I interviewed him at his home in October 1974, but not too vigorously. About a month after the interview, L. Patrick Gray, testifying as a prosecution witness in the Watergate coverup trial, was asked if he had been aware that Felt was suspected of leaking Watergate material in June 1972, the month of the break-in at Democratic headquarters. "Not at that time," Gray replied. "But at a later point, the Attorney General [Richard Kleindienst] told me point-blank to fire him because he was the source of the leaks." Gray never attempted to fire Felt, whom he regarded as a trusted aide. At this writing, Felt was under FBI investigation to determine whether he had provided Watergate-related information and documents to a New York *Times* reporter. In a press statement, Felt denounced the investigation as "ridiculous" and "astounding."

I was not aware of this investigation at the time of the interview, but Felt called my attention to a story in the August 1974 issue of the *Washingtonian,* a local monthly magazine, that was entitled "Getting Deeper into Deep Throat."

FELT: "The writer said, 'Felt could have gone out at all hours of the morning to meet Woodward without arousing any suspicion. Felt's wife would have thought nothing of it, and Felt could have a trusted FBI aide helping him.' My hours were regular: twelve hours a day, five days a week, and five or six hours on Saturday. But I didn't go out at night."

At this point, Felt's wife, Audrey, assured me that she would have noticed if her husband had gone out at two o'clock in the morning.

Felt smiled at his wife and continued: "No, I'm not Deep Throat. I know that the White House thought I was leaking information to the Washington *Post.* I know that if you asked Nixon, he'd say that I was Deep Throat. If you asked Mitchell, he'd say the same thing. I know this was the problem they thought existed in the FBI. The President and Dean talk about Gray playing ball with the White House, but I was their stumbling block. They wanted to make the FBI a political office. In a nutshell, that's what they're talking about. They're talking about Gray not being able to control me, and that he'd have to watch out, that I'm not to be trusted. I was then Associate Director, which was the same position Tolson had for more years than I can recall. I held that job until I retired about a year after Hoover's death. But as Deputy Associate Director under Hoover, I was in the number three spot in the Bureau."

You were moved in ahead of Sullivan?

FELT: "Yes. This was a new position created for that purpose. If you talk to Sullivan, he'll give you a different picture. Sullivan, I think, was probably as close to Hoover as anyone was with the exception of Tolson. Sullivan is an extremely intelligent person. He's more on the academic side than on the investigative side. His background was completely research, an area in which he was excellent. That's what Hoover was trying to do when he moved me into the spot—I was the Chief Inspector for five or six years—and I was supposed to be the disciplinarian and all this sort of thing. I had quite a lot to do with riding herd on Sullivan earlier anyway. I suppose he would have regarded me as a threat at that stage. I was able to slow Sullivan down some. I think I was able to put the lid on certain things."

What is surprising about the feud between Hoover and Sullivan is that the Director's hold on the Bureau seemed shaky at the end.

FELT: "There is no question that Sullivan was freewheeling for a while. That was one of the reasons that this position was created for me, to come in and try to ride herd on Sullivan. In fact, that's the whole reason. Let's go back a little bit. Sullivan was Assistant Director in charge of what they call the Intelligence Division. The Assistant to the Director in charge of the investigative side was Deke DeLoach, who is now a vice president of the Pepsi Cola Company. He and Sullivan were bitter enemies. I don't think Sullivan really had many friends down there. I mean, people either did what Sullivan told them to or he was their enemy, that's all. You either cooperated with him or you were on his blacklist, that's the way that worked. And he did have a tendency to want to freewheel.

"I'm convinced, and Hoover as much as told me, that he was creating this new position so that he could insert me into the line of command ahead of Sullivan. When DeLoach retired [in 1970], Sullivan was appointed to replace him. So after that Sullivan was really in the driver's seat so far as the investigative operations of the FBI were concerned, and I personally don't believe he told Hoover all he was doing in any way. I can tell you that Sullivan bypassed Tolson completely. That's something that wasn't done in the old days, not by Sullivan or anybody else. I think it was because Tolson had Sullivan's number. He knew what he was doing but he couldn't prove it, just like I couldn't, but he was acting as a damper to hold Sullivan down, and then as Tolson's health deteriorated and he wasn't strong enough to do it, then Hoover moved me in to do it."

Why didn't Hoover personally step on Sullivan? Why did he need you to do it?

FELT: "If you'd ever worked in the government, you'd understand a little better. You just don't fire somebody in the government, and I think by this time Sullivan had his contacts with Mardian; he spent half his time at the White House. I think he was becoming too formidable a character for Hoover to take him on. Let's face it, Hoover was past retirement age, he was there at the day-to-day discretion of the President, and I don't think he felt politically strong enough to meet him head on. I think that Sullivan had too much support from the White House. Sullivan is a friend of Haig, apparently a neighbor of Haig at one time, a real close associate. During those last days, Sullivan spent a lot of time down there at the White House. He was the one that gave them all this information and apparently they [in the White House] think it's true about the political abuses of the FBI by prior administrations. This is about ninety percent baloney, it just isn't true, and when they got right down to it, Sullivan couldn't come up with any specifics.

"I'm referring to the charges that past presidents had wiretaps put on newspapermen and this sort of thing. It just wasn't true, but they were talking about that, and you may remember that Senator Hugh Scott released a list of the total number of wiretaps that had been put on by prior administrations—this was information that had been compiled by Ruckelshaus at Richardson's instructions pursuant to a request from the White House. Later on they wanted names. This was because Sullivan was down there telling them that prior administrations had been bugging newsmen, and this just wasn't true. Conceivably there could have been a newsman or an author or somebody, you know, mixed up in there kind of coincidentally. They eventually gave them the names too after I left. I objected to that but there was nothing there and they were never able to do anything with it. There just wasn't anything for them to latch on to, but Sullivan had given them the idea that the FBI, at the behest of former presidents, had been bugging indiscriminately, newspaper people, just like the seventeen wiretaps Kissinger instituted. The only time Hoover ever commented on Sullivan's allegations that he had blackmailed other presidents, Hoover told me, 'That's a damn lie of Sullivan's,' and I'm sure it was. I'm sure Hoover didn't have any intention of doing anything like that. He never had."

Why do you think Sullivan turned the logs over to Mardian?

FELT: "Sullivan was trying to ingratiate himself with the Administration."

There's no question about that in your mind, is there?

FELT: "No question about it. He was trying to get the Director's job. There's just no question about that. And this was just a step to ingratiate himself, and I think that Sullivan was becoming, you know, through the last two or three years, was becoming increasingly frustrated with Hoover."

Is it possible that Sullivan turned over the logs to Mardian because the White House discovered that the wiretap on Halperin overheard fifteen conversations between Halperin and Ellsberg?

FELT: "It's entirely possible, because when a case like that goes to trial, even when they're getting ready for the trial stages, it's almost routine procedure for the Department of Justice to write a little formal note asking the FBI to check what they call the Electronic Surveillance Indices to see whether or not there's ever been an 'overhear.' If there has been a very direct wiretap on that individual, of course, it would show up in the files, but they check this to see whether he's been overheard on somebody else's tap. The files were searched and no record was found. Hoover's response to the Attorney General to that effect was routine. This is done in every case. I'm sure Hoover didn't know about those conversations, or didn't remember. The chances of it being otherwise are extremely remote."

Why didn't the FBI discontinue the wiretaps on Halperin and others after they had left government service?

FELT: "These cases were a little different than ordinary cases. The wiretaps were put on at the request of the White House, and the logs, as a result, were sent to the White House for evaluation. Ordinarily, a wiretap is put on at the request of the FBI and the FBI is getting the material and evaluating it. The FBI was not conducting the investigation to determine the source of the leak. The FBI didn't even know what it was all about other than that these people were suspected of leaking. The FBI was serving in those seventeen cases as a mechanical device to provide the taps and to provide the White House with the results of the taps. There was no FBI investigation. I think it was ridiculous to keep the taps on after they had left the government, but don't put that political responsibility on the back of the FBI. Because, seriously, the FBI did not evaluate these things, they did not know what the charges were, they did not know what the suspicions were, they would not be able to evaluate the stuff on those taps without any background.

"Well, Hoover's dead and there's nobody to defend him. I'm sure Sullivan probably had more conversations with Kissinger than Hoover did. I have no first-hand knowledge of the wiretaps. Sullivan handled all those. All I can tell you is that at the time Sullivan retired in October 1971 there was a general knowledge in the Bureau that he had a whole bunch of confidential files. Nobody knew exactly what they were. I discussed this with Hoover and had a number of dealings and negotiations with Sullivan to get those back. For two or three days, Sullivan kept saying, 'They're over in the other building. I'm going to get them tomorrow and give them to you.' Then on his last day, when I really pushed him and said, 'I want them right now.' Then he said, 'Well, you'll have to talk to the Attorney General.' He just refused to discuss it with me at all."

"Sullivan Had Grandiose Ideas"

John P. Mohr, as noted earlier, has been a close friend of Sullivan's since their days at American University. The first thing Mohr wanted to know when I interviewed him was whether I had talked to Sullivan. "Did he tell you what happened?" Mohr asked me. When I replied that Sullivan had told me his side of it, Mohr asked me if I believed him, and I turned the question around.

MOHR: "I believe everything except the reason he gave for doing it. That's suspicious reasoning that doesn't hold water. He made the statement that he did it because he thought Hoover was going to use that material against the President for some reason, probably to blackmail him into letting him stay on as Director of the FBI, I would assume is what he had in mind. Supposedly Hoover had blackmailed presidents before. That's what he's been quoted in the press as saying even. I don't believe it, because it's not true. After all, if Hoover wanted to use the material, he didn't need the files. What the hell could the President do if Hoover got up and publicly announced that the President had put seventeen wiretaps on newspaper people and White House aides? He would do as much damage as if he had the files. Let's face it, what would he need the files for. I mean, could the President come out and deny it?"

Then why did Sullivan do it? Was he ingratiating himself with the White House?

MOHR: "That's foremost in my mind, that he wanted to be Director. Bill Sullivan had great aspirations. Look, our friendship goes back to 1931, so I know Bill Sullivan. There's no question that Sullivan was wheeling and dealing, but by the same token, until the very end, he wasn't doing it in opposition to Hoover. As far as his relationship with Hoover was concerned, it was— There was no— Let me tell you something. There's something you got to keep straight. Sullivan was the Assistant Director of the Domestic Intelligence Division at the time that DeLoach left in July 1970. The question arose as to a replacement for him, for DeLoach, as Assistant to the Director. Now this is getting right up there near the top. In other words, he would have been the same on the investigative side as I was on the administrative side. Tolson was opposed to Sullivan. Hoover never asked me about whether I thought he should get it or not, but Tolson talked to me about it. I told Tolson that I didn't think that Sullivan temperamentally was the man for that particular job. In other words, you're in charge now of files and all the field activities on the investigative side. I knew, I have always known, that Sullivan had grandiose ideas and anyone who stood in his way was an enemy. Hoover told Tolson that he was going to give it to Sullivan for the simple reason that he was loyal and that loyalty meant more to him than anything else and he could think of nobody with the Bureau who was more loyal than Sullivan. And Sullivan got the job, based on loyalty. It took Sullivan a little over a year to fall off the ladder."

That was when Felt was brought in ahead of him?

MOHR: "Mark Felt was never ahead of him, never. Felt was brought into Tolson's office, and he had no more supervision over Sullivan than he would over the janitor in the basement. Sullivan wouldn't take any instructions from Felt unless he wanted to. Felt was nothing more than a vehicle, a communication vehicle, that's all. He was merely in Tolson's office to assist Tolson in handling the work of the office just as I did when I was an inspector and worked in Tolson's office years ago. Now, after Sullivan gave those logs to Mardian, Felt did acquire some stature because all of the so-called files anybody had were given to Felt to take care of. But Sullivan was gone shortly after that. After Hoover died, then Felt became

Acting Associate Director, the top dog, the number one man under the Director. But until that time, he was just another guy named Joe.

"The trouble with Sullivan began when he opposed Hoover on the expansion of legal attachés in the Bureau overseas. Hoover said he was doing it at the specific request of the President. Sullivan wrote a number of memos, and I agreed with Sullivan. I was opposed to the expansion, but when Hoover told me that it was the President's request, I said, 'Okay, I've said my piece, that's it. Go ahead and do it.' If the President wants it, then he's got to do it, he has no choice in the matter. But not Sullivan. By God, he kept after him. It's possible that Sullivan may have known more than I did, but he kept after him to the point where he actually riled up Hoover. And then, subsequently, we had that issue about the files going to Mardian."

Do you think Sullivan knew that the logs contained conversations between Ellsberg and Halperin?

MOHR: "Yes. Sullivan would know and the guy over in the Domestic Intelligence Division who was handling that paperwork for Brother Sullivan would have known what was in the logs. Hoover himself would have to rely on whoever in the Domestic Intelligence Division was handling it, the Assistant Director over there. Also anything that would have been in those logs had already gone to the White House."

Wiretaps Were Usually Initiated by the Director

Richard Kleindienst is a man of many contradictions. Alarm signals went up all over Washington when he was named Deputy Attorney General under John Mitchell in 1969, and he hardly disappointed his critics when he was quoted as favoring the incarceration of violent dissenters in camps established under the Emergency Detention Act of 1950. Later, he calmly announced the White House's desire to have the act repealed. Along with former Assistant Attorney General William Rehnquist, now a Supreme Court justice, Kleindienst was the author of the policy of mass street arrests during the May Day 1971 anti-war demonstrations in Washington, which was executed under the generalship of Robert Mardian. Yet in this interview on October 7, 1974, he expressed the most liberal views on law enforcement and justice.

KLEINDIENST: "I think there were some in the Nixon Administration who overreacted to some of the social dissenters in our society. I think that they overmagnified the ultimate impact they had upon the ability of our country to function with its normal institutions of government. My approach to dissent was to provide a means for them to articulate their dissent. I always felt that if you had Jane Fonda and three hundred thousand people in the District of Columbia in a big mass meeting, that if you could get her on a platform and put her on national television and give her a microphone and let her give her speech, she would appear irrelevant to ninety-nine point nine percent of the people in this country. If, on the other hand, you suppressed her right to give that speech, she would gain millions of allies in this country, not because of what she said or what she believed in, but because she was denied the right to say it. I think there was an inclination by some to want to silence this kind of dissent.

"It was my responsibility to be in charge of these demonstrations in Washington, D.C., on behalf of the executive branch of the government, and my whole purpose was to provide the means by which they could articulate their dissents, but also to provide the means by which we maintained order so that they wouldn't harm people's lives and destroy property. I've always had a very narrow concept of the justification for the federal government to engage in extraordinary surveillance procedures with respect to citizens, you know, who articulated political dissent."

You sure came in at the wrong time, then, didn't you?

KLEINDIENST: "I was there when I was and I left when I did and I narrow it to that and leave it to your opinion."

As to the seventeen wiretaps—

KLEINDIENST: "I have no knowledge of those."

Did you approve any wiretaps?

KLEINDIENST: "Oh, I was signing national security wiretaps all the time. But they dealt solely with— Well, I signed some before the Keith decision that would be what you would call domestic internal national security wiretaps. I never initiated any of them. They usually came from the FBI with a recommendation from the Director, and I would look at it and determine independently whether the facts were sufficient under the law and whether the conduct was grave enough to justify it. If I didn't think so, I would write on the face of it, 'Need some more information,' or 'I disagree.' If I agreed, I'd sign it. But I was unaware of these so-called seventeen taps that Mr. Mitchell apparently signed. He told me once that he had not authorized them. I was publicly stating that, you know, that they didn't exist. I am confident, without self-serving myself, that I would never have authorized them at that time."

Do you know why Sullivan turned the logs over to Mardian?

KLEINDIENST: "I don't know anything about that."

How about an opinion. Do you think Hoover would have blackmailed Nixon?

KLEINDIENST: "I disbelieve that."

Did you hear anything about it at all?

KLEINDIENST: "No. As a matter of fact, *Time* magazine ran an article once in which it said that Mr. Hoover called me up in anger once when I had asked him to do something and said, 'If you insist on this, I'm going to expose these so-called illegal wiretaps.' That conversation never occurred. Whoever said that was— It was a fiction, or a figment of their imagination. But then there always is fiction in a free society. There's unlimited license given in our country, and I don't disapprove of it, but you have to pay the price for absolute freedom of speech, the right for people to say almost anything they want, particularly about public officials."

"One of the Most Distressing Days of My Life"

Do you know anything about the Ellsberg case?

KLEINDIENST: "All I know about the Ellsberg case is the information that I got in normal channels from the litigating division, the Internal Security Division, with respect to the facts available to the Department and the decision made to prosecute Ellsberg. Then I met with William Olson, who was then the Assistant Attorney General in the Internal Security Division, and a young, very bright, able, fine trial lawyer by the name of [David R.] Nissen, who was designated as the chief attorney in that trial out there. I wanted to have the best support and attorneys prosecuting Ellsberg that we had in the Department of Justice and was keeping pretty much in touch with the preparations and the issues and the trial of Ellsberg."

Did the White House exert pressure on you—

KLEINDIENST: "No, no. I don't think I ever got a call from anybody about Ellsberg. Dependent upon what the facts would have shown and a jury would have done, any time a citizen of this country has in his possession or gets into his possession one way or another, highly classified materials that go to the national security of the United States and in the manner in which allegedly Mr. Ellsberg used such material, the Congress has passed laws which make that a crime; and I wanted to be sure that all the evidence available was brought into court against Mr. Ellsberg and that the full measure of the law was applied to him. One of the most distressing days of my life came about when I was advised by Henry Petersen, then the Assistant Attorney General in the Criminal Division, that the office of Ellsberg's psychiatrist was broken into by, you know, Liddy and Hunt, because on that day I had to go up to the President's office and tell Mr. Nixon that the information had to be made available to Judge Matt Byrne.

"First, we had to determine that no one in the Department of Justice knew about this, and had no information concerning it, and, therefore, it could not have affected or tainted our evidence or our trial of Mr. Ellsberg. Under the law, the government upon learning of it was obligated to give that information to the judge, and the judge then could make a decision whether to give it to the attorneys for Ellsberg or any other disposition of the case he wanted. Judge Byrne dismissed the case, and that was a very sad [long pause] incident as far as I was concerned."

Did Hoover cooperate in the Ellsberg investigation?

KLEINDIENST: "So far as I know he did. There again, my involvement in the Ellsberg case was only of the broadest nature. At that time I was the Attorney General, and believe it or not, if you're the Deputy Attorney General or the Attorney General, because you've got seventeen divisions and fifty thousand employees and a billion and a half budget, you've got an awful lot of responsibility that almost makes it impossible to get deeply involved in the specifics of any situation. If there was any problem involved in the Ellsberg case, I was not aware of it. It would have been something that the Internal Security Division and the trial lawyers in the Department of Justice would have known about."

If they had problems with Hoover, wouldn't they come to you?

KLEINDIENST: "Yes, and I had no such indication from them. We investigated the Ellsberg case and we had sufficient evidence to go to trial, and I had reason to believe if we had been able to finish that trial, we would have gotten a verdict."

Were you aware of the wiretap on Halperin?

KLEINDIENST: "No, I was not. I don't know when I learned of it, but I wasn't aware of it at the time."

Wouldn't that have been cause for dismissal?

KLEINDIENST: "Well, not necessarily a cause for dismissal. You are obligated, the government is obligated to make that information known to the judge."

An Urgent Meeting with the President

It was on April 15, 1973, that John Dean told the Watergate prosecutors about the burglary at Dr. Fielding's office. It didn't take Petersen long to realize what this meant to the Ellsberg trial then being heard in Los Angeles. On April 18, Petersen tried to explain the problem to the President, but before he could really get into it, Nixon cut him short, saying, "I know about that. That is a national security matter. You stay out of that. Your mandate is to investigate Watergate." After a week of soul searching, Petersen brought the problem to his boss. Kleindienst recalled that moment during his testimony before the Watergate Committee:

Mr. Dorsen: When did you first learn of the fact, which apparently is a fact, that White House employees or persons working at the behest of the White House employees burglarized the office of the psychiatrist of Dr. Daniel Ellsberg?

Mr. Kleindienst: I learned that amazing bit of information some time in the morning of Wednesday, April 25, 1973.

Mr. Dorsen: And how did you learn it?

Mr. Kleindienst: Mr. Petersen called me and said that he had a very urgent matter and could he come up to my office. I do not know if I had anybody in there but if I did I got him out. He came up in a minute and handed to me, without saying anything, a copy of a memorandum dated April 16 from Mr. Silbert to himself, a buck slip from him to Mr. Kevin Maroney, the Deputy Assistant Attorney General for the Internal Security Section of the Criminal Division, and a memo from a Mr. John Martin to Mr. Maroney dated some time that week. I do not recall the date of that. It would have been after April 16 and before April 25.

I read the two memos after I had recovered my composure and had uttered some of my abrupt remarks. He and I then began to discuss the dire serious nature of this amazing revelation. We discussed it for some time. It had a—it had a fantastic potential effect upon the trial of the Ellsberg case. It had a—certainly a fantastic potential with respect to the constitutional rights of Mr. Ellsberg, a defendant. And I believe our conversation kicked around until just before noon.

At noon I had an appointment to go with Solicitor General Griswold to the Department of Defense and be with him at a luncheon in his honor by the Judge Advocate General's Corps of the U.S. Army. I remember in the car outlining a hypothetical situation to Dean Griswold as a means by which, as I did quite often to get the benefit of his advice and his wisdom and his counsel.

Prior to the time I went to lunch, Henry and I had arrived without difficulty and simultaneously at two conclusions. No. 1, that we had to transmit this information immediately to Judge Byrne through our chief prosecutor, Mr. Nissen, in Los Angeles, without delay, and No. 2, that because of the explosive—just because of the nature of the situation, that I should immediately contact the President and inform him of this situation and also of what I was going to do.

Before lunch I then placed a call to the White House. Usually when you call and want to see the President they want to know what you want to talk to him about. I was very insistent in this instance to say it was a matter of great urgency but I could not describe the reason for the meeting.

When I got back from my lunch in honor of Dean Griswold, soon thereafter I received a call from the White House that if I could come over right away, I could see the President. I did. I gave him—I had those memos, those papers with me. I had some—I had a couple of cases that, you know, I could discuss, you know, a little note pad, but I did not give those citations. He, without hesitation, one moment's hesitation, said that the course of action that I was going to pursue was the only thing possible to be done. He caused the memos to be Xeroxed. He kept a copy of the memos and I left.

"The Bureau Was Ridden with Factions"

Five days later, President Nixon tearfully announced that Haldeman and Ehrlichman—"two of the finest public servants it has been my privilege to know"—had resigned because it was necessary to restore the public's confidence in the democratic process. Dean and Kleindienst had "also resigned." Then Nixon asked the people to pray for him, and he asked God to "bless America and . . . each and every one of you."

Meanwhile, it had also occurred to Henry Petersen that there might be other bombs lying around that he had neglected to check out. He sent a memo to Kevin Maroney, a former aide of Mardian's, inquiring as to whether Daniel Ellsberg had been overheard on any FBI wiretap. I asked Sullivan if Petersen had called him at that time.

SULLIVAN: "Yes, Petersen called, I think it was in April, but I don't remember offhand. He said, 'Look, do you folks have a wiretap on Ellsberg?' I said, 'I never followed the case myself, I had my men do it, so I'm not filled in on the details, but to my knowledge, we never had a wiretap on Ellsberg.' He said, 'Did Ellsberg walk in on any wiretap?' I said, 'Henry, whenever you have a wiretap on a man, there's always walk-ins.' This is inevitable. I said, 'It's possible, but I don't remember. There were many, many walk-ins on the seventeen taps and Ellsberg could have been one of them, but I don't know from memory.' He said, 'I've got to find out.' 'Well, hell,' I said, 'the only way to do it is to examine the logs and they are all in the Department, in Mardian's safe.' 'No,' he said, 'we looked all over the Department and we can't seem to find them.' That was news to me, because the last I knew back in 1971 Mardian had possession of the logs. So Henry asked me to call Mardian out in Arizona and after I explained the situation, Mardian said, 'There's no problem there. The logs are in a vault over in Ehrlichman's office.' I relayed the information to Petersen and he said, 'Fine, we'll get them.' That's the last I heard of the logs."

It has been suggested that the reason you destroyed the records and turned over the one remaining set of logs to Mardian was not because you thought that Hoover would blackmail the President, but that it was actually an effort to hide the fact that Ellsberg had been overheard on Halperin's wiretap.

SULLIVAN: "No, no. All I knew about it was what came to me through the processing of the logs. I didn't read them. I looked at the first logs that came in, you know, out of curiosity. I kind of wanted to see what the heck was being said there."

Somebody must have been reading them.

SULLIVAN: "The logs were all read carefully in the Bureau. But Ellsberg had nothing to do with what I did. Let's get this right. Hoover said, 'Tell the Washington Field Office to make no duplicates and to send us the original log.' So there was nothing to destroy. The tapes were erased, but we always erased all tapes and used them over again, so there was nothing unique about that, but what was unique was the absence of any duplicates. Then Hoover said, 'I want to keep the logs in my office.' And he did keep them in his office until one day he handed them to me and said, 'I want you to keep them in your office. I don't want them in the files.' Two or three times I said to him, 'We ought to get these things in the files and get them indexed.' 'No,' he'd say, 'this is a White House operation and it's not an FBI operation and we're not going to put them in the FBI files.' Then when the taps were terminated in February 1971 I said, 'Well, now that it's over, let's put them in the files.' He again refused and ordered me to keep them in my office. Later when I got into this feud with him, which was my own decision to deliberately precipitate this conflict, I thought, What in the world am I going to do with these logs when I get forced out? It's dangerous to leave this kind of material in a file cabinet, because I know how FBI material has been abused. As I told you, I know what happened during the McCarthy hearings.

"Oh, God, there's so much of this. There's the Kennedy assassination. Hoover leaked our investigation to the Chicago *Tribune* and the Washington *Evening Star*, thinking that if he got this thing out before the Warren Commission got under way, it would either cut off their own private investigation, or at least it would limit it by dulling the edge of its operations in the eyes of the public. Hoover didn't like the Warren Commission. He didn't like Warren, number one; and, number two, he didn't like the idea of a commission, because there was always the possibility that it might come up with something that we failed to find. He realized the danger, and, of course, he was right. The Commission did come up with criticism of the FBI. At the same time that Hoover leaked this information on Oswald, we also spread the story that Attorney General Katzenbach was the one who had leaked it, because the material had already gone over to the Department, see? Hoover disliked Katzenbach, who was a liberal like Ramsey Clark and Bobby Kennedy, which meant that we should undermine them whenever we could.

"So I had the logs on the seventeen wiretaps and I . . . knew damn well it could be abused, and what bothered me was that the great majority of those people were innocent. I didn't think their names should in any way be put in the press. I was astonished when, I think it was the New York *Times*, printed all the names, because no matter how innocent a man is, you put his name in the press as a man on whom an FBI tap has been placed and suspicion is pointed toward him. That's how I felt about the seventeen wiretaps. I thought, What the hell am I going to do? I was aware that Hoover could use those as blackmail to keep himself in his position or use them as blackmail for some other purpose. He's been well known for doing that, and if the crunch ever comes I can come up with the names and the facts.

"Then I said to myself, 'What the hell difference does it make? I'm going up to New England and I'll never come back again to Washington, I'll never be in government again.' I had a good job lined up, and I said, 'The hell with it. If they want to abuse it, let them abuse it.' Then the next week I'd say to myself, 'It's just not right.' So I vacillated back and forth: Should I leave them where they were or should I put them where they'd be secured?

"Finally, I went over to see Mardian. I knew he knew about the logs, and I said, 'Look, I've got these logs and I'm going to be forced out because of this fight that I'm having with Hoover.' 'Well,' he said, 'God damn it, if you'd go along and do what the Attorney General tells you to do, you wouldn't be forced out.' I said, 'I'm not going along with the Attorney General. I'm going to be forced out. Now what do you people want to do with these logs? I think they should be made secure so they cannot be abused.' He said, 'I can't make the decision, but I agree with you, they should be made secure. Give me a few days and I will talk to people who have the authority to make the decision.'

"He said 'people,' mind you, but he didn't say who, and in a few days, I don't know how long it was, he got in touch with me and he said, 'I am to take possession of the logs on the authority of the Attorney General and on the request of the President of the United States. I will make them secure in my office, in a safe.' I said, 'Wait a minute, I have to give an inventory when I leave,' and he said, 'All you have to do is say that I have possession of the logs and for them to take up the matter with the Attorney General.' And that's exactly what I did when I left the Bureau. I submitted my inventory and I told them that if they had any questions to take it up with the Attorney General.

"The blackmailing idea is something Mardian picked out from all the various ways I mentioned that the files could be abused. I mentioned the name of a man who at one time had been in the Communist Party in Wisconsin, and then had worked on the Democratic National Committee when John Kennedy was running for the Presidency. Hoover hated Kennedy and when he learned that this man was working up there, he gave orders to leak to the press that Kennedy had a Communist working for him on the National Committee, and it got big headlines in the newspapers, and I think it was so embarrassing that Kennedy had to let the man go. So I knew all the various ways this material could be abused. As far as Hoover is concerned, he felt there was something wrong with anybody who had to be wiretapped. And then, you know, the Bureau was ridden with factions, and we were fighting each other viciously, and you have all that damn stuff to contend with.

"As far as the seventeen wiretaps are concerned, don't get the idea that Hoover was opposed to them. For God's sake, he was a thousand percent behind them. He wanted to do the job for the White House, and you can prove it. He initialed every damn piece of mail that went to Kissinger and the President."

Wasn't he following a Presidential order?

SULLIVAN: "So did he take a stand? He didn't have to set up a special courier service so that they rushed the thing over, hand-carried, when the original request was for the letter to go over to Kissinger only. Hoover said, 'No. I want a letter to go to President Nixon also.' He wanted Nixon to get the letter, and he wanted to get the credit from Nixon for getting the letter over to him."

Were you wheeling and dealing with the White House?

SULLIVAN: "Let me tell you of my contacts with the White House. I don't know Ehrlichman, never met him, never talked to him and don't admire him; I never met Mr. Nixon, never talked to him, never received a communication, never sent one; I don't know Haldeman, never talked to him, never sent him a communication, never received one, or from anybody in his office, Krogh, or anybody else. Now, as to John Dean, I wish I had never met him, but I never met him while I was in the FBI. I met him afterward when I went back to the Justice Department as head of ONNI, the Office of National Narcotics Intelligence.

"I knew Tom Huston, who came to see me on his project; I knew Haig, who came to my office. I didn't go to his office. I knew Kissinger. Years ago when he was a professor at Harvard, he used to come to Fritz Kramer's house and sometimes Kramer would call to ask if I wanted to join in their conversation on foreign policy. I don't know anything about foreign policy, but I would sit there and listen to two brilliant minds, Kramer and Kissinger, discuss foreign policy. That's how I got to know Kissinger. When he came to Washington, I never went near him; he never called me. I met him one time at a social event, I think it was at the Gridiron Club, and he came up to me, very nice and very pleasant, and said, 'Why don't you come on over to the office and let's have a chat, let's renew our acquaintanceship.' I thanked him but I never went near him. I had nothing to discuss with him, officially or personally. I didn't want to waste his time and I didn't want to waste my time. Once his secretary called and asked if I would arrange a tour for his former wife and his two children, and I did, and that's all I've ever had to do with Kissinger."

Did you tell John Dean that Hoover had told Coyne about the seventeen wiretaps?

SULLIVAN: "No, now that was completely wrong; he got that garbled. Dean raised some question about the source of the leaks, and he said to me, 'Do you know—' and he mentioned three or four people, including Gray, Rockefeller, Coyne, and so forth. And he said, 'Do you think that any of those people know about the seventeen wiretaps?' I said, 'I think I've heard that Rockefeller did know about them. As a matter of fact, I think I picked up scuttlebutt somewhere that he may have talked to Kissinger about it.' That was the whole thing. How Hoover got into it, the Lord only knows. That must be Dean's imagination. The conversation ran around the President's Foreign Intelligence Advisory Board and who did I know on it that might have knowledge of the wiretaps, and I told him I knew Gray and Coyne, but I didn't know Rockefeller. I've read that Dean thought I was the leak. Well, tell me, don't you think that's stupid? Would I leak information that would cause me all kinds of trouble? I was the operating officer on those wiretaps. Why, it's ridiculous."

"Dean Was Talking for the Benefit of the President"

I would like to go over some of Dean's and Nixon's statements of February twenty-eighth and March thirteenth. Let's begin with what happened in New Jersey. What is that in reference to?

SULLIVAN: "The only thing I can think of is the 1964 Democratic National Convention, which took place in Atlantic City. Johnson requested that a squad of FBI people go up there and be of service to him, particularly in bottling up Robert Kennedy—that is, in reporting on the activities of Bobby Kennedy. He was afraid of what Kennedy might do up there, you know, that it might jeopardize his chances of becoming the nominee.

And we did. For the first time in the history of the FBI, we sent a squad of men to a political convention, and the squad was headed by Deke DeLoach, who was the number three man at the time. He gathered information that was helpful to Johnson. Johnson was always afraid of Bobby, never knew what Bobby would do. He hated the Kennedys with an unreasoning passion, and he hated Bobby above anybody else. Bobby, you know, had taken a position with his brother, Jack, that Johnson should not be the Vice Presidential candidate."

Nixon told Dean that Johnson believed that Bobby bugged him?

SULLIVAN: "No, that's utterly false. Johnson was throwing in a red herring there. If there's any truth at all to any bugging, it would be just the other way around."

Sullivan declined to comment on Walter Jenkins, who was Johnson's FBI liaison until his arrest in the YMCA men's room in the fall of 1964, a development that sent the Johnson campaign headquarters into a frenzy. According to an anonymous FBI source, "Abe Fortas and DeLoach, at the request of President Johnson, went to a doctor who was treating Jenkins and said to him, 'It's apparent that Jenkins has a brain injury and that he's definitely not a homosexual. It's because of this brain injury that he acted in a peculiar, unusual manner on this particular evening. We'd like to have you issue a public statement to that effect.' The doctor refused, and that was the end of it."

What about FBI surveillance of Anna Chennault?

SULLIVAN: "That involved Agnew and so forth? Well, there's not much of a story except that Johnson ordered the surveillance of her, and ordered the telephone calls of Agnew checked, purely a political request. He wanted to know who Agnew was calling, which involved a check of telephone company records. DeLoach was the operative officer. Later, DeLoach and John Mitchell became very close, and after DeLoach went to work for Nixon's friend Don Kendall at Pepsico, Mitchell was going to employ DeLoach on a special basis to handle special assignments for him. According to my information, Kendall delegated to DeLoach the responsibility for setting up the Nixon Library and DeLoach used to be at the White House quite a bit, driving up in a big limousine with a chauffeur and going up there supposedly to facilitate the setting up of the Nixon Library."

Did the FBI bug Goldwater or do surveillance on him?

SULLIVAN: "There was no bug or wiretap on Goldwater, and no surveillance. Johnson did request that we review the FBI files to see if we could come up with derogatory information on Goldwater and members of his staff that he could use in his campaign. He made that specific request and we complied with it, but that was all. We found a bit of information on one member of his staff, as I remember."

Dean quotes you as saying that the Democrats were the only ones who abused the FBI.

SULLIVAN: "No, that's wrong. Dean was talking for the benefit of the President. What I told Dean was—remember this was when Ehrlichman, Haldeman, Dean and Krogh were still fair-haired boys, all clean, and I had no knowledge of anything being wrong*—I said to Dean that when you compared the record of the Nixon Administration with that of Johnson's, it would come out looking very good, and I'd be willing to publicly testify to that fact. I put that into writing, you see, because I believed this very strongly. Johnson's Administration was the worst I ever served under from the standpoint of abusing the FBI; he'd ask us anything. He thought the FBI was his own private investigative agency. I also told Dean that there were only two presidents that I knew of who never made any political requests of the FBI, and they were Truman and Kennedy. Truman detested Hoover. Hell, Hoover was frightened of his life with Truman, I know that personally. During his entire career in the White House, Truman had *nothing* to do with Hoover and wouldn't let Hoover get anywhere close to him. Hoover tried very hard but Truman had General Vaughan in there as a buffer. Truman would have nothing to do with us.

"As for Kennedy, he distrusted Hoover and wouldn't have dared to make a political request of him. On my way out of Dean's office, he said, 'I suppose Kennedy certainly used the FBI for political purposes.' I said, 'No, he never used the FBI for political purposes.' And he said, 'He certainly used the FBI in the steel case, didn't he?' I said, 'That had nothing to do with politics. All that amounted to was getting certain information which involved interviewing an individual we couldn't locate during the day and we went to his home at about eleven in the evening. We woke him up and he delivered a blast. We were the ones who made the decision to

* The Washington *Post* was at this time publishing articles about these men which would lead to the full Watergate scandal.

interview him at night, not Kennedy. It was strictly an economic issue, involved with rolling back steel prices.' Dean didn't like that answer but he said nothing. Later, in his conversation with the President, he said he had asked 'somebody' who had defended the Kennedys, but he didn't tell Nixon that that somebody was me. He concealed that fact from the President because that would kind of destroy the image he was trying to create of me."

In other words, it would defuse the bomb that was going to blow the FBI out of the water?

SULLIVAN: "Exactly. But what bomb would I have? It's just an exaggeration. The whole thing was blown out of proportion and Dean soon lost interest in me when I insisted on keeping things in writing. I didn't want any verbal agreements with Dean, nor did I want anything clandestine, and so following my original meeting with him [in February 1973], which he requested, I sent him a letter that briefly but adequately recapitulated, from my point of view, the main issues. I said, 'Whatever I say to you, I'm willing to go on record publicly.' Dean cooled very quickly. He didn't seem to be much interested after that, and when I didn't hear from him, I called him one day and asked why, and he said, 'Well, they'—whoever *they* were—'they are turning things over in their minds and I haven't heard.' I told him again that I was willing to testify before the Judiciary Committee, but that's the last I heard of him. Which was all right with me.

"I didn't want to go over to his office the first time he called. He pulled rank on me and said, 'I'm the counsel to the President of the United States, and I'm asking you to come to my office to discuss this,' referring to the seventeen wiretaps. I reared back so that when I hung up, my deputy at ONNI said, 'God, you took an awful strong stand with the counsel to the President.' When I got to his office, I told him I didn't feel I ought to be over there discussing the matter, and that's when he said, 'Well, if you want additional authority, I can tell you that Ehrlichman has authorized this interview with you.' I don't know if that was true, and had I known Ehrlichman, I would have called him to check it out. Anyway, I flatly refused to give him the names of the seventeen wiretaps. He never got one name from me."

Why didn't you tell him to ask Ehrlichman?

SULLIVAN: "Of course. If he had discussed the whole thing with

Ehrlichman, he would have known the names of the persons wiretapped. That made me suspicious. I think he knew all about the wiretaps. He wanted to get somebody that he could quote. I think I walked into a trap. It's my opinion that Dean already knew that he was going to go before the Watergate Committee and he was trying to get as many people to quote as possible."

Mitchell has described you as being "a little nuts."

SULLIVAN: "If I ever opened up on Mitchell, there'd be some real head-lines. As I've told you, he was always knocking Hoover, yet when it goes on the record, he'd rather attack me, you see. Mitchell was opposed to my argument with Hoover, and he sent word for me not to argue, but I refused to obey his instructions. My break with Hoover was my own. It had nothing to do with Mitchell or Kleindienst or Mardian or anybody else."

Any truth to the charge that you were bucking to be Director?

SULLIVAN: "No one who wanted to be Director would ever write the kind of letter that I wrote to Hoover. My purpose was to make it so rough and tough that he'd have no other choice except to force me out. In other words, I didn't want to give him a loophole."

Then why were you storming the barricades?

SULLIVAN: "Because I wanted him to force me out and break it out into the open, elevate it to the level of public discussion, hoping that the Administration would wake up after the election and realize that they'd have to get another man for that job. And, of course, it wouldn't be me. And I understand that immediately after the explosion my retirement caused in the press, they held a meeting at the White House of the key people and they were very embarrassed by what I had done. Nixon and Mitchell had been in support of ousting me. Hoover told me that himself. So I was hoping that, by God, this would embarrass them, and it did. They had that meeting and while they said some unkind things about me for causing them all this trouble, they also said, 'We'll get rid of Hoover immediately after the election.' This is what was reported to me, and that satisfied me.

"As far as my wanting to be Director, there are fundamental facts that nobody can refute. I was already preparing to retire as far back as 1969, when I bought this place in New Hampshire. My family had already left Washington and I was living alone when I broke with Hoover, trying to sell my house. I put it up for sale in 1970, but I was having a tough time selling it because I lived in Cheverly, Maryland, and there was this busing problem out there. I finally sold it at a pretty low figure, and all of these things are factual. I was already pulling up my stakes. I don't care who says I wanted to be Director, you can't argue with those facts. You see, this is what you run into in public life. If I had it all to do over again, I would have stayed teaching school, by God, in that little country schoolhouse and lived a happy life."

Enemies Everywhere

Tom Charles Huston was typical of the breed of eager young men who scurried into the bowels of the White House in 1969. A former national chairman of the Young Americans for Freedom, Huston joined the Army after completing his studies at Indiana University Law School. He was trained in intelligence work and assigned to Pentagon duties. Being articulate and a "true believer," he devoted his spare time to boosting the Presidential aspirations of Richard Nixon. After the election, he left the service to join another army across the Potomac called White House aides. His anxiety over the New Left was so acute that even in that hypertensive ambience he gained the attention of those in power. Huston contributed to speeches written for Nixon, but his main preoccupation was with the Movement, and he soon became the resident expert on it. In fact, during the November 1969 moratorium for peace in Vietnam, M Day, as it was called by the protestors, Egil Krogh called on Huston to help coordinate domestic security arrangements.

What made the White House such a congenial place for what Senator Sam Ervin would later term a "Gestapo mentality" was the conviction emanating from the Oval Office that the anti-war unrest on campuses and the violent rhetoric of national black leaders was actually a monstrous plot conceived by foreign enemies to subvert the Presidency of Richard Nixon. The Nixon fantasy was that East European, Egyptian and Cuban money was funding the student movement, while funds for the Black Panthers were coming from the Caribbean and Algeria. Both wings of the CIA, the evaluators and the clandestine operators, were ordered to ferret out the foreign conspirators, and when they reported that the unrest was strictly a domestic problem, Nixon called upon the FBI to continue the quest, at the same time empowering the Bureau to expand its activities in twenty foreign countries. When the FBI also drew a blank, Nixon concluded that both agencies were falling down on the job.* It was at this point that Nixon turned to Tom Charles Huston and his brainstorm for revamping intelligence-gathering practices that would make the CIA and the FBI more aggressive in their approach and more amenable to White House direction.

Here is the way Nixon explained it to the nation in his statement of May 23, 1973:

In the spring and summer of 1970, another security problem reached critical proportions. In March a wave of bombings and explosions struck college campuses and cities. There were 400 bomb threats in one 24-hour period in New York City. Rioting and violence on college campuses reached a new peak after the Cambodian operation and the tragedies at Kent State and Jackson State. The 1969–70 school year brought nearly 1,800 campus demonstrations and nearly 250 cases of arson on campus. Many colleges closed. Gun battles between guerrilla-style groups and police were taking place. Some of the disruptive activities were receiving foreign support.

Complicating the task of maintaining security was the fact that, in 1966, certain types of undercover FBI operations that had been conducted for many years had been suspended. This also had substantially impaired our ability to collect foreign intelligence information. At the same time, the relationships between the FBI and other intelligence agencies had been deteriorating. By May 1970, FBI Director Hoover shut off his agency's liaison with the CIA altogether.

On June 5, 1970, I met with the Director of the FBI (Mr. Hoover), the Director of the Central Intelligence Agency (Mr. Richard Helms), the Director of the Defense Intelligence Agency (Gen. Donald V. Bennett), and the Director of the National Security Agency (Adm. Noel Gayler). We discussed the urgent need for better intelligence operations. I appointed Director Hoover as chairman of an interagency committee to prepare recommendations.

On June 25, the committee submitted a report which included specific options for expanded intelligence operations, and on July 28 the agencies were notified by memorandum of the options approved. After reconsideration, however, prompted by the opposition of Director Hoover, the agencies were notified 5 days later that, on July 28, that the approval had been rescinded. The options initially approved had included resumption of certain intelligence operations which had been suspended in 1966. These in turn had included authorization for surreptitious entry—breaking and entering, in effect—on specific categories of targets in specified situations related to national security.

* One of the reasons advanced by the Watergate burglars was that they were searching for evidence of foreign funds.

Because the approval was withdrawn before it had been implemented, the net result was that the plan for extended intelligence activities never went into effect.

The documents spelling out this 1970 plan are extremely sensitive. They include—and are based upon—assessments of certain foreign intelligence capabilities and procedures, which of course must remain secret.

So much for Nixon's version of the Huston Plan. It was in November 1969, after war protestors had staged a rally at the Justice Department, that Tom Charles Huston got his chance to articulate his vision of a new domestic security order for the nation. That was when John Mitchell, standing on his office balcony, told Martha that it "looks like a Russian Revolution going on."

"Mitchell and those people just didn't know what was happening," Huston later told an interviewer.* "Some paint was thrown at the building and somebody peed on the lawn, and Martha Mitchell got all upset. So he announced that he was going to get the New Mobe for crossing state lines to foment a riot. I knew that no charges were going to stick on some absurd business like that. I asked the FBI for a report on New Mobe involvement with any violence during the moratorium, and they bore me out one hundred percent. I sent the report to Bob Haldeman, and that was the last I heard of it."

Having demonstrated his expertise, Huston finally got Nixon's ear— well, sometimes. "As for the President," Huston told the interviewer, "he never sat down to work out a calculated policy on the Movement. Frankly, it was all I could do at times to get his attention or the attention of his top aides. He would run hot and cold, depending on what was happening and whom he talked to. One day he'd call everybody in and pound the desk and say, 'We've got to stop this violence.' Then he would lose all interest. Weeks would go by before I could get him to listen again."

"Hoover Has to Be Told Who Is President"

Finally, with the full backing of the President, Huston began the task of converting the nation's four top intelligence agencies (FBI, CIA, DIA, NSA) into a secret police. "I was Mr. Greenass," he chuckled, recalling his first meeting with Hoover. "The first thing they told me was 'With Mr. Hoover, you can never be too humble.' Well, normally, I don't act that way, but with Mr. Hoover I *was* humble. You know, he was the last

* Bo Burlingham, *Harper's*, October 1974.

reigning monarch in the Western world. And it's damn lucky he was there, because a guy who was less restrained than he would have been a serious threat."

That was not the way Huston felt on June 5, 1970, when the heads of the four agencies, Hoover, Helms, Bennett and Gayler, along with Haldeman, Ehrlichman, Finch and Huston, met in the Oval Office to hear the President express his hopes for strengthened domestic intelligence. According to Haldeman's Watergate testimony,

The President discussed with these agency heads the nature of the problem, the shortcomings of domestic intelligence, the concern that some of these activities that were underway or being threatened during that period of time were possible, at least, and I think demonstrably, as I recall, connected with foreign activities. Some of the organizations that were declaring themselves out to destroy institutions and in some cases the Government, were doing their training in foreign countries and were studying under foreign dissident organizations and there was a feeling that there was a crossover here that needed to be dealt with in terms of better intelligence, that we didn't know who was causing these things, who was directing them, who was financing them, nor did we know what they were going to be directed to.

Whatever the President didn't know, he was certain that foreigners were in the woodpile. The four directors were instructed to form as a group, with Hoover as chairman, and to prepare a threat assessment of the gaps that existed in intelligence-gathering methods and to give the President a range of options as to what steps he might take to improve the system. A working subcommittee, chaired by William C. Sullivan, with Huston sitting in, was given the task of coming up with the program. When the meeting adjourned, an official photograph was taken of the group with the President.

Huston's humble demeanor soon crumbled as Hoover began balking at the outrageous cloak-and-dagger schemes of this twenty-eight-year-old neophyte. On occasion Huston found it necessary to remind the "Old Man" how to run his business. At one point, when Hoover was trying to explain the need for a "historical view" of objective intelligence, Huston boldly interrupted, with what he evidently considered superior insight: "We're not talking about the dead past—we're talking about the living present."

Contrary to Hoover's objections, when the group again met in the Oval Office on June 25, Huston's views were enshrined in a forty-three-page document entitled "Special Report Interagency Committee on Intelligence (Ad Hoc)." It proposed specific options for expanded intelligence operations, many of them illegal, to wit: surreptitious entry (burglary); electronic surveillance and penetrations of domestic security suspects and foreign diplomats; covert mail coverage (steaming open first-class mail); recruiting FBI campus informers under twenty-one years of age; monitoring of American citizens using international communications facilities; new budgetary methods to cover the increased cost of domestic security; increased CIA coverage of students (and others) living abroad; use of military undercover agents; and other means of gathering intelligence data, including the formation of a new Interagency Group on Domestic Intelligence, with representatives from the White House, FBI, CIA, NSA, DIA, and the three military counterintelligence agencies, and with the FBI Director as its chairman. In short, the report outlined the most oppressive domestic spying program ever conceived by an American government.

There was one hitch: J. Edgar Hoover. Huston's lectures had gone for naught. Whatever his motives, the Old Man turned thumbs down. He was not buying any part of the Huston Plan, and his objections were appended as footnotes under each specific operation: "The FBI is opposed to surreptitious entry," and so forth, right on down the line.

If Huston really believed that Hoover was the "last reigning monarch in the Western world," he didn't act like it. In a "top secret" memorandum to Haldeman in early July, Huston argued that his program was sound and that "Everyone knowledgeable in the field, with the exception of Mr. Hoover, concurs that existing coverage is grossly inadequate. CIA and NSA note that this is particularly true of diplomatic establishments, and we have learned at the White House that it is also true of New Left groups." Huston took after Hoover on each specific objection: "There is no valid argument against use of legal mail covers except Mr. Hoover's concern that the civil liberties people may become upset. This risk is surely an acceptable one and hardly serious enough to justify denying ourselves a valuable and legal intelligence tool. Covert coverage is illegal and there are serious risks involved. However, the advantages to be derived from its use outweigh the risks." In the area of surreptitious entry, Huston noted that "The FBI, in Mr. Hoover's younger days, used to conduct operations with great success and with no exposure. The information secured was invaluable."

And so it went for many pages, with Huston naïvely pleading for his program in the strongest language he could command. It was Hoover's total unreasonableness that was at fault. "His objections are generally inconsistent and frivolous—most express concern about possible embarrassment to the intelligence community (i.e., Hoover) from public disclosure," Huston wrote. This was especially frustrating in view of the total reasonableness of the others involved: "I went into this exercise fearful that the CIA would not cooperate. In fact, Dick Helms was most cooperative and helpful." Why even "Admiral Gayler (NSA) and General Bennett (DIA) were greatly displeased by Mr. Hoover's attitude and his inconsistence on footnoting objections. They wished to raise a formal protest and sign the report only with the understanding that they opposed the footnotes. I prevailed on them not to do so since it would aggravate Mr. Hoover and further complicate our efforts. They graciously agreed to go along with my suggestion in order to avoid a nasty scene and jeopardize the possibility of positive action resulting from the report. I assured them that their opinion would be brought to the attention of the President."

But there was a way of getting around Hoover. Huston saw it as a two-tier process involving the President's conning skill: "Mr. Hoover should be called in privately for a stroking session at which the President explains the decision he has made, thanks Mr. Hoover for his candid advice and past cooperation, and indicates he is counting on Edgar's cooperation in implementing the new report. . . ." Stage two proposed another meeting in the Oval Office of the four intelligence chiefs, where "the President should thank them for the report, announce his decisions, indicate his desires for future activity, and present each with an autographed copy of the photo of the first meeting which Ollie took."

In closing, Huston provided Haldeman with a psychological analysis: "I might add that in my personal opinion Mr. Hoover will not hesitate to accede to any decision which the President makes, and the President should not, therefore, be reluctant to overrule Mr. Hoover's objections. Mr. Hoover is set in his ways and can be bull-headed as hell, but he is a loyal trooper. Twenty years ago he would never have raised the type of objections he has here, but he's getting old and worried about his legend. He makes life tough in this area, but not impossible—for he'll respond to direction by the President, and that is all we need to set the domestic intelligence house in order."

On July 14, Haldeman, also in a top secret memorandum, notified Huston that the President had approved his recommendations, with one reservation: "He does not, however, want to follow the procedure you outlined . . . regarding implementation. He would prefer that the thing simply be put into motion on the basis of his approval." Finally armed with the President's authority, on July 23 Huston issued a "decision" memorandum to the four chiefs rubber-stamping his grandiose scheme. To add insult to injury, Hoover was named chairman of the interagency evaluation committee which he had opposed.

The Huston Plan remained operational all of five days. Huston has testified before the Senate Armed Services Committee that William Sullivan, who had been Hoover's representative on the working committee, called him shortly after Hoover received the decision memorandum to say that the Director was extremely upset. "Hoover went right through the roof," Huston later recalled, and landed in Mitchell's office with such a force that the Attorney General was compelled to persuade the White House to back off. The "decision" memorandum was recalled, but Huston says that it was apparent that each of the documents had been taken apart by the recipient and copied prior to its return.

In a last desperate stand to reactivate the plan, Huston fired off a furious barrage of top secret memos to Haldeman. On August 5, Huston bitterly observed that:

At some point, Hoover has to be told who is President. He has become totally unreasonable and his conduct is detrimental to our domestic intelligence operations. In the past two weeks, he has terminated all FBI liaison with NSA, DIA, the military services, Secret Service—everyone except the White House. He terminated liaison with CIA in May. . . . It is important to remember that the entire intelligence community knows that the President made a positive decision to go ahead and Hoover has now succeeded in forcing a review. If he gets his way it is going to look like he is more powerful than the President. . . . For eighteen months we have watched people in this government ignore the President's order, take actions to embarrass him, promote themselves at his expense, and generally make his job more difficult. It makes me fighting mad, and what Hoover is doing here is putting himself above the President.

It was all too late, of course. With one swat, the Old Man had put the young whippersnapper's political meteor into total eclipse. "There was only one honest way to deal with the problem of Mr. Hoover," Huston later observed, "and that was to remove him. But the White House decided for political reasons that they couldn't get rid of him. So they had to set up the Plumbers. I find that totally indefensible."

This was about the time that John Wesley Dean III came to the White House from the Justice Department as legal counsel to the President. One of his first assignments was to assume responsibility for all matters relating to internal security and domestic intelligence. In his Watergate testimony,

Dean said that having been "told of the Presidentially approved plan that called for bugging, burglarizing, mailcovers, and the like, I was instructed by Haldeman to see what I could do to get the plan implemented. I thought the plan was totally uncalled for and unjustified." Asked if he assumed Huston's responsibilities, Dean said, "I think that you would have to know Tom Huston and my relationship with Tom Huston to know that there was no way I would take over anything regarding Mr. Tom Huston. He is a very brilliant, independent man. He would not, I did not even know what he was doing half the time. In fact, it was some months after he had joined my staff that I learned he had some sort of scrambler phone locked in a safe beside him and he made a lot of calls."

The Paranoia Machine Was Feeding upon Itself

Of course, John Dean was not an innocent. He had received his baptism of paranoia at the Department of Justice. Doug Lea, who now heads the Privacy Project in the Washington office of the American Civil Liberties Union, recalled what it was like in the Justice Department in the summer of 1970 when he interviewed Dean and others for a magazine article on the prospects for a long hot summer.

LEA: "One part of the story was a box on the federal government's intelligence apparatus—not a comprehensive look at it, but some idea of how they would respond to racial outbreaks in cities and things like that. So I went over and talked to John Dean in his office on the fourth floor of the Justice Department. He gave me what turned out to be a pretty complete description of the apparatus that we later saw described in the Huston Plan. That is, in terms of the various committees: the Intelligence Evaluation Committee, the Inter-Departmental Intelligence Unit, IDIU it was called; and, in fact, that same day I later went up and saw this rattletrap computer on the fifth floor of Justice, sitting there, shaking the rafters, and knocking out in sort of an endless stream the names of so-called radicals."

Was this an FBI operation?

LEA: "No, this was run by main Justice, and headed by a fellow named James Devine, who is now over in the Law Enforcement Assistance Administration. I sat there and had a very pleasant talk with Devine, but I had this funny feeling, because all the time we were sitting there, this computer was rattling around, spitting out these names, and it seemed like printout paper was drifting across the floor and out into the corridors. It was a crazy kind of surreal thing. They were getting these names from a variety of sources. A lot of it was simply from newspapers and magazines, and not just radical publications, but *Time* and *Newsweek*, stuff that almost any person generally well informed would know anyway. The information was coming from public sources, public statements by the leaders, the Dellingers and the Susan Sontags and people like that. Intelligence information from federal agencies was also pouring into it.

"I had this strange feeling that this machine and its apparatus, the human apparatus built around the machine, was kind of out of control, and no matter how much data they poured into the machine, it still was hungry. The information was being redisseminated. It came in from multisources, and then it sort of spread back to the same sources. The CIA and the FBI had access to it, and the National Security Agency, Pentagon Intelligence Service, the White House group centered around Huston, and maybe the Plumbers, who would have a pretty easy access to this undiscriminating, unedited massive volume of raw data.

"Paranoia created the machine in the first place and now the machine was increasing the paranoia. Dean had sat across the table from people like David Dellinger and Sam Brown, and he saw that they were human beings and he played politics with them, negotiating, and therefore he wasn't like a Tom Huston or a Robert Mardian or a J. Edgar Hoover, who tended to see these people in the abstract. I think Dean was probably a moderating influence in the White House, trying to tone down these guys who thought there was a massive conspiracy out there somewhere that was about to bring down the republic. While, in fact, all of this information was a lot of horseshit. What you had was this superstructure—an extrasomatic kind of structure that sort of floated above reality and which tied in almost all of the federal agencies that could even plausibly have any kind of investigative or prosecutorial or intelligence function—and it was all just sort of feeding upon itself, back and forth.

"At first Mitchell and Kleindienst were apparently unhappy with the lack of action in the Internal Security Division and that's when they brought in Robert Mardian, who was then busily undermining Finch at HEW. Finch tended to have liberal views and Mardian was sort of a torpedo set right in the midst of it. During the demonstrations, they had command posts set up in the top of the Mayor's building here and over at Justice, with a complicated communications system that tied in the White House. It was like Hitler's bunker. During these periods of demonstrations, Kleindienst, or Mardian, or whoever was his deputy at any given time, was effectively the Mayor of Washington, D.C."

Colson's Reichstag Plot

It was the Pentagon Papers that finally tipped the White House para-noia over the edge.* Until the publication of the first installment of ex-cerpts from the "History of U.S. Decision-Making Process on Viet Nam Policy" in the New York *Times*, the White House's effort to subvert the intelligence community could be charitably characterized as wishful think-ing. But after June 13, 1971, the day the *Times* started its serialization, the White House, by then completely disenchanted with the traditional agencies, finally took that first fateful step toward its own Götter-dämmerung.

Although Daniel Ellsberg, a former Pentagon egghead and Rand Cor-poration think-tank analyst, was immediately discovered and placed under FBI investigation, Nixon promptly instructed Ehrlichman not only to plug the leaks but to supplement the FBI's inquiries by forming a White House Special Investigations Unit. Thus the Plumbers outfit was born, with lines of authority moving directly from the Oval Office: Nixon to Ehrlichman to Egil Krogh, Jr., to David Young, to Jack Caulfield, G. Gor-don Liddy, E. Howard Hunt, Tony Ulasewicz, et al.—the boys in Room 16, a basement office in the Executive Office Building next door to the White House. It was Young, a Kissinger aide on loan to the project, who placed the sign on the door of Room 16: "David Young—Plumber."

Working simultaneously with the Plumbers on the Pentagon Papers caper was Charles Colson, the White House's Heinrich Himmler. The first to fall under his deep suspicion was Morton Halperin, the former Kis-singer aide who had been in overall charge of the McNamara project within the government, and who was now comfortably ensconced in the Brookings Institution, a Washington think tank. Besides, as everybody knew, Halperin was a close friend of Ellsberg's. Convinced that some of the "leaked documents" could be found at the Institution, Colson in-structed Caulfield to retrieve them forthwith. Caulfield dispatched Ulase-

---

* It was in the spring of 1971 that Nixon secretly began taping his conversations for posterity. The Technical Services Division of the Secret Service installed hidden microphones in the Oval Office, in his office in the Executive Office Building, in the Cabinet Room, and on four of his personal telephones. The recording system was linked to an electronic "locator" device operated by security personnel that showed the President's whereabouts by lights for each of seven locations.

wicz to inspect the premises, and according to a chronology later provided by John Dean, the former New York cop reported that the target was impregnable. Upon receiving this regrettable intelligence, Colson told Caulfield that "if necessary he should plant a firebomb in the building and retrieve the documents during the commotion that would ensue." Caulfield complained to Dean, who complained to Ehrlichman, who gently dissuaded Colson from carrying out this Reichstag plot.

In the beginning, Ehrlichman described the Plumbers operation as "a group that was established for the purpose of getting the security people in the departments and agencies to do a better job." Subsequently, "it became an investigative unit," Ehrlichman told the Ervin committee, because "Krogh came to me and said, 'I am having real trouble getting the FBI to move on this.'" Ehrlichman took the problem to Mitchell, who also indicated there was "a very tough problem," because Hoover was a close friend of Ellsberg's father-in-law, Louis Marx, and was taking the position that "interviews of that family are not to take place." "So," Ehrlichman said, he assigned two men in the Plumbers unit who had "considerable investigative experience . . . to follow up" on leads in the file. The two men were Hunt and Liddy.

The FBI had submitted numerous reports on Ellsberg to Ehrlichman, which he routed to Room 16. The problem, as Young expressed it in a memo, was that "The FBI is disposed to thinking that Ellsberg is the sole prime mover." This unpopular thesis was probably the motivating reason for the White House's rejection of the FBI investigation, and for its decision to use Hunt and Liddy for the break-in at the Beverly Hills office of Dr. Lewis Fielding, Ellsberg's psychiatrist. What is remarkable about Ehrlichman's testimony is that the FBI had interviewed Marx about a week after the Pentagon story broke.

"The President Had Shaken Up the Director"

There is something even more remarkable about Ehrlichman's testimony that was never challenged. The testimony quoted here begins on page 2625 of the transcript of the Watergate hearings. Senator Daniel Inouye has just completed his ten-minute interrogation, concentrating on the burglary of Dr. Fielding's office by Hunt and Liddy, when Senator Lowell Weicker begins his series of questions:

Weicker: Mr. Ehrlichman, this morning, I believe you discussed the justification for the Plumbers group. I had a question on my pad which was asked by another member of the committee as to why the Plumbers, why not the FBI?

I believe, and you correct me if I am in any way stating this or paraphrasing it incorrectly, that your response was that you were not getting cooperation from the FBI and had the opposition of the Director, Mr. Hoover, and that was the justification for the Plumbers. Now, is that correct?

Ehrlichman: No. The special unit itself was created in response to a strong feeling by the President that the White House had to more closely supervise the departments, the agencies, in their efforts—that is, in the departments' and agencies' efforts—to do their own job inside the departments and agencies in plugging leaks, finding out who were disseminating these documents [Pentagon Papers], and so forth. So the origin of that unit and the original reason for their being was for that purpose. It was not originally set up as a police organization or an investigatory organization or anything of that kind. But then, when Mr. Krogh ran into this hard place in getting information, it was a last resort to use these two people [Hunt and Liddy] who were in the unit to do this one particular investigatory job [burglary of Dr. Fielding's office].

Weicker: Because, in fact, the information could not be obtained by the FBI, is that correct?

Ehrlichman: Would not, yes.

Weicker: Would not.

I would like to read to you, and I believe your counsel has handed you an exhibit or rather a letter, which I would hope we would make an exhibit, dated August 3, 1971, from the Federal Bureau of Investigation. This was some time before the actual break-in. It is a letter to Mr. Krogh from the Director, J. Edgar Hoover, and I would like to read the letter.

Hon. Egil Krogh.

Deputy Assistant to the President for Domestic Affairs, The White House, Washington, D. C.

Dear Mr. Krogh: By letter dated July 29, 1971, the President advised me that he had directed that you examine in depth the circumstances of the many recent disclosures of Top Secret and other sensitive material to the public. He asked that I forward to you all information acquired to date, including individual reports for interviews, with respect to 17 persons who were named in an attachment to his letter. One of these was Daniel Ellsberg, principal suspect in the disclosure of the "McNamara Study" to various newspapers. He asked that a comprehensive background paper on Ellsberg be sent to you.

Enclosed are 17 memoranda containing the information mentioned by the President. We have interviewed five of the individuals involved in connection with our investigation in the Ellsberg case. We also endeavored to interview a sixth one, Mr. Charles M. Cooke, but he declined to submit to interview by the FBI without the specific clearance of Deputy Attorney General Richard G. Kleindienst.

If you concur, we will proceed with interviews of all the remaining individuals except Daniel Ellsberg.

By separate communication, I am furnishing a copy of each of the enclosures to the Attorney General. Upon removal of the classified enclosures, this transmittal letter may be declassified.

Sincerely yours,

J. Edgar Hoover

Weicker: Would you say this is fairly clear evidence that the FBI was perfectly willing to perform its function insofar as the Ellsberg matter was concerned?

Ehrlichman: Well, I don't think I am able to respond to that, Senator. I think all of us who have had experience with Mr. Hoover recognize that letters of this kind were a method that he had frequently of justifying shortfall in performance by the Bureau. I don't know whether this was window dressing or what this was. It was obvious that the President had, at Mr. Krogh's request, shaken up the Director, and I will say that over a period of a couple of months the result of having appointed the special unit and the result of having—the President having—told Mr. Hoover that he was having to resort to sending two people [Hunt and Liddy?] out there [Dr. Fielding's Beverly Hills office?] from the White House caused the Bureau to wake up on this thing.

This revelation went completely over the committee's head. No member of the committee, or of the press, ever asked Ehrlichman to clarify his statement. The assumption all along has been that Hoover was not aware of the Plumbers unit or of the Fielding burglary on August 25, 1971. We next pick up the interrogation in the middle of page 2627:

Weicker: Would you advise then that every time a department or an agency of this Government falls short that rather than remove the head of that agency or department we set up a similar function on a secret basis? Is that the way we are going to handle it?

Ehrlichman: Oh, no, no, indeed, no indeed, and I think in retrospect, and I think you will recognize that all through this proceeding we keep coming back to Bureau problems, I think in retrospect that the administration would have been far better off if Mr. Hoover had been retired earlier, predating this episode, because many, many of the problems that we encountered were as a result of Mr. Hoover's very fixed views, very sincere. He was alert and he was sincere, he was patriotic but he was certainly fixed in his views, and it made operation very, very difficult.

Now, when you run across a situation where you have a retirement of that kind that is politically sensitive and difficult, sometimes the decision is made to postpone the retirement, and when that happens, then you simply have to find other ways of doing things.

Weicker: In other words, what I gather you are saying he was fixed in his views to the extent that he would not agree to a break-in of Daniel Ellsberg's psychiatrist's office?

Ehrlichman: That of course overstates it dramatically, Senator. What he would not agree to was an investigation of Mr. Marx and others close to Daniel Ellsberg.

Weicker: Well now, Mr. Ehrlichman, we have a letter saying he will agree to go ahead and investigate that is sitting right there before you.

Ehrlichman: Well, frankly, Senator—

Weicker: I am asking you is he lying?

Ehrlichman: No, I don't see for instance Mr. Marx's name in there, and I don't know what the list is that that letter refers to. Maybe Mr. Marx's name is on it.

Weicker: He says "If you will concur, we will proceed with interviews with all the remaining individuals."

Ehrlichman: Who are they, Senator? I honestly don't know. I don't remember ever seeing that letter. I can tell you this: *That by, oh, the 20th of September of that year* [emphasis added], the Bureau was checking on all eight cylinders, they were abroad, and Bureau work was moving ahead, and we were past the problem.

Nothing more was made of this pinpointing of the time that the President apparently shook up the Director. The next day, however, Ehrlichman lost no time in correcting the record.

Weicker: You stated yesterday, Mr. Ehrlichman, that the FBI, through its leadership of Mr. Hoover, was not . . . pushing the Ellsberg investigation, allegedly because of a relationship Mr. Hoover had with Mr. Ellsberg's father-in-law, Mr. Louis Marx. And that it was not until after September 20, 1971, that the FBI "was clicking on all eight cylinders." Would that be correct?

Ehrlichman: I do not think I said "after." If I said after I should have said by, Senator, and the reason that I picked that date is that on or about that date there was a meeting which the Attorney General had with the President where he gave the President a progress report on this matter, and that was the gist of his report at that time. Now, when that commenced I do not need to testify to, because that is not something that I know of my own knowledge.

Not the Most Cooperative Person in the World

With that revised version on the record, Weicker plunged ahead to make his own far less important point that the FBI had interviewed Marx in June, a fact that came as a surprise to Ehrlichman. Intrigued by Ehrlichman's obvious slip of the tongue, I tried to pursue the matter with Senator Weicker in October 1974. He read the transcript pages in question, and then I asked him to interpret Ehrlichman's remarks.

WEICKER: "Well, I'd have to read the entire context of it, but let me say one thing to you right now, because it's been a guideline for everything I've done on Watergate. I wouldn't be alive today, in a figurative sense, unless I followed this ground rule: I don't speculate and I don't interpret. As far as I'm concerned, I deal strictly with facts, and when I go ahead and make statements in my report that the Constitution or this or that was violated, I back it up with a fact that's indisputable, and I'm not going to— The one thing I didn't do in my Watergate report, and I'm not going to do now is to try to speculate and interpret and resolve other people's testimony."

Where do I go from here?

WEICKER: "No, but it's very important because, as I say, I stay out front by my ability to report facts."

All right, what did you learn from the Watergate hearings about Hoover's role vis-à-vis the White House?

WEICKER: "I'd say about the only thing that I could really say with confidence relative to Hoover would be that both the White House and elements within his own Bureau, specifically William Sullivan, obviously didn't think that he was the most cooperative person in the world in going along with the rather unconstitutional methods and procedures which they advocated. They didn't think he was tough enough for what they wanted to do. That you can say.

"You can also say that Sullivan and Hoover obviously didn't see eye to eye because Hoover wasn't tough enough. And you can also say that because they didn't see eye to eye is why Sullivan turned over the Kissinger logs to Mardian, who in turn gave them to Ehrlichman."

You don't think it was because Ellsberg was overheard on the Halperin tap?

WEICKER: "I'm just telling you that that's why Sullivan turned them over to Mardian. He didn't like Hoover. The normal— Obviously, when a man leaves a department, what he does is turn over his material to the department. Why didn't Sullivan turn them over to the department? Obviously, there was a personality clash between he and Mr. Hoover. So, you know, there you are. That, I would say, is the *known*. Everything else, as far as I'm concerned, is speculative."

What about the Huston Plan?

WEICKER: "Sullivan was before the committee in executive session, and I had at least three meetings with Sullivan myself. I know that William Sullivan had a great deal to do with the Huston Plan. He supplied much of the technical input. He was the FBI representative, if you will, in the putting together of this, uh, plan, whatever you want to call it. Yes, definitely. I would say in a psychological sense, he felt that the tough line that the White House wanted followed was proper, and there's no question that it could just as well be termed the Sullivan Plan. He was one of the principal drafters of it."

It seems that the Justice Department, which for some reason your committee did not investigate, was deeply involved in repressive measures. They were not just prosecutors, but acted as investigators, with their own computer up on the fifth floor—

WEICKER: "Oh, yes. There's no question about the fact that all functions were under one roof there. That's what happened when Mardian took over the Internal Security Division of the Justice Department. He combined it with Division Five of the FBI, so that they became the investigative, prosecutorial and— The whole works, in other words, just fell under one heading.

"Remember, there was no concentration of effort in the domestic subversion area until Mardian and the Nixon Administration came along. They really gave a shot in the arm, if you will, to those in the FBI who wanted to concentrate in that area and they built up their staff and their resources, and, you know, once again they were activated, in their own minds. Now, I'm talking about in *their* minds. So that's the reason why you'll find, you know, a great affection between Sullivan and Mardian and the Administration, because these fellows were kind of sitting around dead in the water until the Administration came along and decided to go roaring in on this area of what they termed domestic subversion, and therefore, the loyalties were established between the Administration and Sullivan and also, naturally, then, the split between Sullivan and the Director, and the Director and the Administration, to a certain extent. They were going off into a new area."

More People in the White House Gunning for Hoover Than in Any Other Administration

I asked Felt and Mohr what they thought of Ehrlichman's statement concerning the poor performance of the FBI.

FELT: "This is just a complete phony. It is the act of a desperate man trying to bail himself out of a bad situation. They know that Hoover is dead and that he can't defend himself. If they had any criticism, if the White House was unhappy with the FBI, there I was sitting for quite a long time as Chief Inspector where I would handle critics and criticism, and I was sitting as the Deputy Associate Director during the period of time they're talking about and I certainly never heard of any criticism. I never saw anything in writing. I never heard anybody say anything about it. I never heard Hoover say anything about it. I think they're making it all up."

MOHR: "I think that if Nixon had asked him about the Plumbers, Hoover would have told him he was crazy, that it was a bad thing. Ehrlichman is trying to justify the creation of the Plumbers. I don't think he says that Hoover was told about the break-in at Dr. Fielding's office. All he said was that—I don't know if he ever told it to Hoover—but what he's saying to Weicker is that the White House was sending two men out there to Dr. Fielding's office. Now, as far as the Bureau was concerned, we wouldn't do it. I don't give a damn if Nixon personally asked Hoover. The whole trouble with the White House was that you had a bunch of guys over there that thought that the FBI ought to do this, do that. What they did was a black-bag job, that would be our terminology for a burglary. The Bureau wouldn't do that anymore. Hoover had discontinued this stuff because the public just wouldn't put up with it. Look at the stink it caused. We knew you couldn't get anything worthwhile out of an office file. What they wanted to do was to disgrace or destroy a man who was then on trial. You had Ehrlichman out there talking to the judge, the stupid jerk, offering him a job as Director of the FBI. If he'd had any sense, he wouldn't have done that. What the hell kind of a brain do you call that? Krogh was one of Hoover's primary critics over there. Look at the way Huston was cussing Hoover out. There were many who were try-ing to churn Nixon up into getting rid of Hoover. There's no question about that. But none of them succeeded.

"This is weird because, actually, I think that of all the presidents that he served under, Hoover was closer to Nixon than any other one, yet there were more people in the White House that were out gunning for Hoover than in any other administration that I can remember."

Did he complain to you about it?

MOHR: "No, never. He never indicated that his relationship with Nixon was other than top flight. As far as I know, he and Mitchell got along excellently. As a matter of fact, Ehrlichman and Kissinger and Hal-deman would come over and see Hoover from time to time when they had problems and I'm sure—I've always found this to be true—if the President requested something, he would do it if it was in his prerogative to do it."

The FBI Wouldn't Hesitate to Twist the Arm of an Informant

What about the charge that the FBI refused to do anything about the narcotics traffic?

FELT: "Hoover resisted that through the years for a number of reasons. In the first place, one of the main objectives that he always followed was to keep the FBI as small as possible, and he really believed that there should not be any central federal police agency, that this was a step to-ward a police state."

Did he resist because narcotics is a dirty business?

FELT: "Not entirely. That's only one aspect of it. Another aspect is that for the last ten or fifteen years, every time Congress passed a new law, be-cause of the reputation of the FBI, they'd say, 'Here, have the FBI handle it.' This was getting to the point where it was becoming ridiculous. Now, I don't say that the problem of narcotics investigation is ridiculous, but it's true that an effective investigative agency can't become too big. When it becomes too big, it becomes unwieldy and cumbersome, and if it's a fed-eral agency, one federal agency taking over all federal investigative opera-tions, then you're started on the way to the police state, and this is what

Hoover argued against all the way along the line. Now, he didn't object to the narcotics because it was dirty, he objected to taking over the Narcotics Bureau because of the corruption within its ranks, and because of the fact that it would be impossible to absorb them into the FBI without just mass firings, without all kinds of personnel problems."

I know from personal experience that narcotics agents working the ghettos feel no compunction about latching on to addicted prostitutes and forcing them to inform at great perils to their lives.

FELT: "Well, you're talking about an informant, and the FBI wouldn't hesitate to use an informant."

Would you blackmail them into doing it?

FELT: "No, but you might twist their arm a little bit. It's a question of money or a question of—of—it's arm twisting a lot of times. This is law enforcement. But I was talking about the federal employees in the Narcotics Bureau. They just in no way measured up to the standards of the FBI. You simply couldn't take a large force like that and integrate it into the FBI. You could run it completely separately but that's the way it was being run. The Nixon people wanted us to absorb them into the FBI. It was an impossible situation, not only for Hoover but for the staff, the employees of the FBI. I mean, even when you've got a staff that was as carefully screened as the FBI personnel, you get an occasional rotten apple. So that was Hoover's primary objection."

The Huston Plan Evolved from Hoover's Old Dirty Tricks Stuff

What do you know about the Huston Plan?

FELT: "Who do you think wrote that Huston Plan? It's Sullivan's language all the way through. Sullivan was in charge of the working subcommittee. You see, the committee was Hoover, Helms, Gayler and Bennett, and the working group was Sullivan, Huston, and the aides from these other agencies. Well, that report is just Sullivan from one end to the other."

You don't think Huston did it?

FELT: "I read the memoranda Huston wrote about Hoover and he didn't sound very bright, but that Huston Plan, in my opinion, was written by Sullivan."

Was any pressure put on Hoover to implement the Huston Plan?

FELT: "I'm not sure that there was any pressure put on him for that at all. Hoover attended this meeting at the White House with Helms and the others, and they talked about the problem with the extreme left, they talked about the problem of Russian espionage, and all that sort of thing, and they wanted to overhaul their procedures and guidelines, and I don't think any of them paid very much attention to that meeting at all. They turned the whole thing over to the working group, and when Sullivan brought the report in to Hoover it was probably the first time that Hoover really paid any attention to it. He didn't think along the same lines as Sullivan did at all, and of course he just hit the ceiling when he saw it. He made Sullivan go back and write in a dissenting opinion on every one of the key points: surreptitious entry, opening first-class mail, and so forth. In other words, it was not a unanimous report, there was this dissenting opinion.

"Hoover really felt that the White House would not accept it with his contrary recommendations in it, so he was shocked when he got that decision memorandum from the White House implementing the plan. So Hoover took it to the Attorney General and pointed out how far off the track these people were and convinced him, obviously, because Mitchell went to the White House and told the President that in no way could these things be done. This was the end of it; nobody ever heard anything more about it. It was never officially retracted. What happened was that Sullivan was instructed to retrieve all copies of that instruction memorandum, but some of the fellows had made copies, and that is what Dean latched on to, you see, that he later gave to the Senate Watergate Committee."

John Mohr supplied additional background:

MOHR: "The Huston Plan evolved as a result of Hoover discontinuing what we call 'dirty tricks' stuff. And Sullivan always felt that Hoover was wrong in doing that. Personally, I thought Hoover was right, that the time had come when the American people just wouldn't put up with that stuff, and as it turned out, Hoover was right. Sullivan thought that was wrong, that in order to combat the Communist threat properly through counterespionage and the like you had to use those tactics whether you liked it or not. He also felt that these tactics were necessary in order to combat the groups—you know, we had the SDS and riots and the campus demonstrations and the burning of buildings and all that crap—that these tactics were necessary in order to counteract those people. Hoover said no and he wouldn't go for it. But Sullivan just kept engineering that thing. He had not only Huston but I think he had a couple of other friends over there in the White House who were interested in reinstituting some of that, but the motivating force for most of this stuff came from NSA. They were putting the heat on the Bureau to go back into this business, and Sullivan thought we should, and as a result this group got together over there, NSA and the Army, and I think the CIA to the extent of being advisory, because they weren't permitted to do any of that stuff in this country, you know. But Hoover was against it and he stayed against it. Then this committee came along and they came up with the Huston Plan and Sullivan was a very active, energetic participant in that and obviously he would have been one of those who gave them most of the material."

Sullivan says he wrote a letter opposing the plan—

MOHR: "Well, now wait a minute. They got the plan drawn up and one of the things in there that really wowed me was that Hoover would be the coordinator of this plan. In other words, he would be the coordinator of all these dirty tricks being done by all these agencies, not only the FBI, but he was going to coordinate this whole thing. At first Hoover agreed, however, to go ahead with the plan, then he and Sullivan got together in his office and they went over that thing point by point and Hoover decided this is not for him and he said no and that was the end of the Huston Plan."

In other words, he didn't want to take the responsibility for its execution.

MOHR: "He didn't want to be identified with this stuff. He knew it was going to be bad. As far as backup is concerned, Hoover still could have gotten the Attorney General to approve those things as he had in the past. I think that he was strong enough to get somebody to approve it, but that wasn't the only thing. He knew that this stuff was bad if it became public knowledge, and obviously everybody in the world would say he was right."

"When I Saw How Frightened Hoover Was"

In the final analysis, Sullivan knows more about the Huston Plan—that is, from Hoover's viewpoint—than anybody else. The question, always, is whether anyone ever tells the whole story.

SULLIVAN: "Here's what I know about the Huston Plan. I never knew Huston in my life until one day he appeared in my office and said, 'The President and others in the White House are very dissatisfied at the poor performance the FBI has given. You're not solving the bombings, you're not apprehending the killers, you're not giving us intelligence information on when these violent demonstrations are going to appear, and this has got to be corrected.' And he said, 'I have been given the assignment to see to it that you people improve your operations.' Well, you know, that came right out of the blue to me. And he said, 'I came over to tell you that action is going to be taken.' I said, 'Well, fine, I'll pass that on.' I did pass it on in a memorandum, and the next thing I knew there was a conference at the White House, with Hoover and all the heads of the intelligence community. When Hoover came back, he was quite upset. 'You know,' he said, 'they're dissatisfied with our work.' He said, 'I've been made chairman of this interagency ad hoc group set up to study the intelligence problem and come up with a stronger program so we can solve these problems and see how we can get this straightened out.' Then he said, 'I want you to take charge of the working group.' Of course, I said, 'All right, I'll do it.' So I took charge. I was chairman of the working subcommittee made up of key people in the intelligence community. It is this group that came up with the so-called Huston Plan. It wasn't the product of any one mind."

Did you help write it?

SULLIVAN: "I didn't write one line, not one line. Huston was a member of the subcommittee and he was at every meeting. We met with him at those meetings, and he came over to my office, I don't know, maybe one or two times after that first time. I didn't write one line of it. It was a subcommittee report. I took it up with Hoover and he said, 'I'm willing to go ahead and do this, but the Attorney General is not involved, he is not a member of the committee,' which was true. He said, 'This ad hoc committee is going to go out of existence just as soon as the report is finished. Then when we start to put these programs into effect, where am I going to go to get backup? Where am I going to get approval? That puts the whole thing on my shoulders.' And he said, 'I'm not going to have it on my shoulders.'

"In my opinion, in his position, you ought to make your own decisions, accept the responsibility yourself. That's what you're getting paid for. Unless it's something that demands a legal decision, then you ought to go to the Attorney General and get a ruling. But not if it's intelligence and you've got the President's approval. So when I saw how frightened Hoover was—he was frightened of the whole plan—I said the thing to do is to abort it. I went back to my office and I wrote a memorandum recommending against the plan. And there is a record of it in the Bureau, unless they destroyed it."

Were you in favor of the plan?

SULLIVAN: "Yes, I was in favor of the Huston Plan because it was the basic program which we had been running for years, you know—I might say since I was a boy in the Bureau, since 1941. I was in favor of it and I said to him, 'Mr. Hoover, we've been running these for years and now what about reinstituting at least those that we've been running?' And he said, 'Look, let's wait a year and public opinion might change and then we can go ahead with this program if I can get the Attorney General behind it,' and it was then that I went and dictated a memorandum recommending against the plan, after I saw the condition he was in and how frightened he was over it.

"Remember, it wasn't Hoover who cut out these practices in 1966. It was Ramsey Clark. Prior to 1966 we did this black-bag stuff without the approval of the Attorney General. Then in 1966 Hoover decided he wanted the approval of the Attorney General, and he asked me to prepare a letter. I wrote 'surreptitious entry,' and when it came back from Hoover, he had crossed it out and put in 'burglary.' So we rewrote the letter, and of course Ramsey Clark said no. Now, had Clark given permission, Hoover would have gone ahead with the burglarizing. He wasn't personally opposed to it. All he wanted to do was get the Attorney General to assume the responsibility.

"Now, we never did it politically, per se, you understand, not for any political reasons. But the Huston Plan didn't call for doing it against political objectors. All this plan was, and this can be proven, was to reinstitute the practices that Hoover had done for years.

"Then when we had all the bombings and the killings, the FBI fell down. We were not solving the bombings, we have never solved the Capitol bombing. I think this is a total disgrace. We weren't solving the killings, and this was because Hoover had abolished all our programs."

Are you talking about black-bag stuff?

SULLIVAN: "I was taught how to do these things as a young agent, and Hoover approved every damn one. He approved illegal entries, he approved the opening of mail, and he approved a number of other things of that nature, and so it's a damn lie for anybody to say that Hoover was a holier-than-thou fellow."

Against students or Soviet agents?

SULLIVAN: "Let me explain something. There was no differentiation. It made absolutely no difference whether it was a domestic case or a foreign case. Anybody tries to tell you anything to the contrary, they're lying to you. I engaged in these activities myself, and there's no use of anybody drawing that kind of distinction. This is one of those Johnny-come-lately defenses and it doesn't cut any ice at all. Don't let anybody fool you on that. It was right across the board, and Hoover approved it right across the board."

"Sullivan Wanted to Investigate Everybody"

FELT: "Just to give you an example of the sort of things, of the big arguments I would have with Sullivan, he wanted to conduct an investigation of every member of Students for a Democratic Society. Now, to me, this is just inconceivable. Not only from a policy standpoint, but because probably not more than two or three hundred of all SDS members were the real fanatical radicals that you'd have to watch. Of course, you couldn't be sure, so Sullivan's idea was, Let's take a shotgun approach and we'll investigate every one of them and be sure we got the radicals and the revolutionary violence type pinpointed, and my argument was that we should not open a file on an individual unless there was strong indication that he was disposed toward violence or had committed violence of some sort or other. And this got to be quite a big hassle inside the FBI. Mr. Hoover agreed with me. He said, 'Absolutely not. I agree with Felt.' We restricted the opening of files to a very small number like the Weathermen and others."

MOHR: "Listen, the SDS was ready to have a revolution and they were ready to destroy this country. It was pretty tough going there for a while. I don't know where you were, but I was in Washington when some of those demonstrations took place and I saw them storm the Justice Building, and it wasn't funny. I've seen it happen in other countries and it doesn't take a great deal when you get students riled up like that. Hell, they were bombing, they were burning buildings--the next step was to take over the government. Hoover was of the opinion that we should investigate the SDSers, but who were they? They didn't carry cards, and you just don't go out and investigate everybody. You can't investigate them for having thoughts that you don't agree with or speak words that you don't agree with. It's when they mix action with those words. Sullivan wanted to investigate everybody, but Hoover was still carrying that badge of criticism for the Palmer raids. And he remembered it."

Is there any truth to the charge that Hoover wanted to go easy on Ellsberg's father-in-law, Louis Marx, because they were good friends?

FELT: "That's ridiculous. It's just not true at all. I was sitting in the spot where I saw all the memoranda and all of Hoover's notations going back and forth. What happened, which is the basis for this story, is that a memorandum was submitted by Brennan through Sullivan on up to Hoover, and it pointed out that Marx's daughter was Ellsberg's wife and they requested authority to interview him. Ordinarily, on a lead like that, they wouldn't ask Hoover's authority, but knowing that Marx was someone that Hoover knew, they sent this thing through. And it was pretty much a fishing expedition type of thing.

"When the memorandum came back, Hoover had written on the bottom, 'NOH.' [No. Hoover.] It went to Brennan, who was the Assistant Director in Charge of the Domestic Intelligence Division, and he says, and I believe him, that he thought Hoover had written 'HOK.' And the way Hoover writes, his H is just like a K. Brennan told them to go ahead and interview Marx, which they did, and when Hoover heard about that, he was— I don't think he was so mad that they interviewed Marx, because it was an inconsequential thing, but he was mad because he thought it was just a deliberate, intentional snub to him. He was furious. Brennan was ordered transferred to Cleveland, or Cincinnati, I don't recall which, but Brennan didn't want to go. A couple days later, Mitchell called Hoover to his office and told him to delay the transfer until the Ellsberg case was finished. The reason he gave was that they didn't want to lose continuity. Later on Hoover told me that Mitchell had indicated that this came from the White House, and so, of course, the transfer was canceled. I'm convinced Brennan acted in good faith. What difference would it make to him whether Marx was interviewed or not?"

Unless Sullivan told him to do it.

FELT: "This is possible. He did work right under Sullivan. He was

Sullivan's protégé for years and years and years. He got where he was because of Sullivan. Yes, that's entirely possible. And it's possible that Sullivan got his instructions from the White House. I never thought of that before but this is entirely possible, entirely possible. I talked to Brennan about it and he convinced me that he had acted in good faith. There was just no real benefit to be gained from that interview, and I think essentially that's why Hoover said no."

SULLIVAN: "Let me give you the story on that. One day I was thinking, Where can we locate this guy Ellsberg? Then I thought, Why not go talk to his father-in-law? I called Brennan and said, 'Has anybody talked to Louis Marx?' And he said, 'No, I don't think so.' I told him to go ahead but first to get Hoover's approval because Marx sends down three or four hundred dollars' worth of toys every Christmas for Hoover to give to his friends.

"It so happens that two pieces of mail were prepared simultaneously, one going to Hoover asking for his permission to interview Marx, and the other a letter to the New York Field Office recommending they interview Marx. The New York letter should have been held over until the next day, but it was just one of those mistakes, and we made them every day; we had hundreds of pieces of mail moving. Hoover didn't get to it right away, I guess, and when he did send it back to me, he had written, 'No, I don't want Marx interviewed.' I forwarded it over to Brennan, and he called New York and they said, 'Oh, God, it's too late. We just interviewed him.'

"So we were confronted with a problem. Should we just forget about it? Put it in the files and assume—you do this sometimes—that Hoover would never learn about it? Or should we go ahead and send him a memorandum saying, 'Sorry, Mr. Hoover, but we made a mistake'? We decided to be honest about it, and Hoover went into a rage. He busted Brennan from Assistant Director and transferred him to Cincinnati or Cleveland as Special Agent in Charge. I went to Mardian and told him I'd quit if that thing went through. It was outrageous to transfer a man over this. He could have written him a stinking letter. In the first place, there was no reason for opposing the interview. Marx should have been interviewed, and in fact he was very nice about it."

Did Hoover know about the Plumbers?

SULLIVAN: "God, you raise a hell of an interesting question. I've been told he did, but I can't prove it."

How about yourself?

SULLIVAN: "I didn't know a damn thing about it. It was a strange thing. I knew that the White House was very upset over leaks. They wanted to plug the leaks, and Gordon Liddy came over to our office in early 1971 to discuss leaks, and I couldn't talk to him because I had hijacking cases going that day and I sent him over to the Domestic Intelligence Division over in the Triangle Building. I never heard from him, never saw him again. The first time I heard of the Plumbers was when I read about it in the newspaper. All the time I was in the FBI, I didn't know of their existence. This shows you the extent to which the FBI had disintegrated. For God's sake, we should have known about them. We should not only have known about them, we should have known about their plans, and we should have put it on record and stopped them. To me this is a great tragedy."

The New York *Times* Was Knocking Hoover for Not Doing Any Surreptitious Entries

It was not until June 1971 that Tom Charles Huston wended his way back to Indianapolis, an obscure figure until Watergate would link his name with the White House "horrors."

"In the Nixon White House, it was damn tough for a man of ideas to survive," Huston has written. "For a man of conservative ideas and a modest dose of self-respect, it was virtually impossible."

In September 1974, I asked Huston how he had managed to escape the Watergate quagmire, and his response was: "I made a fortuitous departure." As it now appears, again fortuitously, Huston wasn't privy to very much that went on in the White House.

HUSTON: "I was supposed to be the kingpin that was engineering this great plan of repression and stuff, and I didn't know about the seventeen wiretaps, the Plumbers, the Ellsberg break-in, or about Hoover's Cointelpro.* You know, I've come to the conclusion that I just didn't know

---

* Huston was referring to the counterintelligence programs Hoover operated between 1956 and 1971 to sabotage extremist groups, which first came to light when Attorney General William B. Saxbe, complying with a federal court ruling in a suit brought under the Freedom of Information Act, released FBI documents on December 7, 1973, and November 18, 1974.

what was going on. I was only involved with domestic violence, and both the wiretaps and Ellsberg were related to unauthorized disclosures of classified information. My problem is that there are so many things I don't know anything about, and I hate to say anything because something comes up new every day which makes you look like you're dumber than you are.

"One of the most interesting things, as far as Cointelpro is concerned, was an article that appeared on the front page of the Sunday New York *Times* on October 10, 1971, at a time when there was a fight obviously going on between Hoover and the CIA—you know, the *Times* then would print anything that was critical of Hoover—and one of the criticisms that was being made of him was the fact that he had cut off liaison with the other agencies and that he wasn't doing any surreptitious entries—and they were knocking him for *not* doing it. All this stuff on the front page of the *Times*—so I don't know anymore."

The *Times* charged that Hoover broke off direct liaison with the CIA in February 1970 because Helms would not tell Hoover the name of the special agent who had leaked FBI information to the CIA. From then on, the *Times* said, "the bulk of communication and coordination between the FBI and the CIA has been by telephone and correspondence, with very limited contact approved by Mr. Hoover on an ad hoc basis." Four months later, Hoover "abolished the seven-man section that maintained contact with the Defense Intelligence Agency, the Office of Naval Intelligence, Army Intelligence, Air Force Intelligence, the Air Force Office of Special Investigations, the National Security Agency, the State Department, the Post Office, the Department of Health, Education and Welfare, the United States Information Agency, the Bureau of Customs and the Immigration Service. . . . According to the speculation, he wanted to show that he was not discriminating against the CIA and that all relations could be handled by phone and mail."

By the time I got around to verifying this story with the CIA, Richard Helms was neatly tucked away in the U.S. Embassy in Iran, and the new director, William E. Colby, told me that he had never met Hoover.

COLBY: "I may have shaken his hand once, you know, on some big meeting or something, but I really never had any business with him at all."

How much truth is there to the charge that Hoover broke off liaison with the CIA? This has come up time and again in the Watergate hearings.

COLBY: "I think it's a little exaggerated, quite frankly. But I am a little reluctant to go on the record on something as delicate as this, really. It's not security, it's sort of bureaucratic politeness."

Whatever you can do to set the record straight will be appreciated.

COLBY: "I really don't know enough about it. I just know that the common understanding of a high degree of hostility, I think, is wrong. In other words, I think Mr. Hoover had a very strongly disciplined approach to his responsibilities, and he insisted upon that discipline, you know, being very hardnosed about it. I think this was then interpreted as some kind of hostility which I don't think really existed quite so much. We've always dealt with the Bureau over the years. Obviously, they're responsible for internal security and we're not, by statute. So anything we get in that field we turn over to them, and we've done that for years. In that sense there's been a continuing collaboration."

Specifically, the Times *charged that Hoover broke off direct liaison with the CIA in February 1970 because Helms would not tell Hoover the name of the FBI agent who told one of your employees that the disappearance of Thomas Riha, who was an associate professor of Russian history at the University of Colorado, did not involve foul play, and that Riha had chosen to leave for personal reasons. Any truth to this charge?*

COLBY: "You're really ahead of me. I can't comment on that from personal knowledge, and I really wouldn't want to without looking into it very seriously. Let me check it out and I'll get back to you."

A week later Colby called me at my home in Santa Barbara:

COLBY: "All I can say is that the *Times* story is a fair one. The Agency cannot take issue with it."

Mark Felt was convinced that Sullivan was behind the *Times* story. "That and four or five of the Evans and Novak stories were actually, no question about it, written by Sullivan," Felt said. "I mean, his favorite words and all this sort of stuff were in there, right down the line with arguments that he used and so forth."

I told Sullivan of Felt's charge, but he declined to answer.

SULLIVAN: "I won't answer that question. All I can say is that the article was accurate. The CIA was completely right in the matter. Being with the FBI, I'd like to be able to say that the FBI was right, but we weren't;

we were completely wrong, and the relationship should never have been broken."

An Intelligence Operation Is Not All Milk and Honey

The *Times* went on to observe that the Bureau's "ability to neutralize foreign spies" had been weakened because "Mr. Hoover is so intent on preventing any embarrassment to the FBI or any sullying of his reputation that he avoids the risks of counter-espionage work. As an example of such risks, the [intelligence] officials point out that an FBI man might find himself apprehended by the police when he does a 'bag job'—surreptitious piece of counter-espionage sometimes involving illegal activity. Or, they say, if an FBI man approaches a foreign diplomat and asks him to defect or spy, the bureau runs the risk of a refusal and possibly a diplomatic uproar."

Both the *Times* and Huston were then unaware of Cointelpro, and both had arrived at an indentical conclusion: The fear of sullying his legend had rendered Hoover officially impotent. It is ironic to note that when the existence of Cointelpro was revealed after Hoover's death, the Los Angeles *Times* lamented in an editorial that "Counterintelligence carried to these lengths smacks of police-state tactics. . . . Society faces many dangers. Not the least is the apparent belief by the FBI that police agencies can set aside the Constitution at will."

Initiated in 1956, Cointelpro, the acronym used within the Bureau to identify seven counterintelligence programs, was discontinued on April 28, 1971, three days after Hale Boggs accused the FBI of employing "secret police tactics." This was a month after the FBI office in Media, Pennsylvania, was burglarized and FBI documents detailing various harassment and disruption tactics were distributed to the press. It was also shortly before Hoover terminated Cointelpro that the Bureau came under fire for allegedly using *agents provocateurs* in several cases, the most notable being the one in which Father Philip F. Berrigan and six other anti-war activists were accused—and later acquitted—of conspiring to kidnap Henry Kissinger.

According to the report released by Saxbe, Cointelpro was directed at the Communist Party, USA, from 1956 to 1971; the Socialist Workers Party, 1961 to 1970; the Ku Klux Klan and white hate groups, including the Minutemen, the American Nazi Party, and the National States Rights Party, 1964 to 1971; black extremists, including the Southern Christian

Leadership Conference headed by Martin Luther King, the Congress on Racial Equality, the Student Nonviolent Coordinating Committee, the Revolutionary Action Movement, the Black Panthers, and the Nation of Islam, 1967 to 1971; the New Left, including the Weathermen, the Students for a Democratic Society, the Progressive Labor Party, and the Young Socialist Alliance, 1968 to 1971. Two Cointelpro efforts were aimed at "hostile foreign intelligence services" and "foreign Communist organizations and individuals connected with them."

Most of the documents reflected Hoover's concern that the programs remain secret. In one memo he noted that "under no circumstance should the existence of the program be made known outside the bureau and appropriate within-office security should be afforded this sensitive operation." The field offices were instructed not to initiate action "without specific bureau authorization."

The modus operandi in all seven programs was pretty well standardized. In the case of black nationalists, for example, Hoover advised, "When an opportunity is apparent to disrupt or neutralize black nationalist, hate-type organizations through the cooperation of established local news media contacts or through such contact with sources available to the seat of government (i.e., Washington), in every instance careful attention must be given to the proposal to insure [that] the targeted group is disrupted, ridiculed or discredited through the publicity and not merely publicized. Consideration should be given to techniques to preclude violence-prone or rabble-rouser leaders of hate groups from spreading their philosophy publicly or through various mass communication media."

In a May 11, 1970, memo, Hoover established a separate program aimed at the Black Panther Party. His memo noted it would be "effected through close coordination on a high level with the Oakland or San Francisco Police Department." The memo suggested various techniques for a "disruptive-disinformation operation" against the party's national office in Oakland. One method of spreading distrust and dissension among party members was the use of true documents, "documents subtly incorporating false information, and entirely fabricated documents" to be mailed anonymously to the residences of key Panther leaders. "These documents would be on the stationery and in the form used by the Police Department or by the FBI in disseminating information to the police," Hoover wrote. "FBI documents, when used, would contain police routing or date received notations, clearly indicating they had been pilfered from police files. Alleged police or FBI documents could be prepared pinpointing Panthers as police or FBI informants; ridiculing or discrediting Panther leaders through their ineptness or personal escapades; espousing personal philosophies and promoting factionalism among BPP members; indicating electronic coverage or other counter-actions; revealing misuse or misappropriation of Panther funds; pointing out instances of political disorientation."

In a memo on the New Left, Hoover urged increased interrogation of members because "it will enhance the paranoia endemic in these circles and will further serve to get the point across there is an FBI agent behind every mailbox."

In specific acts against individuals, Saxbe cited forty-three instances in which a person's employer, creditor or prospective employer was notified of his "illegal, immoral, radical and Communist party activities," and in twelve instances, "among the most troubling" in the study, "the FBI acted to influence political or judicial processes. Examples include sending an anonymous letter to a target group member who was running for mayor to create distrust toward his 'comrades,' furnishing records on a candidate's arrest and questionable marital status to news media contacts, and giving an individual's arrest records to his employer, who later fired him, and to a court that had earlier given him a suspended sentence."*

Although Saxbe found Cointelpro "involved isolated instances of practices that can only be considered abhorrent in a free society," he pointed out that "it is important to understand that these improper activities were not the purpose or indeed even the major characteristic of the FBI's efforts."

* One report included this notation: "investigating the love life of a group leader for dissemination to the press." The group leader was later identified by the Justice Department as Martin Luther King. Arthur Murtagh, a retired agent, was quoted in the New York *Times* on March 8, 1975, to the effect that the moves against King were second in size "only to the way they went after Jimmy Hoffa." Murtagh and a former senior Bureau official, the *Times* said, "confirmed the Bureau tried to disrupt plans for a banquet in Atlanta in 1964 by business leaders to laud King's winning of the Nobel Prize. It included covert contacts with community leaders with charges about King's personal life." Other officials confirmed that a "monograph on King's personal life was circulated among government officials by the Bureau during the Kennedy Administration. President Kennedy became aware of what was going on and ordered Hoover to retrieve every copy of the monograph." Other officials told the *Times* that the Bureau "routinely sought to prevent King from receiving honorary degrees from colleges and universities by planting stories about his personal life, including charges that he directed SCLC funds to his own use and to Swiss bank accounts." And there "were anonymous telephone calls, sometimes to make false fire alarm reports at locations where King was to speak and in other instances to friends and associates of King trying to sow distrust among them."

In a press release, FBI Director Clarence M. Kelley noted that Cointelpro took place at a time when violence-prone groups sought "to bring America to its knees. . . . For the FBI to have done less under the circumstances would have been an abdication of its responsibilities to the American people."

In explaining why he ordered the program, Hoover wrote that the FBI "is highly concerned that the anarchistic activities of a few can paralyze institutions of learning, induction centers, cripple traffic and tie the arms of law enforcement officials, all to the detriment of our society." He concluded that "Law and order is mandatory for any civilized society to survive."

I asked Huston if he still thought that Hoover had rejected his plan because he was afraid to tarnish his reputation.

HUSTON: "I think that's what it was. I mean, that's what I thought, but I may be wrong. I'm not saying I'm right. That was my impression and I have no reason necessarily to believe that it wasn't true."

If his reputation was his primary concern, why would he initiate Cointelpro?

HUSTON: "I don't know what he did in Cointelpro. There has been a lot of implications that he used *agents provocateurs*, but none of the material I've seen indicated that it was true. The memos that Saxbe released didn't give any indication that he used those means. They talk in abstractions about disruptions and stuff. I don't know what he was doing, and I don't know how much of it he knew about, or what he didn't, all I know is what he was doing as far as I was concerned. I think the main thrust there probably was simply the threat he saw to his own operation. Obviously, in Cointelpro he wouldn't even let the Justice Department or the Attorney General know what was going on. He obviously didn't want anybody being in a position to review what was happening."

In his press statement, Kelley maintained that the program was known to all attorneys general from Rogers to Mitchell, but Nicholas Katzenbach, Ramsey Clark and Richard Kleindienst have since denied any knowledge of the Bureau's disruptive tactics. In October 1974, I posed that question to Attorney General Saxbe, and his response was "I don't know." Then I asked him how he got involved in the investigation.

SAXBE: "When they broke into the FBI office in Media, Pennsylvania, and they took the FBI files, there were directives in there concerning

Cointelpro. NBC newsman Carl Stern brought a suit under the Freedom of Information Act, and some of these practices were confirmed. Well, when I came in here, I had been following this—not directly, but I was aware of it—and I said, 'Well, I'm going to establish a committee and we'll investigate Cointelpro.' So we had a committee headed by Henry Petersen and it took about two months, and I went over it and they went over it and made a report. I took the report up to the Oversight Committee of the Senate—Senators Ervin, Bob Byrd, Eastland, Hruska, and I don't recall who else—and gave them the report. They decided that no good purpose would be served by further ventilation. I then made an offer to Chairman Rodino and Mr. Hutchinson that I would come up and give it to them, and I am suggesting that rather than just a Senate oversight committee that there be a joint House-Senate oversight committee for the FBI. Now, Mr. Rodino has been busy, as you know, with Watergate material, and we haven't been able to get together with him and Mr. Hutchinson, but we will."

Saxbe's successor, Edward H. Levi, found a more receptive Congress—see Afterword. In May, 1975, in a letter to the House Judiciary Committee, Levi disclosed five additional counterintelligence programs. Three "were in the area of foreign intelligence and are classified secrets," Levi said; the fourth was directed against "militant groups" seeking Puerto Rican independence; and the fifth, code-named Operation Hoodwink, was designed to pit two of the FBI's prime foes—the Mafia and the Communist Party USA—against each other. Conducted between October, 1966, and July, 1968, Hoodwink consisted of four anonymous letters addressed to Mafia bosses, the *Daily Worker,* and a union local. One letter to a Mafia figure included an article the FBI had written to appear as if it were the work of CPUSA—it attacked labor practices at a business run by the Mafia boss. A second letter, again made to appear as if it had been written by American communists, went to three Mafia leaders—it denounced them for their alleged role in bombing CPUSA's New York headquarters. With these disclosures, Levi said that the "FBI's search of their files is now complete."

John Mohr was convinced that William Sullivan was behind Cointelpro.

MOHR: "That was Sullivan, that was engineered by Sullivan. He was behind most of that. You see, that was the investigative side of the Bureau, and the Domestic Intelligence Division would have handled, generally, a lot of that stuff. Principally, it was intelligence gathering, but it also included harassment."

SULLIVAN: "Of course I was involved in Cointelpro, and I think it was a fine program. I can't understand all the damn misinformation that's been put out about it. I can't go into detail on it, but the essence of it is this: Are you going to spend millions of taxpayer dollars going around ringing doorbells and asking questions of people who know nothing, or are you going to very systematically and very carefully penetrate these organizations like the Ku Klux Klan and the Black Panthers and disrupt them from within at a cost of almost nothing, and that's precisely what we did, we disrupted them. I just can't understand all the damn nonsense that's been issued, and certainly I'm amazed at Saxbe confusing the matter."

He found part of the program abhorrent.

SULLIVAN: "Aw, he doesn't know what he's talking about. You've got to see the program as a whole. Now, what the hell do people think an intelligence operation is about? Do they think it's all milk and honey? It's a rough, tough business. The question is, does this country want intelligence operations or does it not? But don't blame the people who engage in this activity with the approval of United States policy."

But it was not approved by the Attorney General.

SULLIVAN: "There are any number of operations that the FBI engages in that aren't approved by the Attorney General. We don't have to get everything approved by the Attorney General. We made independent decisions, that's what we are getting paid for, and the fact that the Attorney General didn't know about all of our operations is no criticism of our operations."

"It's Time to Lay Low"

Did Hoover stop the programs after Hale Boggs charged that Hoover was using secret police tactics?

SULLIVAN: "Yes, but that was just peripheral. Boggs' main charge was that we had a wiretap on him. Hoover was right on that. Now, I'm all on Hoover's side in regard to Boggs. Boggs was completely wrong and Hoover was completely right. We didn't have any tap on Hale Boggs, or on any-

body else up on the Hill. Why, it would be stupid. But others have
charged the same thing. Johnson thought we had tapped him when he
was a senator, and every once in a while he'd call Hoover and say, 'Now,
I'm going to ask you again. Tell me now, did you have a tap on me when
I was a senator?' Of course, the answer was no, which was the truth, but
Johnson had a hell of a guilty conscience. I guess he assumed that if we
had a tap on him when he was a senator, he'd be in real trouble. And I
can believe that a hundred percent."

*If Hoover was so preoccupied with preserving his legend, why did he
sanction Cointelpro as long as he did while at the same time opposing
the Huston Plan?*

SULLIVAN: "The question is whether you're jeopardizing your legend
more if you run twenty questionable programs or two or three. It's just a
question of cutting down the risk. Let me explain how most good programs begin. Take Cointelpro, for instance, it began by the men in the
field suggesting new methods and procedures, which were reviewed by supervisors, who in turn bucked memoranda up the line through section
chiefs, branch inspectors and so on until it finally got to Mohr and me.
We'd look it over and send it to Hoover. All ideas come from the working
level, because, hell, you've got to understand that the position of people
like myself is administrative. We didn't have any time to sit around thinking up counterintelligence operations.

"Cointelpro goes way back to the 1954 Supreme Court decision that
resurrected the Ku Klux Klan. We first tested this program against the
Klan and we found it to be damn good and we raised hell with the Klan.
Don't confuse this with what we did against the Communist Party.
Strictly speaking, that wasn't a part of this program at the beginning.
We'd been using different techniques to disrupt the Party. It became a
real program when we hit the Klan, and then we moved from the white
hate groups to the black hate groups, from the Klan to the Black Panthers.
Later, we broadened it to include all those organizations Saxbe mentioned
in his report.

"I still think it was a good program. When I took over, the Klan was
handled by the Criminal Division and nothing was being done. I personally asked Hoover to take it over. I had a real interest in breaking up the
Klan. If you'll pardon a personal allusion, my father led the battle against
the Klan years ago in this town [Bolton, Massachusetts] in which I

grew up in. I can remember the fiery crosses burning up on the hilltop, and it used to— You know, it would frighten a kid.

"My idea was that we ought to use intelligence and security techniques against the Klan and not just criminal investigative methods. When we took it over, the Klan had more than fourteen thousand very active members, and when I left in 1971 it had been reduced to forty-three hundred completely disorganized and impotent individuals. But the problem with the business of law enforcement, and Hoover, of course, knew this very well, is that you can't win. You're damned if you do and damned if you don't.

"I was opposed to Hoover discontinuing Cointelpro. I went over all the programs with him and his reasoning was the same as with the Huston Plan: 'The climate of public opinion,' and he said, 'You know, we can resurrect this later on. It might be a year, it might be a year and a half, but right now it's time to lay low.' He wasn't opposed to it from the standpoint of invasion of privacy, or anything like that, but purely because of public opinion. Lay low because things might break.

"Now I'm going to throw out an idea that's intrigued me for a long time, but I guess nobody will ever know the answer. I'm wondering whether Hoover knew far more about what was going on over at the White House than any of us did, and if so, would he reason that sooner or later the thing was going to blow up and he'd better trim his sails to avoid getting tarred with the same brush. However, in all honesty, I must say that he never gave any indication of this, but the old boy was real clever and he was a very close personal friend of Nixon's."

Could it be that since he was getting along in years, he wanted to set his house in order—he didn't want to die and leave these programs on the books for others to discover?

SULLIVAN: "Yes. He knew he had high blood pressure. Of course, he kept telling us that he was in perfect health, but I learned later on from a very authoritative source that Hoover knew he had high blood pressure and was not in good health. You're right. He might have been cleaning things up, not wanting to leave anything that would be a blemish on his record. Even so, when Ruckelshaus came in, he raised some hell as it was. He said what the FBI needed was another Pope John to open up the windows and let in some fresh air and reform and reorganize everything. But with Kelley in there now, Hoover's secrets are safe."

AFTERWORD

At this writing, in the spring of 1975, no fewer than five Congressional bodies were investigating charges that Hoover had abused his immense power. In fact, Congress was in a furor over the entire U.S. intelligence community. In Hoover's case, however, it appeared to be more a consequence of the Watergate syndrome than a matter of new evidence. What had ignited the firestorm against Hoover were news stories that a private cache of files derogatory to several presidents and seventeen senators and representatives, two of whom were still serving, had been found in his office after his death. There was speculation that he had purged some files in the year before his death, and others were either shredded by his secretary immediately after his death, or were moved to his home to be placed in the custody of Clyde Tolson. The testimony of Director Kelley before a House committee that the material shredded and/or given to Tolson consisted of personal correspondence and memorabilia had little effect on the rumor mill.

This was followed by a barrage of rehashes of old stories with a few new flourishes and conclusions. Lyndon Johnson, said *Time*, "had a voracious appetite for gossip" and Hoover fed him with the "hottest files on important people . . . when it suited his power-hungry purpose." Not only had he provided presidents with these lubricious morsels whenever it suited his purpose, said *Newsweek*, but "he had willingly obeyed requests from the White House that he try to dredge up still more."

What an ironic twist this premise presents. If only somebody had told Nixon. He could have used Hoover instead of opting for outsiders like Jack Caulfield and Tony Ulasewicz to conduct scores of investigations on the morals of his political opponents. What a waste, when one contemplates the turn history might have taken if Nixon had prevailed on Hoover to do his dirty work.

Congress, of course, was outraged. It was perfectly fine for the FBI to have 6.8 million files and 55 million index cards on private citizens, but seventeen folders on the philandering and drinking habits of lawmakers heralded nothing short of the "destruction of our form of government because of intimidation of members of Congress," said Representative Robert W. Kastenmeier, who headed one of the investigating groups. Senator John Q. Pastore thought it was a "sad commentary on a democratic and open society." "There's no point in its being there if they are not going to use it," said Senator Gale W. McGee of the files. "Obviously, it's to be held in reserve for some kind of blackmail. The Gestapo operated that way, too. They were just collecting records." Most lawmakers quoted in news stories were convinced that the files were held in reserve "for some kind of blackmail."

The fact that not one individual would or could stand up and make the charge stick seemed of little moment to anybody. Politicians are notoriously thin-skinned, but there is nothing wrong with their instinct for the jugular. Or, for that matter, with their instinct for knowing the precise moment to flog a dead horse. It took them three years to get around to Hoover. By then they were not only pretty convinced that he was dead, but his entire high command was in retirement, and Tolson was on his deathbed—he died on April 14, 1975.

I don't mean to take issue with the investigations. On the contrary, I fully subscribe to the thesis that police and intelligence agencies should be accountable to elected officials. What I do question are some of the motives behind the wholesale airing of dirty linen, much of it more trumped up than based on solid data.

In the wake of Watergate, there is, as one observer phrased it, a gullibility gap—a disposition in the nation to believe anything bad about anybody. The leakers, for whatever motives, are having a field day. Many are reaping windfalls in the book bonanza exploited by Nixon felons. Reputations are falling by the wayside without a second glance. Contentious claims are accepted at face value. The likes of John Dean have become our post-Watergate oracles. While some of their tall tales may be true, they are not unaware that truth that is stranger than fiction will sell better in a market already jaded by exotic overexposure.

Of all the allegations made against Hoover, none have been more damaging than the one made by Sullivan to Mardian that the Director had blackmailed presidents. Without a shred of evidence to support it, it has inspired instant credibility. It is now an accepted fact in much of the media that Hoover blackmailed presidents. When I asked Helen Gandy, who was Hoover's secretary for fifty-four years, what she thought of this charge, she could only laugh in frustration. "Some people," she said, "have nightmares in broad daylight." I'm inclined to agree with her, particularly when I think of the presidents he served under: Hoover, Roosevelt, Truman, Eisenhower, Kennedy, Johnson, Nixon. It is possible that one or two were intimidated by their own guilty conscience in the belief that the files contained their innermost secrets, but actual blackmail requires something quite different.

In his last appearance before the House Appropriations subcommittee, Hoover was in good form. "Mr. Chairman," he said, addressing his old friend, John Rooney, "I have a philosophy: you are honored by your friends and you are distinguished by your enemies. I have been very distinguished."

Yes, indeed, distinguished and honored, in a career that spanned nearly one-third of our history as a nation. He was, whatever his failings, an extraordinary man, truly one of a kind.

APPENDIXES

APPENDIXES

WILL - John Edgar Hoover

I, John Edgar Hoover, a resident citizen of Washington, District of Columbia, being of sound and disposing mind, do hereby declare this to be my last will and testament, specifically revoking any and all wills heretofore made by me.

The following bequests I desire to be carried out:

(1) The perpetual care of the burial plots of my father, my mother, my sister Marguerite and myself in the Congressional Cemetery in Washington, D. C.

(2) To Helen W. Gandy, absolutely, the sum of five thousand dollars.

(3) To James E. Crawford, two thousand dollars to be paid over a period of three years.

(4) To John Edgar Ruch, my platinum watch with white gold wrist band, and two pairs of cuff links.

(5) To John Edgar Nichols, my small star sapphire ring, and two pairs of cuff links.

(6) To James E. Crawford and W. Samuel Noisette, equal distribution of all personal wearing apparel.

(7) To Annie Fields, three thousand dollars to be paid over a period of one year.

I would like Clyde Tolson to keep, or arrange for a good home, or homes for my two dogs.

I give, devise and bequeath all the rest, residue and remainder of my estate, both real and personal, unto Clyde A. Tolson, his heirs, executors, administrators and assignees forever.

In the event Clyde A. Tolson's death should occur prior to or simultaneously with mine, then the residue of my estate, both real and personal, after the above stated bequests are satisfied, is given, devised and bequeathed to the Boys' Clubs of America, Inc., and the Damon Runyon Memorial Fund for Cancer Research, Inc., equally.

I hereby nominate and appoint Clyde A. Tolson as Executor of this my last will and testament and direct that he serve with no bond.

In witness whereof, I subscribe my name and set my seal this 19th day of July, 1971.

John Edgar Hoover

The foregoing instrument was on the 19th day of July, 1971, signed and sealed and declared by the testator as his last will and testament in the presence of each of us, who, at the same time and in his presence, and in the presence of each other, hereunto subscribe our names as witnesses.

Erma D. Metcalf

Edna M. Held

WITNESSES

UNITED STATES DISTRICT COURT FOR THE DISTRICT OF COLUMBIA
Holding a Probate Court

In re Estate of
   JOHN EDGAR HOOVER   )
   also known as   )   Administration No. _____
     J. EDGAR HOOVER,   )
            Deceased)   Address of Petitioner:

4936 - 30th Place, N.W.
Washington, D.C. 20008

PETITION TO PROBATE WILL
AND FOR LETTERS TESTAMENTARY

The petition of Clyde A. Tolson respectfully represents:

1. The petitioner Clyde A. Tolson is a citizen of the
United States and a resident of the District of Columbia, of adult
age, and not under any legal disability. The petitioner makes
this application as the executor nominated in the will of the
above-named decedent.

2. John Edgar Hoover, also known as J. Edgar Hoover,
late an adult citizen of the United States domiciled in the District
of Columbia, died on or about May 2, 1972, leaving a paper writing
dated July 19, 1971 in the nature of a will and testament. Said
paper writing is now on file in the Office of Register of Wills for
the District of Columbia. No other paper writing in the nature of
a testamentary disposition of said decedent's estate has been found,
although diligent search therefor has been made. The petitioner
believes that such paper writing is in fact decedent's last will
and testament.

3. The decedent was survived by the following persons
who are the only heirs-at-law and next-of-kin of decedent, who
are all of adult age and sui juris, and whose respective names,
addresses, places of residence and relationships are as follows:

Fred G. Robinette, nephew
(son of decedent's deceased sister)
5401 Whitfield-Chapel Road
Lanham, Maryland 20801

Mrs. Dorothy Robinette, niece
(daughter of decedent's deceased sister)
P.O. Box 911
Delano, California 93215

Mrs. Marjorie A. Stromme, niece
(daughter of decedent's deceased sister)
2040 Federal Avenue
Costa Mesa, California 92626

Mrs. Anna Hoover Kienast, niece
(daughter of decedent's deceased brother)
12004 Lisborough Road
Mitchellville, Maryland 20716

Mrs. Margaret Hoover Fennell, niece
(daughter of decedent's deceased brother)
12313 Shelter Lane
Bowie, Maryland 20715

Dickerson N. Hoover, Jr., nephew
(son of decedent's deceased brother)
The Rocks
Route 2, Box 107
Charlestown, West Virginia 25414

Decedent was not survived by a wife, child or descendants or by
any parent or by a brother or sister or descendants thereof except
as stated above.

4. The decedent at the time of his death owned the
following described real estate in the District of Columbia:

4936 - 30th Place, N.W., known for purposes

of taxation as lot 806 in square 2274, assessed

for real estate tax purposes at $40,437, un-

encumbered.

Decedent at the time of his death did not own or possess any other
real estate or interest therein in the District of Columbia or elsewhere, except as indicated in paragraph 5 hereof.

5. The decedent owned at the time of his death approximately forty oil, gas and mineral leases (or parts thereof) for

interests in Texas and Louisiana, some of which may be considered
as real estate interests, the estimated value of which insofar as
petitioner can determine at this time is approximately $125,000.

6.   The decedent at the time of his death was possessed
of personal property of a total estimated value of $326,500, con-
sisting of the following:

Stocks and bonds	$122,000.
Cash in banks and loan associations	84,000.
Insurance payable to estate	45,000.
Contributions to Civil Service retirement	45,000.
Unpaid salary and annual leave	18,000.
Household effects	7,500.
Jewelry	5,000.
	$326,500.

7.   The decedent, so far as petitioner has been able to
ascertain, after diligent search and inquiry, left no debts except
(a) funeral expenses in the approximate amount of $5,000, which
have not been paid and (b) miscellaneous current expenses in the
approximate amount of $1,000, which have not been paid.

WHEREFORE, the petitioner prays:

1.   That notice by citation or by publication or both
as may be necessary, shall issue to the above-named heirs-at-law
and next-of-kin.

2.   That said paper writing dated July 19, 1971, be
admitted to probate and record as the last will and testament
of John Edgar Hoover as a will of both real and personal property.

3.   That letters testamentary issue to the petitioner
as the executor named in the will.

4. And for such other and further relief as the nature
of the case may require and to this Court may seem proper.

Clyde A. Tolson
Petitioner

HOGAN & HARTSON

By *George E. Monk*
George E. Monk

and

Robert J. Elliott
Robert J. Elliott

815 Connecticut Avenue, N.W.
Washington, D.C. 20006
298-5500

ATTORNEYS FOR PETITIONER

District of Columbia ss:

I, the undersigned, ___Clyde A. Tolson___, do
solemnly swear that I have read the foregoing and annexed petition
by me subscribed and know the contents thereof; that I verily
believe the facts as stated in said petition to be true.

Clyde A. Tolson

Subscribed and sworn to before me this _____ day of
_____, 1972.

Elizabeth S. Well
Notary Public

My commission expires:

____MAY 22, 1973____

I personally guarantee the payment of costs not to exceed $15.00.

...*S. George E. Monk*

Attorney

Form No. 57

No. 967-72

United States District Court for the District of Columbia

We, The undersigned, appointed by the said Court to examine and appraise the personal estate of John Edgar Hoover, also known as J. Edgar Hoover, D. C. late of _____ The District of Columbia _____, deceased, do hereby certify that the following schedule is a true and correct appraisement of said estate in so far as it has come to our knowledge, a return of which we have made to the Court of even date herewith:

		$	
Master Bed Room	Maple four poster double bed and bedding	150	00
	Maple open front stand with deck and drawer	20	00
	Footed glass case	2	00
	Brass base table lamp	10	00
	Indian woven basket	3	00
	Platform rocker	20	00
	Mahogany stand with 2 drawers and chinese brass pulls	40	00
	Antique metal table lamp	45	00
	Needle point upholstered foot stool	25	00
	Desk clock	5	00
	Mexican cigarette box, footed wooden bowl, and miniture book rack	10	00
	Maple open front stand	15	00
	Maple chest of 5 drawers	85	00
	Apple jar, slide rule, candle stand and enamel decorated bottle	5	00
	Carved wooden figure of J. Edgar Hoover in glass case	100	00
	Maple chest of 5 drawers, small chest of drawers, and bureau with 4 drawers and detached glass	250	00
	AMOUNT CARRIED FORWARD,	785	00

	$	
RCA color television in maple cabinet	100	00
Electric clock	5	00
Gotham travel clock	5	00
Bullet paper weight, metal shield on wooden base and thermometer	5	00
Red lacquer framed mirror	15	00
Pair of maple glasses	8	00
Wooden case thermometer, hydrometer and barometer	15	00
FBI shield	5	00
Pair of brass base table lamps	15	00
3 wooden trays, wooden covered box, wicker covered box and copper tray	8	00
Ivory tray and ivory buffer and case	15	00
5 piece sterling silver vanity set	25	00
Oak cane back rocker with eagle finial	90	00
Maple open front stand with sliding glass doors	25	00
Everlast exercycle	100	00
Stained wooden jewel case	15	00
Small maple chair	15	00
Valet stand	15	00
Chaise lounge	50	00
Maple 2 deck stand	40	00
Wooden base table lamp	70	00
Maple chest of drawers with safety glass top	75	00
Pen reciver with desk lighter	15	00
Mahogany tray	15	00
Heating pad	2	00
Leather suitcase and overnight case	30	00
Amount carried forward,	1,563	00

	Chrome thermos and tray	$ 5	00
	Sony AM/FM radio	50	00
	General Electric clock	5	00
	Maple note stand with 2 drawers	35	00
	Carved Chinese chest	150	00
	Approximately 210 volumes of books, some autographed	125	00
	Hooked rug with "Department of Justice" seal	100	00
	Small hooked satter rug	45	00
	4 panel invitation and match cover screen	20	00
	3 water colors of houses, miniture landscapes, oil palm scene, 2 seascapes, "Joshua Free" by Sacks, shelf bracket, framed photographs and animal pastels	55	00
	Circular lead glass of saint	20	00
	Bokhara oriental rug, 3' x 6'	100	00
	Green domestic carpet 12' x 18'	50	00
	10 various plant holders	5	00
Closet	2 leather and 2 metal suitcases	30	00
Den	Oil paintings, "Spanish House" Alice Dutton, "Landscape" C. Backers, "Spanish Hacienda" Joan Cromwell, and "Clown" signed J.M. and 5 miniture landscapes	125	00
	2 Desert scene landscapes in shadow box frames	5	00
	Desk	45	00
	Red vinyl swivel chair	25	00
	5 vitrine bookcases	80	00
	2 floor lamps	15	00
	Green vinyl arm chair	25	00
	Red leather arm chair	55	00
	Indian side table	20	00
	Pottery chinese style lamp	5	00
	Amount carried forward,	2,758	00

Match cover screen , 4 panel	$ 20	00
Blue pottery jardiniere on stand	10	00
Glass top book stand	10	00
Metal ashtray stand	7	00
Pedestal stand	18	00
Bowl stand, footed stool and basket	4	00
Butterfly table	15	00
Needlepoint framed horses, ship print, mottos framed miniature pictures, figurines, ashtrays, desk accessories, and variour bibelots	60	00
Night stand	7	00
Cowboy figurine, Lincoln bookends, electric clock, jade top match box	22	00
Semca clock-barometer	15	00
Approximately 1,000 volumes of books, many autographed by such people as Herbert Hoover, Robert Kennedy, Richard Nixon, Peter Marshall, Dwight D. Eisenhower, Eddie Rickenbacker, and Bob Considine	1,000	00
Night stand	7	00
Electric clock, barometer, thermometer, desk lamp, file cases, lacquer bowl, pewter clock, and airplane ash tray	30	00
FM radio	5	00
Seahorse lamp	7	00
Plaster figurine of nude, 2 El Camino Real bells, and paper weight	8	00
3 pieces of luggage	15	00
Jewel case and boxes	3	00
Sterling silver decanter and 12 tumblers	35	00
2 rugs, "Department of Justice", "Horse and Colt"	75	00
Miscellaneous vases, figurines, leather boxes, and lighters	10	00
Guest Room / various Navajo rugs	350	00
Amount carried forward,	4,491	00

Mahogany double bed with box spring and mattress	$ 45	00
Carved Chinese night table with marble top	100	00
Chinese mahogany lamp table with cabinet base	40	00
3 fold match cover screen	15	00
Mahogany chest of drawers with safety glass top	50	00
Lacquer decorated corner stand with safety glass top	45	00
All upholstered wing back arm chair with down cushion	60	00
Victorian marble top table	45	00
Small maple double drop leaf stand	20	00
Victorian oval marble top table	75	00
Sylvania color television on stand	250	00
Upholstered seat side chair	5	00
Wooden chest of drawers with safety glass top	35	00
Mirrored waste basket	5	00
Pair of porcelain base table lamps	8	00
Shaving mirror with drawer base	15	00
Carved wooden bear brush	10	00
Copper candle lamp and metal candle lamp	5	00
Plaster statue of Nude woman	5	00
Large antique chinese porcelain vase	200	00
Vinyl waste basker and 2 pillows	2	00
Pair of marble bookends	15	00
Antique brass oil lamp with glass globe	45	00
Pottery ash tray and indian figurine	5	00
Silver plated ash tray	1	00
Sterling silver cigarette box	25	00
Amount carried forward,	5,617	00

	Jade relief on carved wooden stand	$ 150	00
	Carved Chinese mirror	35	00
	Art noveau figure of dancing nude on marble pedestle	25	00
	Metal ash tray lamp	5	00
	Wall clock	10	00
	Framed etching "San Francisco" signed Alec Stern	20	00
	Framed etching "The road in the valley" signed Bauand	50	00
	Framed print "Notre Dame de Laon" signed John Taylor Armstrong	20	00
	Small framed etching "European city" signed Macumber	15	00
	Framed print of Charles Dickens	10	00
	Framed autographed picture of Theodore Roosevelt	15	00
	Framed print of nude maiden with Knight	2	00
	Framed print of George Washington	15	00
	2 framed photographs of Sundquist	5	00
	Framed etching "Silver Light" signed Woiceske	30	00
	Alarm clock	1	00
	Framed motto	2	00
Bath Room	Bath scale, mat and hamper	5	00
	Whirlpool bath	35	00
Hall	Framed color print of 2 nudes	8	00
	Collection of various political cartoons, autographed letters, pictures and documents, by such people as Harry Truman, Dwight D. Eisenhower, John F. Kennedy, Robert Kennedy, Ladybird Johnson, Lyndon B. Johnson, Franklin Roosevelt etc.	1,000	00
	Framed warrant signed by Abraham Lincoln	300	00
	Framed autographed letter signed Alexander Hamilton	250	00
	Amount carried forward,	7,625	00

	Framed autograph picture of John Hay, American statesman	$ 20	00
	Framed note written and signed Samuel Clemens	100	00
	Colt 22 cal. single action revolver, gold plated with mother of pearl grips in wooden case	200	00
	Japanese cloisonne plate	75	00
	Mahogany double drop leaf stand	100	00
Linen closet	Lot of assorted bed and bath linen	50	00
Bath room	Hamper, floor mat, waste basket, shaving mirror and bath scale	25	00
	Framed black and white engraving, signed Cadmut	25	00
	Corner cabinet, metal cabinet, wall fan, and framed print	15	00
Hall cond.	Gilt framed wall mirror with 2 candles	35	00
	Mahogany corner cabinet	50	00
	Framed oil on canvas "Mountain landscape" signed but illegible	50	00
	Golden railroad spike, mounted	35	00
	Framed bronze relief	35	00
	Large black pottery bowl signed Marie Juilian	300	00
	Cinnabar figure of Hoti on stand	45	00
	Indian hand painted bowl with 2 spouts	5	00
	Framed color engraving of "Berne"	20	00
	Framed etching, "Harbor Scene" signed Whistler 1859	350	00
	Framed etching, "Hurlingham" signed with the Whistler Butterfly	300	00
	7 various framed etchings	150	00
	Carved ivory relief	35	00
	Miniture framed oil on ivory, portrait of woman	50	00
	Autographed letter signed Lucien Powell	15	00
	Amount carried forward,	9,710	00

Attic	Captain's desk	$ 75	00
	Marble vase	5	00
	Glasses, icebox, waste basket, bronze figurine wooden box, Plates, wooden horse and hassock	35	00
	Miscellaneous china and clock	3	00
	Motorola television and vacuum cleaner	no value	
	Fountain, cart, buffalo rug, and bear rug	25	00
	Television stand, shoe shine stand, cigar box, floral pieces and radio	30	00
	Cannon, Marble tray, humidor box, and paper backs	10	00
	Chinese chow table	125	00
	Eagle figurine, ash trays, bookends, coasters, 2 leather boxes, and mats	30	00
	Framed needle point	10	00
	Small lot of assorted knives and swords	50	00
	4 wicker garden chairs	15	00
	Persian vase with silver inlay	125	00
	Andirons	6	00
	Circular plant stand	25	00
	Miscellaneous framed mementos	50	00
	Small lot of linen	20	00
	2 deer heads mounted and antlers mounted	20	00
	4 pieces of wicker lawn furniture, coffee table and wrought iron table	35	00
	Crate	1	00
	7 fishing rods	8	00
	23 American Indian rugs, various sizes	450	00
	3 Mexican throw rugs	10	00
	Brass candelabra	5	00
	Bowl table, elephant hoofs, 2 lamps, flags, and miscellaneous tables	35	00
	Amount carried forward,	10,913	00

French style fire screen, fan type	$	100	00
World electric clock		10	00
Electric toaster, bar equiptment and misc-ellenious FBI bibelots		15	00
6 bookcases		60	00
2 easy chairs, slip covers and cushions		40	00
4 panel match cover screen		20	00
Lot of miscellaneous volumes of books		350	00
Miscellaneous lot of vases, hurricane globes fan, persian lamp, plaques, figurines, novelties, tomahawks, medals, horns and memorabilia		200	00
Oil painting, american indian prints, tile table, mexican chair, prints and presentation gifts		170	00
Metal file cabinet		10	00
Maple chair		7	00
Brass cigar box, tray "Master of Deceit"		15	00
Mexican tray		10	00
Japanese wooden bell		2	00
FBI tile cocktail table		75	00
Planters plant stand		5	00
Air plane propellar and oar		50	00
Miscellaneous glassware, china, framed prints fishing reel, and english china bowl		65	00
2 sun lamps, nut cracker, steak boards, miscellaneous vases, bed tray, cookwares, framed nude pastel, Havanna cigar box, dolphin mounted		45	00
Lot of autographed pictures of such people as Hoover, White, Sullivan, and Moses		60	00
Television snack tables		3	00
Lot of autographed pictures of Hollywood personalities		35	00
2 framed horse prints by Brewer		100	00
Amount carried forward,		12,360	00

		$	
	Personal mementos, given and signed by historical and famous personages	75	00
	Miscellaneous pottery, as is monogramed JEH	10	00
	Round garden table	6	00
	Records, tin lamp, Christmas decorations, law books and miscellaneous books	15	00
	Bar barrel	5	00
	4 pieces of luggage	12	00
Porch 2nd floor	Metal chaise lounge, metal arm chair, and metal glass top table	20	00
	7 various pottery plant holders	3	00
Entrance Hall	Oriental rug, 4' x 6'	175	00
	Oriental rug, 3' x 4'	50	00
	Oriental rug, 4' x 9'	125	00
	Bokhara scatter rug	35	00
	Shiraz scatter rug	20	00
	Carved Chinese stand with marble inserted top	350	00
	Cast bronze figure, "The Thorn Picker"	250	00
	Phyfe style card table	150	00
	Pair of ivory candle holders	50	00
	Kindell Indian, pottery	10	00
	Wooden carved bas relief of JEH on guest book cover	25	00
	Plaster nude torso base table lamp	100	00
	Letter opener	2	00
	Silver envelope shaped covered box	50	00
	Framed Chinese embroidery, Lao Tzu	150	00
	Small carved Chinese stand with marble inserted top	150	00
	Bronze statue, "The Archers"	215	00
	Gossip stand and bench	20	00
	Amount carried forward,	14,433	00

	"Elgin" wooden case wall clock	$ 50	00
	Marble fragment of Adolph Hitler's book-case	25	00
	Pair of 19th century Chinese vases in wooden wall cases	75	00
	Gilt framed oil on canvas, "Nude with glass" Roy Crawler	200	00
	Wooden and matted framed mosaic, FBI seal	75	00
	Oriental rug, 3' x 5'	75	00
	Korean lacquer desk sign with mother of pearl inlay	25	00
	5 wooden backed wall plaques honoring J. Edgar Hoover	200	00
	Plaster wall relief, 3 nude torsos	45	00
	Gilt framed color engraving of "The United States Capial"	50	00
	2 gilt framed Japanese wall plaques	40	00
	Toned framed oil on panel, "Indian Woman"	35	00
	Ebony and matted framed silk embroidery, "Pagoda"	75	00
	Circular sterling silver plate, monogramed	25	00
	Banjo style thermometer, hydrometer and barometer	50	00
	Framed photograph, Lincoln with his son	25	00
	Gilt framed death mask of "Dante"	50	00
	Small ebony framed painting of "Cathedral"	10	00
Bath Room	Japanese calligraphy	15	00
	Framed Chinese embroidery	50	00
	Framed oil landscape	15	00
	Hamper, mat and mirror	2	00
	Framed color print "Ocean"	15	00
Living Rm. Entrance	Contents of Vitrine number one		
	2 Jade panels, stand with Squirrels	125	00
	Amount carried forward,	15,785	00

Gilded "Kuan Yin" with two deitys	$ 100	00
26 ivory, crystal, teak, bronze, and bisque Elephants	300	00
Chinese rose quartz urn on stand, early 19th century	250	00
Ivory sterling silver pipe, ball and Buddha	45	00
Pair of jade and semi-precious stone floral groups each in stand	350	00
5 Chinese wine cups, 9 beaded boxes, lucite paper weight, geode, sea shells, Scorpion, 2 Counch shells, 2 tomahawks, Arabic scabbard, 2 American Indian bowls, 2 Roman lamps, ivory scrimshaw, Pre Columbian idol, pair of Chinese Buffalos and gavel	175	00
Contents of Vitrine number two		
Milk glass vase, 5 Easter eggs, plaster Madonna, ivory figurines and Satsuma vases	150	00
Purple pendant on stand, Green jade animal shape pitcher on stand, and 6 green jadite wine cups	350	00
2 Chinese opium pipes, rock crystal figure of Kuan Yin, Japanese kitchen gods, crystal Bull and Buffalo	125	00
Alabaster figure of "David"	15	00
Pewter mug, Japanese ivory house, ivory figurine, pottery mug, historical atom fragment, Staffordshire mugs, Roman lamp, 7 shells, feather belt, ivory otter, and copper knife	110	00
American Indian bead work, geode, steel box, Satsuma shell cloisonne bone knife, and rose quartz	100	00
Living Rm. 8 wooden horses	16	00
12 ivory horses on stand	48	00
Oil, "Mexican bull fighter"	20	00
Miniture bookcases	15	00
2 oil "Landscapes" and oil painting of "Indian"	20	00
Chinese plant stand with marble top	125	00
Amount carried forward,	18,099	00

Pottery vase and Japanese Cloisonne vase	$ 10	00
Pair of English Chinese Chippendale wall brackets	450	00
Bronze figure of "Wrestler"	300	00
Chinese marble top plant stand	125	00
Framed miniture, "Piano Player"	15	00
Chien Lung figure of "Kuan Yin" on stand	175	00
Brass andirons, French style fire screen fan, Peruvian stirrups	170	00
Chinese blue porcelain figure of "Taoist Man"	30	00
Garnet Dragon finial stand	50	00
Pair of brass hurricane lamps	15	00
Pair of red amber figures of "Kuan Yin" each on stand	200	00
Scrimshaw of J. Edgar Hoover	40	00
Garnet bell	155	00
Japanese daruma	15	00
Pair of porcelain Foo dogs	15	00
Jade sleeve holder on stand	25	00
Pair of pink quartz Phoenix birds on stands	250	00
Pair of sterling silver lanterns on stand	50	00
Pair of "Royal Worcester" dogs	45	00
Jade Phoenix bird on stand	35	00
Ivory Chinese immortal, pair of immortal figurines, and 8 immortals	125	00
Jade, sterling silver box on stand	25	00
Coral figure of "Kuan Yin" on stand	150	00
Green jade figure of "Kuan Yin"	175	00
Alabaster figure of "Hoi Tai"	10	00
Turquoise figure of "Child" on stand	75	00
Blue vase, "Chien Lung"	75	00
Amount carried forward,	20,874	00

Celluloid figure of Buddha	$ 1	00
Ivory, 4 Buddhas, Monkey, Rooster, and Sandpan	15	00
Ivory "Kuan Yin" and child	20	00
Set of Japanese heads, mounted on board	20	00
Gilt framed oil on canvas, "Grand Canyon" Lucien W. Powell	350	00
Pair of Mexican plaques	10	00
Elephant foot with silver top	150	00
Bronze figure of "Mercury"	275	00
Indian stand	25	00
"Landscape", Cromwell	20	00
Black framed water color sketch, Lucien W. Powell	150	00
Gilt framed porcelain painting, "Nymph"	120	00
Corner shelf	15	00
Chinese deity, 3 alabaster vases, miniture animal figurine, bronze incense burner, Japanese box and flask	70	00
Tea cart	25	00
Cabinet, basket, bar equipment, and silver plated ice bucket	10	00
Brass wood basket	20	00
Wooden base flag stand	15	00
Tibetian pipe	85	00
Wooden plaque with Presidential pen	5	00
Sterling silver covered box with Dominican Republic seal	45	00
Chinese silver covered box	40	00
Pair of carver wooden bookends, FBI entrance	50	00
Pair of lift top curio stands	250	00
32 Bronze, silver Commeration medals	350	00
Pottery dish with "Department of Justice" seal	15	00
Amount carried forward,	23,025	00

"Smith & Wesson" 38 Cal. revolver with gold inlay and Department of Justice seal	250	00
"Stieff" pewter cup	10	00
Green leather cigarette case, Eisenhower trip 1954	50	00
2 safety metal plastic cases	5	00
14kt yellow gold TRA plaque	25	00
Japanese pipe	5	00
Police plaque	5	00
Porcelain thumb print ash tray	30	00
2 miniture mother of pearl revolvers	50	00
4 wooden commemorative plaques	60	00
2 mounted Presidental pens	10	00
Pottery covered bowl, with Cherry finial	25	00
Miniture wooden cart	15	00
Bronze plaque of "Apollo"	15	00
Russian gold coin	15	00
Mahogany kidney shaped lamp table	45	00
6 silver plated ash trays with glass liners	8	00
Small covered box monogramed JEH	35	00
Indian letter opener	2	00
Glazed pottery figure of "Ho Tai"	150	00
Carved Chinese stand	50	00
Royal Doulton "Sine de Buff" vase	75	00
2 gilt framed paintings of "Geisha Girls"	50	00
Framed jade vase with flowers	50	00
Gilt framed oil on canvas, "Mountain of Holy Cross"	300	00
2 small bronze figurines, "Gold Panner" and "Hired Gun"	150	00
Bronze figure, "Forward", Philip Kraczkowski	100	00
Amount carried forward,	24,610	00

Carved gilt decorated wooden boat from Thailand	$ 100	00
Pair of brass cannon bookends	150	00
Bronze figure of "Nude", Harriet W. Frishmuth, Roman Bronze Works	300	00
Sterling silver presentation tray, with embossed gold signatures and set with 25 round cut diamonds	400	00
Pair of mounted Partridge bookends	100	00
"Fisher" AM/FM radio and phonograph in mahogany case	75	00
Nest of 3 glass top tea tables	50	00
Open arm chair	15	00
All upholstered arm chair	40	00
Combination desk clock and calander	35	00
Sterling silver covered box, presented by the government of Thailand	30	00
Elaborately carved Chinese stand with marble inserted top	125	00
Chinese porcelain figure of "Ho Tai", seated	85	00
Provincial record cabinet	40	00
Sterling silver hat shaped tray	25	00
Figural letter opener	10	00
Leather bill fold with Department of Justice seal set with 13 diamonds	50	00
Bronze statue, "Trooper's Return", Philip Kraczkowski	100	00
Bronze statue, "Sergeant, North West Mounted Police, 1885" Philip Kraczkowski	100	00
Approximately 40 miscellaneous records and sterio tapes	60	00
Electric clock with Department of Justice seal	75	00
Set of 6 carved ivory elephants on wooden stand	100	00
Amount carried forward,	26,675	00

Chinese red lacquer stand	$ 70	00
Small red lacquer chest	35	00
Gilt framed embrodered bird figure, with glass chips and moasic inlay	50	00
Mahogany corner what-not shelf	75	00
Red lacquer bowl	15	00
Pair of Venetian glass bird figures	10	00
Italian carver wooden figurine, "Mother and Child"	35	00
2 carved figural vases	30	00
Small Bohemian glass cup	5	00
Carved jade buckle	50	00
Miniture silver oil lamp	10	00
Pair of carved ivory vases	40	00
2 small Satsuma vases	10	00
Pair of Foo dog salt and peppers	3	00
Small red laquer tray	10	00
Plaster figure of dog	1	00
Glass and marble base table lamp	25	00
Pair of Thai floral decorated flower vases	90	00
2 mounted Presidental pens	10	00
Small sterling silver boxe, monogramed "21"	20	00
Wooden mother of pearl inlayed septre	15	00
"Cybis" figure of horse, number 123	350	00
Wooden gavel	25	00
English silver spoon	5	00
Approximately 110 miscellaneous metals, keys, and medallions	100	00
Sterling silver pen holder with quill	10	00
Gilt framed porcelain under glass, portrait of semi-nude woman	200	00
Amount carried forward,	27,974	00

Mahogany corner shelf	$ 20	00
Limoges porcelain bowl	5	00
2 framed illuminated ivories of nude women	85	00
Wooden curio cabinet with glass shelves	100	00
Persian framed illuminated cathedral window	20	00
Italian carved wooden figure of semi-nude	10	00
Pair of carved ivory horse figures each on stand	100	00
2 carved ivory nude female figurines	75	00
Metal key figure	3	00
Bronze figure of Fox	20	00
Carved marble figure of semi-nude woman on stand	35	00
Hawaii statehood medal in plastic housing	10	00
Sterling silver beaker, monogramed	10	00
Porcelain dish on stand	5	00
Royal Doulton figure of "Mermaid"	50	00
Presidental pen on stand	10	00
"Baccarat" crystal star	50	00
Tusk letter opener	25	00
Sterling silver juicer ash tray	10	00
Marble paper weight	10	00
Autographed picture of LBJ	15	00
3 medals	20	00
Sterling silver bowl, monogramed	40	00
Sterling silver cigarette case	30	00
"Steuben" glass "Excalibur", monogramed	300	00
"Steuben" glass salt and pepper shaker	50	00
Pewter mug, monogramed	35	00
Lot of miscellaneous LP records	30	00
Amount carried forward,	29,147	00

Bronze figure of male moving bolder on marble base	$ 100	00
Bronze figure of Bull with ivory horns	50	00
Composition bust of "Abraham Lincoln"	15	00
Steel figure of Knight	20	00
Bronze figure of Gladiator	25	00
Metal figure of Atlas holding world on shoulders	50	00
Chinese bronze incense burner on stand	50	00
Head of Buddha, 16th century , Thai	150	00
Spanish sword	50	00
Hoover bust, not appraised		
Austrian figure of American Indian	10	00
Bronze figure of "Hercules"	20	00
Japanese metal figure of Eagle	150	00
Bronze figures of "Sileno" and "Narciso"	40	00
Silver plated army helmet on stand, mono.	20	00
Carver ivory thermometer in glass case	25	00
Indian peace pipe, monogramed	50	00
Bisque figure of 2 children	10	00
Antique South American drinking cup, in shape of warrior, 800 AD, Peruvian	150	00
Antique carved African figurine on stand	45	00
Bronze statue of Gladiator sheating sword, as is	100	00
American Security Council award, 1964	10	00
Glass FBI plaque dated, 5-10-1924	20	00
Carved ivory figure of "The Pied Piper"	150	00
2 small bronze figurines, "Buffalo Hunter" and "Buffalo Prayer"	150	00
Cast metal figure of "Pony Express"	10	00
Fish fossil on stand	40	00
Amount carried forward,	30,657	00

Carved Chinese tusk on lacquer pedèstal	$ 250	00
German bronze figure of Gladiator on stand	75	00
Metal figure of nude children on marble pedestal	5	00
Brass pen holder with ink pot, 1884	35	00
Chrome "Mack" bull dog	5	00
Carved African bust of nude woman	40	00
Bronze figure of "Discus Thrower" on marble pedestal	100	00
Carved stone head of Buddha, Gandahara	300	00
Carved wooden Congo figurine, 14th Century	50	00
Small bronze figure of "Discus Thrower" on marble pedestal	50	00
Plaster figural group "The Lovers"	10	00
German bronze figure of nude male with club	75	00
Plaster bust of J. Edgar Hoover, not appraised		
Porcelain nude figure, torso, on stand	15	00
Carved stone totem pole on stand	50	00
Pewter mug with glass bottom, monogramed	10	00
Pair of gilt bronze figures, "Pan" and nude woman	40	00
Wooden gavel and plastic gavel	15	00
Carved Thai figure of semi-nude woman	30	00
Stone building fragment with seal	3	00
Carved wooden Mexican figure of Madonna	50	00
Carved ivory thread spool, as is	20	00
Bronze figure of "Rabbit", P. J. Mene	200	00
Bronze figure of nude male with shoulder pouch	20	00
Carved wooden nude torso of female	35	00
Carved wooden figure of Eagle	35	00
Amount carried forward,	32,175	00

	$	
India figure of dancer on lotus flower base	75	00
Pair of dog figural bookends	35	00
Korean lacquer plaque	50	00
FBI mug	5	00
Sheet brass sword in case	20	00
Alaska stone carving of Eskimo and Walrus	100	00
Japanese carved wooden figure of trout	35	00
Chou bronze ceremonial wine vessel	200	00
Reproduction of Tang horse	50	00
Girka knife	35	00
Carved wooden gavel	25	00
Shrunken head from New Guinea, in glass case	150	00
Alaska stone carving of Eskimo and Bear	100	00
Chinese brass incense burner with handle	50	00
Pottery figure of dog	15	00
Wooden gavel from George Washington's tree	25	00
Copper book plate jewel box	20	00
Carved wooden figure of bird	60	00
Fern fossil	20	00
Carved Hatian wood figurine, woman on donkey	25	00
Carved German figurine, "Mushroom Picker"	40	00
Pair of carved wooden bookends, Scotty dog and Yorkshire Terrier	60	00
Copper model of Balsa log raft	50	00
Mercury figural decorated oil lamp	25	00
Rabinical silver lamp	100	00
Framed print of Arab	10	00
Wooden Chinese wall relief	15	00
Amount carried forward,	33,570	00

Plaster bust of Lady Godiva	$ 15	00
Bull Fighter collage	15	00
Rose damask upholstered arm chair	35	00
Metal base floor lamp	25	00
Moroccan table with pearl inlay	150	00
Sterling silver leaf shaped letter opener	5	00
Sterling silver cigarette box, monogramed	20	00
Table lighter	5	00
Glass ash tray, monogramed	1	00
"Toledo" steel broad sword	100	00
Glass flower vase and artificial flowers	2	00
Mother of Pearl decorated box	75	00
Mahogany stool	25	00
Large antique Chinese cloisonne vase	250	00
Swiss pewter wine pot	75	00
Moroccan inlayed table with safety glass top	45	00
Chinese yellow porcelain vase, Phoenix bird design	150	00
Pair of carved Chinese tables with marble inserted tops	100	00
Glass base table lamp with nude figure	20	00
5 carved ivory elephants on parade, as is	10	00
Magazine stand with drawer	20	00
Green upholstered arm chair	45	00
Pair of mahogany end tables with drawer base	80	00
Carved Chinese stand with marble top	150	00
Silver plated bronze statue, woman and lovers	50	00
"Angelus" desk clock with barometer	75	00
Sterling silver case thermometer	5	00
Pair of sterling silver ash trays	10	00
Amount carried forward,	35,128	00

Pair of brass bud vases	$ 6	00
Upholstered settee with down cushions and 3 pillows	200	00
Ship's wheel barometer	5	00
Alabaster ashtray with silver plated horse figure attached	5	00
Pair of metal base table lamps with silk shades	100	00
Mahogany end table with deck	35	00
Microscope base table lamp	25	00
Silver plated cigarette box	10	00
Silver plated ashtray	5	00
Glass top curio coffee table	50	00
Mirrored top coffee table	50	00
Persian oriental rug, 9' x 12'	800	00
Bokhara oriental rug, 3'8" x 5'	140	00
Oriental rug, 4' x 5' 9"	175	00
Persian oriental rug, 4'7" x 6'10", as is	150	00
Nixon and Humphrey ashtrays	10	00
Vietnamese green porcelain Foo dog	75	00
English "Billy Club" on stand with badge	35	00
Ashtray and cigarette box, monogramed J. Edgar Hoover	10	00
Japanese porcelain figure of Eagle under plastic case	200	00
Pair of Chinese artifical plants	40	00
Chinese brass incense burner on stand	150	00
Silver cigarette box with glass top	10	00
Carved ivory cup	50	00
Brass derringer table lighter	10	00
Table lighter	5	00
Library shears monogramed from Lawrence Welk	3	00
Amount carried forward,	37,482	00

	Pair of heavy glass ashtrays	$ 6	00
	Chinese dagger with Kwai decorated handle	75	00
	Collection of approximately 39 miscellaneous bronze medals, plaques and medallions	400	00
Porch	4 pieces of cast iron lawn furniture	75	00
	Wicker chaise lounge	20	00
	Metal arm chair	35	00
	Pair of porcelain jardineres	70	00
	Wrought metal glass top table	10	00
	Pair of tile top coffee tables	70	00
	Few grass scatter rugs	10	00
	Metal pot holder, copper platter, pottery dish, 2 Moroccan pitchers, faiance plate, and wall barometer	100	00
	2 metal pot stands, bell, wall pot holder, and cast iron eagle	30	00
Garage	"Toro" snow blower	60	00
	Lawn vacuum	50	00
	"Cooper" lawn mower	45	00
	3 aluminum ladders	30	00
	2 lawn chairs	2	00
	Lot of assorted garden tools	25	00
	Bronze statue of Gladiator	50	00
Dining Rm	Shelf vitrine cabinet	20	00
	Collection of wooden dog figurines, German wood carvings	75	00
	Bronze figure of "Hercules"	325	00
	Vitrine, 3 shelves	95	00
	LBJ bust	15	00
	Rose quartz figure of "Kuan Yin"	100	00
	Rock crystal figure of "Kuan Yin and Foo Dog"	150	00
	Amount carried forward,	39,425	00

Item		$	
4 porcelain dogs, Fox, crystal Elephant, Buffalo, 2 ebony Elephants and Panther		150	00
Tiger skull decorated with sterling silver, used as cigarette, pipe and match holder		250	00
Chinese plant stand with marble top		100	00
Japanese candle stand		20	00
Chinese plant stand with 4 legs.		60	00
Italian bronze figure of "Athlete"		300	00
2 Japanese lacquer stands		20	00
Pair of Japanese cloisonne vases on stand		65	00
Aquarium with pump		32	00
Pair of Hurricane electrified lamps		10	00
Bar table		18	00
Model of a Church		20	00
Sligh mahogany dining table, oval with glass top		165	00
Sligh dining chairs, 2 arm, 6 side, "Adam" style		195	00
Sligh china cabinet, buffet and 4 drawer chest		250	00
Chinese gong stand, Bat design		90	00
Electric clock, star shape		3	00
Oil painting, "Monk"		75	00
Corner shelf		5	00
Bronze figure of "Napoleon", Egyptian head, and Jewish bronze clock		70	00
Chinese red gourd vase		60	00
Chinese stand, ornate carving		60	00
Chinese wall brackets		20	00
Pair of Chinese cinnabar vases on stands		50	00
Pair of brass hurricane lamps		35	00
Pair of carved wooden plaques, "Ho Tai"		60	00
Amount carried forward,		41,608	00

Pair of District of Columbia and New York etchings	$ 60	00
Oil painting, "Seascape", Robert Wood	250	00
Italian bronze "Gladiator"	300	00
4 panel laquer and oil decorated screen	70	00
Pair of Victorian sconces	35	00
Chinese stand with marble top	100	00
Chinese cloisonne covered urn	350	00
Oil painting, "San Clemente"	150	00
Pair of Chinese silhouettes	5	00
Pair of Chinese cloisonne plates on stands	200	00
Lamp, "George Washington at Valley Forge"	200	00
Corner shelf, mirror	3	00
Ivory figure of "Confucius"	125	00
Framed Japanese calligraphy	10	00
Pair of "Waterford" crystal candelabra	300	00
Crystal decanter	20	00
Cut crystal hurricane candelabra	175	00
6 porcelain plates, cut crystal goblets monogramed, wines, old fashions, brandies, cordials and assorted stemware	95	00
Sterling silver cigarette box, monogramed.	35	00
Sterling silver lighter, silver plated silent butler, lucite box, sterling silver tray, salts, and wooden fruit carving	55	00
Cut crystal shallow bowl	25	00
Silver cake knife	5	00
2 sterling silver candelabra	16	00
Pair of pewter candlesticks	20	00
Cut glass celery dish	15	00
Plastic tray	1	00
Cut crystal bon bon dish with handle	20	00
Amount carried forward,	44,248	00

Cut crystal bowl	$ 10	00
Small lot of miscellaneous linen	30	00
Pair of sterling silver 3 lite candelabra monogramed JEH	200	00
Sterling silver punch set, consisting of bowl, 12 cups and ladel	500	00
Pair of silver plated covered vegetable dishes	75	00
International sterling silver Revere style bowl, monogramed and dated 1960	150	00
Sterling silver Revere style bowl, monogramed and dated 1961	150	00
8 sterling silver Mint Julip cups, mon.	100	00
Silver plated covered vegetable dish	20	00
Black, Star and Gorham sterling silver 2 handled bowl	200	00
Silver cigarette box	10	00
Table lighter	5	00
Brass bell in stand	5	00
Small Revere style sterling silver bowl	10	00
Crystal bell with silver overlay	30	00
Sterling silver Revere style bowl, monogramed H	150	00
Sterling silver pitcher, monogramed	65	00
12 silver plated cups	50	00
Small silver plated coffee pot	35	00
Crystal cruet	40	00
Song bird in cage	25	00
Oval sterling silver 2 handled tray	45	00
Persian oriental rug, 9' x 12'	1,000	00
Turkoman oriental rug, 3' x 6'	135	00
9 sterling silver salt and peppers, 7 coasters and 6 silver plated ash trays	20	00
Amount carried forward,	47,308	00

Table mats, shell mats, and trays	$ 10 00
Approximately 169 pieces of sterling silver and coin silver flatware	550 00
Hanging lamp	20 00
Silver plated circular tray	35 00
Sterling silver 2 handled presentation tray	90 00
Sterling silver presentation tray, Mexican	65 00
Sterling silver presentation tray, dated 1964, Mexican	40 00
Silver plated wine bottle holder from "21" club	7 00
Pewter bowl	6 00
Silver plated gravy boat	5 00
Sterling silver Revere style pitcher, Mon.	75 00
Silver plated tree/well platter	15 00
12 sterling silver goblets	150 00
Silver plated shell shaped dish, Monogramed	40 00
6 steak knives	3 00
Mahogany dish with sterling silver base	15 00
Italian silver plated bucket	5 00
Sterling silver tray, monogramed	5 00
8 Stag horn handled steak knives	10 00
2 trays, enamel and wood	8 00
Miscellaneous lot consisting of asparagus gravy spoons, tongs, etc.	35 00
Approximately 52 pieces of "Royal Arch Mason" sterling silver flatware	166 00
2 sterling silver spoons	6 00
Pantry Hoover vacuum machine	15 00
2 fire extinguishers	5 00
Miscellaneous vases and cachepots	4 00
Amount carried forward,	48,693 00

	Miscellaneous crystal goblets, old fashions, wines, slad plates, salad bowls, brass candelabra, tea pots and carafe sets	$ 110	00
	12 Limoges plates	48	00
	Pottery plates, monogramed	20	00
	7 asparagus plates	14	00
	FBI mugs	4	00
	Pottery plates, glass dishes, crystal bowl, aluminum tray, asparagus dishes, pottery bowls and mugs	20	00
Kitchen	Miscellaneous vases, crystal, glassware and silver plated brandy	10	00
	Miscellaneous Lenox china cups, saucers, dinner plates, demitasse cups, salad bowl, carafe set, and pitchers	30	00
	Electric can opener, toaster, radio and broiler	10	00
	Persian tile	8	00
	Miscellaneous cookware, ladder, metal table, chair, pyrex ware, pottery ware, and linen	10	00
Basement	Bar with brass rail	25	00
	Linen, iron	5	00
Bedroom	Chinese rug, as is	15	00
	Single bed	8	00
	Japanese lamp, silver overlay	30	00
	Arm chair	8	00
	Chest of drawers and mirror	18	00
	Wing chair	10	00
	Floor lamp	2	00
	Desk	5	00
	Chair	2	00
Basement cond.	Traveling Pak, portable bar	25	00
	Miscellaneous vases	6	00
	Amount carried forward,	49,136	00

2 boxes of cards, Danish vase, wooden case clock, brass scale, salt glaze mug, Japanese vase, pottery setter and mug	37	00
Silver plated pitcher, English pitcher, sterling silver Mexican tray, silver plated urn, pitcher, Limoges tray, Satsuma vase, and Japanese vase	70	00
Japanese tray, vase/silver overlay, cranberry vase, Kutani vase, Italian figurine, Sake vase and 2 odd vases	35	00
Murano vase, Danish vase, opaline vase, pottery seal, carafe set, 2 thermoware trays, tole candlestick, electric coffee pot	10	00
Pottery tray, pottery rooster, Limoges tray, silver plated tray, blue opaline bottle, 2 ducks, 3 wooden gavels, bowl, copper mug, silver plated box, sterling silver mexican box, silver plated box and tray	65	00
6 sterling silver mugs, overlay	30	00
2 TV lucite lamps, shell pattern	10	00
Sterling silver flask, crystal	8	00
Pottery vase and pottery mug, Kutani vase, 2 Chien Lung vases with stands, pistol grip, ginger jar and onyx tray	75	00
Ceramic hat, Pewter box and tray	8	00
Chinese ice bucket	10	00
Carton of miscellaneous books	8	00
Pair of sterling silver hurricane globes, mahogany case	65	00
Metal plaque	8	00
2 mirrors, paper weight, stone	10	00
Historical Senate flag	50	00
Jewish medal, 2 old fashion glasses, D'orsay jar, wooden box, 3 Bohemian cups, bird pottery jar, and 2 candy jars	35	00
2 Kutani vases, murano vase, cranberry glass cut glass pitcher, sterling silver coaster, Bohemian vase, 2 decanters, cut crystal vase and decanter	150	00
Amount carried forward,	49,820	00

	$	
2 cut crystal trays, pitcher, blue pitcher, and cut crystal bowl	75	00
Zenieth transistor radio	15	00
2 Sony radios	50	00
Sound 6, radio	15	00
Sony transistor	15	00
6 covered bean pots	10	00
Silver plated Revere style bowl with ladle	20	00
Lot of assorted art books	25	00
Tortoise box and tray	15	00
Cigar box, wooden, porcelain musical box, pottery jar, Scottie trays, Cinnabar box, leather box, 2 indian boxes, pair bookends, 2 Irish Belleck vases	120	00
2 Chinese Ox blood vases, lynox vase, cut crystal vase, mug, 2 cloisonne vases, Chinese vase, and blue and white vase	175	00
Miscellaneous lot of books	10	00
Tray, vases, cut crystal tray, 6 glasses, cranberry glass, pottery tray, cut crystal vase,	80	00
Danish vase, German vase, Swedish vase, and German ash trays	12	00
Cut crystal pitcher, Fosteria candlesticks, milk glass bottle, bronze tray, and chamber candlestick	30	00
Cannon wine bottle, Lebanise medals, Lilique Buffalo, brush, apple jars, novelty art ware	20	00
Cuspidor, tray, 2 ash trays, 2 mirrored trays, brass tray, cloisonne trays, cigar box, Indian box and tray	20	00
Persian vase, cloisonne vase, silver plated vase, pair of Murano vases, Italian pitcher, Sterling silver pepper mill, and cheese covers	35	00
2 Lalique Quails	120	00
4 goblets	10	00
Shoe polisher	3	00
Amount carried forward,	50,695	00

Flag set, rare photographs, mottos, and Hummel figurine	135	00
Krlmar camera with zoom lens	100	00
Binoculars and case	25	00
Pair of Leitz binoculars	50	00
Binoculars and case	10	00
Baush and Lomb binoculars and case	75	00
Zoom scope binoculars and case	100	00
Miniture brandy snifter	5	00
Miscellaneous autographed books	20	00
ash tray, pottery, crystal, Blinko leather, blue opaline, German crystal, Murano, Fostoria copper bowl, ashtrays, and assorted bowls	35	00
12 Wedgwood Historical plates, and 1 chop plate	200	00
Album chess set, bookends, and collection of bills	75	00
Cigar humidor box, and Indian Kashmir steak set	40	00
Martini set, ivory opener, bronze bull and bear, and helmet covered statue	70	00
Leather Bound books, Iranian and sterling silver covered	45	00
12 Bohemian wine glasses	70	00
Swedish candlestick, Austrian bowl, cups and ladle	35	00
3 ice buckets	12	00
Bohemian vase, cut crystal vase, Japanese cloisonne vase, cut satin cameo vase and 2 cloisonne vases	300	00
Bar equiptment, novelties, corkscrew, and boxes	8	00
3 wooden covered cigar boxes	30	00
Jar, music mug, vase, Victorian vase, Lenox vase, murano vase, and Rockwood vase	15	00
2 blankets and golf covers	10	00
Amount carried forward,	52,160	00

	$	
Lucite box, sterling silver box, vase, Chinese box, crystal ashtray, Borghese box, tray, Chinese pewter tray, Japanese lighter, trays and spoons	15	00
Blanket	5	00
6 glasses, wood carving, cork screw, trays, porcelain ppener, Quail, electric clock, Staffordshire creamer and sugar bowl	25	00
Hi ball glasses	6	00
Ball players	4	00
3 art books	12	00
Lucite tray and thermos pitcher	5	00
8 Hi ball glasses and ice bucket	10	00
12 "Steuben" old fashion glasses	150	00
Pyrex casserole	4	00
Pepper mill	2	00
Sterling silver dagger, enameled Iran lacquer tray, Italian belts, agate egg, lighter knife, alabaster jar, vase, 2 berry spoons, 2 fish knives, sterling silver tart server, and 2 frames	95	00
Japanese tea pot	8	00
2 pottery cows	10	00
Bar glasses	3	00
Art glass, musical vase, alabaster vase, tray, goblets, miscellaneous ashtrays, bowls carved Indian figurine	25	00
6 Copper mugs	8	00
Brass box	125	00
6 glasses	1	00
14 thermos glasses	5	00
Old fashion glasses, Hi ball and Manhattan glasses	10	00
Brass box, 4 trays, gun showcase, and Phillipine box	20	00
2 spirit burners, brandy glass, and cookie jar	10	00
Amount carried forward,	52,718	00

Bean pots, and cordial glasses	$ 15	00
Twirling glasses and miscellaneous glasses	6	00
Plaques, Korea, Thi, Roman stone, 2 cloisonne vases, atom rock, hand grenade, sterling silver vase, weight horse, pair of bookends and wooden plaques	85	00
Miscellaneous Danish candles	8	00
Silver plated trays, antique pewter ashtrays portable music box and 2 planters	20	00
Lacquer box	3	00
4 decanter set and case	75	00
Cane, letter opener, tray and brass opener	20	00
Silver plated English tankard	75	00
Silver plated letter opener, bookends, Bronze boy, and letter opener	75	00
Taiwan Foo dog	20	00
Globe, decanter, water jug, table lighter, and brass incense burner	15	00
Spanish ship model	20	00
Jade planter on stand	500	00
Ashtrays, murano glass, cloisonne, pewter deer, candlestick holder, African carving, bluevase, Mexican onyx pottery head, ceramic doll, Murano ashtrays, 2 Ho Tai stone Buddhas Onyx turtle, Eskimo art and head	150	00
10 crystal decanters, crystalware, wooden	40	00
Books	6	00
Brass hatchet, party favors, novelities, pressed glass and pottery animals	10	00
English plaque	10	00
Old paper weight, Staffordshire plates, mug, 10 wood carvings, and 4 Wedgwood trays	25	00
Mounted Sailfish	100	00
Framed oil on canvas, "Sierra Nevada" Leonidgechtoff, 30-1/4" x 34"	100	00
4 picture spot lamps	20	00
Amount carried forward,	54,116	00

Oil on canvas, "Yosemite Falls" Lucien Powell	$ 500	00
Oil on canvas, "Yuccas" Ruth Boyce	75	00
Oil on canvas, "Grand Canyon" Lucien Powell	450	00
Glass Christmas Tree	25	00
"Gentilehomme" French case mantle clock	500	00
Pair of carved Phillipine figurines	30	00
Pair of porcelain Foo dogs	10	00
Carved wooden figure of Mystic	20	00
Carven wooden figure of "Quan Yin"	50	00
Wooden ash tray	1	00
Pottery ash tray	1	00
Chinese porcelain figure of "Quan Yin"	15	00
Pottery figure of Rooster	5	00
Pair of pottery wine bottles, figural dec.	6	00
Carved wooden figure of Oriental Priest	5	00
Art Noveau figure of woman	35	00
Metal figure of Oriental woman	15	00
Cast metal figure of Partridge	20	00
Pottery figure of bird	3	00
Bone bird carving	10	00
Pair of West Virginia goblets	8	00
Blue pitcher, pottery ashtray with bisque design and 2 enamel ashtrays	10	00
Brass ash tray, Cedar memo pad, and lucite picture frame	15	00
6 footed glass jars and bowling ball jar	5	00
Note pad and Bronze by Y. Lerch	45	00
3 Stork Club ash trays, pottery bowl, and ash tray	3	00
Pair of Cinnabar lacquer vases with stands	100	00
Amount carried forward,	56,078	00

Box of miscellaneous books	$ 10	00
5 steak platters	10	00
Afghan	35	00
Leather dagger wall plaque	10	00
Carved wooden Korean jewel chest	10	00
Pair of redwood bookends	15	00
Pair of Lincoln bookends	20	00
Wall prayer	2	00
Limoges "Jockey" ashtray and covered jar	8	00
Lacquer bowl	5	00
Wooden box	2	00
Hobnail glass bowl	5	00
Silver plated salt housing	5	00
Italian glass vase	5	00
French porcelain ash tray	2	00
Chinese bud vase	35	00
Staffordshire covered jar	5	00
Luster cup	30	00
Large luster footed bowl	40	00
Blown glass bowl with ribbon edge	20	00
Rosenthal bowl	35	00
California porcelain bowl	1	00
Footed luster wine cup	50	00
Cut crystal bowl	40	00
"Libbey" crystal bowl	25	00
Blown crystal decanter	20	00
Leather bottle coaster	20	00
2 boxes of FBI ashtrays	50	00
Italian glass ash tray	5	00
Amount carried forward,	56,598	00

Rock crystal ashtray	$ 3	00
3 paper weights	50	00
Rosenthal crystal ash tray	10	00
Pair of blown blue glass ash trays, vase shaped	10	00
6 enamel ashtrays	10	00
Cast iron ashtray	3	00
Crystal perfume bottle and pottery ash tray	3	00
4 teak match box holders	2	00
Brass wick clipper	3	00
Leather jewel case	5	00
4 sterling silver grapefruit spoons	10	00
Desk calander	1	00
Desk clock	15	00
Billfold and binoculars and case	10	00
Metal paper weight and bottle opener comb.	3	00
Telephone dial clock	15	00
Leather jewel box	5	00
Leather pad holder	1	00
Leather jewel box, 2 cuticle sets, desk pad turf kit, note pad, 4 pocket calanders, leather pad, 15 billfolds, letter holder, key rings and 2 desk sets	100	00
Pair of porcelain vases and crystal decanter	40	00
Bohemian decanter	40	00
Antique blown blue glass bottle with stopper	35	00
Pair of Bohemian vases with covers	100	00
Pottery vase	2	00
Cloisonne vase	50	00
Pottery cup	1	00
Pair of Bohemian glass cups	30	00
Amount carried forward,	57,155	00

Ice-o-matic ice crusher	$ 5	00
Antique English silver letter opener	35	00
Marble ash tray	2	00
Hand brush	2	00
4 shoe horns	4	00
"Toledo" steel dagger and India carving knife	20	00
Green and clear glass vase	1	00
2 pair of aluminum candlesticks with shades	10	00
Glass pitcher	3	00
German porcelain covered jar	5	00
Martini set	3	00
Hungarian luster decorated vase, circa 1870	100	00
Italian red glass vase	1	00
Welded ship model on rock	20	00
Silver plated serving spoon	5	00
Pair of metal Japanese vases	10	00
Pair of Swedish, blue and green vases	15	00
Bohemian glass vase	45	00
Silver plated ashtray with coin insert	2	00
Brandy glass candle	5	00
Porcelain tea pot with gilt decoration	8	00
Antique George IV, half pint tankard, 1820	100	00
Box of large pine cones	5	00
2 etched crystal wine glasses	4	00
Mexican pottery ashtray	1	00
Pen lighter, lighter, belt buckle and pipe holder	10	00
Calander travel clock and case	10	00
Parker pen and pencil	8	00
Amount carried forward,	57,594	00

	$	
Basket	2	00
Paraguay carved steer	10	00
8 Indian old fisher glasses	2	00
2 Electric razors and double edge razor	15	00
Wooden and glass coasters	2	00
Pottery ash tray and china tea pot, cups and trays	35	00
Pair of German binoculars, 7'x50'	25	00
Lot of assorted paper weights	10	00
Waltham brass desk calendar	10	00
2 Pair binoculars	40	00
Hunting knife	5	00
Parker and Onyx desk set	10	00
Finnish hunting knife	5	00
2 Autograph footballs	20	00
Pair of colt Revolvers bookends	75	00
Shell paper weight	5	00
Marble pen receiver	15	00
Cigarette holder	1	00
Police decorated pen receiver	2	00
Box of miscellaneous pottery	10	00
1962 Royal Copenhagen plate	100	00
Scottish Rite Centinental plate	5	00
Cheese board	3	00
Wm. 4th Antique pewter tankard, circa 1830	100	00
Belguim shot glasses and decanter	5	00
Box of colored cordial glasses	2	00
Pottery hat, wooden stork, pair of English pottery ash trays	10	00
Rectangular shaped Japanese porcelain dish	10	00
Austrain porcelain covered mantle vase	50	00
Pitcher and four cordial glasses and 6 Sweedish crystal footed glasses	10	00
7 Clear heavy crystal cordials	7	00
Amount carried forward,	58,195	00

Heavy clear and green crystal vase	$ 10	00
Box of assorted vases	20	00
Antique George IV half-pint tankard	100	00
Dice cup	1	00
Japanese cloisonne vase	40	00
Pewter pepper mill	20	00
Taiwan brass cannon	10	00
2 Rooster head stoppers	2	00
Chrome cocktail shaker	1	00
Rosenthal figure of Poodle	10	00
Southern Comfort bank	2	00
Box of miscellaneous pottery plates, glass plate and clock	25	00
Antique colbalt wine glass	20	00
Glass pitcher and 2 glasses	3	00
2 Japanese lacquered bowls	40	00
Porcelain ashtray	1	00
Holland pewter pitcher	10	00
Kit of monkey pod wooden small dishes	1	00
Silver gilt ship model	10	00
Swedish brass candle lamp with glass shade	5	00
Large cookie jar	1	00
18 plastic riders, letter opener, world clock wooden handled flatware in case, wooden cocktail tray and framed engraving	50	00
Ice bucket in false book housing	5	00
7 blue plastic bowls, wooden salad bowl and coasters, kit of velva glasses, pitcher cooler, Baten lightoiler and 2 reading lamps	20	00
Revolver base florescent desk lamp	50	00
Kit of VFW glasses, FBI bookends, Czech. vase 2 pitchers, tile, Swiss cow bell, plastic figurine, air plane lighter, horse figurine plastic bust and paper weight	40	00
amount carried forward,	58,692	00

	$	
Carved wooden Nativity set	100	00
Hawaiian Pig board	10	00
Sterling silver picture frame, silver plated oval tray, sterling silver footed bon bon 7½", 2 kits of steak knives, lenox ash tray, 2 Dozen cordials	35	00
Frosted glass cup, combination lock, coffee cup, print wooden panel, 4 sterling silver cordials, red leather jewel box	100	00
Enamel bowl, silver picture frame, brown silver tray and silver plated tray	10	00
Metal devil mash bowl, brass bowl, silver plated cocktail tray, carved wooden horse figure, leather covered bottle, pair of wooden busts of natives, pottery bowl and stopper	45	00
Jade handled spirit burner	75	00
8 Glasses	4	00
Wooden tray, Kwai decorated with brass mounts	55	00
Oil on panel, 'Dawn In Mountains'	45	00
Composition Aztec decorated chess set	25	00
German pottery dish	2	00
Wooden lazy susan tray	11	00
Pair of Japanese bronze elephant heads	100	00
Pair of wood bookends, and nut cracker, 2 coffee cups	10	00
Framed D.C. notes	10	00
Set of salt and pepper, 2 salt and pepper mugs and lot of biblots	15	00
Ivory letter opener	10	00
Saddle seat	4	00
Coffee urn	8	00
Motorola transister '600'	25	00
Sterling silver 5-arm candalabra, weighted	40	00
Cut glass bowl	35	00
Cut glass vase	25	00
Cut glass relish dish	30	00
Amount carried forward,	59,521	00

	$	
6 Pearl handle fruit knives and case	20	00
Sterling silver overlay vase	30	00
Silver plated relish dish	8	00
Wedgwood black basket, pot creamer and sugar	50	00
18 Miscellaneous stirrups, high balls	36	00
Wine rack	6	00
Tantalizer set, three decanters	15	00
Sterling silver 2-arm candalabra	25	00
Chinese export bowl, circa 1780	150	00
2 Lacquer trays, enameled	6	00
Eagle sumi drawing, Kakemono	75	00
2 Bohemian blue glasses	25	00
12 high ball glasses	5	00
Books, (4) LBJ, miscellaneous books	20	00
8 High ball and old fashions	10	00
8 High ball glasses	8	00
Carved wooden stallion	30	00
12 Steuben champaign glasses	150	00
6 Silver plated berry spoons	12	00
6 VIP glasses	6	00
Sterling silver Reed and Barton goblets, three salts and peppers, spoon, blue liner	35	00
Alligator album	15	00
Silver plated trivet, pair bookends, dagger, letter holder, Spanish milk glass	25	00
Cork screw, wood carvings, 2 monks, covered box, 2 Phillipine figurines	20	00
6 Tulip shaped wine glasses	6	00
Lucite bookends, FBI	15	00
4 Silver plated condiment liners	6	00
Japanese bronze eagle, as is	20	00
Leather attache case	20	00
Ice bucket	7	00
Amount carried forward,	60,377	00

	$	
Brief case, toilet article	10	00
Wooden bowl, stainless steel tray, pyrex, coffee maker, Eskimo doll	25	00
Miscellaneous lot of books and records	30	00
Pottery mugs, trays and pot	8	00
Cocktail pick, lalique bowl, bone horn books	40	00
Bookends	10	00
Korean Kakemono	6	00
2 Chinese stands, martini shaker, napkin holder, attache case	25	00
6 High-ball glasses, horse head	12	00
2 Wooden trays	6	00
Leather album	3	00
Decanter, cordial (8) twist glasses	15	00
Cocktail tree	3	00
Seiko desk clock	10	00
Books and records	2	00
Cldsonne insense burner, Ming	250	00
12 Tumblers, engraved	12	00
16 Old fashions, glasses	6	00
Mein Kampf historical volume, leather bound volume sent to Hoover. This particular volume was presented to Field Von Epp, Governor of Bavaria by Hitler and was found in Von Epp's home in Manick	500	00
Wood tray	8	00
Iran photo album	15	00
Houdon plaster cast of George Washington	25	00
Pair of Behm Canadian geese	200	00
Cocktail glasses, tray	6	00
Broggi suitcase	15	00
Amount carried forward,	61,619	00

Plated key chain	$ 3	00
Calander pad	1	00
3 cocktail picks, 5 letter openers, brush, figa luck horn, lobster pick, opener and salad set	20	00
Gold nugget	25	00
Jewelry case, Parker pen, cigar cutter, lighter and box	10	00
Brush, clip, flask, lighter, pen, pencil, dog heads, picks, dispenser, pistol cigar lighter	15	00
Warming tray	12	00
Luggage	10	00
Silver plated compote	25	00
Italian table	7	00
Billy club, few swords and canes	40	00
Desk lamp	8	00
Rim pistol	10	00
Lalique bird figure	15	00
Sterling silver letter opener	3	00
2 silver spoons and kit of silver shot glasses	10	00
2 desk clocks	15	00
Playing cards, traveling kit, pen, pen knife, Ronson lighter and pencil caddy	20	00
Lighter clock	20	00
Pen and ruler, letter pad, letter opener and pad	10	00
Sterling silver case, 800 fine	10	00
Sterling silver lighter and paper weight	5	00
Money clip watch	10	00
Key chain dated 1895	15	00
Pair of 14kt yellow gold cuff links	15	00
Amount carried forward,	61,953	00

Jewelry
residence

JEWELRY-Residence-		$	
	Coral bird, bracelet, stand	95	00
	Sterling silver money clip, monogramed J.E.H. with FBI seal	20	00
	Pair of yellow gold cuff links, each set with 4 small rubies	250	00
	Pair of Tiffany 14k yellow gold cuff links 'Department of Justice' seal	100	00
	Gilt metal tie bar, 'Royal Police' seal and matching cuff links	20	00
	Yellow gold tie pin with attached sterling silver saddle pendant	25	00
	Sterling silver money clip, monogramed J.E.H.	15	00
	Pair of sterling silver U.S. Senate cuff links	10	00
	Pair of tortis cuff links, monogramed J.E.H.	10	00
	Three tie pins with stirrup pendants, monogramed J.E.H.	30	00
	4 Yellow gold tie tacks	8	00
	Pair of sterling silver cuff links, monogramed '50th'	10	00
	2 Key rings and 1 key	10	00
	9 FBI Service award pins, 4 set with diamonds	50	00
	Lobster shaped tie bar	5	00
	14k Yellow gold money clip	10	00
	Benrus watch	65	00
	14k Yellow gold cuff links, (pair)	5	00
	10k Justice cuff links	10	00
	8 Rings set with semi precious stones and 2 jade rings	80	00
	Silver dollar key ring, 1882	50	00
	Agate cuff / tie rack	10	00
	Belt, gold filled key chain	8	00
	Gold zodiac pin	2	00
	Three 14k star sapphires	45	00
	Amount carried forward,	62,896	00

	$	
Cartier gold pin	15	00
Coin chain, 1887	15	00
Costume cuff links	75	00
4 Gold cuff links, (pair)	20	00
Garnet cuff links	20	00
14k Calendar cuff links, ruby	40	00
Pair of gold coin $10. cuff links, 1895	100	00
Menuki sword, cuff link tie	75	00
Lot of costume and sterling silver jewelry, pins, cuff links, tie tacks, etc.	150	00
Pair of 14k yellow gold cuff links	15	00
2 Yellow gold studs, each set with diamonds	20	00
Pair of gold nugget cuff links	20	00
Box of assorted cuff links, tie tacks, table lighter, etc.	35	00
Cultured pearl pin	15	00
14k Studs, marqueterie	15	00
Amount carried forward,	63,526	00

Jewelry Riggs Bank		$	
	7 Collar ties	2	00
	4 Costume tie clips	10	00
	14k Yellow gold tie clip with monogramed pendant attached	15	00
	Three silver and three gold wash money clips	75	00
	14k Yellow gold tie clasp set with small diamonds 10 pints	50	00
	4 Yellow gold money clips, 2 monogramed	100	00
	Costume tie clip with signature of J.E. Hoover	20	00
	Yellow gold tie clasp set with sapphire, monogramed J.E.H.	75	00
	LBJ campaign tie clasp	5	00
	Platinum tie pin set with 1 OSC diamond, 25 points	75	00
	2 Stick pins	1	00
	Pen knife, clock key, key in case	75	00
	Three masonic pins, 1 set with 3 diamonds 1 set with ruby and small diamond	30	00
	14k Yellow gold tie tack	25	00
	14k Yellow gold tie tack, monogramed 'H'	15	00
	Costume pearl tie tack	1	00
	Yellow gold patent pencil, dated 1876	20	00
	Silver case pencil	10	00
	Silver case patent pencil	15	00
	Yellow gold '$20.00' gold coin money clip	150	00
	One belt buckle set with 8 diamonds, monogramed J.E.H. Yellow gold	50	00
	Three belt buckles, all monogramed	10	00
	14k Yellow gold belt buckle, monogramed J.E.H.	35	00
	'Cartier' platinum case wrist watch with 14k and white gold band	200	00
	Longines white gold case wrist watch with metal band	15	00
	Vacheron & Constantin platinum case wrist watch with metal band	100	00
	Amount carried forward,	64,705	00

	$	
Litwin 14k Yellow gold case wrist watch, yellow gold band, case set with 76 diamonds	400	00
Litwin 14k yellow gold watch with silk band	100	00
Platinum case, longines pocket watch face set with Roman Numerals, diamond studded	350	00
Elgin yellow gold open face pocket watch	50	00
Elgin pocket watch with St. Christopher metal	20	00
Movado traveling watch	15	00
2 Leather watch bands and 1 metal watch band	10	00
1 White gold and three yellow gold watch chains and Pan-Am key chain	65	00
6 Pieces dress set, set with sapphire, three studs, 1 button, and cuff links	30	00
Lot of Italian cuff buttons	5	00
Mother of Pearl pocket knife and yellow gold maltese cross	25	00
Elephant hair sapphire ring	3	00
English wooden enamel ring and wooden ring	5	00
Three pair sterling silver cuff links, 1 pair Teak cuff links and 1 pair porcelain 'finger print' cuff links	40	00
2 Pair yellow gold cuff links, shaped initial J.E.H.	100	00
1 Pair yellow gold 'Peter Pan' cuff links	40	00
Pair of 14k Cartier cuff links, enamel decorated	50	00
Pair of Mother of Pearl and Shild cuff links	30	00
Pair of yellow gold cuff links, monogramed JEH	40	00
Pair of yellow gold cuff links each set with 12 diamonds, 10 points each	600	00
Pair of yellow gold enamel decorated cuff links	30	00
Pair of 14k white gold cuff links each set with 4 diamonds	150	00
Pair of sterling silver cuff links each set with turquoise	40	00
Tie slide enamel, Scotty dog	3	00
Yellow gold ring set with Moss Agate panel	10	00
Amount carried forward,	66,916	00

Large yellow gold ring set with green scarab	$ 50	00
Yellow gold ring set with small scarab	25	00
Friendship ring	15	00
Yellow gold ring set with onyx	25	00
4 yellow gold masonic rings, 1 set with small diamond	80	00
2 sterling silver rings, 1 set with turquoise 1 set with onyx and turquoise	40	00
Yellow gold ring inscribed JEH	50	00
Platinum ring set with star sapphire flanked by 6 diamonds	800	00
Platinum diamond ring set with medium round cut diamond and 2 sapphires, diamond 100 pts	600	00
Yellow gold ring set with medium round cut diamond, 50 points	200	00
Yellow gold Masonic ring, 33rd degree, set with 1 diamond, 50 points	400	00
Lucien Piccard 14kt white gold dress set consisting of cuff links and 3 studs	100	00
14kt yellow gold dress set, set with mother of pearl, 4 buttons, three studs and pair of cuff links	150	00
Pair of 14kt white gold cuff links set with Lynde star sapphire	75	00
Pair of 14kt yellow gold cuff links, monogramed "21"	20	00
2 yellow gold tie clips and yellow gold pen knife	25	00
Pro-football dress set	15	00
Yellow gold ring set with amethyst, surrounded by seed pearls	45	00
Cultured pearl necklace	75	00
Gilt metal necklace with 2 jade pendents	100	00
Yellow gold tie clip	5	00
Pair of fabric cuff links	10	00
Yellow gold chain and tie pin and gilt metal chain	20	00
Amount carried forward,	69,841	00

		$	
STOCKS— Wg	125 Shares, Common Stock, Allied Stores, Corp., Appraised at 35-7/8	4,484	38
Wg	220 Shares, Common Stock, American Electric Power Company, Inc., Appraised at 28-1/8	6,187	50
Wg	100 Shares, Common Stock, Altantic City Electric Company Appraised at 21-3/4	2,175	00
Wg	100 Shares, Common Stock, The Brooklyn Union Gas Company Appraised at 24½	2,450	00
Wg	100 Shares, Common Stock, Central Hudson Gas & Electric Corp., Appraised at 23-3/4	2,375	00
Wg	200 Shares, Common Stock, Central Illinois Light Company Appraised at 23-3/8	4,675	00
Wg	100 Shares, Common Stock, Central Maine Power Company Appraised at 17-1/8	1,712	50
Wg	100 Shares, Common Stock, The Cincinnati Gas & Electric Company Appraised at 23	2,300	00
Wg	100 Shares, Common Stock, Columbus & Southern Ohio Electric Company Appraised at 27-1/8	2,712	50
Wg	100 Shares, Common Stock, Consolidated Natural Gas Company Appraised at 28-7/8	2,887	50
Wg	100 Shares, Common Stock, Continental Mortgage Investors Appraised at 13-3/8	1,337	50
Wg	100 Shares, Common Stock, Creole Petroleum Corp., Appraised at 20-3/4	2,075	00
Wg	200 Shares, Common Stock, Crown Cork & Seal Co., Inc., Appraised at 21-½	4,300	00
Wg	320 Shares, Common Stock, General Public Utilities Corp., Appraised at 21¼	6,800	00
Wg	102 Shares, Common Stock, Howard Johnson Co., Appraised at 52-5/8	5,367	75
	Amount carried forward,	121,680	63

Wg	100 Shares, Common Stock, Inland Steel Co., Appraised at 34-7/8	3,487	50
Pg	1 Share, Common Stock, Dallas Uranium & Oil Corp., NOW:, International Airlines, Inc. Appraised at 11¢		11
Wg	50 Shares, Common Stock, Ford Motor Company, Appraised at 68-¼	3,412	50
Wg	111 Shares, Common Stock, Washington Gas-Light Company, Appraised at 22-3/8	2,483	63
Wg	100 Shares, Common Stock, The Washington Water Power Co., Appraised at 21-7/8	2,187	50
Wg	100 Shares, Common Stock, Wisconsin Public Service Corp., Appraised at 16-7/8	1,687	50
Wg	100 Shares, Common Stock, National Fuel Gas Co., Appraised at 25-5/8	2,562	50
Wg	300 Shares, Common Stock, New England Electric System, Appraised at 23-3/4	7,125	00
Wg	43 Shares, Series A $4.50 Preferred Stock, Newmont Mining Corp., Appraised at 111	4,773	00
Wg	100 Shares, Common Stock, Pacific Lighting Corp., Appraised at 24-1/2	2,450	00
Wg	100 Shares, Common Stock, Pennsylvania Power & Light Co., Appraised at 24-5/8	2,462	50
Wg	224 Shares, Common Stock, Philadelphia Electric Company, Appraised at 22-7/8	5,124	00
Wg	100 Shares, Common Stock, Public Service Electric & Gas Co., Appraised at 24-5/8	2,462	50
Wg	100 Shares, Common Stock, Southern California Water Co., Appraised at 14-3/4	1,475	00
Wg	53 Shares, Common Stock, Standard Oil of California, Appraised at 56-3/8	2,987	88
	100 Shares, Common Stock, General Motors Corporation, Appraised at 77.9375	7,793	75
	Amount carried forward,	174,155	50

		$	
Wg	52 Shares, Common Stock, Standard Oil of New Jersey, Appraised at 70	3,640	00
Wg	200 Shares, Common Stock, Telcom Inc., Appraised at 5-3/4	1,150	00
Wg	200 Shares, Common Stock, Texas Oil and Gas Corp., Appraised at 56	~~11,~~200	00
Wg	50 Shares, Common Stock, Union Pacific Corp., Appraised at 55-3/8	2,768	75
Wg	100 Shares, Common Stock, Utah-Idaho Sugar Co., Appraisedcat 13-5/8	1,362	50
Bonds Wg	3 $1,000 6-7/8% Registered Bonds, Loew's Theatres, Inc., Due 1993, Appraised at 86	2,580	00
Wg	$100 Registered Bond, Loew's Theatres, Inc., Appraised at 86	86	00
	TOTAL xxxxxxxxxxxxxxx	$196,942	75

RECAPITULATION

	Household effects,	59,780	00
	Jewelry,	7,928	00
	Stocks,	124,435	75
	Bonds,	2,666	00
	Books,	2,133	00
	Stock and fixtures,		
	Automobile,		
	Total,	$196,942	75

WITNESS our hands and seals this _____20th_____ day of _____July_____, A.D. 19 72

Thomas G. Meal (SEAL)

Barry Gagen (SEAL)

Appraisers.

DISTRICT OF COLUMBIA, *to wit:*

I, the undersigned, Clyde A. Tolson, Executor _____ xxx

of _____the estate of John Edgar Hoover, also known as J. Edgar_____, late of
Hoover
_____the District of Columbia_____, deceased,

do solemnly swear that the foregoing schedule is a true and perfect Inventory of the Goods, Chattels, and Personal Estate of said deceased, except money belonging to, and debts due, the deceased, that have come to _____my_____ hands or possession at the time of the making thereof, and that what hath since, or shall hereafter, come to _____my_____ hands or possession _____I_____ will return an additional inventory of; that _____I_____ know of no concealment of any part of the deceased's estate by any person whatsoever, and that if _____I_____ shall hereafter discover any concealment, or suspect any to be, _____I_____ will acquaint the Court with the same.

Clyde A. Tolson

Sworn to and subscribed before me this _____ day of _____ July _____, A.D. 19 ...

Elizabeth S. Willingham

Register of Wills for the District of Columbia,
Clerk of the Probate Court.

NOTARY PUBLIC, D. C.

My Commission Expires Feb. 28, 1973

Form No. 57

No. 967-72

United States District Court for the District of Columbia

RE-APPRAISAL

DOCKET:

We, The undersigned, appointed by the said Court to examine and appraise the personal estate

of _____ John Edgar Hoover, etc. _____

late of _____ The District of Columbia _____, deceased,

do hereby certify that the following schedule is a true and correct appraisement of said estate in so

far as it has come to our knowledge, a return of which we have made to the Court of even date

herewith:

			$	
Wg	NOTE; Item number 3 on page 52 of original appraisal reads as follows;			
	200 Shares, Common Stock, Texas Oil and Gas Corp., Appraised at 56	11,200.00		
Wg	CORRECTION; Do to a stock split which did not belong as date of death, the above should read as follows;			
	100 Shares, Common Stock, Texas Oil and Gas Corp., Appraised at 56		5,600	00
	Original Total	$196,942.75		
	Corrected	$191,342.75		
	AMOUNT CARRIED FORWARD,			

RECAPITULATION

	Household effects,	$59,780	00
	Jewelry,	7,928	00
	Stocks,	118,835	75
	Bonds,	2,666	00
	Books,	2,133	00
	Stock and fixtures,		
	Automobile,		
	Total,	$191,342	75

WITNESS our hands and seals this ___24th___ day of ___August___ A.D. 19 72

(signature) (SEAL)

(signature) (SEAL)

Appraisers.

DISTRICT OF COLUMBIA, *to wit:*

_____ and

_____

of _____, late of

_____, deceased,

do solemnly swear that the foregoing schedule is a true and perfect Inventory of the Goods, Chattels, and Personal Estate of said deceased, except money belonging to, and debts due, the deceased, that have come to _____ hands or possession at the time of the making thereof, and that what hath since, or shall hereafter, come to _____ hands or possession _____ will return an additional inventory of; that _____ know of no concealment of any part of the deceased's estate by any person whatsoever, and that if _____ shall hereafter discover any concealment, or suspect any to be, _____ will acquaint the Court with the same.

_____

_____

Sworn to and subscribed before me this _____ day of _____, A.D. 19___

_____
Register of Wills for the District of Columbia,
Clerk of the Probate Court,

Form No. 57

No. 967-72

United States District Court for the District of Columbia

HOLDING PROBATE COURT

A D D I T I O N A L

We, The undersigned, appointed by the said Court to examine and appraise the personal estate

of _____ John Edgar Hoover, etc. _____

late of _____ the District of Columbia _____, deceased,

do hereby certify that the following schedule is a true and correct appraisement of said estate in so

far as it has come to our knowledge, a return of which we have made to the Court of even date

herewith:

		$	
Riggs Bank			
JEWELRY-	Platinum ring set with sapphire and 6 rose cut diamonds	400	00
	Pair of platinum star sapphire cuff links	400	00
511 R.I. Ave Northeast	Teak Bokhara oriental rug	150	00
	Small oriental mat	80	00
	Oriental rug, 9'x12'	500	00
STOCKS	2,000 Shares, Trustee Certificate Little Tavern, Inc., Appraised at lot (Letter)	24,000	00
	-1- TOTAL Amount carried forward,	$25,530	00

RECAPITULATION

Household effects,	$ 730	00
Jewelry,	800	00
Stocks,	24,000	00
Bonds,		
Books,		
Stock and fixtures,		
Automobile,		
Total	$25,530	00

WITNESS our hands and seals this ____14th____ day of ____September____ A.D. 19_72_

Thomas A. Mead (SEAL)

Larry J. Lyon (SEAL)
Appraisers.

DISTRICT OF COLUMBIA, *to wit:*

____I, the undersigned, Clyde A. Tolson____ XXXXXXXXXXXXXXXXXX and

Bank, Exeuctor of the estate

of ____John Edgar Hoover, etc.,____ , late of

____the District of Columbia____ , deceased,

do solemnly swear that the foregoing schedule is a true and perfect Inventory of the Goods, Chattels, and Personal Estate of said deceased, except money belonging to, and debts due, the deceased, that have come to ___its___ hands or possession at the time of the making thereof, and that what hath since, or shall hereafter, come to ___its___ hands or possession ___it___ will return an additional inventory of; that ___it___ know of no concealment of any part of the deceased's estate by any person whatsoever, and that if ___it___ shall hereafter discover any concealment, or suspect any to be, ___it___ will acquaint the Court with the same.

Clyde A. Tolson
Clyde A. Tolson

Sworn to and subscribed before me this __20__ day of _Sept._ , A.D. 19_72_

Elizabeth D. Williamson
Register of Wills for the District of Columbia,
Clerk of the Probate Court.

NOTARY PUBLIC, D. C.

My Commission Expires Feb. 23, 1973

Administration No. ___967-72___

United States District Court for the District of Columbia

INVENTORY OF MONEY AND DEBTS DUE TO DECEASED

Cash on deposit:		
The Riggs National Bank of Washington, D. C.		
Checking a/c #10-03-246-292	$ 7,289	86
American Federal Savings & Loan Assn.		
Savings a/c #1-002990-2	8,854	52
Certificates of deposits:		
#1-600594-0 6% dated 3/2/70	28,154	33
#1-600594-0 6% dated 4/21/70	31,000	00
#1-602413-9 6% dated 4/24/72	10,601	31
U. S. Civil Service Commission		
Terminal Leave	16,507	44
Accrued Salary to 5/2/72	1,791	39
Contributions to retirement plan	59,147	11
Federal Employees Group Life Insurance		
Proceeds of group policy #17000G	45,000	00
Miscellaneous:		
B. Altman & Co., refund of credit balance	3	70
Hat Corporation of America, refund of credit balance	54	00
J. H. Small & Sons, refund of credit balance	59	22
The Wayside Gardens Co., refund of credit balance	2	72
Aetna Life Insurance Co., refund auto insurance	52	00
Allen Oil Company - Director's fee 5/1/72	100	00
Cash found among effects	297	94
	$208,915	54

DOCKETED

FILED

AUG 13 1972

PETER J. McLAUGHLIN
REGISTER OF WILLS D. C.
Clerk of Probate Court

DISTRICT OF COLUMBIA, to wit:

I, Clyde A. Tolson ~~and~~

Executor of the estate

of John Edgar Hoover A/K/A J. Edgar Hoover ___ late of

the District of Columbia ___, deceased,

do solemnly swear that the foregoing schedule is a true and perfect inventory of all the MONEY belonging to the deceased, and of all the DEBTS due the said deceased, which have come to ___my___ hands or knowledge and that ___I___ will well and truly charge ___myself___ with all money and all and every such debt or debts as shall hereafter come to ___my___ knowledge or possession.

Clyde A. Tolson

Sworn to and subscribed before me this ___11___ day of ___Aug___ A. D. 19 72

Elizabeth S. Williamson

Register of Wills for the District of Columbia.
Notary Public   Clerk of the Probate Court

My Commission Expires Feb. 28, 1973

INDEX

Adams, Sherman, 143n, 148–49
Agnew, Spiro, 258, 280
Air Force: Intelligence, 311; Office of Special Investigations, 311
Air Force One, 21
Air Force Two, 203
Alcohol Tax Bureau, 146
Alexander, Jack, 4, 60, 72
Ali, Muhammad, 205
Allen, George E., 10–11, 16, 21, 25, 28–31, 35, 107, 110, 161
Amerasia case, 125
American Bar Association, 25, 100, 131, 178
American Broadcasting Co. (ABC), 65
American Civil Liberties Union (ACLU), 204, 205, 291
American Heart Association, 87
American Jewish League Against Communism, 98
American Legion, 95, 96, 215
American Liberty League, 95
American Medical Association, 179
American Nazi Party, 313
Americans for Democratic Action, 114
Anderson, Jack, 13, 15, 193–94, 222
Andretta, Salvatore, 130, 134, 135
Anslinger, Harry, 138
Anson, George, 14
Apalachin, N.Y., 137, 138, 140, 145, 199, 200
Army: Department, 28, 115, 304; Engineers, 120; Intelligence, 311
Army-McCarthy hearings, 160
Atlanta *Constitution*, 193
Attorney General, 91, 104–5, 113, 119–49 passim, 175–204 passim, 221–31 passim, 238, 239, 249, 266, 276–77, 305, 306, 316, 318

Baker, Bobby, 188
Barbara, Joe, 137n
Barker, Ma, 53, 81
Barkley, Alben, 118
Barnett, Ross, 169
Barrow, Clyde, 53
Baughman, Frank, 7, 9–10
Baumgartner, Lady, 131
Bay of Pigs operation, 179
Beck, Dave, 173
Beecher, William, 246–47, 248
Belding, Don, 94
Belmont, Al, 84, 85
Bennett, Dave, 110
Bennett, Donald V., 285, 287, 289, 302
Bentley, Elizabeth, 115
Bernstein, Carl, 262
Berrigan, Daniel J., 128n, 210, 232, 234, 235
Berrigan, Philip F., 128n, 210, 232, 234, 235, 313
Biddle, Francis, 105, 121–33 passim, 149
Big Frenchy, 25
Billingsley, Sherman, 24
Binion, Benny, 145
Birdman of Alcatraz, 6
Bishop, Jim, 14
Bishop, Thomas, 167, 196, 246
Black Panther Party, 126, 127, 225, 284, 314–19 passim
Bloch, Emanuel, 156
Boardman, Lee, 85
Bogalusa, Miss., 202
Boggs, Hale, 166–67, 313, 318
Bolshevism, 51
Bowie, Md., 22, 24; race track, 35
Boyle, Bill, 112
Bradlee, Benjamin, 193
Brady, Tom P., 95

Brandon, Henry, 248
Bremer kidnaping case, 69
Brennan, Charles, 252, 308
Brewster, Kingman, 196
Brinkman, Jesse, 18
Brookings Institution, 293
Brown, Sam, 292
Brownell, Herbert, 108, 131, 136, 144, 147, 192
Brownell, Mrs. Herbert, 131
Buchanan, Patrick, 257-58
Bureau of the Budget, 113
Bureau of Investigation, 51, 52
Burger, Warren, 148
Burlingham, Bo, 286n
Byars, B. B. (Billy), 11, 14
Byrd, Robert, 317
Byrne, Matthew, 272, 274

Cabinet, 91, 105
Cain, Effie, 15
Cain, Wofford, 15
Callahan, Nicholas P., 214
Callaway, Howard (Bo), 95
Calomaris, Anthony, 39-48
Cardinal Spellman Trust Foundation, 98
Carusi, Ugo, 54-59
Caulfield, John, 249, 293, 321
Celler, Emanuel, 22, 48, 98, 164-66
Census Bureau, 120
Center, Tex., 89
Central Intelligence Agency (CIA), 104, 260, 284-92 passim, 304, 311
Chambers, Whittaker, 115
Chappaquiddick case, 21, 249
Charlestown race track, 35
Chennault, Anna, 258, 280
Cheshire, Maxine, 96-97
Chicago, Ill., 70, 110, 140, 142, 152, 222
Chicago Tribune, 276
Choate School, 172
Christian Anti-Communist Crusade, 95
Civil Code, 130
Civil Rights Act (1964), 205, 206
Civil Service, 58, 61, 198
Civil Service Commission, 115, 135
Clark, Ramsey, 48, 105, 119, 126-27, 129, 135-36, 157, 188, 208-9, 215, 221-29, 276, 306, 316
Clark, Tom C., 48, 104-5, 119-36 passim, 157, 186, 188

Clawson, Kenneth W., 48, 208-13, 220
Clay, Henry, 28
Clay, Shorty, 18, 23
Clifford, Clark, 107, 113-14
Coast and Geodetic Survey, 3
Cobb, Ty, 170
Cohn, Roy, 17, 48, 97, 98, 154-58, 159-62
Cointelpro, 310, 313-20
Colby, William, 311-12
Cold War, 116
Collier, Rex, 63, 64
Collins, Patricia, 48, 130-37, 148
Colson, Charles, 293
Commager, Henry Steele, 75
Communist Party, 17, 51, 52, 62, 85, 87, 114, 116, 119, 125, 137, 138, 142, 154-65 passim, 186, 187, 196, 213, 225, 277, 303, 313-19 passim
Condon, John F., 60
Congress, 55, 56, 58, 82, 112-27 passim, 151, 152, 153, 163, 164, 166, 168, 178, 183, 199-205 passim, 230, 239, 240, 246, 272, 317, 321, 322
Congress on Racial Equality, 314
Connally, Tom, 105
Connelly, Matt, 102
Cooke, Charles M., 296
Coolidge, Calvin, 52, 54
Cooper, Courtney Ryley, 65
Coplon, Judith, 115, 125
Corcoran, Thomas (Tommy the Cork), 106
Corcoran, Mrs. Thomas, 106
Costello, Frank, 25, 107, 108, 145
Coughlin, Father, 165
Counter Intelligence Corps (CIC), 113
Cowley, Samuel, 69, 71, 72
Coyne, Patrick, 257, 258, 279
Crawford, Dorothea, 32-39 passim
Crawford, James E., 32-46 passim, 92
Criminal Code, 130
Cromie, Robert, 70
Crosby, Bing, 12, 15
Crowley, Edward J., 14-16
Crusaders, 95
Cuba, 178, 181, 284
Cummings, Homer, 55, 56, 123, 130, 132
Customs Service, 60, 146, 311

Daily Worker, 317
Damon Runyon Fund, 87

Daugherty, Harry M., 52
Daughters of the American Revolution, 95
Davidson, Daniel I., 248
Dean, John, 253–63 passim, 273–83 passim, 290, 291, 292, 294, 303, 322
Defense Department, 160, 247, 274
Defense Intelligence Agency (DIA), 285–90 passim, 311
Dellinger, David, 292
Del Mar race track, 13, 16
Del Mar Turf Club, 16, 31
DeLoach, Cartha (Deke), 31, 68, 94, 141, 188–94 passim, 202, 212, 214–15, 223, 224, 225, 246, 257–64 passim, 280
Democratic National Committee, 245, 277
Dennis, Eugene, 124–25, 137
Devine, James, 291
Dewey, Thomas, 145
DeWitt, John L., 119–20
Dies, Martin, 117
Dillinger, John, 53, 54, 56, 69–72, 79, 81, 207, 226
Dillon, C. Douglas, 189
Douglas, Boyd F. Jr., 235
Dulles, Allen, 169, 175
Duncan, Harry, 22, 35
Dunne, Irene, 21
Dyer Act, 53, 127, 240

Eastland, James, 261, 317
Ehrlichman, John, 250–56 passim, 274–87 passim, 293–301 passim
Eisenhower, Dwight D., 11, 43, 62, 111, 143n, 148, 149, 152, 156, 169, 178, 180, 216, 260, 323
Eisenhower, Milton, 120
Ellsberg, Daniel, 92, 220, 250, 253, 256, 266–75 passim, 293–98 passim, 309, 310–11
Emergency Detention Act (1950), 269
Emerson, Ralph Waldo, 78
Employee Loyalty Program, 115
Enemies List (Nixon's), 81
Engels, Friedrich, 51
Ervin, Sam, 258, 284, 317
Evans, Courtney, 139, 142, 174, 175, 179–88 passim, 212

Federal Bureau of Investigation (FBI): Academy, see Quantico, Va.; and CIA, 290, 311; and civil rights, 202–3, 205–7; Crime Records Division, 63, 87, 189, 198, 202; Domestic Intelligence Division, 87, 91, 198, 214, 264, 268, 269, 308, 310, 317; Electronic Surveillance Indices, 266; and espionage, 61, 112, 114; field offices, 71, 82, 84, 98, 253, 257, 275, 309; integrating, 38, 187, 205; and Justice Department, 132; and narcotics, 301–2; No Contact List, 81; and organized crime, 138–40, 145–47, 181–82, 199–200, 208, 223; other divisions, 64, 65, 198, 200; publicity for, 63–68, 87; and radicals, 284, 288, 292; and Secret Service, 60–62, 179, 290; and wiretapping, 106, 140–41 passim, 166, 222–23, 248–67 passim, 275–83 passim
Federal Record Center, 168
Felt, Audrey, 263
Felt, W. Mark, 48, 214, 217–18, 250–68 passim, 300, 301–3
Fennell, Margaret (niece), 5–9, 23
Ferguson, Homer, 118
Fielding, Lewis, 273, 294, 295, 296, 300
Fields, Annie, 32, 37, 41–42, 47
Finch, Robert, 251, 287, 292
Floyd, Pretty Boy, 53, 54
Fogelson, Buddy, 14
Fonda, Jane, 270
Forand Bill, 89
Ford, Henry, 165
Foreign Intelligence Advisory Board, 279
Forrestal, James V., 169
Fortas, Abe, 257, 261, 280
Fort Monmouth case, 160
Freedom of Information Act, 310n, 317
Freedoms Center, 96
Freedoms Foundation, 90, 94, 96, 99, 100
Fund for Public Education, 100

Gale, James, 80, 200
Gandy, Helen, 26, 73–74, 85, 91–92, 323
Garson, Greer, 14
Gayler, Noel, 285, 287, 289, 302
General Intelligence Division, 51, 57
George Washington Award, 90, 94
Gestapo, 166, 322

Goldberg, Arthur, 181
Goldfine, Bernard, 139, 143
Goldwater, Barry, 230, 251, 258, 281
Golos, Jacob, 115
Goodwin, Guy, 251
Gordon, Maxie, 25
Goulden, Joseph C., 95, 96
Gouzenko, Igor, 115
Graham, Wallace, 107
Grand Bahama Island, 14
Gray, L. Patrick, 239, 253–63 passim, 279
Griswold, Erwin, 274
Gross, H. R., 141
Gurney, Edward, 261
Guthman, Ed, 201

Hadnott vs. Amos, 205
Haig, Alexander, 249, 252, 254, 265, 278
Haldeman, H. R., 252, 274–91 passim, 301
Halperin, Morton H., 248, 250, 253, 258, 266, 273, 275, 293, 298
Hamilton, Polly, 70
Harding, Warren G., 52, 61
Hargis, Billy, 95
Harney, Malachi, 59–62
Harriman, W. Averell, 169
Harrington, Don, 14
Harris, Phil, 15
Harrisburg case, 128
Harvard University, 172, 247, 248, 249, 278
Harwood, Richard, 191
Hauptmann, Bruno Richard, 59–60
Havre de Grace race track, 35
Hays Office, 29
Health, Education and Welfare Department, 251, 311
Heller, Walter, 181
Hellis, William, 23
Helms, Richard, 285, 287, 289, 302, 311
Heymsfeld, Ralph, 89
Himmler, Heinrich, 293
Hiss, Alger, 116, 155
Hitler, Adolf, 165, 166
Hitz, John (great-uncle), 3
Hoffa, James, 173, 315n
Hogan, Frank, 153
Hogan, Lawrence J., 167–68
Holley, William, 17, 22

Hook, Charles R., 95
Hoover, Annie M. S. (mother), 3, 4, 5–6, 8
Hoover, Dickerson N. (father), 3, 8
Hoover, Dickerson N. Jr. (brother), 3, 4, 5, 8
Hoover, Herbert, 111, 323
Hoover, J. Edgar: and anti-Communism, 116, 118, 123–24, 137, 153, 164, 225; and Attorneys General, 130–37; birth, 3; business ambitions, 28–29; and civil rights, 202–3, 204–6; and Congress, 55, 56–57, 61; and criticism, 11; death, 32; and discipline, 57, 125, 197–98, 218; and domestic intelligence, 287–90, 302–7, 310–20; early years with Justice Department, 51–53, 54–55; and freeloading, 13–19; and homosexuality, 30, 90, 106–7; and horse racing, 17, 35; inventory, appraisal and re-appraisal of estate, 331–87; last will and testament, 327; money and debts due to, 388; and mother, 5–6; and narcotics, 301–2; and organized crime, 138–40, 145–47, 181, 199–200, 221; pets, 6, 34–35, 45, 46; and politics, 28–29, 153, 238; power of, 93–94; as practical joker, 22–25; and the press, 11, 189; and publicity, 63–68; and radicals, 126–27, 225–26, 241, 285, 287–91, 308, 313–17; retirement, 173, 181, 186; schooling, 3–4; and secret files, 57, 82, 104, 123, 149, 152–53, 164, 256; and Secret Service, 62–63; senility, 209–10, 218, 219, 220, 237; swearing, 85–86; vacations, 11–18 passim; and Watergate, 245–48; and wiretapping, 140–43, 146–47, 166, 184–85, 192–93, 249, 253–55, 265, 271, 276, 279–80, 318–19; and women, 8, 25
Hoover, Lillian (sister), 3, 9
Hoover Foundation, 88, 90, 95–97, 100
Hoover Library on Communism and Totalitarianism, 96, 99
Horan, Mike, 113
House: Appropriations Committee, 164, 323; Civil Service Committee, 115; Judiciary Committee, 164, 245, 247n, 256n, 317; Un-American Activities Committee, 114, 115–16, 117
Howard, Bill, 11–12, 18, 24–25, 26

Hruska, Roman, 261, 317
Hughes, Howard, 29
Humphrey, George, 16, 62
Hundley, William, 48, 137–43, 145, 146, 157
Hunt, E. Howard, 272, 293, 294, 295, 296
Huston, Tom Charles, 48, 245, 256, 259, 278–92 passim, 299–320 passim
Hutchins, Robert Maynard, 75
Hutchinson, Edward, 317
Hutton, Edward F., 95

Immigration Bureau, 138, 148, 311
Inouye, Daniel, 294
Internal Revenue Service (IRS), 58, 60, 111, 137, 196
Irey, Elmer L., 59, 60, 61

Jackson, Robert H., 132
James, Jesse, 112, 207
Japanese-American internment, 119–22, 133
Jenkins, Walter, 187–88, 257, 261, 280
John Birch Society, 74, 95
Johnson, Lyndon B., 43, 104, 123, 136, 149, 166, 178–89, 202, 203, 212, 215, 226, 255–62 passim, 279–80, 281, 319, 321, 323
Jones, W. Alton, 11
Justice Department, 51, 54, 62, 64, 78, 86, 112, 115, 119, 130–57 passim, 178, 189, 199, 201, 208, 215, 221, 222, 224–60 passim, 266, 272, 276, 278, 286, 290, 291, 292, 299, 307, 315n, 316; Criminal Division, 122, 133, 233, 272, 273, 319; Internal Security Division, 137, 141, 251, 255, 271, 272, 292, 299; Office of National Narcotics Intelligence (ONNI), 254n, 260, 278, 282; Organized Crime Division, 137, 138, 139, 145, 221, 233; other divisions, 119, 122, 148, 228, 255

Kalb, Marvin, 248
Karpis, Alvin, 53, 69, 81
Kastenmeier, Robert W., 322
Katzenbach, Nicholas, 188, 215, 276, 316
Kaufman, Irving, 156

Kefauver, Estes, 138, 145
Keith decision, 248, 270–71
Kelley, Clarence M., 253n, 316, 320, 321
Kelly, Machine Gun, 53, 54, 69
Kendall, Donald, 188, 281
Kennedy, Edward, 249
Kennedy, Ethel, 134, 135
Kennedy, Jacqueline, 135, 171, 193
Kennedy, John F., 43, 140, 141, 143, 168–87, 192, 193, 205, 214, 247, 248, 249, 261, 276, 277–78, 280, 281–82, 315n, 323
Kennedy, Patrick B., 171
Kennedy, Robert F., 108, 130–43 passim, 166–77 passim, 186–212 passim, 221–24, 229, 257, 261, 276, 279–80
Kennedy family, 22, 212, 249
Keogh case, 139
Kerr, Robert, 178
Khrushchev, Nikita, 76
Kienast, Anna (niece), 5–9
Kilpatrick, John, 196
King, Barbara, 19
King, Coretta, 194
King, Donald E., 19
King, Leslie, 19
King, Martin Luther Jr., 183, 190–95, 205, 206, 223, 224, 225, 227, 261, 314, 315n
Kissinger, Henry, 128n, 210, 233, 234, 246–57 passim, 265, 267, 278, 279, 293, 298, 301, 313
Klein, Herb, 14
Kleindienst, Richard, 48, 230–35, 236–38, 256–74 passim, 283, 292–93, 296, 316
Kopechne, Mary Jo, 249
Korean War, 89
Kraft, Joseph, 249
Kramer, Fritz, 278
Krogh, Egil Jr., 256, 278, 281, 284, 293–94, 295, 296, 301
Ku Klux Klan, 313, 318, 319–20

Ladd, D. Milton (Mickey), 65, 91
Lait, Jack, 107
La Jolla, Cal., 11, 13, 15, 17, 26, 29
Lake, Anthony, 248, 250, 258
Lamour, Dorothy, 11, 12
Lansky, Meyer, 97
Laurel, Md., 8; race track, 35, 126

Law Enforcement Assistance Administration, 291
Lawrence, Bill, 176
Lea, Doug, 48, 291–93
Leahy, W. D., 107
Lehman, Herbert, 156
Leinbaugh, Harold, 208, 213
Lenin, V. I., 52
LeRoy, Kitty, 21
LeRoy, Mervyn, 10, 21–22, 27, 29, 67–68
Lester, Louise, 12
Levi, Edward H., 317
Library of Congress, 4
Liddy, G. Gordon, 245, 272, 293, 294, 295, 296, 310
Life magazine, 13, 80
Lincoln, Abraham, 43, 60
Lincoln, Evelyn, 180
Lincoln, Todd, 43
Lindbergh, Charles A., 60
Lindbergh, Charles A. Jr., 60
Lindbergh kidnaping case, 53, 55, 59–60
Lindbergh Law, 53
Little Augie, 25
Loftus, Matt, 172
London Sunday Times, 248
Lord, Winston, 248
Los Angeles, Cal., 12, 15, 92, 121, 273
Los Angeles Times, 13, 313
Lucas, Scott, 118
Lulley, Birdie, 24
Lulley, Julius, 17–18, 23, 24, 36
Lynch, William S., 233

McAlister, Elizabeth, 233, 235
McCarran, Pat, 118
McCarran Internal Security Act, 114, 117, 118
McCarthy, Jeannie, 161
McCarthy, Joseph, 17, 101, 108, 109, 114, 125, 142, 154–65 passim, 251, 276
McClellan, John, 142
McClellan Committee, 139, 173, 174
McCone, John, 169
McCormack, John, 118
McGee, Gale W., 322
McGovern, George, 80
McNamara, Robert, 169, 171, 180, 247, 293, 295

Madden, Owney, 24–25
Maddox, Lester, 95
Mafia, 25, 137, 138, 145, 200, 207, 317
Manion, Clarence A., 95
Manion Forum, 95
Mardian, Robert, 216, 230, 251–56 passim, 265–83 passim, 292–93, 298, 299, 309, 322
Maroney, Kevin, 251, 273, 275
Marshall, Burke, 192, 201
Marshall, Thurgood, 105, 189
Marshall Plan, 116
Martin, John, 273
Marx, Karl, 51
Marx, Louis, 92, 294, 297, 308, 309
Mason, Alpheus T., 52
Mayo Clinic, 27
Mental Retardation Bill (1963), 169
Meredith, James, 169
Merrill, Dory, 15
Messick, Hank, 97, 158
Miami, Fla., 17, 21, 92, 172, 179
Miller, Merle, 101, 105, 106
Mintener, Bradshaw, 117
Minutemen, 313
Missouri National Guard, 101
Mitchell, John N., 136, 209, 229–36 passim, 245–55 passim, 263, 269, 271, 280–308 passim, 316
Mitchell, Martha, 286
Mohr, John P., 30, 48, 83–84, 162, 163–64, 194, 214, 216–17, 218–19, 250, 256, 267–69, 300–1, 303–4, 317–18, 319
Monroe, Marilyn, 43
Morgan, Charles Jr., 204–8
Morgenthau, Henry, 121, 123
Morgenthau, Robert, 155, 158, 159
Mortimer, Lee, 107
Moyers, Bill, 203
Mundt, Karl, 108, 118
Mundt-Nixon Bill, 114, 117–18
Murchison, Clint, 13–17 passim, 88
Murphy, Charlie, 114
Murphy, Frank, 25, 123, 129, 131
Murtagh, Arthur, 315n
Muskie, Edmund, 250

Narcotics Bureau, 138, 139, 302
National Association for the Advancement of Colored People (NAACP), 38, 113

National College of Defense Lawyers, 100
National College of District Attorneys, 100
National Security Agency (NSA), 285–92 passim, 304, 311
National Security Council, 160, 180, 246, 247, 248, 250, 258
National States Rights Party, 313
Nation of Islam, 314
Navy Department, 115
Nelson, Baby Face, 53, 54, 71
New Deal, 95
New Jersey State Police, 59
New Left, 126, 241, 284, 288, 314, 315
Newsweek magazine, 292, 321
New York, N.Y., 92, 108, 137–45 passim, 152, 153, 158, 159, 160, 161, 210, 222, 285, 317
New York City Police, 59
New Yorker, 4, 60, 72
New York Herald Tribune, 66
New York Joint Legislative Committee on Crime, 89
New York Times, 176, 194, 246, 248, 263, 276, 293, 310, 311, 313, 315n; Magazine, 157
Nichols, Louis B., 10, 63–73 passim, 87–101 passim, 158–59, 189–90
Nissen, David R., 271, 274
Nixon, Donald, 250
Nixon, Richard M., 14, 21, 43, 47–48, 81, 93, 108, 116, 117, 118, 188, 208, 215, 230, 231, 238, 245–55 passim, 267–310 passim, 320, 321–22, 323
Nixon Library, 280
NKVD, 115
Nobel Peace Prize, 190, 195, 206, 315n
Noisette, Sam, 28, 33, 36, 92, 103
Novello, Angie, 134

Oakland (Cal.) Police Department, 314
Oberdorfer, Louis, 133, 201
O'Brien, John Lord, 51
O'Donnell, Kenneth, 48, 168, 170, 173–89
Office of Naval Intelligence, 311
Olney, Warren III, 145
Olson, Culbert L., 122
Olson, William, 271
Omnibus Crime Bill (1961), 199

Orangeburg massacre, 223
Oswald, Lee Harvey, 276

Palmer, A. Mitchell, 51, 52, 57, 163, 308
Parker, Mack Charles, 202
Parsons, Louella, 11–12
Pastore, John Q., 322
Patterson, Gene, 193
Patton, Mrs. James B., 95
Penn, Lemuel, 202
Pentagon, 28, 246, 284, 293; Intelligence Service, 292; Papers, 220, 250, 256, 293, 295
Perez case, 160
Petersen, Henry, 272, 273, 275, 317
Peterson, 174
Pew, Mrs. J. Howard, 95
Phillips, Kevin, 257
Pimlico race track, 35
Pinkston, Joseph, 70
Plumbers, White House, 160, 245, 250, 256, 290–300 passim, 310
Pollack, Milton, 158
Post Office Department, 311
Potsdam Conference, 110
Powell, Lucien, 46
Powers, Dave, 48, 168–73, 175
President, 91, 248–49
President's Temporary Commission on Employee Loyalty, 115
Prisons Bureau, 148
Progressive Labor Party, 314
Prohibition, 24
Pulitzer Prize, 66
Purvis, Melvin, 56, 69, 70, 71–72, 80–81

Quantico, Va. (FBI Academy), 38, 75, 83–84, 100, 148

Ramparts magazine, 13
Ray, James Earl, 223, 224
Rayburn, Sam, 28, 105, 118
Reconstruction Finance Corp., 11, 107
Rehnquist, William, 269
Reis, Harold, 133
Remington, William, 155
Revolutionary Action Movement, 314
Reynolds vs. Sims, 205
Ribicoff, Abraham, 176
Richardson, Elliot, 265

Richardson, Sid, 14, 16
Robinette, Fred (nephew), 9
Robinette, Marjorie (niece), 9
Rockefeller, Nelson, 254, 257, 279
Rodino, Peter, 317
Rogers, William P., 21, 48, 108, 131, 139, 140, 144–54, 200, 316
Rooney, John, 163, 164, 323
Roosevelt, Franklin D., 11, 55, 59, 95, 106, 122, 123–24, 132, 156, 180, 192, 248, 323
Roosevelt, Theodore, 61
Rosen, Alex, 214
Rosenberg, Julius and Ethel, 155, 156–57, 165
Rosenstiel, Lewis, 65, 89–99 passim
Royal Canadian Mounted Police, 247
Ruckelshaus, William, 265, 320
Rusk, Dean, 169, 171, 180

Sage, Anna, 70, 71
Salinger, Pierre, 175
SALT talks, 250
Samish, Artie, 145
San Diego Evening Tribune, 161n
San Francisco Police Department, 314
Sawyer, W. C. (Tom), 90, 95
Saxbe, William B., 238–41, 310n, 313–18 passim
Schine, G. David, 17, 154
Schlesinger, Arthur, 175
Schneir, Walter and Miriam, 156
Schorr, Daniel, 210
Scotland Yard, 151, 224
Scott, Hugh, 265
Scripps Clinic and Research Foundation (Cal.), 14, 101
Secret Service, 54–63 passim, 112, 114, 169, 174, 175, 180, 250, 290, 293n
Sedition Act, 52
Senate: Appropriations Committee, 178; Armed Services Committee, 290; Foreign Relations Committee, 249; Judiciary Committee, 230, 261, 262, 282; Oversight Committee, 317; Permanent Investigations Subcommittee, 155; Public Works Committee, 178; Watergate Committee, 250, 253, 258, 273, 283, 287, 290, 294, 303
Sessions, Cliff, 201
Shaw, Jack, 210, 220
Sihanouk, Norodom, 246

Silvermaster, Nathan Gregory, 115
Simon, William G., 98
Smathers, George, 178
Smith, Don, 12–13, 16–17, 26–27
Smith, Hedrick, 248
Smith, Howland (Howling Mad), 17
Smith, Margaret Chase, 108
Smith, Worthington, 33, 36
Smith Act, 137
Smithsonian Institution, 110
Snyder, John, 110
Sobell, Morton, 156
Sobeloff, Irene, 136
Sobeloff, Simon, 136, 148
Socialist Workers Party, 313
Sokolsky, George, 98
Sonnenfeldt, Helmut, 248
Sontag, Susan, 292
Sorensen, Theodore, 175
Southern Christian Leadership Conference, 192, 313–14, 315n
Soviet Union, 114–15, 157, 166, 178, 203, 222, 250, 307
Spencer, Charles, 31–32
Spingarn, Stephen, 48, 112–19 passim
Stalin, Joseph, 116
State Department, 115, 123, 135, 162–63, 188, 311
Steamboat Inspection Service, 3
Stern, Carl, 317
Stewart, Jimmy, 20, 27, 67
Stone, Harlan F., 52, 55, 125, 129, 221
Strategic Air Command (SAC), 219
Strider, Jesse, 12
Student Nonviolent Coordinating Committee, 314
Students for a Democratic Society (SDS), 303, 307–8, 314
Stukenbroeker, Fern, 87, 88
Stump, Felix B., 95
Subversive Activities Control Board, 117
Sullivan, Joe, 202
Sullivan, William C., 30, 31, 48, 74–94 passim, 99, 100, 162–63, 194–220 passim, 229–30, 235–36, 246–90 passim, 298–322 passim
Supreme Court, 95, 105, 119, 123, 124, 131, 132, 137, 205, 248, 269, 319

Tamn, Quinn, 212
Tax Reform Act (1969), 96, 100
Taylor, Maxwell, 169

Temple, Shirley, 46, 76
Thomas, J. Parnell, 117
Thompson, Robert, 14
Time magazine, 195n, 251, 253, 254, 255, 260, 271, 292, 321
Tolson, Clyde A., 9–44 passim, 64, 65, 67–68, 77–92 passim, 100, 101, 103, 126, 149, 161, 196, 197, 198, 202, 211, 214, 218, 228–29, 246, 250, 253n, 264, 268, 321, 322; petition of, 328–32
Treasury agents, 59, 60
Treasury Department, 61, 62, 112, 113, 115, 146, 160
Trotsky, Leon, 52
Truman, Bess, 109–10, 111
Truman, Harry S, 11, 101–19 passim, 132, 148, 156, 248, 281, 323
Truman, Margaret, 109
Truman Committee, 102

Ulasewicz, Tony, 293, 321
United Nations, 155
U.S. Information Agency, 311
U.S. News and World Report, 119

Valachi, Joseph, 138–39
Vaughan, Harry, 23–24, 48, 101–12, 281
Vietnam, 169, 214–15, 220, 226, 246, 247, 260, 284, 293
Viner, Harry, 22
Viner, Rae, 22
Vinson, Fred, 107, 110
Voorhis, Jerry, 117

Wall Street Journal, 14
Walsh, Eugene, 214
War Emergency Division, 51
Warner, Jack, 67
War Relocation Authority, 120
Warren, Earl, 122
Warren Commission, 276
Washington, D.C., 15, 28, 29, 32, 47, 52, 67, 92, 98–109 passim, 140, 151, 154–55, 173, 176, 196, 224, 225, 233, 236, 248, 251, 269, 270, 277, 278, 283, 293, 307, 314
Washingtonian magazine, 263
Washington *Post,* 169, 192, 193, 208, 213, 221, 262, 263, 281n
Washington *Star,* 64, 141, 169, 276
Watergate scandal, 101, 154, 155, 160–61, 164, 245, 255, 256, 263, 273, 285n, 298, 310, 317, 322
Wayne, John, 94
Weathermen, 307, 314
Weicker, Lowell, 48, 253, 254, 294–300
Weinfeld, Edward, 156
Welk, Lawrence, 12, 20–21
Wells, Kenneth D., 95, 99
Wessel, Milton, 140, 145, 199
Western Defense Command, 119
West Point (Military Academy), 61
Whelan, Dick, 258
White, Harry Dexter, 62, 160
Whitehead, Don, 59–60, 66–72 passim
White House, 54, 81, 107–17 passim, 132, 135, 160, 166–83 passim, 194, 205–13 passim, 222, 230, 239, 248–69 passim, 276–310 passim, 320, 321
Wick, Robert, 30, 48, 189–204 passim
Wicker, Tom, 157, 160
Williamsburg, Va., 163, 196, 213, 216
Wilson, Woodrow, 51
Winchell, Walter, 25, 96
Winstead, Charles B., 70, 79, 80–81
Witwer, Allan, 13–14, 15–16
Woodward, Bob, 262, 263
World War II, 45, 61, 114

YMCA, 64, 257, 280
Young, David, 256, 293, 294
Young, Milton, 20
Young American Medal for Bravery, 170
Young Americans for Freedom, 284
Young Socialist Alliance, 314

Zimbalist, Efrem Jr., 28, 67–77 passim, 195
Zwillman, Longie, 25